SOMEONE LIKE ME

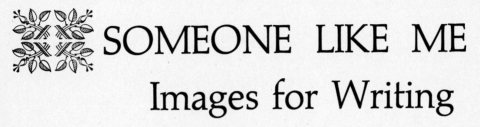

SOMEONE LIKE ME
Images for Writing
Third Edition

Sheena Gillespie
Linda Stanley

Queensborough Community College

WINTHROP PUBLISHERS, INC.

Cambridge, Massachusetts

Library of Congress Cataloging in Publication Data

Gillespie, Sheena, comp.
  Someone like me.

  Includes bibliographical references.
  1. College readers.   I.   Stanley, Linda,
joint comp.   II.   Title.
PE1417.G5   1977   808'.04275   77-13440
ISBN 0-87626-857-2

Acknowledgments begin on page xix.

Cover design by Sandra Rigney, adapted from photo by Jim Holland,
    Stock, Boston.
Interior design by Sandra Rigney.

Photos on pages xxvi, 80, 136 and 214 by Linda Stanley.
Photos on pages 280 and 368 by Lawrence Goldberg.

To Hana and Kurt, with a poignant awareness of the miracle of your survival of the concentration camps. For despite the atrocities to which you were subjected, you have given to your children Eva, John, Susan and Dana an unusual legacy: a faith in man, a respect for truth and a love of beauty.

To Lawrence Mason Stanley, who lived one excellent minute and with whom a world died.

To Joyce and Sylvia, with respect and affection.

 Contents

 # Preface

The third edition of *Someone Like Me: Images for Writing* continues with the inductive approach to the development of writing style, which was the major feature of the first two editions. Essay models are directly utilized to suggest various writing techniques. The book thus combines the features of the essay anthology with many aspects of the rhetoric.

Moreover, the thematic units are synchronized with the rhetorical units to help the student see the logical need for the various methods of essay development as well as understand good writing techniques such as selecting a topic, organizing the essay, writing paragraphs and achieving coherence.

The book includes essays, short stories and poems selected on the hypothesis that students become more involved in essay models when they can sense a person behind the pen. Consequently, all essays are written in the first person—about a third are autobiographical—and they discuss six essential areas of personal experience and ideas: people, places, events and experiences, emotions, choices and philosophies. As in the first two editions, the short stories and poems further develop the thematic thrust of the chapter and often the organizational principles as well.

However, while retaining these significant features of the first two editions, we have made important changes, based on colleagues' comments and our own experience. In addition to changing about fifty percent of the selections in a continuing effort to reflect students' current interests, we have also added one essay to each chapter, for a total of five essays, two short stories and three poems in each of the six sections of the book. A wide selection of approaches is thus available to instructors and students alike.

As well as the additional essay per chapter, we have also included in an appendix short biographical sketches of the writers, which the personal nature of the text suggests. Finally, questions on vocabulary have been included where applicable under "Probing for Method." Although every effort has been made to choose selections that do not have highly sophisticated vocabularies, some essays with more abstract vocabularies have also been included.

Changes as well as additions have been made. In order to move the students' own writing from experiential to expository modes earlier in the semester, we have shifted slightly the focus of Chapter III ("Events and Experiences"). Essay models and writing assignments now stress narrative for expository purposes rather than for its purely personal value.

The third edition thus calls for experiential writing in the first two chapters but stresses expository writing in the last four chapters, reflecting the need many instructors have felt for students to grapple at greater length with the formulation and presentation of ideas. In retaining the experiential approach in the first two chapters and stressing the personal nature of writing throughout the book, we still recognize the act of writing as personal communication for which experience as well as ideas forms an important foundation.

The second change occurs in Chapter VI ("Philosophies"), in which the writing technique has been changed from analysis to forms of illustration: analogy, allegory, example and metaphor. This shift retains the complexity of theme of the final chapter but also introduces the student to a method of handling complex material that he or she can more readily comprehend and reproduce.

As in the first editions, the chapters have been devised to accommodate the instructor who may wish to use the anthology but not the rhetorical sections. Questions after each selection have likewise been divided into two sections: "Probing for Meaning" and "Probing for Method." For those instructors wishing to use the rhetorical sections, Chapters I through IV each contain discussions of two rhetorical devices and Chapters V and VI, because of their thematic complexity, develop one writing technique.

In the rhetorical sections, we have tried to be as helpful as possible to the student. Each of these sections contains three subdivisions: an "Illustration" division, pointing out how the essay writer developed the skill in his or her essay; an "Induction" division, stating rhetorical principles based on the observations made in the "Illustration" section; and a section on "Imitation," indicating ways in which the student can implement in his own writing the techniques he has observed in the essay models.

Finally, each chapter includes suggestions for essay topics in "Topics for Imitation." This section offers two types of essays: one encourages the student to develop his own experiences and ideas; the second, on which we have placed far greater emphasis in this edition, calls for critical evaluation of the ideas presented in the chapter selections.

We wish to acknowledge the assistance of the following people in preparing this third edition: Joyce Sigurdsson and Jon Ripley for aid in selecting the table of contents and writing the questions; Evelyn Pomann and Margaret Cavanaugh for the typing of the manuscript; and Paul O'Connell for his continued support throughout.

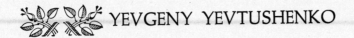

YEVGENY YEVTUSHENKO

People

No people are uninteresting.
Their fate is like the chronicle of planets.

Nothing in them is not particular,
and planet is dissimilar from planet.

And if a man lived in obscurity
making his friends in that obscurity
obscurity is not uninteresting.

To each his world is private,
and in that world one excellent minute.

And in that world one tragic minute.
These are private.

In any man who dies there dies with him
his first snow and kiss and fight.
It goes with him.

They are left books and bridges
and painted canvas and machinery.

Whose fate is to survive.
But what has gone is also not nothing:

by the rule of the game something has gone.
Not people die but worlds die in them.

Whom we knew as faulty, the earth's creatures.
Of whom, essentially, what did we know?

Brother of a brother? Friend of friends?
Lover of lover?

We who knew our fathers
in everything, in nothing.

They perish. They cannot be brought back.
The secret worlds are not regenerated.

And every time again and again
I make my lament against destruction.

# Introduction

In his poem "People," Yevtushenko seeks to convey the uniqueness of each individual:

Nothing in them is not particular,
and planet is dissimilar from planet.

Paradoxically, however, while people are dissimilar, they also have many qualities in common. In this anthology, you will encounter people who have had experiences, felt emotions and developed thoughts which are common to all human beings. In reading about them, you will no doubt recognize yourself.

The selections are written by writers of many ethnic backgrounds who have sought to clarify their own experiences and ideas. In each essay, story and poem, the author has tried to capture in words the meaning of an aspect of his or her life. You may have expressed yourself in another medium: music, painting or photography. Each attempt of an individual to capture a thought or experience in some concrete way is an indication of a desire to prolong it because of its intellectual or emotional value.

This book offers a new medium through which you can crystallize your thoughts and experiences—the essay. You may feel, like Jonathan Swift, that "there are words enough already," but perhaps by the end of the book, you will agree more with Arthur Miller, who has expressed his reason for writing in the following words: "One had to write because other people needed news of the inner world, and without such news they would go mad with the chaos of their lives." You also may have something that other people "need" to know, even if those people are simply your friends. In writing these essays, you will develop your powers of written communication, aided by the rhetorical sections in each chapter.

Many of the essays in the first three chapters on people, places and experiences are autobiographical. The essays you write based on these models can be considered part of your autobiography. You may think that nothing as unusual has happened to you as to them, but you will find as you read their selections that the authors are writing about ordinary people and experiences—people like some you have known and experiences similar to those you have had.

In the last three chapters of *Someone Like Me*, you will read about emotions, choices and philosophies which the various writers have analyzed. Writing in these chapters primarily for others about subjects in which they have some expertise, these writers provide essays which are not only models of good writing but also supply information and stimulate thought about aspects of life and society important to us all.

Yevtushenko writes that,

In any man who dies there dies with him
his first snow and kiss and fight.
It goes with him.

They are left books and bridges
and painted canvas and machinery

Whose fate is to survive.

We are all captives of time, and in order to bring dimension to our lives, we must think of our experiences and ideas as significant enough to clarify for ourselves and others.

 # Acknowledgments

Sherwood Anderson, "Discovery of a Father." *Sherwood Anderson's Memoirs*, edited by Ray Lewis White, The University of North Carolina Press, 1969. Reprinted by permission.

W. H. Auden, "The Unknown Citizen." Copyright 1940 and renewed 1968 by W. H. Auden. Reprinted from *Collected Poems*, by W. H. Auden, edited by Edward Mendelson, by permission of Random House, Inc.

Dee Brown, "The Flight of the Nez Percés." From *Bury My Heart at Wounded Knee* by Dee Brown. Copyright © 1970 by Dee Brown. Reprinted by permission of Holt, Rinehart and Winston, Publishers.

Anthony Burgess, "Is America Falling Apart?" © 1971 by The New York Times Company. Reprinted by permission.

Albert Camus, "Summer in Algiers." From *Lyrical and Critical Essays*, by Albert Camus, edited by Philip Thody, translated by Ellen Conroy Kennedy. Copyright © 1968 by Alfred A. Knopf, Inc. Copyright © 1967 by Hamish Hamilton, Ltd. and Alfred A. Knopf, Inc. "The Guest." From *Exile and the Kingdom*, by Albert Camus, translated by Justin O'Brien. Copyright © 1957, 1958 by Alfred A. Knopf, Inc. Reprinted by permission of Alfred A. Knopf, Inc.

Eldridge Cleaver, "A Day in Folsom Prison." From *Soul on Ice* by Eldridge Cleaver. Copyright © 1968 by Eldridge Cleaver. Used with permission of McGraw-Hill Book Company.

James Dickey, "Adultery." Copyright © 1966 by James Dickey. Reprinted from *Poems 1957-1967* by permission of Wesleyan University Press.

Emily Dickinson, "My Life Closed Twice." Reprinted by permission of the publishers and Trustees of Amherst College from *The Poems of Emily Dickinson*, edited by Thomas H. Johnson, Cambridge, Mass.: The Belknap Press of Harvard University Press. Copyright © 1951, 1955 by the President and Fellows of Harvard College.

Richard Eberhart, "If I could only live at the pitch that is near madness." From *Collected Poems 1930-1976* by Richard Eberhart. Copyright © 1960, 1976 by Richard Eberhart. Reprinted by permission of Oxford University Press, Inc. and Chatto and Windus Ltd.

Nora Ephron, "Fantasies." Copyright © 1972 by Nora Ephron. Reprinted from *Crazy Salad: Some Things About Women*, by Nora Ephron, by permission of Alfred A. Knopf, Inc.

Kenneth Fearing, "American Rhapsody (2)." From New and Selected Poems by Kenneth Fearing. Copyright © 1956 by Kenneth Fearing. Reprinted by permission of Indiana University Press.

E. M. Forster, "My Wood." From *Abinger Harvest*, copyright 1936, 1964, by E. M. Forster. Reprinted by permission of Harcourt Brace Jovanovich, Inc. and Edward Arnold (Publishers) Ltd.

Ernest J. Gaines, "The Sky Is Gray." Excerpted from *Bloodline* by Ernest J. Gaines. Copyright © 1963, 1964, 1968 by Ernest J. Gaines. Reprinted by permission of The Dial Press.

Gary Gildner, "First Practice." Reprinted from *First Practice* by Gary Gildner by permission of the University of Pittsburgh Press. © 1969 by the University of Pittsburgh Press.

Herbert Gold, "Let's Kill the First Red-Haired Man We See . . ." Copyright © 1970 by Herbert Gold. Reprinted from *The Magic Will*, by Herbert Gold, by permission of Random House, Inc.

Suzanne Gordon, "The Geography of Loneliness." From *Lonely in America* by Suzanne Gordon. Copyright 1976 by Suzanne Gordon. Reprinted by permission of Simon & Schuster, Inc.

Alex Haley, "My Furthest-Back Person—'The African'." Copyright © 1972 by Alex Haley. Reprinted by permission of Paul R. Reynolds, Inc., 12 East 41st Street, New York, N.Y. 10017.

Ernest Hemingway, "Soldier's Home." Reprinted by permission of Charles Scribner's Sons from IN OUR TIME by Ernest Hemingway. Copyright © 1925 Charles Scribner's Sons.

Ted Hughes, "Secretary." From *The Hawk in the Rain* by Ted Hughes. Copyright © 1957 by Ted Hughes. Reprinted by permission of Harper & Row, Publishers, Inc.

Alfred Kazin, "The Kitchen." From *A Walker in the City*, copyright, 1951, by Alfred Kazin. Reprinted by permission of Harcourt Brace Jovanovich, Inc.

Helen Keller, "Three Days to See." Copyright © by The Atlantic Monthly Company, Boston, Mass. Reprinted with permission.

William Melvin Kelley, "Saint Paul and The Monkeys." From *Dancers on the Shore* by William Melvin Kelley. Copyright © 1963 by The Curtis Publishing Company. Reprinted by permission of Doubleday & Company, Inc.

Pär Lagerkvist, "Father and I." Reprinted with the permission of Farrar, Straus & Giroux, Inc. from *The Marriage Feast* by Pär Lagerkvist, translated by Alan Blair. Copyright 1954 by Albert Bonniers Förlag.

Doris Lessing, "Notes from a Case History." From *A Man and Two Women* by Doris Lessing. Copyright 1958, 1962, 1963, by Doris Lessing. Reprinted by permission of Simon & Schuster, Inc.

Robert Jay Lifton and Eric Olson, "Death—The Lost Season." From *Living and Dying* by Robert Jay Lifton and Eric Olson. © 1974 by Robert Jay Lifton and Eric Olson. Reprinted by permission of Praeger Publishers, Inc., New York. Excerpts from "Starlight" by Tom Rush used with permission; from the poem "Insensibility," by Wilfred Owen from *War*

Poems. Copyright Chatto & Windus, Ltd. 1946, © 1963. Reprinted by permission of New Directions Publishing Corporation, The Owen Estate, and Chatto & Windus Ltd.; from *Looking Back* by Joyce Maynard, copyright © 1972, 1973. Used by permission of Doubleday & Company, Inc.; from "I-Feel-Like-I'm-Fixin'-To-Die Rag" by Country Joe Macdonald, © by Tradition Music Co. (BMI); from "Golden Slumbers" by Lennon/McCartney, copyright © 1969 Northern Songs Ltd.; from "God" by John Lennon; copyright © 1971 Northern Songs Ltd. All rights for the U.S.A., Canada, Mexico and the Philippines controlled by MacLean Music, Inc., c/o ATV Music Group. Used by permission. All rights reserved. International copyright secured.

Anne Morrow Lindbergh, "Channelled Whelk." From *Gift from the Sea*, by Anne Morrow Lindbergh. Copyright © 1955 by Anne Morrow Lindbergh. Reprinted by permission of Pantheon Books, a division of Random House, Inc.

Bernard Malamud, "The Prison." Reprinted with the permission of Farrar, Straus & Giroux, Inc. from *The Magic Barrel* by Bernard Malamud, copyright © 1950, 1952, 1953, 1954, 1955, 1956, 1958 by Bernard Malamud.

Rollo May, "Our Schizoid World." Reprinted from *Love and Will* by Rollo May. By permission of W. W. Norton & Company, Inc. Copyright © 1969 by W. W. Norton & Company, Inc.

Joyce Maynard, "The Lion Tamers." From *Looking Back*, copyright © 1972, 1973 by Joyce Maynard. Used by permission of Doubleday & Company, Inc.

Carson McCullers, "The Sojourner." From *Collected Short Stories and the Novel, The Ballad of the Sad Café.* Copyright 1955 by Carson McCullers. Reprinted by permission of Houghton Mifflin Company.

Edna St. Vincent Millay, "Spring." From *Collected Poems*, by Harper & Row. Copyright, 1921, 1948, by Edna St. Vincent Millay and Norma Millay Ellis.

Howard Nemerov, "To David, About His Education." From *The Next Room of the Dream*, copyright 1962 by the University of Chicago Press. Reprinted by permission of the author.

Anaïs Nin, "Refusal to Despair." From *A Woman Speaks* by Anaïs Nin. Copyright © 1975 by Anaïs Nin. Edited by Evelyn J. Hinz. Published by The Swallow Press, Chicago. Reprinted by permission of the author's representative, Gunther Stuhlmann.

Tillie Olsen, "I Stand Here Ironing." Excerpted from *Tell Me a Riddle* by Tillie Olsen. Copyright © 1956 by Tillie Olsen. Reprinted by permission of Delacorte Press/Seymour Lawrence.

George Orwell, "Reflections on Gandhi." From *Shooting an Elephant and Other Essays* by George Orwell, copyright, 1945, 1946, 1949, 1950, by Sonia Brownell Orwell; copyright, 1973, 1974, by Sonia Orwell. Reprinted by permission of Harcourt Brace Jovanovich, Inc., Sonia Brownell Orwell, and Secker & Warburg.

Ann Petry, "Like A Winding Sheet." From *Miss Muriel and Other Stories.* Copyright © 1971 by Ann Petry. Reprinted by permission of Houghton Mifflin Company.

Norman Podhoretz, "The Brutal Bargain." From *Making It*, by Norman Podhoretz. Copyright © 1967 by Norman Podhoretz. Reprinted by permission of Random House, Inc.

Jack Harrison Pollack, "Are Teachers Fair to Boys?" From *Today's Health* (April 1968). Reprinted by permission of the author.

Martin Ralbovsky, "A Little Foul Play, the Coach's Way." Copyright © 1974 by Martin Ralbovsky. From *Lords of the Locker Room*, published by Peter H. Wyden, a division of David McKay Co., Inc. Reprinted by permission of the publishers.

Santha Rama Rau, "Return to India." Reprinted by permission of William Morris Agency, Inc. Copyright © 1960 by Reporter Magazine Company.

Alastair Reid, "Curiosity." Reprinted by permission; © 1959 The New Yorker Magazine, Inc.

Theodor Reik, A selection from LOVE AND LUST by Theodor Reik. Copyright © 1941, 1944, 1957 by Theodor Reik. Copyright © by Farrar, Straus and Company (now Farrar, Straus & Giroux, Inc.). Reprinted with the permission of Farrar, Straus & Giroux, Inc.

Adrienne Rich, "Anger and Tenderness." Reprinted from *Of Woman Born* by Adrienne Rich. By permission of W. W. Norton & Company, Inc. Copyright © 1976 by W. W. Norton & Company, Inc. "Trying to Talk with a Man." Reprinted from *Diving into the Wreck, Poems, 1971–1972* by Adrienne Rich. By permission of W. W. Norton & Company, Inc. Copyright © 1973 by W. W. Norton & Company, Inc.

Theodore Roethke, "Elegy for Jane." Copyright © 1950 by Theodore Roethke from *Collected Poems of Theodore Roethke*. Reprinted by permission of Doubleday & Company, Inc.

Bertrand Russell, "Marriage." Reprinted from *Marriage and Morals* by Bertrand Russell. By permission of Liveright Publishing Corporation. Copyright 1929 by Horace Liveright, Inc. Copyright renewed 1957 by Bertrand Russell.

Anne Sexton, "The Rowing Endeth." From *The Awful Rowing Toward God*. Copyright © 1975 by Loring Conant, Jr., Executor of the Estate of Anne Sexton. Reprinted by permission of Houghton Mifflin Company.

William Stafford, "The Star in the Hills." From *Traveling Through the Dark* (1962) by William Stafford. Copyright © 1957 by William Stafford. Reprinted by permission of Harper & Row, Publishers, Inc.

James Thurber, "The Secret Life of Walter Mitty." Copyright © 1942 by James Thurber. Copyright © 1970 by Helen Thurber. From *My World and Welcome to It*, published by Harcourt Brace Jovanovich. Originally printed in *The New Yorker*.

Chad Walsh, "Port Authority Terminal, 9:00 a.m. Monday." Reprinted from *The End of Nature*, © 1969 by Chad Walsh, by permission of The Swallow Press, Inc., Chicago.

Hana Wehle, "Birkenau-Auschwitz, July 1944." Reprinted by permission of the author.

E. B. White, "Once More to the Lake—August 1941." From *One Man's Meat* by E. B. White. Copyright 1941 by E. B. White. Reprinted by permission of Harper & Row, Publishers, Inc.

Tom Wicker, "Kennedy Without Tears." Reprinted by permission of William

Morrow & Company, Inc. from *Kennedy Without Tears* by **Tom Wicker**. Copyright © 1964 by Tom Wicker.

William Carlos Williams, "Tract." From *Collected Earlier Poems*. Copyright 1938 by New Directions Publishing Corporation. Reprinted by permission of New Directions Publishing Corporation.

Tom Wolfe, "Las Vegas (What?) Las Vegas (Can't hear you! Too noisy) Las Vegas!!!!" Reprinted with the permission of Farrar, Straus & Giroux, Inc. from *The Kandy-Kolored Tangerine-Flake Streamline Baby* by Tom Wolfe, copyright © 1963, 1964, 1965 by Thomas K. Wolfe, Jr. Copyright © 1963, 1964, 1965 by New York Herald Tribune, Inc.

Yevgeny Yevtushenko, "People." From *Selected Poems*, translated by Robin Milner-Gulland and Peter Levi, S.J. (Penguin Modern European Poets, 1962). Translation copyright © Robin Milner-Gulland and Peter Levi, 1962. Reprinted by permission of Penguin Books Ltd.

Al Young, "Lonesome in the Country." Copyright © 1968 by Al Young. Reprinted with permission of the author.

SOMEONE LIKE ME

ONE

PEOPLE

"no people are uninteresting"

"A man of few days and full of troubles" is how Tom Wicker describes John Kennedy in his essay from *Kennedy Without Tears*. And Mahatma Gandhi, says George Orwell in "Reflections on Gandhi," "was an interesting and unusual man who enriched the world simply by being alive."

While we are impressed by these famous and heroic men of our time, we are influenced even more keenly by those about us who share our daily lives. In "Discovery of a Father" Sherwood Anderson begins, "A boy wants something very special from his father." Norman Podhoretz speaks of Mrs. K., an English teacher in high school who decided he was "a gem in the rough and who took it upon herself to polish me to as high a sheen as she could manage and I would permit." We all have been exposed to diverse people in our lives, both past and present, publicly and privately. Parents, teachers, lovers, friends and national figures have all influenced us, for better or for worse.

Three essays in this chapter are autobiographical—each author writes of a person he has known who has influenced him. You will see the change in a boy's relationship with his father, the disgust a team manager feels for his high school coach, and the ambivalent feelings a student has for a former teacher. George Orwell and Tom Wicker attempt to unlock the key to the fascinating personalities of Gandhi and Kennedy.

The short stories dramatize the lives of very different people: Walter Mitty, who tries to escape his boring, frustrating

1

life through extravagant fantasies, and a Southern black
woman who faces her poverty-stricken life squarely and with
amazing courage.

The poems have unlikely subjects for poetry: a secretary,
a typical citizen and a student. Poets can make any person interesting. Can you?

Choosing an Effective Topic and Selecting Vocabulary and Tone

As you read the essays in this chapter, look for the two
aspects of good writing that will be emphasized here: 1. how
the writers choose the material to include in their essays from
all the facts that they know about their subjects—all the conversations, incidents and events that they and the people they
write about shared; 2. how the writers select words to express
appropriately their ideas and attitudes.

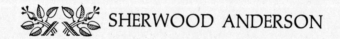 SHERWOOD ANDERSON

Discovery of a Father

You hear it said that fathers want their sons to be what
they feel they cannot themselves be, but I tell you it also works
the other way. A boy wants something very special from his father. I
know that as a small boy I wanted my father to be a certain thing he
was not. I wanted him to be a proud, silent, dignified father. When I
was with other boys and he passed along the street, I wanted to feel a
flow of pride. "There he is. That is my father."

But he wasn't such a one. He couldn't be. It seemed to me
then that he was always showing off. Let's say someone in our town
had got up a show. They were always doing it. The druggist would be
in it, the shoe-store clerk, the horse doctor, and a lot of women and
girls. My father would manage to get the chief comedy part. It was,
let's say, a Civil War play and he was a comic Irish soldier. He had to
do the most absurd things. They thought he was funny, but I didn't.

I thought he was terrible. I didn't see how mother could stand it. She even laughed with the others. Maybe I would have laughed if it hadn't been my father.

Or there was a parade, the Fourth of July or Decoration Day. He'd be in that, too, right at the front of it, as Grand Marshal or something, on a white horse hired from a livery stable.

He couldn't ride for shucks. He fell off the horse and everyone hooted with laughter, but he didn't care. He even seemed to like it. I remember once when he had done something ridiculous, and right out on Main Street, too. I was with some other boys and they were laughing and shouting at him and he was shouting back and having as good a time as they were. I ran down an alley back of some stores and there in the Presbyterian Church sheds I had a good long cry.

Or I would be in bed at night and father would come home a little lit up and bring some men with him. He was a man who was never alone. Before he went broke, running a harness shop, there were always a lot of men loafing in the shop. He went broke, of course, because he gave too much credit. He couldn't refuse it and I thought he was a fool. I had got to hating him.

There'd be men I didn't think would want to be fooling around with him. There might even be the superintendent of our schools and a quiet man who ran the hardware store. Once I remember there was a white-haired man who was a cashier of the bank. It was a wonder to me they'd want to be seen with such a windbag. That's what I thought he was. I know now what it was that attracted them. It was because life in our town, as in all small towns, was at times pretty dull and he livened it up. He made them laugh. He could tell stories. He'd even get them to singing.

If they didn't come to our house they'd go off, say at night, to where there was a grassy place by a creek. They'd cook food there and drink beer and sit about listening to his stories.

He was always telling stories about himself. He'd say this or that wonderful thing had happened to him. It might be something that made him look like a fool. He didn't care.

If an Irishman came to our house, right away father would say he was Irish. He'd tell what county in Ireland he was born in. He'd tell things that happened there when he was a boy. He'd make it seem so real that, if I hadn't known he was born in southern Ohio, I'd have believed him myself.

If it was a Scotchman the same thing happened. He'd get a burr into his speech. Or he was a German or a Swede. He'd be anything the other man was. I think they all knew he was lying, but they seemed to like him just the same. As a boy that was what I couldn't understand.

And there was mother. How could she stand it? I wanted to ask but never did. She was not the kind you asked such questions.

I'd be upstairs in my bed, in my room above the porch, and father would be telling some of his tales. A lot of father's stories were about the Civil War. To hear him tell it he'd been in about every battle. He'd known Grant, Sherman, Sheridan and I don't know how many others. He'd been particularly intimate with General Grant so that when Grant went East to take charge of all the armies, he took father along.

"I was an orderly at headquarters and Sim Grant said to me, 'Irve,' he said, 'I'm going to take you along with me.'"

It seems he and Grant used to slip off sometimes and have a quiet drink together. That's what my father said. He'd tell about the day Lee surrendered and how, when the great moment came, they couldn't find Grant.

"You know," my father said, "about General Grant's book, his memoirs. You've read of how he said he had a headache and how, when he got word that Lee was ready to call it quits, he was suddenly and miraculously cured.

"Huh," said father. "He was in the woods with me.

"I was in there with my back against a tree. I was pretty well corned. I had got hold of a bottle of pretty good stuff.

"They were looking for Grant. He had got off his horse and come into the woods. He found me. He was covered with mud.

"I had the bottle in my hand. What'd I care? The war was over. I knew we had them licked."

My father said that he was the one who told Grant about Lee. An orderly riding by had told him, because the orderly knew how thick he was with Grant. Grant was embarrassed.

"But, Irve, look at me. I'm all covered with mud," he said to father.

And then, my father said, he and Grant decided to have a drink together. They took a couple of shots and then, because he didn't want Grant to show up potted before the immaculate Lee, he smashed the bottle against the tree.

"Sim Grant's dead now and I wouldn't want it to get out on him," my father said.

That's just one of the kind of things he'd tell. Of course the men knew he was lying, but they seemed to like it just the same.

When we got broke, down and out, do you think he ever brought anything home? Not he. If there wasn't anything to eat in the house, he'd go off visiting around at farmhouses. They all wanted him. Sometimes he'd stay away for weeks, mother working to keep us fed, and then home he'd come bringing, let's say, a ham. He'd got it from some farmer friend. He'd slap it on the table in the kitchen. "You bet I'm going to see that my kids have something to eat," he'd say, and mother would just stand smiling at him. She'd never say a word about all the weeks and months he'd been away, not leaving us a cent for food. Once I heard her speaking to a woman in our street. Maybe the woman had dared to sympathize with her. "Oh," she said, "it's all right. He isn't ever dull like most of the men in this street. Life is never dull when my man is about."

But often I was filled with bitterness, and sometimes I wished he wasn't my father. I'd even invent another man as my father. To protect my mother I'd make up stories of a secret marriage that for some strange reason never got known. As though some man, say the president of a railroad company or maybe a Congressman, had married my mother, thinking his wife was dead and then it turned out she wasn't.

So they had to hush it up but I got born just the same. I wasn't really the son of my father. Somewhere in the world there was a very dignified, quite wonderful man who was really my father. I even made myself half believe these fancies.

And then there came a certain night. He'd been off somewhere for two or three weeks. He found me alone in the house, reading by the kitchen table.

It had been raining and he was very wet. He sat and looked at me for a long time, not saying a word. I was startled, for there was on his face the saddest look I had ever seen. He sat for a time, his clothes dripping. Then he got up.

"Come on with me," he said.

I got up and went with him out of the house. I was filled with wonder but I wasn't afraid. We went along a dirt road that led down into a valley, about a mile out of town, where there was a pond. We walked in silence. The man who was always talking had stopped his talking.

I didn't know what was up and had the queer feeling that I was with a stranger. I don't know whether my father intended it so. I don't think he did.

The pond was quite large. It was still raining hard and there were flashes of lightning followed by thunder. We were on a grassy bank at the pond's edge when my father spoke, and in the darkness and rain his voice sounded strange.

"Take off your clothes," he said. Still filled with wonder, I began to undress. There was a flash of lightning and I saw that he was already naked.

Naked, we went into the pond. Taking my hand he pulled me in. It may be that I was too frightened, too full of a feeling of strangeness, to speak. Before that night my father had never seemed to pay any attention to me.

"And what is he up to now?" I kept asking myself. I did not swim very well, but he put my hand on his shoulder and struck out into the darkness.

He was a man with big shoulders, a powerful swimmer. In the darkness I could feel the movement of his muscles. We swam to the far edge of the pond and then back to where we had left our clothes. The rain continued and the wind blew. Sometimes my father swam on his back and when he did he took my hand in his large powerful one and moved it over so that it rested always on his shoulder. Sometimes there would be a flash of lightning and I could see his face quite clearly.

It was as it was earlier, in the kitchen, a face filled with sadness. There would be the momentary glimpse of his face and then again the darkness, the wind and the rain. In me there was a feeling I had never known before.

It was a feeling of closeness. It was something strange. It was as though there were only we two in the world. It was as though I had been jerked suddenly out of myself, out of my world of the school-boy, out of a world in which I was ashamed of my father.

He had become blood of my blood; he the strong swimmer and I the boy clinging to him in the darkness. We swam in silence and in silence we dressed in our wet clothes, and went home.

There was a lamp lighted in the kitchen and when we came in, the water dripping from us, there was my mother. She smiled at us. I remember that she called us "boys."

"What have you boys been up to," she asked, but my father did not answer. As he had begun the evening's experience with me in silence, so he ended it. He turned and looked at me. Then he went, I thought, with a new and strange dignity out of the room.

I climbed the stairs to my own room, undressed in the darkness and got into bed. I couldn't sleep and did not want to sleep. For the first time I knew that I was the son of my father. He was a story teller as I was to be. It may be that I even laughed a little softly there in the darkness. If I did, I laughed knowing that I would never again be wanting another father.

PROBING FOR MEANING

1. In the first part of the essay, what impression of his father does Anderson create? What examples of his father's behavior are given to achieve this impression?

2. What does the boy discover is different about his father in the swimming scene?

3. Explain the phrase "a face filled with sadness" which is used at least twice in this second part of the essay.

4. Anderson gains recognition about himself and his father as a result of this encounter. What does he find out?

5. What kind of man was Anderson's father? Why was he a clown? Why didn't he support his family? Would a father like Anderson's have embarrassed and angered you if you had been in Anderson's place? How important are the roles which society has given us to play?

Choosing an Effective Topic

ILLUS-
TRATION

How did Anderson choose an effective topic?   In writing an autobiographical essay on his father, Anderson has gone through a selective process in choosing material. By analyzing his essay, one is able to reconstruct this process. Obviously, he has not given a complete chronological account of his father's life, for to do so would involve more writing than he has space for. He chooses, then, to begin limiting his topic by concentrating on the span of years in which he was part of his father's life.

He further limits his topic to that time in their relationship in which he came to understand his father. One event, when they went swimming together one night, serves best to indicate what he learned about his father. By limiting his account to one dramatic event, Anderson has written an absorbing as well as an informative essay.

INDUCTION

Principles for choosing an effective topic.   Why does an author writing about another person usually include a crucial moment in their relationship? One reason might be that the author thought about this person only at the time when the important event occurred. Often, we do not really see the people we are with every day. Frequently, it takes something extraordinary to make us aware of them.

Another good reason for emphasizing a climactic moment is that people are often revealed more fully in this dramatic situation than through their daily routines. An account of a person's entire life might tell less than one "high point."

A final reason for focusing the account of a relationship is a practical one. A narrative focused on one specifically revealing or climactic event makes more interesting reading than a narrative relating several vaguely described events.

Your choice of topic must necessarily be limited by the projected length of your writing assignment. It is much more effective to devote full attention to a character exploration of one episode than to try to "tell everything" in a short space.

IMITATION

Procedures to follow in choosing an effective topic.
A. Choose a general topic which interests you and about which you have some knowledge.
B. Jot down what you know about your topic.
C. Determine how much writing would be necessary to develop these points specifically.

D. If you find that you have too much material for the length of your paper, reexamine your list for an aspect or aspects which could be developed specifically in the allotted space.

E. Once you have limited your general topic to an effective topic, make an exhaustive list of your knowledge on the latter to determine that you do not still have too much material to enable you to write a specific paper, or that you have not limited your topic so much that you have left yourself with too little material.

F. State your effective topic in the form of a sentence to clarify for yourself exactly what you intend to write about. Be as specific as possible. For example, Anderson's "thesis" sentence might have been, "While for many of my childhood years I was ashamed of my clown-like father, I one night came to realize his serious side which made me proud to be his son."

 NORMAN PODHORETZ

The Brutal Bargain

One of the longest journeys in the world is the journey from Brooklyn to Manhattan—or at least from certain neighborhoods in Brooklyn to certain parts of Manhattan. I have made that journey, but it is not from the experience of having made it that I know how very great the distance is, for I started on the road many years before I realized what I was doing, and by the time I did realize it I was for all practical purposes already there. At so imperceptible a pace did I travel, and with so little awareness, that I never felt footsore or out of breath or weary at the thought of how far I still had to go. Yet whenever anyone who has remained back there where I started—remained not physically but socially and culturally, for the neighborhood is now a Negro ghetto and the Jews who have "remained" in it mostly reside in the less affluent areas of Long Island—whenever anyone like that happens into the world in which I now live with such perfect ease, I can see that in his eyes I have become a fully acculturated citizen of a country as foreign to him as China and infinitely more frightening.

That country is sometimes called the upper middle class; and indeed I am a member of that class, less by virtue of my income than by virtue of the way my speech is accented, the way I dress, the way I furnish my home, the way I entertain and am entertained, the way I educate my children—the way, quite simply, I look and I live. It appalls me to think what an immense transformation I had to work on myself in order to become what I have become: if I had known what I was doing I would surely not have been able to do it, I would surely not have wanted to. No wonder the choice had to be blind; there was a kind of treason in it: treason toward my family, treason toward my friends. In choosing the road I chose, I was pronouncing a judgment upon them, and the fact that they themselves concurred in the judgment makes the whole thing sadder but no less cruel.

When I say that the choice was blind, I mean that I was never aware—obviously not as a small child, certainly not as an adolescent, and not even as a young man already writing for publication and working on the staff of an important intellectual magazine in New York—how inextricably my "noblest" ambitions were tied to the vulgar desire to rise above the class into which I was born; nor did I understand to what an astonishing extent these ambitions were shaped and defined by the standards and values and tastes of the class into which I did not know I wanted to move. It is not that I was or am a social climber as that term is commonly used. High society interests me, if at all, only as a curiosity; I do not wish to be a member of it; and in any case, it is not, as I have learned from a small experience of contact with the very rich and fashionable, my "scene." Yet precisely because social climbing is not one of my vices (unless what might be called celebrity climbing, which very definitely *is* one of my vices, can be considered the contemporary variant of social climbing), I think there may be more than a merely personal significance in the fact that class has played so large a part both in my life and in my career.

But whether or not the significance is there, I feel certain that my long-time blindness to the part class was playing in my life was not altogether idiosyncratic. "Privilege," Robert L. Heilbroner has shrewdly observed in *The Limits of American Capitalism*, "is not an attribute we are accustomed to stress when we consider the construction of *our* social order." For a variety of reasons, says Heilbroner, "privilege under capitalism is much less 'visible,' especially to the favored groups, than privilege under other systems" like feudalism. This "invisibility" extends in America to class as well.

No one, of course, is so naïve as to believe that America is a classless society or that the force of egalitarianism, powerful as it has been in some respects, has ever been powerful enough to wipe out class distinctions altogether. There was a moment during the 1950's, to be sure, when social thought hovered on the brink of saying that the country had to all intents and purposes become a wholly middle-class society. But the emergence of the civil-rights movement in the 1960's and the concomitant discovery of the poor—to whom, in helping to discover them, Michael Harrington interestingly enough applied, in *The Other America*, the very word ("invisible") that Heilbroner later used with reference to the rich—has put at least a temporary end to that kind of talk. And yet if class has become visible again, it is only in its grossest outlines—mainly, that is, in terms of income levels—and to the degree that manners and style of life are perceived as relevant at all, it is generally in the crudest of terms. There is something in us, it would seem, which resists the idea of class. Even our novelists, working in a genre for which class has traditionally been a supreme reality, are largely indifferent to it—which is to say, blind to its importance as a factor in the life of the individual.

In my own case, the blindness to class always expressed itself in an outright and very often belligerent refusal to believe that it had anything to do with me at all. I no longer remember when or in what form I first discovered that there was such a thing as class, but whenever it was and whatever form the discovery took, it could only have coincided with the recognition that criteria existed by which I and everyone I knew were stamped as inferior: we were in the *lower* class. This was not a proposition I was willing to accept, and my way of not accepting it was to dismiss the whole idea of class as a prissy triviality.

Given the fact that I had literary ambitions even as a small boy, it was inevitable that the issue of class would sooner or later arise for me with a sharpness it would never acquire for most of my friends. But given the fact also that I was on the whole very happy to be growing up where I was, that I was fiercely patriotic about Brownsville (the spawning-ground of so many famous athletes and gangsters), and that I felt genuinely patronizing toward other neighborhoods, especially the "better" ones like Crown Heights and East Flatbush which seemed by comparison colorless and unexciting—given the fact, in other words, that I was not, for all that I wrote poetry and read books, an "alienated" boy dreaming of escape—my confrontation with the issue of class would probably have come later rather than sooner if not for an English teacher in high school who decided that I was a gem in the rough and who took it upon herself to polish me to as high a sheen as she could manage and I would permit.

I resisted—far less effectively, I can see now, than I then thought, though even then I knew she was wearing me down far more than I would ever give her the satisfaction of admitting. Famous throughout the school for her altogether outspoken snobbery, which stopped short by only a hair, and sometimes did not stop short at all, of an old-fashioned kind of patrician anti-Semitism, Mrs. K. was also famous for being an extremely good teacher; indeed, I am sure that she saw no distinction between the hopeless task of teaching the proper use of English to the young Jewish barbarians whom fate had so unkindly deposited into her charge and the equally hopeless task of teaching them the proper "manners." (There were as many young Negro barbarians in her charge as Jewish ones, but I doubt that she could ever bring herself to pay very much attention to them. As she never hesitated to make clear, it was punishment enough for a woman of her background—her family was old-Brooklyn and, she would have us understand, extremely distinguished—to have fallen among the sons of East European immigrant Jews.)

For three years, from the age of thirteen to the age of sixteen, I was her special pet, though that word is scarcely adequate to suggest the intensity of the relationship which developed between us. It was a relationship right out of *The Corn Is Green*, which may, for all I know, have served as her model; at any rate, her objective was much the same as the Welsh teacher's in that play: she was determined that I should win a scholarship to Harvard. But whereas (an irony much to the point here) the problem the teacher had in *The Corn Is Green* with her coal-miner pupil in the traditional class society of Edwardian England was strictly academic, Mrs. K.'s problem with me in the putatively egalitarian society of New Deal America was strictly social. My grades were very high and would obviously remain so, but what would they avail me if I continued to go about looking and sounding like a "filthy little slum child" (the epithet she would invariably hurl at me whenever we had an argument about "manners")?

Childless herself, she worked on me like a dementedly ambitious mother with a somewhat recalcitrant son; married to a solemn and elderly man (she was then in her early forties or thereabouts), she treated me like a callous, ungrateful adolescent lover on whom she had humiliatingly bestowed her favors. She flirted with me and flattered me, she scolded me and insulted me. Slum child, filthy little slum child, so beautiful a mind and so vulgar a personality, so exquisite in sensibility and so coarse in manner. What would she do with me, what would become of me if I persisted out of stubbornness and perversity in the disgusting ways they had taught me at home and on the streets?

To her the most offensive of these ways was the style in which I dressed: a tee shirt, tightly pegged pants, and a red satin jacket with the legend "Cherokees, S.A.C." (social-athletic club) stitched in large white letters across the back. This was bad enough, but when on certain days I would appear in school wearing, as a particular ceremonial occasion required, a suit and tie, the sight of those immense padded shoulders and my white-on-white shirt would drive her to even greater heights of contempt and even lower depths of loving despair than usual. *Slum child, filthy slum child.* I was beyond saving; I deserved no better than to wind up with all the other horrible little Jewboys in the gutter (by which she meant Brooklyn College). If only I would listen to her, the whole world could be mine: I could win a scholarship to Harvard, I could get to know the best people, I could grow up into a life of elegance and refinement and taste. Why was I so stupid as not to understand?

In those days it was very unusual, and possibly even against the rules, for teachers in public high schools to associate with their students after hours. Nevertheless, Mrs. K. sometimes invited me to her home, a beautiful old brownstone located in what was perhaps the only section in the whole of Brooklyn fashionable enough to be intimidating. I would read her my poems and she would tell me about her family, about the schools she had gone to, about Vassar, about writers she had met, while her husband, of whom I was frightened to death and who to my utter astonishment turned out to be Jewish (but not, as Mrs. K. quite unnecessarily hastened to inform me, *my* kind of Jewish), sat stiffly and silently in an armchair across the room, squinting at his newspaper through the first *pince-nez* I had ever seen outside the movies. He spoke to me but once, and that was after I had read Mrs. K. my tearful editorial for the school newspaper on the death of Roosevelt—an effusion which provoked him into a full five-minute harangue whose blasphemous contents would certainly have shocked me into insensibility if I had not been even more shocked to discover that he actually had a voice.

But Mrs. K. not only had me to her house, she also—what was even more unusual—took me out a few times, to the Frick Gallery and the Metropolitan Museum, and once to the theatre, where we saw a dramatization of *The Late George Apley*, a play I imagine she deliberately chose with the not wholly mistaken idea that it would impress upon me the glories of aristocratic Boston.

One of our excursions into Manhattan I remember with particular vividness because she used it to bring the struggle between us to rather a dramatic head. The familiar argument began this time on the subway. Why, knowing that we would be spending the afternoon together "in public," had I come to school that morning improperly dressed? (I was, as usual, wearing my red satin club jacket over a white tee shirt.) She realized, of course, that I owned only one suit (this said not in compassion but in derision) and that my poor parents had, God only knew where, picked up the idea that it was too precious to be worn except at one of those bar mitzvahs I was always going to. Though why, if my parents were so worried about clothes, they had permitted me to buy a suit which made me look like a young hoodlum she found it very difficult to imagine. Still, much as she would have been embarrassed to be seen in public with a boy whose parents allowed him to wear a zoot suit, she would have been somewhat less embarrassed than she was now by the ridiculous costume I had on. Had I no consideration for her? Had I no consideration for myself? Did I want everyone who laid eyes on me to think that I was nothing but an ill-bred little slum child?

My standard ploy in these arguments was to take the position that such things were of no concern to me: I was a poet and I had more important matters to think about than clothes. Besides, I would feel silly coming to school on an ordinary day dressed in a suit. Did Mrs. K. want me to look like one of those "creeps" from Crown Heights who were all going to become doctors? This was usually an effective counter, since Mrs. K. despised her middle-class Jewish students even more than she did the "slum children," but probably because she was growing desperate at the thought of how I would strike a Harvard interviewer (it was my senior year), she did respond according to form on that particular occasion. "At least," she snapped, "they reflect well on their parents."

I was accustomed to her bantering gibes at my parents, and sensing, probably, that they arose out of jealousy, I was rarely troubled by them. But this one bothered me; it went beyond banter and I did not know how to deal with it. I remember flushing, but I cannot remember what if anything I said in protest. It was the beginning of a very bad afternoon for both of us.

We had been heading for the Museum of Modern Art, but as we got off the subway, Mrs. K. announced that she had changed her mind about the museum. She was going to show me something else instead, just down the street on Fifth Avenue. This mysterious "something else" to which we proceeded in silence turned out to be the college department of an expensive clothing store, de Pinna. I do not exaggerate when I say that an actual physical dread seized me as I followed her into the store. I had never been inside such a store; it was not a store, it was enemy territory, every inch of it mined with humiliations. "I am," Mrs. K. declared in the coldest human voice I hope I shall ever hear, "going to buy you a suit that you will be able to wear at your Harvard interview." I had guessed, of course, that this was what she had in mind, and even at fifteen I understood what a fantastic act of aggression she was planning to commit against my parents and asking me to participate in. Oh no, I said in a panic (suddenly realizing that I *wanted* her to buy me that suit), I can't, my mother wouldn't like it. "You can tell her it's a birthday present. Or else I will tell her. If I tell her, I'm sure she won't object." The idea of Mrs. K. meeting my mother was more than I could bear: my mother, who spoke with a Yiddish accent and of whom, until that sickening moment, I had never known I was ashamed and so ready to betray.

To my immense relief and my equally immense disappointment, we left the store, finally, without buying a suit, but it was not to be the end of clothing or "manners" for me that day—not yet. There was still the ordeal of a restaurant to go through. Where I came from, people rarely ate in restaurants, not so much because most of them were too poor to afford such a luxury—although most of them certainly were—as because eating in restaurants was not regarded as a luxury at all; it was, rather, a necessity to which bachelors were pitiably condemned. A home-cooked meal was assumed to be better than anything one could possibly get in a restaurant, and considering the class of restaurants in question (they were really diners or luncheonettes), the assumption was probably correct. In the case of my own family, myself included until my late teens, the business of going to restaurants was complicated by the fact that we observed the Jewish dietary laws, and except in certain neighborhoods, few places could be found which served kosher food; in midtown Manhattan in the 1940's, I believe there were only two and both were relatively expensive. All this is by way of explaining why I had had so little experience of restaurants up to the age of fifteen and why I grew apprehensive once more when Mrs. K. decided after we left de Pinna that we should have something to eat.

The restaurant she chose was not at all an elegant one—I have, like a criminal, revisited it since—but it seemed very elegant indeed to me: enemy territory again, and this time a mine exploded in my face the minute I set foot through the door. The hostess was very sorry, but she could not seat the young gentleman without a coat and tie. If the lady wished, however, something could be arranged. The lady (visibly pleased by this unexpected—or was it expected?—object lesson) did wish, and the so recently defiant but by now utterly docile young gentleman was forthwith divested of his so recently beloved but by now thoroughly loathsome red satin jacket and provided with a much oversized white waiter's coat and a tie—which, there being no collar to a tee shirt, had to be worn around his bare neck. Thus attired, and with his face supplying the touch of red which had moments earlier been supplied by his jacket, he was led into the dining room, there to be taught the importance of proper table manners through the same pedagogic instrumentality that had worked so well in impressing him with the importance of proper dress.

Like any other pedagogic technique, however, humiliation has its limits, and Mrs. K. was to make no further progress with it that day. For I had had enough, and I was not about to risk stepping on another mine. Knowing she would subject me to still more ridicule if I made a point of my revulsion at the prospect of eating nonkosher food, I resolved to let her order for me and then to feign lack of appetite or possibly even illness when the meal was served. She did order—duck for both of us, undoubtedly because it would be a hard dish for me to manage without using my fingers.

The two portions came in deep oval-shaped dishes, swimming in a brown sauce and each with a sprig of parsley sitting on top. I had not the faintest idea of what to do—should the food be eaten directly from the oval dish or not?—nor which of the many implements on the table to do it with. But remembering that Mrs. K. herself had once advised me to watch my hostess in such a situation and then to do exactly as she did, I sat perfectly still and waited for her to make the first move. Unfortunately, Mrs. K. also remembered having taught me that trick, and determined as she was that I should be given a lesson that would force me to mend my ways, she waited too. And so we both waited, chatting amiably, pretending not to notice the food while it sat there getting colder and colder by the minute. Thanks partly to the fact that I would probably have gagged on the duck if I had tried to eat it—dietary taboos are very powerful if one has been conditioned to them—I was prepared to wait forever. And in fact it was Mrs. K. who broke first.

"Why aren't you eating?" she suddenly said after something like fifteen minutes had passed. "Aren't you hungry?" Not very, I answered. "Well," she said, "I think we'd better eat. The food is getting cold." Whereupon, as I watched with great fascination, she deftly captured the sprig of parsley between the prongs of her serving fork, set it aside, took up her serving spoon and delicately used those two esoteric implements to transfer a piece of duck from the oval dish to her plate. I imitated the whole operation as best I could, but not well enough to avoid splattering some partly congealed sauce onto my borrowed coat in the process. Still, things could have been worse, and having more or less successfully negotiated my way around that particular mine, I now had to cope with the problem of how to get out of eating the duck. But I need not have worried. Mrs. K. took one bite, pronounced it inedible (it must have been frozen by then), and called in quiet fury for the check.

Several months later, wearing an altered but respectable conservative suit which had been handed down to me in good condition by a bachelor uncle, I presented myself on two different occasions before interviewers from Harvard and from the Pulitzer Scholarship

Committee. Some months after that, Mrs. K. had her triumph: I won the Harvard scholarship on which her heart had been so passionately set. It was not, however, large enough to cover all expenses, and since my parents could not afford to make up the difference, I was unable to accept it. My parents felt wretched but not, I think, quite as wretched as Mrs. K. For a while it looked as though I would wind up in the "gutter" of Brooklyn College after all, but then the news arrived that I had also won a Pulitzer Scholarship which paid full tuition if used at Columbia and a small stipend besides. Everyone was consoled, even Mrs. K.: Columbia was at least in the Ivy League.

The last time I saw her was shortly before my graduation from Columbia and just after a story had appeared in the *Times* announcing that I had been awarded a fellowship which was to send me to Cambridge University. Mrs. K. had passionately wanted to see me in Cambridge, Massachusetts, but Cambridge, England was even better. We met somewhere near Columbia for a drink, and her happiness over my fellowship, it seemed to me, was if anything exceeded by her delight at discovering that I now knew enough to know that the right thing to order in a cocktail lounge was a very dry martini with lemon peel, please.

PROBING FOR MEANING

1. What "journey" did Podhoretz take? Why does he say that he did not know where he was going until he arrived? Why did he feel that taking this journey made him guilty of "treason"?

2. Why does Podhoretz claim that class in America is invisible? What class distinctions does he admit are made in this country?

3. What kind of person is Mrs. K.? What mixture of attitudes does she have toward Podhoretz? Why is she ambivalent?

4. How great an influence does Mrs. K. really exert on Podhoretz' life?

5. Do you know anyone as aware of class distinction as Mrs. K.? Are class distinctions still widely made in America today? On what basis do we distinguish between classes? Should there be class distinctions? Explain.

PROBING FOR METHOD

Which episode in his relationship with his English teacher does the author emphasize? Why does he limit his topic to dramatizing that one event? Why doesn't he also highlight, for example, their meeting after his graduation from Columbia?

Selecting Vocabulary and Tone

ILLUS-
TRATION

What factors influenced Podhoretz in his selection of words? Podhoretz is obviously writing for a literate, sophisticated audience. Words like "imperceptible" and "acculturated" (paragraph 1), "inextricably" and "variant" (paragraph 3), "idiosyncratic" (paragraph 4), and "egalitarianism" (paragraph 5) emanate from a rather extensive vocabulary and presume a sophisticated readership. What other words can you find in the essay which suggest this level of audience?

Podhoretz selects words to fulfill various purposes as well. He chooses "journey" which suggests that a long time span is involved in moving from one point to another. He might have chosen "trip" which implies a movement involving less time. Why is journey closer to what Podhoretz means than trip? Likewise, why does he use the word "treason" (paragraph 2) when in terms of actual meaning "disloyalty" would be more appropriate?

As a skilled writer, Podhoretz' effective use of words does much of his work. Actually, he is taking advantage of the distinction between the *denotative* and the *connotative* meanings of certain words. Every word has a denotative meaning; this is the literal meaning as found in a dictionary. Many words have also a connotative meaning; this is the emotional meaning the word has when used in a certain situation with a specific audience. For example, "bitch" has a denotative meaning when used by an author describing a dog show, but it has definite connotative meaning when used by an author to describe a female character!

Another excellent example of Podhoretz' use of connotation is his use of "blindness" (paragraphs 2, 3, 4) when he is not literally "blind" but perhaps "unaware." What meaning does "blind" connote that "unaware" does not?

What attitude toward Mrs. K. does Podhoretz convey in his description of her? In paragraph 8, he describes her as "old-fashioned." Does this word have a favorable connotation? In the same sentence he adds that she is "patrician." What denotation does this word have? What connotation might it have in our democratic society? Finally, by terming her "anti-Semitic," Podhoretz, himself Jewish, must feel some degree of antagonism toward her. In the next sentence, however, he asserts that she is "an extremely good teacher." Can you cite other words or phrases from the essay which indicate that Podhoretz both likes and dislikes Mrs. K.?

When employing satire in depicting a topic, a writer presents his subject apparently in a serious manner but, through subtle exaggeration, actually mocks it. To some extent, Podhoretz is satirizing Mrs. K. For example, in the last paragraph he describes her delight over both his fellowship at Cambridge University and his knowing how to act in a cocktail lounge. Since these accomplishments are obviously not of equal value, Podhoretz is mocking her values. What other evidences of satire can you find? Would you say that he is primarily satirizing Mrs. K. or appreciating her?

Compare the vocabulary used by Sherwood Anderson with that used by Podhoretz. Anderson is writing to a different audience and has a different goal in mind. How does Anderson's language reflect what he is trying to accomplish? That he has limited his vocabulary does not mean that he has not chosen his words carefully, nor does it mean that he has not let connotation work for him. Find examples of connotative diction in Anderson's essay.

INDUCTION   *Principles of word selection.*   The right words do not automatically flow from the pen of the good writer, who agonizes when searching for the precise word that is wanted. The poet James Emanuel once said that he exhausted sixty-six words before finally discovering one that satisfied him completely. Of course, poets specialize in language and make it their business to know many synonyms for each word. A good thesaurus, however, will help you as a beginning writer to expand your vocabulary.

In determining your choice of words, you must first consider your audience. Vocabulary levels vary, even among adult audiences, as is evidenced by an examination of the degrees of verbal sophistication found in magazines on the newsstand. Usually, but not always, the educational level of the audience determines the level of vocabulary which the writer will use. For example, phrases in Podhoretz' essay, if intended for a less sophisticated audience, might be rewritten as follows:

1. "Fully acculturated citizen of a country" (paragraph 1) to "fully a part of a country"

2. "Concurred in the judgment" (paragraph 2) to "agreed with the judgment"

3. "Altogether idiosyncratic" to "just my hangup" (colloquial) (paragraph 4)

You also consider connotation as well as denotation in your choice of words. Words which have similar dictionary definitions often have different cultural associations. "Clang" and "ring" may be listed as synonyms in the thesaurus, but "clang" has the connotation of being louder than "ring." "Slim" has the same denotative meaning as "skinny" but a very different connotation.

Words are also writers' most effective tools in conveying their attitude toward their subject, or in conveying *tone.* The tone of a piece of writing can be delighted, depressed, critical, humorous, satirical, ambivalent, or objective. The writer chooses words which communicate a consistent tone.

Selection of details also helps to transmit tone. A writer wishing to convey a humorous tone, for example, would select humorous details and omit those which do not transmit humor.

IMITATION   *Procedures to follow in choosing vocabulary.*

A. Determine as precisely as possible who your audience will be. If you are writing in a classroom situation, you can assume that your teacher is your audience.

B. Decide what your attitude toward your audience will be. Usually in student themes you will adopt an informal but not familiar or colloquial tone.

C. Decide next what attitude you will take toward your subject. In student themes, the writer usually attempts to be objective and impartial in tone, for writing humor or satire is difficult. Above all, be consistent in your attitude or explain any inconsistency, as Podhoretz does in describing his ambivalent attitude toward Mrs. K.

D. Be precise in your choice of words. Aim for clarity in considering connotation of words. You should use a thesaurus, while being careful at the same time not to "over write" by using words whose meanings you do not fully comprehend.

 TOM WICKER

From *Kennedy Without Tears*

Shortly after President Kennedy was shot, the following inscription appeared on a plaque in one of the private bedrooms of the White House:

In this room Abraham Lincoln slept during his occupancy of the White House as President of the United States, March 4, 1861–April 13, 1865.

In this room lived John Fitzgerald Kennedy with his wife Jacqueline Kennedy during the two years, ten months and two days he was President of the United States, January 20, 1961–November 22, 1963.

Before many years pass, that deliberate linkage of two Presidents, that notice chiseled upon history by Jacqueline Kennedy, may seem as inevitable as the Washington Monument. Already, airports and spaceports and river bridges and a cultural center have been named for her husband. Six months after his death books about him, even phonograph records, were at floodtime; many more were being written or planned. *Profiles in Courage* seemed destined to be a perennial best-seller. It was almost as if he had never called businessmen sons of bitches, sent troops to Ole Miss, the refugees to the Bay of Pigs, or kicked the budget sky-high.

Thus, John F. Kennedy is certain to take his place in American lore as one of those sure-sell heroes out of whose face or words or monuments a souvenir dealer can turn a steady buck. There he soon will stand, perhaps in our lifetime—cold stone or heartless bronze, immortal as Jefferson, revered as Lincoln, bloodless as Washington. One can imagine the graven words on his pedestal:

Ask not what your country can do for you. Ask what you can do for your country.

What his country inevitably will do for John Kennedy seems a curious fate for the vitality and intensity, the wry and derisive style of the man who was the Thirty-fifth President of the United States. His wit surely would have seared the notion of John F. Kennedy International Airport, much less Cape Kennedy—for this was the man who once told the great-great-grandson of John Adams, "It is a pleasure to live in your family's old house, and we hope that you will come by and see us."

One suspects the Eternal Flame might have embarrassed him as much as the Navy did that brilliant Pacific day when the strutting admirals put him literally on a flag-draped pedestal aboard an aircraft carrier while the band played *Hail to the Chief* and the jets screamed overhead on taxpayers' money; one of his favorite quips, after all, was that he had gone from Lieutenant J.G. to Commander-in-Chief without any qualifications at all.

I can almost hear that amused Boston voice inquiring, as he once did after reading a favorable Gallup Poll, where all those people who admired him so much were when Congress turned down his school bill in 1961. Staring from Valhalla at himself cast in stone in the middle of some downtown Washington traffic circle, he might well whisper to earthly passersby what he once told 12,000 Democrats in Harrisburg, Pennsylvania:

"I will introduce myself. I am Teddy Kennedy's brother."

And when children rise reverently in some future Fourth of July pageant to recite the chiastic prose of the Kennedy Inaugural Address—the stirring words that raced so many pulses among that "new generation of Americans" to which he appealed—some may recall instead the same rhythm, the same rhetoric, but different words and a more subtle imagination at work:

"We observe tonight not a celebration of freedom but a victory of party, for we have sworn to pay off the same party debt our forebears ran up nearly a year and three months ago. Our deficit will not be paid off in the next hundred days, nor will it be paid off in the first one thousand days, nor in the life of this Administration. Nor, perhaps, even in our lifetime on this planet. But let us begin— remembering that generosity is not a sign of weakness and that ambassadors are always subject to Senate confirmation. For if the Democratic party cannot be helped by the many who are poor, it cannot be saved by the few who are rich. So let us begin."

In much the same vein were Kennedy's remarks at a dinner of

the White House Correspondents Association in April, 1962. The organization had just raised its dinner ticket prices—and Kennedy had just forced the steel companies to rescind a somewhat more important price increase.

"The sudden and arbitrary action of the officers of this association," he said to the correspondents, "in increasing the price of dinner tickets by $2.50 over last year constitutes a wholly unjustifiable defiance of the public interest . . . In this serious hour in our nation's history, when newsmen are awakened in the middle of the night to be given a front page story, when expense accounts are being scrutinized by Congress, when correspondents are required to leave their families for long and lonely weekends at Palm Beach, the American people will find it hard to accept this ruthless decision made by a tiny handful of executives . . ."

Now a politician who could laugh at parodies of his noblest speech and his moment of most spectacular success—let alone make the parodies himself, as Kennedy did the foregoing—obviously was something more intricate in life than the mere sum of the virtues symbolized by the Eternal Flame: purity, steadfastness, warmth, light. A President delighted by the political caricature of Everett McKinley Dirksen, but impatient with the solemn earnestness of Chester Bowles obviously had a wide streak of Honey Fitz down his spine; yet that same President, confronted with an adulatory mob of hundreds of thousands of cheering Europeans, could not bring himself to respond with more than a halfhearted jab of the arm from the chest—something like a halfback straight-arming a tackler, apologetically. But let us not imagine that he was merely unemotional; those who saw it are not likely to forget his flashing anger when a reporter asked him at a news conference about two "security risks" in the State Department.

In the early days of Kennedy's New Frontier (there was bound to be something roguish about a man who could bring the Ivy Leaguers—and himself—to Washington with a slogan that evoked echoes of the Wild West, which appalled most of them), I thought Richard Nixon was perhaps a more interesting *man* than Kennedy. I thought Nixon was, as Conrad wrote of Lord Jim, "one of us." But Kennedy, I thought then, for all his charm and fire and eloquence, was a straightforward political man, who listened to his own rhetoric, contrived his "image" in the comforting faith that a statesman had to get elected before he could do anyone any good, and believed sincerely that his causes were not only right but actually offered solutions to human problems. I thought Kennedy had what someone has called the perfect political mentality—that of a football coach, combining the will to win with the belief that the game is important.

Now, I think that what Kennedy really had of that mentality was a rather peculiar form of the will to win. He wanted power, all right, but something more; "This ability," he once said, "to do things well, and to do them with precision and with modesty, attracts us all." It was a theme to which he often returned—the pursuit of excellence. And as the probability of his political canonization turns toward certainty, and the sad calcification of his humanity into stone and bronze continues, there is not much football coach in the man Kennedy who recalls himself to me most strongly.

If that human Kennedy still seems to me to have been altogether too detached and too controlled to have been, as were Nixon and Lord Jim, "one of us," with all those fascinating hesitancies and inadequacies and torments out of which literature is made, nevertheless he *was* a man "of few days and full of trouble," and for all I know he may even have played "such fantastic tricks before high heaven as to make the angels weep." But the statues will tell us nothing of that.

PROBING FOR
MEANING

1. Why does Wicker feel that comparisons of Kennedy with Lincoln are a "curious fate" for Kennedy? On which qualities of Kennedy does Wicker concentrate?

2. How does the example of what Kennedy said to the great-great-grandson of John Adams show the former's wry humor? What does his speech to the White House correspondents demonstrate about Kennedy?

3. What contrast does Wicker present between Kennedy and Nixon? What similarity do Nixon and Lord Jim have?

4. Why does Wicker feel that Kennedy had a perfect political mentality? What unique quality did Kennedy contribute to this mentality?

5. What attributes of Kennedy does Wicker feel will unfortunately be forgotten?

PROBING FOR
METHOD

1. How does Wicker structure the first paragraph of the essay? How effective is it as an introduction?

2. What category of evidence does Wicker employ to counteract the "canonization" of Kennedy?

3. What does the last sentence refer to? Is it an effective final point? Explain the technique Wicker has used here for concluding his essay.

4. a. What does the word "chiastic" mean? Could Wicker have used a more familiar word? Why didn't he?

b. What do "caricature," "canonization" and "calcification" mean? How do their various connotations reflect our different attitudes toward Kennedy since his death?

 GEORGE ORWELL

Reflections on Gandhi

Saints should always be judged guilty until they are proved innocent, but the tests that have to be applied to them are not, of course, the same in all cases. In Gandhi's case the questions one feels inclined to ask are: to what extent was Gandhi moved by vanity—by the consciousness of himself as a humble, naked old man, sitting on a praying mat and shaking empires by sheer spiritual power—and to what extent did he compromise his own principles by entering politics, which of their nature are inseparable from coercion and fraud? To give a definite answer one would have to study Gandhi's acts and writings in immense detail, for his whole life was a sort of pilgrimage in which every act was significant. But this partial autobiography,[1] which ends in the nineteen-twenties, is strong evidence in his favor, all the more because it covers what he would have called the unregenerate part of his life and reminds one that inside the saint, or near-saint, there was a very shrewd, able person who could, if he had chosen, have been a brilliant success as a lawyer, an administrator or perhaps even a businessman.

At about the time when the autobiography first appeared I remember reading its opening chapters in the ill-printed pages of some Indian newspaper. They made a good impression on me, which Gandhi himself at that time did not. The things that one associated with him—home-spun cloth, "soul forces" and vegetarianism—were unappealing, and his medievalist program was obviously not viable in a backward, starving, over-populated country. It was also apparent that the British were making use of him, or thought they were making use of him. Strictly speaking, as a Nationalist, he was an enemy, but since in every crisis he would exert himself to prevent violence—which, from the British point of view, meant preventing any effective action whatever—he could be regarded as "our man." In private this was sometimes cynically admitted. The attitude of the Indian millionaires was similar. Gandhi called upon them to repent, and naturally they preferred him to the Socialists and Communists who, given the

[1] *The Story of My Experiments with Truth.* By M. K. Gandhi.

chance, would actually have taken their money away. How reliable such calculations are in the long run is doubtful; as Gandhi himself says, "in the end deceivers deceive only themselves"; but at any rate the gentleness with which he was nearly always handled was due partly to the feeling that he was useful. The British Conservatives only became really angry with him when, as in 1942, he was in effect turning his non-violence against a different conqueror.

But I could see even then that the British officials who spoke of him with a mixture of amusement and disapproval also genuinely liked and admired him, after a fashion. Nobody ever suggested that he was corrupt, or ambitious in any vulgar way, or that anything he did was actuated by fear or malice. In judging a man like Gandhi one seems instinctively to apply high standards, so that some of his virtues have passed almost unnoticed. For instance, it is clear even from the autobiography that his natural physical courage was quite outstanding: the manner of his death was a later illustration of this, for a public man who attached any value to his own skin would have been more adequately guarded. Again, he seems to have been quite free from that maniacal suspiciousness which, as E. M. Forster rightly says in *A Passage to India*, is the besetting Indian vice, as hypocrisy is the British vice. Although no doubt he was shrewd enough in detecting dishonesty, he seems wherever possible to have believed that other people were acting in good faith and had a better nature through which they could be approached. And though he came of a poor middle-class family, started life rather unfavorably, and was probably of unimpressive physical appearance, he was not afflicted by envy or by the feeling of inferiority. Color feeling when he first met it in its worst form in South Africa, seems rather to have astonished him. Even when he was fighting what was in effect a color war, he did not think of people in terms of race or status. The governor of a province, a cotton millionaire, a half-starved Dravidian coolie, a British private soldier were all equally human beings, to be approached in much the same way. It is noticeable that even in the worst possible circumstances, as in South Africa when he was making himself unpopular as the champion of the Indian community, he did not lack European friends.

Written in short lengths for newspaper serialization, the autobiography is not a literary masterpiece, but it is the more impressive because of the commonplaceness of much of its material. It is well to be reminded that Gandhi started out with the normal ambitions of a young Indian student and only adopted his extremist opinions by degrees and, in some cases, rather unwillingly. There was a time, it is interesting to learn, when he wore a top hat, took dancing lessons, studied French and Latin, went up the Eiffel Tower and even tried to learn the violin—all this was the idea of assimilating European civilization as thoroughly as possible. He was not one of those saints who are marked out by their phenomenal piety from childhood onwards, nor one of the other kind who forsake the world after sensational debaucheries. He makes full confession of the misdeeds of his youth, but in fact there is not much to confess. As a frontispiece to the book there is a photograph of Gandhi's possessions at the time of his death. The whole outfit could be purchased for about £5, and Gandhi's sins, at least his fleshly sins, would make the same sort of appearance if placed all in one heap. A few cigarettes, a few mouthfuls of meat, a few annas pilfered in childhood from the maidservant, two visits to a brothel (on each occasion he got away without "doing anything"), one narrowly escaped lapse with his landlady in Plymouth, one outburst of temper—that is about the whole collection. Almost from childhood onwards he had a deep earnestness, an attitude ethical rather than religious, but, until he was about thirty, no very definite sense of direction. His first entry into anything describable as public life was made by way of vegetarianism. Underneath his less ordinary qualities one feels all the time the solid middle-class businessmen who were his ancestors. One feels that even after he had abandoned personal ambition he must have been a resourceful, energetic lawyer and a hard-headed political organizer, careful in keeping down expenses, an adroit handler of committees and an indefatigable chaser of subscriptions. His character was an extraordinarily mixed one, but there was almost nothing in it that you can put your finger on and call bad, and I believe that even Gandhi's worst enemies would admit that he was an interesting and unusual man who enriched the world simply by being alive. Whether he was also a lovable man, and whether his teachings can have much value for those who do not accept the religious beliefs on which they are founded, I have never felt fully certain.

Of late years it has been the fashion to talk about Gandhi as though he were not only sympathetic to the Western Left-wing movement, but were integrally part of it. Anarchists and pacifists, in particular, have claimed him for their own, noticing only that he was opposed to centralism and State violence and ignoring the otherworldly, anti-humanist tendency of his doctrines. But one should, I think, realize that Gandhi's teachings cannot be squared with the belief that Man is the measure of all things and that our job is to make life worth living on this earth, which is the only earth we have. They make sense only on the assumption that God exists and that the world of solid objects is an illusion to be escaped from. It is worth considering the disciplines which Gandhi imposed on himself and which—though he might not insist on every one of his followers observing every detail—he considered indispensable if one wanted to serve either God or humanity. First of all, no meat-eating, and if possible no animal food in any form. (Gandhi himself, for the sake of his health, had to compromise on milk, but seems to have felt this to be a backsliding.) No alcohol or tobacco, and no spices or condiments even of a vegetable kind, since food should be taken not for its own sake but solely in order to preserve one's strength. Secondly, if possible, no sexual intercourse. If sexual intercourse must happen, then it should be for the sole purpose of begetting children and presumably at long intervals. Gandhi himself, in his middle thirties, took the vow of *brahmacharya*, which means not only complete chastity but the elimination of sexual desire. This condition, it seems, is difficult to attain without a special diet and frequent fasting. One of the dangers of milk-drinking is that it is apt to arouse sexual desire. And finally—this is the cardinal point—for the seeker after goodness there must be no close friendships and no exclusive loves whatever.

Close friendships, Gandhi says, are dangerous, because "friends react on one another" and through loyalty to a friend one can be led into wrong-doing. This is unquestionably true. Moreover, if one is to love God, or to love humanity as a whole, one cannot give one's preference to any individual person. This again is true, and it marks the point at which the humanistic and the religious attitude cease to be reconcilable. To an ordinary human being, love means nothing if it does not mean loving some people more than others. The autobiography leaves it uncertain whether Gandhi behaved in an inconsiderate way to his wife and children, but at any rate it makes clear that on three occasions he was willing to let his wife or a child die rather than administer the animal food prescribed by the doctor. It is true that the threatened death never actually occurred, and also that Gandhi—with, one gathers, a good deal of moral pressure in the opposite direction—always gave the patient the choice of staying alive at the price of committing a sin: still, if the decision had been solely his own, he would have forbidden the animal food, whatever the risks might be. There must, he says, be some limit to what we will do in order to remain alive, and the limit is well on this side of chicken broth. This attitude is perhaps a noble one, but, in the sense which—I think—most people would give to the word, it is inhuman. The essence of being human is that one does not seek perfection, that one *is* sometimes willing to commit sins for the sake of loyalty, that one does not push asceticism to the point where it makes friendly intercourse impossible, and that one is prepared in the end to be defeated and broken up by life, which is the inevitable price of fastening one's love upon other human individuals. No doubt alcohol, tobacco, and so forth, are things that a saint must avoid, but saint-hood is also a thing that human beings must avoid. There is an obvious retort to this, but one should be wary about making it. In this yogi-ridden age, it is too readily assumed that "non-attachment" is not only better than a full acceptance of earthly life, but that the ordinary man only rejects it because it is too difficult: in other words, that the average human being is a failed saint. It is doubtful whether this is true. Many people genuinely do not wish to be saints, and it is probable that some who achieve or aspire to sainthood have never felt much temptation to be human beings. If one could follow it to its psychological roots, one would, I believe, find that the main motive for "non-attachment" is a desire to escape from the pain of living, and above all from love, which, sexual or non-sexual, is hard work. But it is not necessary here to argue whether the other-worldly or the humanistic ideal is "higher." The point is that they are incompatible. One must choose between God and Man, and all "radicals" and "progressives," from the mildest Liberal to the most extreme Anarchist, have in effect chosen Man.

However, Gandhi's pacifism can be separated to some extent from his other teachings. Its motive was religious, but he claimed also for it that it was a definite technique, a method, capable of producing desired political results. Gandhi's attitude was not that of most West-ern pacifists. *Satyagraha*, first evolved in South Africa, was a sort of non-violent warfare, a way of defeating the enemy without hurting him and without feeling or arousing hatred. It entailed such things as civil disobedience, strikes, lying down in front of railway trains, enduring police charges without running away and without hitting back, and the like. Gandhi objected to "passive resistance" as a translation of *Satyagraha:* in Gujarati, it seems, the word means "firmness in the truth." In his early days Gandhi served as a stretcher-bearer on the British side in the Boer War, and he was prepared to do the same again in the war of 1914–18. Even after he had completely abjured violence he was honest enough to see that in war it is usually necessary to take sides. He did not—indeed, since his whole political life centred round a struggle for national independence, he could not—take the sterile and dishonest line of pretending that in every war both sides are exactly the same and it makes no difference who wins. Nor did he, like most Western pacifists, specialize in avoiding awkward questions. In relation to the late war, one question that every pacifist had a clear obligation to answer was: "What about the Jews? Are you prepared to see them exterminated? If not, how do you propose to save them without resorting to war?" I must say that I have never heard, from any Western pacifist, an honest answer to this question, though I have heard plenty of evasions, usually of the "you're another" type. But it so happens that Gandhi was asked a somewhat similar question in 1938 and that his answer is on record in Mr. Louis Fischer's *Gandhi and Stalin*. According to Mr. Fischer, Gandhi's view was that the German Jews ought to commit collective suicide, which "would have aroused the world and the people of Germany to Hitler's violence." After the war he justified himself: the Jews had been killed anyway, and might as well have died significantly. One has the impression that this attitude staggered even so warm an admirer as Mr. Fischer, but Gandhi was merely being honest. If you are not prepared to take life, you must often be prepared for lives to be lost in some other way. When, in 1942, he urged non-violent resistance against a Japanese invasion, he was ready to admit that it might cost several million deaths.

At the same time there is reason to think that Gandhi, who after all was born in 1869, did not understand the nature of totalitarianism and saw everything in terms of his own struggle against the British government. The important point here is not so much that the British treated him forbearingly as that he was always able to command publicity. As can be seen from the phrase quoted above, he believed in "arousing the world," which is only possible if the world gets a chance to hear what you are doing. It is difficult to see how Gandhi's methods could be applied in a country where opponents of the régime disappear in the middle of the night and are never heard of again. Without a free press and the right of assembly, it is impossible not merely to appeal to outside opinion, but to bring a mass movement into being, or even to make your intentions known to your adversary. Is there a Gandhi in Russia at this moment? And if there is, what is he accomplishing? The Russian masses could only practice civil disobedience if the same idea happened to occur to all of them simultaneously, and even then, to judge by the history of the Ukraine famine, it would make no difference. But let it be granted that non-violent resistance can be effective against one's own government, or against an occupying power: even so, how does one put it into practice internationally? Gandhi's various conflicting statements on the late war seem to show that he felt the difficulty of this. Applied to foreign politics, pacifism either stops being pacifist or becomes appeasement. Moreover the assumption, which served Gandhi so well in dealing with individuals, that all human beings are more or less approachable and will respond to a generous gesture, needs to be seriously questioned. It is not necessarily true, for example, when you are dealing with lunatics. Then the question becomes: Who is sane? Was Hitler sane? And is it not possible for one whole culture to be insane by the standards of another? And, so far as one can gauge the feelings of whole nations, is there any apparent connection between a generous deed and a friendly response? Is gratitude a factor in international politics?

These and kindred questions need discussion, and need it urgently, in the few years left to us before somebody presses the button and the rockets begin to fly. It seems doubtful whether civilization can stand another major war, and it is at least thinkable that the way out lies through non-violence. It is Gandhi's virtue that he would have been ready to give honest consideration to the kind of question that I have raised above; and, indeed, he probably did discuss most of these questions somewhere or other in his innumerable newspaper articles. One feels of him that there was much that he did not understand, but not that there was anything that he was frightened of saying or thinking. I have never been able to feel much liking for Gandhi, but I do not feel sure that as a political thinker he was wrong in the main, nor do I believe that his life was a failure. It is curious that when he was assassinated, many of his warmest admirers exclaimed sorrowfully that he had lived just long enough to see his life work in ruins, because India was engaged in a civil war which had always been foreseen as one of the by-products of the transfer of power. But it was not in trying to smooth down Hindu-Moslem rivalry that Gandhi had spent his life. His main political objective, the peaceful ending of British rule, had after all been attained. As usual the relevant facts cut across one another. On the other hand, the British did get out of India without fighting, an event which very few observers indeed would have predicted until about a year before it happened. On the other hand, this was done by a Labour government, and it is certain that a Conservative government, especially a government headed by Churchill, would have acted differently. But if, by 1945, there had grown up in Britain a large body of opinion sympathetic to Indian independence, how far was this due to Gandhi's personal influence? And if, as may happen, India and Britain finally settle down into a decent and friendly relationship, will this be partly because Gandhi, by keeping up his struggle obstinately and without hatred, disinfected the political air? That one even thinks of asking such questions indicates his stature. One may feel, as I do, a sort of aesthetic distaste for Gandhi, one may reject the claims of sainthood made on his behalf (he never made any such claim himself, by the way), one may also reject sainthood as an ideal and therefore feel that Gandhi's basic aims were anti-human and reactionary: but regarded

simply as a politician, and compared with the other leading political
figures of our time, how clean a smell he has managed to leave
behind!

1. What are the two central questions that form the basis for
Orwell's inquiry into whether Gandhi can be considered a saint?

2. Since Gandhi did not have the military strength to enable him
to remain in power, how did he manage to do so?

3. What characteristics of sainthood does Orwell find in Gandhi?
In what way is Gandhi atypical for a saint?

4. What is the humanistic attitude? Why is it not compatible with
Gandhi's political philosophy and religious beliefs? Why were love and
friendships dangerous to Gandhi?

5. What does Orwell mean when he calls Gandhi "inhuman"?
How does Orwell contrast being a saint with being human? Which is
more virtuous, in his opinion?

6. How does Orwell separate Gandhi's pacifism (*Satyagraha*) from
his other teachings?

7. Why does Orwell admire Gandhi's willingness to answer the
"awkward questions" that many pacifists avoid?

8. What criticisms of Gandhi's political thinking does Orwell
include in the essay?

9. In the final analysis, how does Orwell view Gandhi's life?

1. There are many instances in which the author inserts his own
biases into this essay. Do you feel that Orwell is sufficiently objective
about Gandhi? Explain.

2. How well does Orwell answer the two central questions that
he poses in the introduction?

3. In the later stages of the essay, Orwell broadens the focus
for a more general discussion. How is this accomplished?

4. Of the following words Orwell uses in this essay, which are
synonyms? Which are antonyms? What one connotation do all the words
have, regardless of the denotation of each? Why would the author choose
words with this particular connotation in writing about Gandhi?

abjured
adroit
asceticism
coercion
debaucheries
unregenerate

 MARTIN RALBOVSKY

A Little Foul Play, the Coach's Way

By the turn of the 1950s, thousands of veterans from World War II had used their GI loans to transform the forests and the farmlands of rural America into what is now known, somewhat derisively, as Middle America. They left their rented cold-water flats in the decaying cities, and they moved their families out to suburbia. They bought their own homes. In 1952, my family moved from the ethnic ghetto that was called Flockie Boulevard in Schenectady, New York, to a suburb of that city called Rotterdam. (People in upstate New York were very big on naming their cities after current or ancient European capitals; besides Rotterdam, there are now, in upstate New York, an Amsterdam, a Berlin, a Rome, a Naples, a Troy, a Carthage, an Athens, a Warsaw, a Hamburg, a Dunkirk, and, of course, an Attica.)

It was in Rotterdam, in the middle of the 1950s, as I entered a junior high school named after some fellow named John Bigsbee, that I encountered my first real, live coach. Everybody said he was a nice guy. Everybody said that Sunday followed Saturday. His name, let's say, was Benchley Steele. In gym classes, Benchley Steele made fun of kids who happened to be lacking in coordination; he had derogatory nicknames for kids he didn't particularly like; he swore regularly at kids who happened to be rowdy, and every once in a while he would punch one. Benchley Steele was a fanatic about the game of soccer; most of the time, at the beginning of gym classes Benchley Steele would throw out a brown soccer ball, blow his silver whistle, and instruct us to go at each other with maniacal fervor. Benchley Steele would stand off to the side, chain-smoking cigarettes, and watch the mayhem that ensued, with, I always suspected, a certain amount of sadistic pleasure. Whenever a kid got kicked in the shins and started to cry, Benchley Steele would berate him for acting like a sissy. Nice guy, my first coach.

But it wasn't until my sophomore year in a spanking, new high school, in the late 1950s, that I experienced rather genuine problems with Benchley Steele. (The spanking, new high school was christened "Mohonosen"; they held a contest, and a kid named Vincent Bowers thought up the name, splicing together the first three letters of three decimated Indian nations that had once occupied the very same land, the Mohawks, the Onondagas, and the Senecas. He won five dollars.) The coach, Benchley Steele, followed us from the old junior high school to the spanking, new high school, and he became the head coach of basketball there. Now, since I was a kid who had roots that traced back to the obliterated inner city, I already was something of a fanatic about the game of basketball. I was totally obsessed with it. By the time I got to the tenth grade, I already had five or six years of shooting jump shots under my belt; the jump shots were not merely shot in the stifling heat of summer, or in the gentle warmth of spring, or in the rustic coziness of autumn. They were also shot in the dead of winter, in temperatures that were twenty-three degrees below zero, with my hands wrapped in gloves, a skiing cap pulled over my head and ears, two sweaters and two jackets covering my chest, black, buckled galoshes over dirty black sneakers on my feet. I shot jump shots on large patches of ice, dribbling the ball deftly, bouncing the ball off cracks in the ice and using the ricochets as lead passes; if you knew how to use the ice to your advantage, and you bounced the ball at the right speed and the right angle off the cracks and the crevices, the ricochets would come back to you in the form of perfectly thrown lead passes from imaginary teammates. My nose would run, the mucous would freeze in a straight line between my nostrils and my lips. My face looked like Niagara Falls, frozen over. People did not know whether my nose had suddenly begun to grow stalactites or my upper lip had suddenly begun to grow stalagmites. But I loved it. The neighbors, of course, recommended to my parents that I be whisked off to undergo psychiatric examination; surely, normal kids were not to be found outside during roaring blizzards, shooting a basketball, while dressed to resemble a refugee from Outer Mongolia. I got even with my neighbors during the summers. They mowed their own lawns.

After a while, I could shoot jump shots quite well in such things as freezing rain, sleet, high winds, and snowstorms. Wearing sneakers and shorts, and being inside a warm gymnasium, and shooting at a basket that happened to have a net dangling off the end of it were luxuries. I used to shoot two hundred jump shots a day, every day; I used to run off streaks of thirty-five or forty-five in a row. I kept score on myself. I never went into the house to eat supper (or because of darkness) without first popping a parting jumper. *Swish.* Even though there was never a net on the basket in my backyard, the imagined sound of rippling cords brought about by a soft-touch jump shot set the tuning forks in my brain to gyrating, and *that sound* made all the more palatable the waiting bowls of hot chicken soup. To this day, I can go over to the schoolyard in my neighborhood, bounce a basketball a few times, and start popping jump shots, stringing together seven, eight, and nine in a row. A boyhood spent in a blighted industrial city shooting jump shots is a boyhood not altogether wasted; little kids in my neighborhood are impressed today. My coach back then wasn't.

He cut me from the basketball team.

I remember the tryouts as if they occurred yesterday. It was a three-on-one drill that did me in. There I was, in my brand-new white, high-topped P.F. Keds, wearing red satin shorts with white stripes down the sides and a sparkling white sweatshirt, dribbling up the court in the image of Mr. Jump Shot himself, Paul Arizin. There was a kid on my right, streaking down the right side of the court; there was a kid to my left, running down the left side of the court. In front of me was the defensive player, tall and strong and experienced, with airplane wings for arms, stretched out wide like a middle linebacker waiting to devour his prey. I dribbled to the top of the key; the defensive player approached me, stalking, and trying to look intimidating. The other two kids were free, waving their arms in each corner of the court. I ignored them both. I opted for the jump shot; the ball left my fingertips softly, and it was perfectly arched and perfectly aimed. Impeccable trajectory. *Swish*. The cords rippled sensuously. The kids on the sidelines began cheering wildly. They appreciated artistry, no doubt.

Benchley Steele blew his whistle. He ordered me off the floor.

"Drive, goddammit, drive," he yelled at me.

The next day, I got a second chance. Three-on-one drills again. I was placed in the middle again, and I started dribbling up court as soon as the coach yelled, "Go!" I didn't want to drive smack into the defensive player. I didn't want to challenge him and run the risk of his getting his hand on the ball and cramming it straight back down my throat, which happened to be the insult of all insults. No sir. The jump shot was my equalizer. I had such confidence in the accuracy of my jump shot that I was convinced it was the most accurate thing inside that gymnasium; I was convinced that its chances of going into the basket were just as good as any other kid's layup was. But coaches such as Benchley Steele, I discovered, preferred layups to jump shots; percentages, the cliché goes. So I came up the floor, and somewhere around mid-court I decided to prove my point. Dribbling to my right, to my favorite spot on the floor, three feet beyond the perimeter of the keyhole, I went up. The ball sailed toward the basket with the lightness of a floating feather; the cords of the net danced ever so slightly—that soft *swish* was the result of a shooting touch that every kid in the gymnasium envied, which is why every kid in the gymnasium broke into spontaneous applause as soon as the ball had dropped through.

Benchley Steele blew his whistle again.

"Out!" he said, bristling. "Get out!"

I showered and got dressed, and I cried all the way home. The tears froze to my cheeks. I could not understand what had befallen me. This coach, this Benchley Steele, had just rejected the best damn jump shot in the whole school, and he was settling instead for a bunch of tall, strong, unpolished goons who had spent their summers husking corn instead of shooting baskets. He was picking the plumbers over the artist, damn him. I was convinced that there wasn't a kid in the school who could have beaten me in a game of one-on-one; I knew—and all the other kids knew, too—that I could string together seven, eight jump shots in a row and totally demoralize them, which is the secret to winning in one-on-one. (I already held the school record for winning the greatest number of unfinished one-on-one matches; with the scores at 9–2 or 8–1, my favor, my opponents would quit, rather than suffer the embarrassment of consummated defeat.) Size is not necessarily a factor in being successful in one-on-one; talent most definitely is. But size certainly was a factor in making the junior varsity basketball team; talent, I concluded that night, wasn't. I pretended I was sick when I got home. I took the next two days off from school, and I sulked. I could not bear to face the humiliation that I knew was waiting for me at school, at the hands of my own peer group. I knew that dozens of kids were salivating at the very prospect of my showing up at school, so that they could ease up beside me in the hall, between classes, and say, "Best jump shot, my ass."

A couple of weeks later, one of the kids who had made the junior varsity team stopped me in the hall and said, "Coach wants to see you."

I immediately presumed that Benchley Steele had finally reacquired his senses; surely, nobody, not even Benchley Steele, could pass over such a jump shot—he was just teaching me a lesson, Mr. Steele was, for not following orders. I ran down the hall to the gym. I stopped abruptly at the door. I took a deep breath. Then I walked through the swinging doors, with all of the correctness and the composure of a British butler. The coach was sitting on the bottom row of the bleachers; the rest of the bleachers were folded up into the wall. I calmly walked over to him.

"You want to see me, Coach?" I asked, faking nonchalance.

"Sit down," he said.

I suspected that Benchley Steele was going to give me that old have-you-learned-your-lesson? routine. (I had been through that once already, in Little League, swinging at a 3-and-0 pitch instead of taking.) I wanted to spare him the embarrassment of elaborating on the merits of humility and conformity; I was quite willing to say, "Yes, Coach, I have learned my lesson. Layups from now on." But he surprised me; Benchley Steele did not say what I was expecting him to say.

He said, "I need a manager."

A manager? *Manager!* I was simultaneously mortified and outraged. Who in hell wanted to be a manager? Gathering up all of the dirty, sweaty, stinking towels after practice; sweeping off the court; pumping air into lifeless basketballs; keeping score at games. How could he do this to me? I felt that he was insulting me with his offer. *Manager.* Managers were gawky kids who had trouble with their eyesight, or else they were elfish kids who had no talent whatsoever but wanted to be a part of the team anyway. Jocksniffers. Kids who had the best jump shot in their schools definitely were not managers. No sir. It was clearly a matter of pride with me.

I did not answer him.

Then he said, "Look, I already got kids who are going to collect towels and sweep and all of that. I need somebody to be a scorekeeper at games. You're the only kid in school who seems to know what a box score is." He was pretty close to being right; most of the kids in that school didn't read newspapers. "I'll let you practice with the varsity every day. Then, next year, you'll have the inside track at tryouts. What more can you ask for? You go to all the games, home and away, free, and you practice every day with the varsity. All you have to do is keep score at games. What do you expect me to do? Make a scorekeeper out of Nicky Bernardino? He can't add four and six."

The coach had thrown me a curve. He had offered me a spot on the periphery: part of the team, but not really part of the team. I immediately envisioned myself working out with the varsity, tossing in endless strings of jump shots over the distorted and frustrated faces of first-stringers, looking so impressive and so confident and so suave that Benchley Steele would finally take me aside some afternoon after practice and tell me to suit up for the game on Friday night. Then, of course, there was the prospect of all those one-on-one games before practices began; whoever heard of a manager beating the varsity star in one-on-one, in front of the rest of the team? *I'll show them.* I said to myself, *I'll show him. Head manager . . .*

"Yes, I'll do it," I said to him.

The coach smiled at me, and he tapped me on the knee.

"Good," he said.

The first game that season was against Heatly High School in Green Island, New York. Now, if you happen to know where the city of Cohoes, New York, is located, or where the city of Lansingburgh, New York, is located, or where the cities of Watervliet, Menands and Mechanicville, New York, are located, then you certainly will know where the village of Green Island is located. If not, suffice to say that the village of Green Island is located on the northernmost banks of the Hudson River. Green Island is not green; it is burned-charcoal gray, courtesy of the belching smokestacks of the Ford Motor Company plant there.

Before the game, Benchley Steele gave me my instructions: He said that he wanted to personally inspect the scorebook at half time of every game; he said that he wanted to see exactly who was doing what. Now, keeping score in basketball is not a difficult assignment. When a player makes a basket, you make an entry that looks like this: X. When a player attempts a free throw, you make an entry that looks like this: O. If the player makes the free throw, then you fill in the O with an X. So, if a player named Kelly, say, scores four baskets and converts three out of five free throws, for 11 points, his line in the scorebook would consist of the following:

	G. (Goals)	F. (Free Throws)	P. (Points)
Kelly.	4	3–5	11

Heatly High School had a tremendous player on its team; his name was Dick Kendall. He scored 22 points in the first half. I dutifully brought the scorebook to the coach at half time; smoking a cigarette in the hallway, adjacent to the locker room, he scanned the X's and the O's. He also scanned the column that was reserved for each player's personal fouls; when a player committed a foul, the entry was: p-1. The second foul was p-2. And so on. Five fouls and he was out of the game. I quickly learned that Benchley Steele liked the personal-foul column the best of all. He liked to see a lot of p-5's in the personal-foul column. Of the other team.

As he scanned the personal-foul column, the coach abruptly stopped, and he began screaming at me. Benchley Steele bellowed:

"What is this, two fouls on Kendall? *What is this?* Are you daydreaming or something? The kid's been fouling all night long; he must have four on him by now. Whose side are you on, anyway? Goddammit!"

I gulped.

I was sure that Dick Kendall had committed only two fouls. He had been too busy scoring points to commit fouls. Then I realized what my coach was up to: He was intimidating me. Benchley Steele was intimidating me for a reason. He wanted me to think that I had incurred his displeasure; he wanted me to go out there in the second half and eliminate Dick Kendall from the game with my mathematics. Then he would be happy, and I would be vindicated in his eyes. He wanted me to go out there in the second half and sneak in a quick p-3 and a quick p-4 on Dick Kendall when the other scorekeeper wasn't looking. That way, Dick Kendall would foul out of the game quicker. When Dick Kendall fouled out of the game, he would have to sit on the bench. He couldn't score any points while sitting on the bench. Then, my team could win the game.

Benchley Steele wanted me to cheat.

In the second half, he kept leaving the bench and coming over to the scorer's table. He kept asking me the same question:

"How many fouls on Kendall?"

"Two."

"Two? *Two?* Can you count past two? It's three."

After a while, I was afraid to answer him. Dick Kendall wasn't fouling anybody. He was just scoring points. He had 34 points after three quarters. My team was being obliterated by one player. Nobody could have stopped him but me. I could have penciled him out of the game. I didn't have the guts to do it. We lost. Dick Kendall wound up with 44 points in the game. I wound up with a tongue-lashing from Benchley Steele after the game. He was not very happy with me. He said:

"I got a moron for a scorekeeper. I not only get beat badly, but I got a moron for a scorekeeper. A *moron!*"

I had to make a decision that weekend. It was a pretty big decision for a fourteen-year-old boy to make: Either I was going to give the coach what he wanted, and I was going to cheat and doctor up the scorebook to foul out the other teams' best players, or else I was going to have to turn in my pencil. I wrestled with the decision all weekend. Integrity was not the only thing at stake. My future as a basketball player was on the line as well. If I quit, and if I told the coach to shove his pencil into a dark and creviced spot, my chances of making the team the following year would be nil. I could swish fifteen jump shots in a row, I could bank layups, play defense, and throw perfect lead passes, but I still would be cut. The coach had placed me in one hell of a spot.

There was no one with whom to discuss the situation, either. My father, a reasonably honest man, would have advised me to quit immediately. He always told me that man could not live by basketball alone. If I had gone to the school principal—which I considered doing for a moment or two—he would have called the coach into his office and confronted him with my verbal evidence. Then the scenario would have gone like this: The coach would have said, "The kid's lying. He's just trying to get back at me for cutting him from the team. He thinks he's got a great jump shot, you know. You don't really think I would tell him to cheat, do you?" Then the principal would have agreed with him. I would have been out as the score-keeper, too.

So, I did the only thing that any other fourteen-year-old kid with a great jump shot would have done under the circumstances. I decided to cheat.

The first time I did it was in a game against the Pebble Hill School in Syracuse. How a private, affluent, elite, Anglo-Saxon preparatory school ever wound up on our basketball schedule mysti-fied me anyway. It was an all-male school; on the day we played them, a Saturday afternoon, the school had imported some cheer-leaders from a private, affluent, elite, Anglo-Saxon girls' prep school nearby. The kid who was the scorekeeper for Pebble Hill was paying a lot of attention to the girls; it looked as if he had never seen any before. Every time there was a timeout, he would ogle the cheer-leaders. While he was ogling, I was finagling.

I got the two best Pebble Hill players out of the game early in the third period. They never knew what hit them. As they left the floor and headed for the bench, they had bewildered looks on their faces. They said, "I've only got three, Coach; I've only got three." The scorebook said five. Out. The Pebble Hill coach, however, was a gentleman. He never came over to the scorer's table to demand a detailed accounting. It was obvious to me that he was so much of a gentleman that it never dawned upon him that a fourteen-year-old scorekeeper that he had never seen before was actually cheating him out of the game right before his very eyes. My school won that game.

After the game, my coach winked at me; it was one of those "nice job" winks. I got the message.

The second time I did it was in a game at Waterford, New York. Waterford is near Green Island; it is landlocked. Waterford High School had a superb basketball player named John Anderson. He had 12 points in the first period. I knew he had to go. Now, Waterford High School apparently didn't have enough boys in its student body to spare one as its scorekeeper; either that, or the male students were very poor in math. The Waterford scorekeeper was a girl. It was like taking candy from a baby. During a timeout in the second period, I slipped in a p-3 on John Anderson. Early in the third period, while the coaches and the referees were discussing a slippery spot on the court, I slipped in a p-4 on John Anderson. Just before the third period ended, damned if John Anderson didn't go ahead and commit p-5 himself.

I pressed the button that sounded the buzzer. The referee came over to the scorer's table. He asked what was wrong.

"That's five on Anderson," I said.

The girl scorekeeper next to me was mortified.

"Five?" she gasped. "I've, uh, only got him down for three."

She stuttered and became nervous; she just did not have the necessary steadfastness to back up her statistics. She panicked. Besides, she was only a girl. What did she know about keeping score?

"How long you been keepin' score, son?" the referee asked me.

"Two years," I said, lying.

"How long you been keepin' score, miss?" he said.

"I, uh, just started," she said.

The referee called the Waterford coach over to the scorer's table.

"That's five on Anderson," he announced.

The Waterford coach went into a fit of apoplexy. He began screaming at his scorekeeper. She began to cry. Benchley Steele came over to the table, and he told the Waterford coach to stop screaming at that poor little innocent girl.

"What kind of man are you?" my coach asked the Waterford coach.

Sufficiently embarrassed, the Waterford coach apologized to his scorekeeper. He sent in a substitute for John Anderson. We won that game, too.

That summer, while playing basketball at all the local playgrounds, I carried around in the pit of my stomach this horrible feeling. I felt as if I were a criminal. Some days I rationalized my actions by telling myself that what I had done was done in the best interests of my basketball career. Surely, after winning three games for him from the scorer's table, the coach wouldn't cut me again. Surely, I had ingratiated myself with him; there would be a spot for me. I had earned it. I had showed him that I could follow orders correctly; I had showed him that I could be daring and yet discreet; I had showed him what a good scorekeeper could do, and that he could pattern all of his future scorekeepers after me. But meanwhile, it was time I got mine. My reward was going to be a place on the varsity team.

I was wrong, of course.

He cut me from the team again, after a spectacular showing in tryouts. I drove to the basket and feinted, sending defensive stalwarts flying in all directions; I banked layups, dropped in jump shots from the far corners of the floor, and, on defense, stole basketballs from players' grasps or else slapped them loose and scooped them up myself. On the last day, when I was coming off the floor for the last time, all the other players applauded me. The coach then put up three pieces of paper on the bulletin board outside the gym.

The first list was headed by the words: "The following players have been selected to the freshman team . . ."

My name was not on that list.

The second list was headed by the words: "The following players have made the junior varsity team . . ."

My name was not on that list.

The third list was headed by the words: "The following players have made the varsity team . . ."

Nope. Cut again.

I didn't cry this time. I silently thought about cutting the coach's heart out with a pair of scissors and feeding it to the neighborhood stray cat. After having showered and gotten dressed, I walked slowly out of the locker room, hoping to bump into some smallish player so that I could start a fight with him and beat him up. The coach was waiting for me in the hall.

He motioned for me to follow him into the dark gymnasium. He sat on the first row of the bleachers again. He said to me:

"I need you again. Just like last year. You're more valuable to me as a scorekeeper than you are as a player. No way you're gonna win three games for me as a player. As a scorekeeper, you could win six, or eight."

I nodded, not saying a word.

"Now, look," he said, "I know you feel bad. But we'll have the same arrangement we had last year. You work out with the varsity all week. You keep scores at games, I'll get you a letter. I'll get you into the varsity club. I'll get you the sports column in the school paper. Put yourself in my shoes. You got a kid like you, what're you gonna do with him? Sit him on the bench as a player? Or let him win games for you as a scorekeeper?"

He put his arm around me, and he said: "I like you. You're one of my favorite kids. I've got a soft spot right here for you."

He pointed to somewhere below his left nipple. I was hooked.

"Okay," I said. "I'll do it."

We were in a new league that year, a league called the Suburban Council. It consisted of schools exactly like mine: new, glass fishbowls of schools that were pancaked over vast acres of rolling grassland. I was in the vanguard of the suburban-high-school explosion in America. The Suburban Council was supposed to be the model organization for upstate New York schools; it was going to be the prestige league. The sophisticated suburban kids were supposed to be more intelligent, more aware, than all of those rowdies left behind in the medieval city high schools. We wouldn't be playing in Green Island or Waterford any more; now we were going to be playing on real farmland, in schools that were called "Niskayuna," and "Shaker," and "Guilderland" and "Schalmont." Even the team nicknames were exotic: One school selected "Sabres," another "The Dutchmen," a third "The Blue Bison."

The gymnasiums were lavish, well-lighted, large, and acoustically correct.

When the basketball season started, I quickly realized that the scorekeepers in the Suburban Council were, indeed, a lot more sophisticated and a lot more aware than the scorekeepers I had bilked the year before.

Everybody cheated in the Suburban Council.

A kid from Schalmont, a tall Italian who said his name was Danny, actually had the audacity to attempt to sneak in a p-3 on me. Niskayuna had two scorekeepers, one to keep score and one to watch the other scorer so that he didn't pull any funny stuff. I realized right away that my work was going to be cut out for me. The other kids apparently had coaches just like mine. Their coaches apparently told them the same things that mine told me.

I ran out the string that season. The next year, my senior year in high school, I took a part-time job as a sports stringer for the evening newspaper in town, the *Union-Star*. Sports stringers are people who cover high-school basketball games on Friday and Saturday nights during the winter. They are paid five dollars a game. The job got me off the hook with Benchley Steele. He got himself a new cheater. I didn't see Benchley Steele much that season. In fact, the last time I saw him and spoke to him at any length was one Monday afternoon in the gym office. I had covered one of my own school's games the Friday night before. I had written the story that appeared in the Saturday paper. My school had lost. When I walked into the gym office, I could tell that Ol' Benchie Steele was mad.

"What the hell kind of headline was that?" he growled at me.

"What headline?" I asked.

"The one in Saturday's paper," he said.

The headline in the Saturday paper, I remembered, read: NISKAS ROUT MOHONS, 72–58.

"What was wrong with it?" I asked.

He said, "What is this 'rout' business? We were only ten down with two minutes left. Tell me, is that a rout? Now, is it?"

I tried to explain to him that in newspaper offices the people who write the stories do not write the headlines. People who are called "Deskmen" do. Benchley Steele did not believe my explanation. He said:

"You're selling me out, right down the river."

Then he walked away.

But I'm not really mad at my first coach today. In fact, every time I think about him I smile. When he retired, I heard that the people gave him a testimonial banquet. Beautiful. But he taught me one of the first real hard lessons that all young men must learn before they succeed in America: He taught me the art of cheating within the system. There is a big difference between cheating within the system and cheating outside the system. When you cheat within the system, you are praised for being smart, alert, and mature. When you cheat outside the system, you go to jail. Doctoring scorebooks in basketball games is cheating within the system. Doctoring blank checks that belong to somebody else is cheating outside the system. Cheating within the system is very big in America, even today.

Grown men cheat companies with fake expense accounts and by calling in sick when they feel chipper but feel like playing a round of golf instead of working. I knew old ladies who cheated at bingo games; they doctored up their transparent, round tokens with half-numbers. If they needed a 4 for bingo and there was a 1 on the card, they slipped their half-4 button over the 1. Then the 1 would look like a 4. Bingo.

In America today, it is entirely possible that millions of young males acquire their first lessons in cheating in the playgrounds of the neighborhood schools. The coaches do the honors. What do you think players practice every night? How to be nice, and legal, and gentlemanly? No sir. They practice deceptive plays until they get them down pat. Deception in sports, for the ultimate good of the team, is revered. Parents and educators do not question the pick in basketball, or the curve ball in baseball, on moral grounds. But they become outraged when there is a little teamwork in the classroom, in the form of sharing test answers. Sports are separate entities; they have their own moral criteria.

Coaches rule these little empires. The only thing standing between coaches and moral anarchy is the referee. And sometimes even he doesn't help. Benchley Steele used to chew out referees at games very often. He chewed them out so often, and so loudly, that the referees became intimidated. They started worrying if they were going to be invited back to earn their fifteen dollars the following week. Then they started ignoring fouls, or else they started making judgment calls in my coach's favor. When that happened, they were always invited back. Someday Ol' Benchie Steele is going to make a deal with Lucifer—I just know it.

PROBING FOR MEANING

1. How is Benchley Steele described? Which of his characteristics does Ralbovsky emphasize?

2. Is the author typical of high school students? After he is cut from the team and is offered the job of manager, what prompts him to accept?

3. How does the author feel about cheating while in high school? Why does he decide to cheat? Why doesn't he simply quit the team? How does Benchley Steele coerce him to doctor the scorebook?

4. What is the theme of the essay? What does the experience of the author say about the American sports system? How are sports a reflection of the morality of American society? Explain.

5. Is the argument that sports are deceptive in nature and therefore lacking in morality a good one? Explain.

PROBING FOR METHOD

1. What is the tone of the essay? How does the tone contribute to the meaning?

2. The opening paragraph of the essay describes the postwar migration to the suburbs. How is this introduction connected to what follows? How effective is it as an opening paragraph?

3. What is the purpose of the description of the author's solitary winter practices? Is this description exaggerated? Why?

4. How does the conclusion contribute to the central statement of the essay?

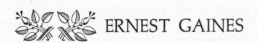 ERNEST GAINES

The Sky Is Gray

1

Go'n be coming in a few minutes. Coming round that bend down there full speed. And I'm go'n get out my handkerchief and wave it down, and we go'n get on it and go.

I keep on looking for it, but Mama don't look that way no

more. She's looking down the road where we just come from. It's a long old road, and far 's you can see you don't see nothing but gravel. You got dry weeds on both sides, and you got trees on both sides, and fences on both sides, too. And you got cows in the pastures and they standing close together. And when we was coming out here to catch the bus I seen the smoke coming out of the cows's noses.

I look at my mama and I know what she's thinking. I been with Mama so much, just me and her, I know what she's thinking all the time. Right now it's home—Auntie and them. She's thinking if they got enough wood—if she left enough there to keep them warm till we get back. She's thinking if it go'n rain and if any of them go'n have to go out in the rain. She's thinking 'bout the hog—if he go'n get out, and if Ty and Val be able to get him back in. She always worry like that when she leaves the house. She don't worry too much if she leave me there with the smaller ones, 'cause she know I'm go'n look after them and look after Auntie and everything else. I'm the oldest and she say I'm the man.

I look at my mama and I love my mama. She's wearing that black coat and that black hat and she's looking sad. I love my mama and I want put my arm round her and tell her. But I'm not supposed to do that. She say that's weakness and that's crybaby stuff, and she don't want no crybaby round her. She don't want you to be scared, either. 'Cause Ty's scared of ghosts and she's always whipping him. I'm scared of the dark, too, but I make 'tend I ain't. I make 'tend I ain't 'cause I'm the oldest, and I got to set a good sample for the rest. I can't ever be scared and I can't ever cry. And that's why I never said nothing 'bout my teeth. It's been hurting me and hurting me close to a month now, but I never said it. I didn't say it 'cause I didn't want act like a crybaby, and 'cause I know we didn't have enough money to go have it pulled. But, Lord, it been hurting me. And look like it wouldn't start till at night when you was trying to get yourself little sleep. Then soon 's you shut your eyes—ummm-ummm, Lord, look like it go right down to your heartstring.

"Hurting, hanh?" Ty'd say.

I'd shake my head, but I wouldn't open my mouth for nothing. You open your mouth and let that wind in, and it almost kill you.

I'd just lay there and listen to them snore. Ty there, right 'side me, and Auntie and Val over by the fireplace. Val younger than me and Ty, and he sleeps with Auntie. Mama sleeps round the other side with Louis and Walter.

I'd just lay there and listen to them, and listen to that wind out there, and listen to that fire in the fireplace. Sometimes it'd stop long enough to let me get little rest. Sometimes it just hurt, hurt, hurt. Lord, have mercy.

2

Auntie knowed it was hurting me. I didn't tell nobody but Ty, 'cause we buddies and he ain't go'n tell nobody. But some kind of way Auntie found out. When she asked me, I told her no, nothing was wrong. But she knowed it all the time. She told me to mash up a piece of aspirin and wrap it in some cotton and jugg it down in that hole. I did it, but it didn't do no good. It stopped for a little while, and started right back again. Auntie wanted to tell Mama, but I told her, "Uh-uh." 'Cause I knowed we didn't have any money, and it just was go'n make her mad again. So Auntie told Monsieur Bayonne, and Monsieur Bayonne came over to the house and told me to kneel down 'side him on the fireplace. He put his finger in his mouth and made the Sign of the Cross on my jaw. The tip of Monsieur Bayonne's finger is some hard, 'cause he's always playing on that guitar. If we sit outside at night we can always hear Monsieur Bayonne playing on his guitar. Sometimes we leave him out there playing on the guitar.

Monsieur Bayonne made the Sign of the Cross over and over on my jaw, but that didn't do no good. Even when he prayed and told me to pray some, too, that tooth still hurt me.

"How you feeling?" he say.

"Same," I say.

He kept on praying and making the Sign of the Cross and I kept on praying, too.

"Still hurting?" he say.

"Yes, sir."

Monsieur Bayonne mashed harder and harder on my jaw. He mashed so hard he almost pushed me over on Ty. But then he stopped.

"What kind of prayers you praying, boy?" he say.

"Baptist," I say.

"Well, I'll be—no wonder that tooth still killing him. I'm going one way and he pulling the other. Boy, don't you know any Catholic prayers?"

"I know 'Hail Mary,' " I say.

"Then you better start saying it."

"Yes, sir."

He started mashing on my jaw again, and I could hear him praying at the same time. And, sure enough, after while it stopped hurting me.

Me and Ty went outside where Monsieur Bayonne's two hounds was and we started playing with them. "Let's go hunting," Ty say. "All right," I say; and we went on back in the pasture. Soon the hounds got on a trail, and me and Ty followed them all 'cross the pasture and then back in the woods, too. And then they cornered this little old rabbit and killed him, and me and Ty made them get back, and we picked up the rabbit and started on back home. But my tooth had started hurting me again. It was hurting me plenty now, but I wouldn't tell Monsieur Bayonne. That night I didn't sleep a bit, and first thing in the morning Auntie told me to go back and let Monsieur Bayonne pray over me some more. Monsieur Bayonne was in his kitchen making coffee when I got there. Soon 's he seen me he knowed what was wrong.

"All right, kneel down there 'side that stove," he say. "And this time make sure you pray Catholic. I don't know nothing 'bout that Baptist, and I don't want know nothing 'bout him."

3

Last night Mama say, "Tomorrow we going to town."

"It ain't hurting me no more," I say. "I can eat anything on it."

"Tomorrow we going to town," she say.

And after she finished eating, she got up and went to bed. She always go to bed early now. 'Fore Daddy went in the Army, she used to stay up late. All of us sitting out on the gallery or round the fire. But now, look like soon 's she finish eating she go to bed.

This morning when I woke up, her and Auntie was standing 'fore the fireplace. She say: "Enough to get there and get back. Dollar and a half to have it pulled. Twenty-five for me to go, twenty-five for him. Twenty-five for me to come back, twenty-five for him. Fifty cents left. Guess I get little piece of salt meat with that."

"Sure can use it," Auntie say. "White beans and no salt meat ain't white beans."

"I do the best I can," Mama say.

They was quiet after that, and I made 'tend I was still asleep.

"James, hit the floor," Auntie say.

I still made 'tend I was asleep. I didn't want them to know I was listening.

"All right," Auntie say, shaking me by the shoulder. "Come on. Today's the day."

I pushed the cover down to get out, and Ty grabbed it and pulled it back.

"You, too, Ty," Auntie say.

"I ain't getting no teef pulled," Ty say.

"Don't mean it ain't time to get up," Auntie say. "Hit it, Ty."

Ty got up grumbling.

"James, you hurry up and get in your clothes and eat your food," Auntie say. "What time y'all coming back?" she say to Mama.

"That 'leven o'clock bus," Mama say. "Got to get back in that field this evening."

"Get a move on you, James," Auntie say.

I went in the kitchen and washed my face, then I ate my breakfast. I was having bread and syrup. The bread was warm and hard and tasted good. And I tried to make it last a long time.

Ty came back there grumbling and mad at me.

"Got to get up," he say. "I ain't having no teefes pulled. What I got to be getting up for?"

Ty poured some syrup in his pan and got a piece of bread. He didn't wash his hands, neither his face, and I could see that white stuff in his eyes.

"You the one getting your teef pulled," he say. "What I got to get up for. I bet if I was getting a teef pulled, you wouldn't be getting up. Shucks; syrup again. I'm getting tired of this old syrup. Syrup, syrup, syrup. I'm go'n take with the sugar diabetes. I want me some bacon sometime."

"Go out in the field and work and you can have your bacon," Auntie say. She stood in the middle door looking at Ty. "You better be glad you got syrup. Some people ain't got that—hard 's time is."

"Shucks," Ty say. "How can I be strong."

"I don't know too much 'bout your strength," Auntie say; "but I know where you go'n be hot at, you keep that grumbling up. James, get a move on you; your mama waiting."

I ate my last piece of bread and went in the front room. Mama was standing 'fore the fireplace warming her hands. I put on my coat and my cap, and we left the house.

4

I look down there again, but it still ain't coming. I almost say, "It ain't coming yet," but I keep my mouth shut. 'Cause that's something else she don't like. She don't like for you to say something just for nothing. She can see it ain't coming, I can see it ain't coming, so why say it ain't coming. I don't say it, I turn and look at the river that's back of us. It's so cold the smoke's just raising up from the water. I see a bunch of pool-doos not too far out—just on the other side the lilies. I'm wondering if you can eat pool-doos. I ain't too sure, 'cause I ain't never ate none. But I done ate owls and blackbirds, and

I done ate redbirds, too. I didn't want kill the redbirds, but she made
me kill them. They had two of them back there. One in my trap, one
in Ty's trap. Me and Ty was go'n play with them and let them go, but
she made me kill them 'cause we needed the food.

"I can't," I say. "I can't."

"Here," she say. "Take it."

"I can't," I say. "I can't. I can't kill him, Mama, please."

"Here," she say. "Take this fork, James."

"Please, Mama, I can't kill him," I say.

I could tell she was go'n hit me. I jerked back, but I didn't
jerk back soon enough.

"Take it," she say.

I took it and reached in for him, but he kept on hopping to
the back.

"I can't, Mama," I say. The water just kept on running down
my face. "I can't," I say.

"Get him out of there," she say.

I reached in for him and he kept on hopping to the back. Then
I reached in farther, and he pecked me on the hand.

"I can't, Mama," I say.

She slapped me again.

I reached in again, but he kept on hopping out my way. Then
he hopped to one side and I reached there. The fork got him on the
leg and I heard his leg pop. I pulled my hand out 'cause I had hurt
him.

"Give it here," she say, and jerked the fork out my hand.

She reached in and got the little bird right in the neck. I heard
the fork go in his neck, and I heard it go in the ground. She brought
him out and helt him right in front of me.

"That's one," she say. She shook him off and gived me the
fork. "Get the other one."

"I can't, Mama," I say. "I'll do anything, but don't make me
do that."

She went to the corner of the fence and broke the biggest
switch over there she could find. I knelt 'side the trap, crying.

"Get him out of there," she say.

"I can't, Mama."

She started hitting me 'cross the back. I went down on the
ground, crying.

"Get him," she say.

"Octavia?" Auntie say.

'Cause she had come out of the house and she was standing
by the tree looking at us.

"Get him out of there," Mama say.

"Octavia," Auntie say, "explain to him. Explain to him. Just don't beat him. Explain to him."

But she hit me and hit me and hit me.

I'm still young—I ain't no more than eight; but I know now; I know why I had to do it. (They was so little, though. They was so little. I 'member how I picked the feathers off them and cleaned them and helt them over the fire. Then we all ate them. Ain't had but a little bitty piece each, but we all had a little bitty piece, and everybody just looked at me 'cause they was so proud.) Suppose she had to go away? That's why I had to do it. Suppose she had to go away like Daddy went away? Then who was go'n look after us? They had to be somebody left to carry on. I didn't know it then, but I know it now. Auntie and Monsieur Bayonne talked to me and made me see.

5

Time I see it I get out my handkerchief and start waving. It's still 'way down there, but I keep waving anyhow. Then it come up and stop and me and Mama get on. Mama tell me go sit in the back while she pay. I do like she say, and the people look at me. When I pass the little sign that say "White" and "Colored," I start looking for a seat. I just see one of them back there, but I don't take it, 'cause I want my mama to sit down herself. She comes in the back and sit down, and I lean on the seat. They got seats in the front, but I know I can't sit there, 'cause I have to sit back of the sign. Anyhow, I don't want sit there if my mama go'n sit back here.

They got a lady sitting 'side my mama and she looks at me and smiles little bit. I smile back, but I don't open my mouth, 'cause the wind'll get in and make that tooth ache. The lady take out a pack of gum and reach me a slice, but I shake my head. The lady just can't understand why a little boy'll turn down gum, and she reach me a slice again. This time I point to my jaw. The lady understands and smiles little bit, and I smile little bit, but I don't open my mouth, though.

They got a girl sitting 'cross from me. She got on a red overcoat and her hair's plaited in one big plait. First, I make 'tend I don't see her over there, but then I start looking at her little bit. She make 'tend she don't see me, either, but I catch her looking that way. She got a cold, and every now and then she h'ist that little handkerchief to her nose. She ought to blow it, but she don't. Must think she's too much a lady or something.

Every time she h'ist that little handkerchief, the lady 'side her say something in her ear. She shakes her head and lays her hands in her lap again. Then I catch her kind of looking where I'm at. I smile at her little bit. But think she'll smile back? Uh-uh. She just turn up her little old nose and turn her head. Well, I show her both of us can turn us head. I turn mine too and look out at the river.

The river is gray. The sky is gray. They have pool-doos on the water. The water is wavy, and the pool-doos go up and down. The bus go round a turn, and you got plenty trees hiding the river. Then the bus go round another turn, and I can see the river again.

I look toward the front where all the white people sitting. Then I look at that little old gal again. I don't look right at her, 'cause I don't want all them people to know I love her. I just look at her little bit, like I'm looking out that window over there. But she knows I'm looking that way, and she kind of look at me, too. The lady sitting 'side her catch her this time, and she leans over and says something in her ear.

"I don't love him nothing," that little old gal says out loud.

Everybody back there hear her mouth, and all of them look at us and laugh.

"I don't love you, either," I say. "So you don't have to turn up your nose, Miss."

"You the one looking," she say.

"I wasn't looking at you," I say. "I was looking out that window, there."

"Out that window, my foot," she say. "I seen you. Everytime I turned round you was looking at me."

"You must of been looking yourself if you seen me all them times," I say.

"Shucks," she say, "I got me all kind of boyfriends."

"I got girlfriends, too," I say.

"Well, I just don't want you getting your hopes up," she say.

I don't say no more to that little old gal 'cause I don't want have to bust her in the mouth. I lean on the seat where Mama sitting, and I don't even look that way no more. When we get to Bayonne, she jugg her little old tongue out at me. I make 'tend I'm go'n hit her, and she duck down 'side her mama. And all the people laugh at us again.

6

Me and Mama get off and start walking in town. Bayonne is a little bitty town. Baton Rouge is a hundred times bigger than Bayonne. I went to Baton Rouge once—me, Ty, Mama, and Daddy. But that was 'way back yonder, 'fore Daddy went in the Army. I wonder when we go'n see him again. I wonder when. Look like he ain't ever coming back home. . . . Even the pavement all cracked in Bayonne. Got grass shooting right out the sidewalk. Got weeds in the ditch, too; just like they got at home.

It's some cold in Bayonne. Look like it's colder than it is home. The wind blows in my face, and I feel that stuff running down my nose. I sniff. Mama says use that handkerchief. I blow my nose and put it back.

We pass a school and I see them white children playing in the yard. Big old red school, and them children just running and playing. Then we pass a café, and I see a bunch of people in there eating. I wish I was in there 'cause I'm cold. Mama tells me keep my eyes in front where they belong.

We pass stores that's got dummies, and we pass another café, and then we pass a shoe shop, and that bald-head man in there fixing on a shoe. I look at him and I butt into that white lady, and Mama jerks me in front and tells me stay there.

We come up to the courthouse, and I see the flag waving there. This flag ain't like the one we got at school. This one here ain't got but a handful of stars. One at school got a pile of stars—one for every state. We pass it and we turn and there it is—the dentist office. Me and Mama go in, and they got people sitting everywhere you look. They even got a little boy in there younger than me.

Me and Mama sit on that bench, and a white lady come in there and ask me what my name is. Mama tells her and the white lady goes on back. Then I hear somebody hollering in there. Soon 's that little boy hear him hollering, he starts hollering, too. His mama pats him and pats him, trying to make him hush up, but he ain't thinking 'bout his mama.

The man that was hollering in there comes out holding his jaw. He is a big old man and he's wearing overalls and a jumper.

"Got it, hanh?" another man asks him.

The man shakes his head—don't want open his mouth.

"Man, I thought they was killing you in there," the other man says. "Hollering like a pig under a gate."

The man don't say nothing. He just heads for the door, and the other man follows him.

"John Lee," the white lady says. "John Lee Williams."

The little boy juggs his head down in his mama's lap and holler more now. His mama tells him go with the nurse, but he ain't thinking 'bout his mama. His mama tells him again, but he don't even hear her. His mama picks him up and takes him in there, and even when the white lady shuts the door I can still hear little old John Lee.

"I often wonder why the Lord let a child like that suffer," a lady says to my mama. The lady's sitting right in front of us on another bench. She's got on a white dress and a black sweater. She must be a nurse or something herself, I reckon.

"Not us to question," a man says.

"Sometimes I don't know if we shouldn't," the lady says.

"I know definitely we shouldn't," the man says. The man looks like a preacher. He's big and fat and he's got on a black suit. He's got a gold chain, too.

"Why?" the lady says.

"Why anything?" the preacher says.

"Yes," the lady says. "Why anything?"

"Not us to question," the preacher says.

The lady looks at the preacher a little while and looks at Mama again.

"And look like it's the poor who suffers the most," she says. "I don't understand it."

"Best not to even try," the preacher says. "He works in mysterious ways—wonders to perform."

Right then little John Lee bust out hollering, and everybody turn they head to listen.

"He's not a good dentist," the lady says. "Dr. Robillard is much better. But more expensive. That's why most of the colored people come here. The white people go to Dr. Robillard. Y'all from Bayonne?"

"Down the river," my mama says. And that's all she go'n say, 'cause she don't talk much. But the lady keeps on looking at her, and so she says, "Near Morgan."

"I see," the lady says.

7

"That's the trouble with the black people in this country today," somebody else says. This one here's sitting on the same side me and Mama's sitting, and he is kind of sitting in front of that preacher. He looks like a teacher or somebody that goes to college. He's got on a suit, and he's got a book that he's been reading. "We don't question is exactly our problem," he says. "We should question and question and question—question everything."

The preacher just looks at him a long time. He done put a toothpick or something in his mouth, and he just keeps on turning it and turning it. You can see he don't like that boy with that book.

"Maybe you can explain what you mean," he says.

"I said what I meant," the boy says. "Question everything. Every stripe, every star, every word spoken. Everything."

"It 'pears to me that this young lady and I was talking 'bout God, young man," the preacher says.

"Question Him, too," the boy says.

"Wait," the preacher says. "Wait now."

"You heard me right," the boy says. "His existence as well as everything else. Everything."

The preacher just looks across the room at the boy. You can see he's getting madder and madder. But mad or no mad, the boy ain't thinking 'bout him. He looks at that preacher just 's hard 's the preacher looks at him.

"Is this what they coming to?" the preacher says. "Is this what we educating them for?"

"You're not educating me," the boy says. "I wash dishes at night so that I can go to school in the day. So even the words you spoke need questioning."

The preacher just looks at him and shakes his head.

"When I come in this room and seen you there with your book, I said to myself, 'There's an intelligent man.' How wrong a person can be."

"Show me one reason to believe in the existence of a God," the boy says.

"My heart tells me," the preacher says.

" 'My heart tells me,' " the boy says. " 'My heart tells me.' Sure, 'My heart tells me.' And as long as you listen to what your heart tells you, you will have only what the white man gives you and nothing more. Me, I don't listen to my heart. The purpose of the heart is to pump blood throughout the body, and nothing else."

"Who's your paw, boy?" the preacher says.

"Why?"

"Who is he?"

"He's dead."

"And your mom?"

"She's in Charity Hospital with pneumonia. Half killed herself, working for nothing."

"And 'cause he's dead and she's sick, you mad at the world?"

"I'm not mad at the world. I'm questioning the world. I'm questioning it with cold logic, sir. What do words like Freedom, Liberty, God, White, Colored mean? I want to know. That's why *you* are sending us to school, to read and to ask questions. And because we ask these questions, you call us mad. No sir, it is not us who are mad."

"You keep saying 'us'?"

" 'Us.' Yes—us. I'm not alone."

The preacher just shakes his head. Then he looks at everybody in the room—everybody. Some of the people look down at the floor, keep from looking at him. I kind of look 'way myself, but soon 's I know he done turn his head, I look that way again.

"I'm sorry for you," he says to the boy.

"Why?" the boy says. "Why not be sorry for yourself? Why are you so much better off than I am? Why aren't you sorry for these other people in here? Why not be sorry for the lady who had to drag her child into the dentist office? Why not be sorry for the lady sitting on that bench over there? Be sorry for them. Not for me. Some way or the other I'm going to make it."

"No, I'm sorry for you," the preacher says.

"Of course, of course," the boy says, nodding his head. "You're sorry for me because I rock that pillar you're leaning on."

"You can't ever rock the pillar I'm leaning on, young man. It's stronger than anything man can ever do."

"You believe in God because a man told you to believe in God," the boy says. "A white man told you to believe in God. And why? To keep you ignorant so he can keep his feet on your neck."

"So now we the ignorant?" the preacher says.

"Yes," the boy says. "Yes." And he opens his book again.

The preacher just looks at him sitting there. The boy done forgot all about him. Everybody else make 'tend they done forgot the squabble, too.

Then I see that preacher getting up real slow. Preacher's a great big old man and he got to brace himself to get up. He comes over where the boy is sitting. He just stands there a little while looking down at him, but the boy don't raise his head.

"Get up, boy," preacher says.

The boy looks up at him, then he shuts his book real slow and stands up. Preacher just hauls back and hit him in the face. The boy falls back 'gainst the wall, but he straightens himself up and looks right back at that preacher.

"You forgot the other cheek," he says.

The preacher hauls back and hit him again on the other side. But this time the boy braces himself and don't fall.

"That hasn't changed a thing," he says.

The preacher just looks at the boy. The preacher's breathing real hard like he just run up a big hill. The boy sits down and opens his book again.

"I feel sorry for you," the preacher says. "I never felt so sorry for a man before."

The boy makes 'tend he don't even hear that preacher. He keeps on reading his book. The preacher goes back and gets his hat off the chair.

"Excuse me," he says to us. "I'll come back some other time. Y'all, please excuse me."

And he looks at the boy and goes out the room. The boy h'ist his hand up to his mouth one time to wipe 'way some blood. All the rest of the time he keeps on reading. And nobody else in there say a word.

8

Little John Lee and his mama come out the dentist office, and the nurse calls somebody else in. Then little bit later they come out, and the nurse calls another name. But fast 's she calls somebody in there, somebody else comes in the place where we sitting, and the room stays full.

The people coming in now, all of them wearing big coats. One of them says something 'bout sleeting, another one says he hope not. Another one says he think it ain't nothing but rain. 'Cause, he says, rain can get awful cold this time of year.

All round the room they talking. Some of them talking to people right by them, some of them talking to people clear 'cross the room, some of them talking to anybody'll listen. It's a little bitty room, no bigger than us kitchen, and I can see everybody in there. The little old room's full of smoke, 'cause you got two old men smoking pipes over by that side door. I think I feel my tooth thumping me some, and I hold my breath and wait. I wait and wait, but it don't thump me no more. Thank God for that.

I feel like going to sleep, and I lean back 'gainst the wall. But I'm scared to go to sleep. Scared 'cause the nurse might call my name and I won't hear her. And Mama might go to sleep, too, and she'll be mad if neither one of us heard the nurse.

I look up at Mama. I love my mama. I love my mama. And when cotton come I'm go'n get her a new coat. And I ain't go'n get a black one, either. I think I'm go'n get her a red one.

"They got some books over there," I say. "Want read one of them?"

Mama looks at the books, but she don't answer me.

"You got yourself a little man there," the lady says.

Mama don't say nothing to the lady, but she must've smiled, 'cause I seen the lady smiling back. The lady looks at me a little while, like she's feeling sorry for me.

"You sure got that preacher out here in a hurry," she says to that boy.

The boy looks up at her and looks in his book again. When I grow up I want be just like him. I want clothes like that and I want keep a book with me, too.

"You really don't believe in God?" the lady says.

"No," he says.

"But why?" the lady says.

"Because the wind is pink," he says.

"What?" the lady says.

The boy don't answer her no more. He just reads in his book.

"Talking 'bout the wind is pink," the old lady says. She's sitting on the same bench with the boy and she's trying to look in his face. The boy makes 'tend the old lady ain't even there. He just keeps on reading. "Wind is pink," she says again. "Eh, Lord, what children go'n be saying next?"

The lady 'cross from us bust out laughing.

"That's a good one," she says. "The wind is pink. Yes sir, that's a good one."

"Don't you believe the wind is pink?" the boy says. He keeps his head down in the book.

"Course I believe it, honey," the lady says. "Course I do." She looks at us and winks her eye. "And what color is grass, honey?"

"Grass? Grass is black."

She bust out laughing again. The boy looks at her.

"Don't you believe grass is black?" he says.

The lady quits her laughing and looks at him. Everybody else looking at him, too. The place quiet, quiet.

"Grass is green, honey," the lady says. "It was green yesterday, it's green today, and it's go'n be green tomorrow."

"How do you know it's green?"

"I know because I know."

"You don't know it's green," the boy says. "You believe it's green because someone told you it was green. If someone had told you it was black you'd believe it was black."

"It's green," the lady says. "I know green when I see green."

"Prove it's green," the boy says.

"Sure, now," the lady says. "Don't tell me it's coming to that."

"It's coming to just that," the boy says. "Words mean nothing. One means no more than the other."

"That's what it all coming to?" that old lady says. That old lady got on a turban and she got on two sweaters. She got a green sweater under a black sweater. I can see the green sweater 'cause some of the buttons on the other sweater's missing.

"Yes ma'am," the boy says. "Words mean nothing. Action is the only thing. Doing. That's the only thing."

"Other words, you want the Lord to come down here and show Hisself to you?" she says.

"Exactly, ma'am," he says.

"You don't mean that, I'm sure?" she says.

"I do, ma'am," he says.

"Done, Jesus," the old lady says, shaking her head.

"I didn't go 'long with that preacher at first," the other lady says; "but now—I don't know. When a person say the grass is black, he's either a lunatic or something's wrong."

"Prove to me that it's green," the boy says.

"It's green because the people say it's green."

"Those same people say we're citizens of these United States," the boy says.

"I think I'm a citizen," the lady says.

"Citizens have certain rights," the boy says. "Name me one right that you have. One right, granted by the Constitution, that you can exercise in Bayonne."

The lady don't answer him. She just looks at him like she don't know what he's talking 'bout. I know I don't.

"Things changing," she says.

"Things are changing because some black men have begun to think with their brains and not their hearts," the boy says.

"You trying to say these people don't believe in God?"

"I'm sure some of them do. Maybe most of them do. But they don't believe that God is going to touch these white people's hearts and change things tomorrow. Things change through action. By no other way."

Everybody sit quiet and look at the boy. Nobody says a thing. Then the lady 'cross the room from me and Mama just shakes her head.

"Let's hope that not all your generation feel the same way you do," she says.

"Think what you please, it doesn't matter," the boy says. "But it will be men who listen to their heads and not their hearts who will see that your children have a better chance than you had."

"Let's hope they ain't all like you, though," the old lady says. "Done forgot the heart absolutely."

"Yes ma'am, I hope they aren't all like me," the boy says. "Unfortunately, I was born too late to believe in your God. Let's hope that the ones who come after will have your faith—if not in your

God, then in something else, something definitely that they can lean on. I haven't anything. For me, the wind is pink, the grass is black."

9

The nurse comes in the room where we all sitting and waiting and says the doctor won't take no more patients till one o'clock this evening. My mama jumps up off the bench and goes up to the white lady.

"Nurse, I have to go back in the field this evening," she says.

"The doctor is treating his last patient now," the nurse says. "One o'clock this evening."

"Can I at least speak to the doctor?" my mama asks.

"I'm his nurse," the lady says.

"My little boy's sick," my mama says. "Right now his tooth almost killing him."

The nurse looks at me. She's trying to make up her mind if to let me come in. I look at her real pitiful. The tooth ain't hurting me at all, but Mama say it is, so I make 'tend for her sake.

"This evening," the nurse says, and goes on back in the office.

"Don't feel 'jected, honey," the lady says to Mama. "I been round them a long time—they take you when they want to. If you was white, that's something else; but we the wrong color."

Mama don't say nothing to the lady, and me and her go outside and stand 'gainst the wall. It's cold out there. I can feel that wind going through my coat. Some of the other people come out of the room and go up the street. Me and Mama stand there a little while and we start walking. I don't know where we going. When we come to the other street we just stand there.

"You don't have to make water, do you?" Mama says.

"No, ma'am," I say.

We go on up the street. Walking real slow. I can tell Mama don't know where she's going. When we come to a store we stand there and look at the dummies. I look at a little boy wearing a brown overcoat. He's got on brown shoes, too. I look at my old shoes and look at his'n again. You wait till summer, I say.

Me and Mama walk away. We come up to another store and we stop and look at them dummies, too. Then we go on again. We pass a café where the white people in there eating. Mama tells me keep my eyes in front where they belong, but I can't help from seeing them people eat. My stomach starts to growling 'cause I'm hungry.

When I see people eating, I get hungry; when I see a coat, I get cold.

A man whistles at my mama when we go by a filling station. She makes 'tend she don't even see him. I look back and I feel like hitting him in the mouth. If I was bigger, I say; if I was bigger, you'd see.

We keep on going. I'm getting colder and colder, but I don't say nothing. I feel that stuff running down my nose and I sniff.

"That rag," Mama says.

I get it out and wipe my nose. I'm getting cold all over now—my face, my hands, my feet, everything. We pass another little café, but this'n for white people, too, and we can't go in there, either. So we just walk. I'm so cold now I'm 'bout ready to say it. If I knowed where we was going I wouldn't be so cold, but I don't know where we going. We go, we go, we go. We walk clean out of Bayonne. Then we cross the street and we come back. Same thing I seen when I got off the bus this morning. Same old trees, same old walk, same old weeds, same old cracked pave—same old everything.

I sniff again.

"That rag," Mama says.

I wipe my nose real fast and jugg that handkerchief back in my pocket 'fore my hand gets too cold. I raise my head and I can see David's hardware store. When we come up to it, we go in. I don't know why, but I'm glad.

It's warm in there. It's so warm in there you don't ever want to leave. I look for the heater, and I see it over by them barrels. Three white men standing round the heater talking in Creole. One of them comes over to see what my mama want.

"Got any axe handles?" she says.

Me, Mama and the white man start to the back, but Mama stops me when we come up to the heater. She and the white man go on. I hold my hands over the heater and look at them. They go all the way to the back, and I see the white man pointing to the axe handles 'gainst the wall. Mama takes one of them and shakes it like she's trying to figure how much it weighs. Then she rubs her hand over it from one end to the other end. She turns it over and looks at the other side, then she shakes it again, and shakes her head and puts it back. She gets another one and she does it just like she did the first one, then she shakes her head. Then she gets a brown one and do it that, too. But she don't like this one, either. Then she gets another one, but 'fore she shakes it or anything, she looks at me. Look like she's trying to say something to me, but I don't know what it is. All I know is I done got warm now and I'm feeling right smart better. Mama shakes this axe handle just like she did the others, and shakes her head and says something to the white man. The white man just looks at his pile of axe handles, and when Mama pass him to come to the front, the white man just scratch his head and follows her. She tells me come on and we go on out and start walking again.

We walk and walk, and no time at all I'm cold again. Look like I'm colder now 'cause I can still remember how good it was back there. My stomach growls and I suck it in to keep Mama from hearing it. She's walking right 'side me, and it growls so loud you can hear it a mile. But Mama don't say a word.

10

When we come up to the courthouse, I look at the clock. It's got quarter to twelve. Mean we got another hour and a quarter to be out here in the cold. We go and stand 'side a building. Something hits my cap and I look up at the sky. Sleet's falling.

I look at Mama standing there. I want stand close 'side her, but she don't like that. She say that's crybaby stuff. She say you got to stand for yourself, by yourself.

"Let's go back to that office," she says.

We cross the street. When we get to the dentist office I try to open the door, but I can't. I twist and twist, but I can't. Mama pushes me to the side and she twist the knob, but she can't open the door, either. She turns 'way from the door. I look at her, but I don't move and I don't say nothing. I done seen her like this before and I'm scared of her.

"You hungry?" she says. She says it like she's mad at me, like I'm the cause of everything.

"No, ma'am," I say.

"You want eat and walk back, or you rather don't eat and ride?"

"I ain't hungry," I say.

I ain't just hungry, but I'm cold, too. I'm so hungry and cold I want to cry. And look like I'm getting colder and colder. My feet done got numb. I try to work my toes, but I don't even feel them. Look like I'm go'n die. Look like I'm go'n stand right here and freeze to death. I think 'bout home. I think 'bout Val and Auntie and Ty and Louis and Walter. It's 'bout twelve o'clock and I know they eating dinner now. I can hear Ty making jokes. He done forgot 'bout getting up early this morning and right now he's probably making jokes. Always trying to make somebody laugh. I wish I was right there listening to him. Give anything in the world if I was home round the fire.

"Come on," Mama says.

We start walking again. My feet so numb I can't hardly feel them. We turn the corner and go on back up the street. The clock on the courthouse starts hitting for twelve.

The sleet's coming down plenty now. They hit the pave and bounce like rice. Oh, Lord; oh, Lord, I pray. Don't let me die, don't let me die, don't let me die, Lord.

11

Now I know where we going. We going back of town where the colored people eat. I don't care if I don't eat. I been hungry before. I can stand it. But I can't stand the cold.

I can see we go'n have a long walk. It's 'bout a mile down there. But I don't mind. I know when I get there I'm go'n warm myself. I think I can hold out. My hands numb in my pockets and my feet numb, too, but if I keep moving I can hold out. Just don't stop no more, that's all.

The sky's gray. The sleet keeps on falling. Falling like rain now—plenty, plenty. You can hear it hitting the pave. You can see it bouncing. Sometimes it bounces two times 'fore it settles.

We keep on going. We don't say nothing. We just keep on going, keep on going.

I wonder what Mama's thinking. I hope she ain't mad at me. When summer come I'm go'n pick plenty cotton and get her a coat. I'm go'n get her a red one.

I hope they'd make it summer all the time. I'd be glad if it was summer all the time—but it ain't. We got to have winter, too. Lord, I hate the winter. I guess everybody hate the winter.

I don't sniff this time. I get out my handkerchief and wipe my nose. My hands's so cold I can hardly hold the handkerchief.

I think we getting close, but we ain't there yet. I wonder where everybody is. Can't see a soul but us. Look like we the only two people moving round today. Must be too cold for the rest of the people to move round in.

I can hear my teeth. I hope they don't knock together too hard and make that bad one hurt. Lord, that's all I need, for that bad one to start off.

I hear a church bell somewhere. But today ain't Sunday. They must be ringing for a funeral or something.

I wonder what they doing at home. They must be eating. Monsieur Bayonne might be there with his guitar. One day Ty played with Monsieur Bayonne's guitar and broke one of the strings. Monsieur Bayonne was some mad with Ty. He say Ty wasn't go'n ever 'mount to nothing. Ty can go just like Monsieur Bayonne when he ain't there. Ty can make everybody laugh when he starts to mocking Monsieur Bayonne.

I used to like to be with Mama and Daddy. We used to be happy. But they took him in the Army. Now, nobody happy no more. . . . I be glad when Daddy comes home.

Monsieur Bayonne say it wasn't fair for them to take Daddy and give Mama nothing and give us nothing. Auntie say, "Shhh, Etienne. Don't let them hear you talk like that." Monsieur Bayonne say, "It's God truth. What they giving his children? They have to walk three and a half miles to school hot or cold. That's anything to give for a paw? She's got to work in the field rain or shine just to make ends meet. That's anything to give for a husband?" Auntie say, "Shhh, Etienne, shhh." "Yes, you right," Monsieur Bayonne say. "Best don't say it in front of them now. But one day they go'n find out. One day." "Yes, I suppose so," Auntie say. "Then what, Rose Mary?" Monsieur Bayonne say. "I don't know, Etienne," Auntie say. "All we can do is us job, and leave everything else in His hand . . ."

We getting closer, now. We getting closer. I can even see the railroad tracks.

We cross the tracks, and now I see the café. Just to get in there, I say. Just to get in there. Already I'm starting to feel little better.

12

We go in. Ahh, it's good. I look for the heater; there 'gainst the wall. One of them little brown ones. I just stand there and hold my hands over it. I can't open my hands too wide 'cause they almost froze.

Mama's standing right 'side me. She done unbuttoned her coat. Smoke rises out of the coat, and the coat smells like a wet dog.

I move to the side so Mama can have more room. She opens out her hands and rubs them together. I rub mine together, too, 'cause this keep them from hurting. If you let them warm too fast, they hurt you sure. But if you let them warm just little bit at a time, and you keep rubbing them, they be all right every time.

They got just two more people in the café. A lady back of the counter, and a man on this side the counter. They been watching us ever since we come in.

Mama gets out the handkerchief and count up the money. Both of us know how much money she's got there. Three dollars. No, she ain't got three dollars, 'cause she had to pay us way up here. She ain't got but two dollars and a half left. Dollar and a half to get my tooth pulled, and fifty cents for us to go back on, and fifty cents worth of salt meat.

She stirs the money round with her finger. Most of the money is change 'cause I can hear it rubbing together. She stirs it and stirs it. Then she looks at the door. It's still sleeting. I can hear it hitting 'gainst the wall like rice.

"I ain't hungry, Mama," I say.

"Got to pay them something for they heat," she says.

She takes a quarter out the handkerchief and ties the handkerchief up again. She looks over her shoulder at the people, but she still don't move. I hope she don't spend the money. I don't want her spending it on me. I'm hungry, I'm almost starving I'm so hungry, but I don't want her spending the money on me.

She flips the quarter over like she's thinking. She's must be thinking 'bout us walking back home. Lord, I sure don't want walk home. If I thought it'd do any good to say something, I'd say it. But Mama makes up her own mind 'bout things.

She turns 'way from the heater right fast, like she better hurry up and spend the quarter 'fore she change her mind. I watch her go toward the counter. The man and the lady look at her, too. She tells the lady something and the lady walks away. The man keeps on looking at her. Her back's turned to the man, and she don't even know he's standing there.

The lady puts some cakes and a glass of milk on the counter. Then she pours up a cup of coffee and sets it 'side the other stuff. Mama pays her for the things and comes on back where I'm standing. She tells me sit down at the table 'gainst the wall.

The milk and the cake's for me; the coffee's for Mama. I eat slow and I look at her. She's looking outside at the sleet. She's looking real sad. I say to myself, I'm go'n make all this up one day. You see, one day, I'm go'n make all this up. I want say it now; I want tell her how I feel right now; but Mama don't like for us to talk like that.

"I can't eat all this," I say.

They ain't got but just three little old cakes there. I'm so hungry right now, the Lord knows I can eat a hundred times three, but I want my mama to have one.

Mama don't even look my way. She knows I'm hungry, she knows I want it. I let it stay there a little while, then I get it and eat it. I eat just on my front teeth, though, 'cause if cake touch that back tooth I know what'll happen. Thank God it ain't hurt me at all today.

After I finish eating I see the man go to the juke box. He drops a nickle in it, then he just stand there a little while looking at the record. Mama tells me keep my eyes in front where they belong. I turn my head like she say, but then I hear the man coming toward us.

"Dance, pretty?" he says.

Mama gets up to dance with him. But 'fore you know it, she done grabbed the little man in the collar and done heaved him 'side the wall. He hit the wall so hard he stop the juke box from playing.

"Some pimp," the lady back of the counter says. "Some pimp."

The little man jumps up off the floor and starts toward my mama. 'Fore you know it, Mama done sprung open her knife and she's waiting for him.

"Come on," she says. "Come on. I'll gut you from your neighbo to your throat. Come on."

I go up to the little man to hit him, but Mama makes me come and stand 'side her. The little man looks at me and Mama and goes on back to the counter.

"Some pimp," the lady back of the counter says. "Some pimp." She starts laughing and pointing at the little man. "Yes sir, you a pimp, all right. Yes sir-ree."

13

"Fasten that coat, let's go," Mama says.

"You don't have to leave," the lady says.

Mama don't answer the lady, and we right out in the cold again. I'm warm right now—my hands, my ears, my feet—but I know this ain't go'n last too long. It done sleet so much now you got ice everywhere you look.

We cross the railroad tracks, and soon's we do, I get cold. That wind goes through this little old coat like it ain't even there. I got on a shirt and a sweater under the coat, but that wind don't pay them no mind. I look up and I can see we got a long way to go. I wonder if we go'n make it 'fore I get too cold.

We cross over to walk on the sidewalk. They got just one sidewalk back here, and it's over there.

After we go just a little piece, I smell bread cooking. I look, then I see a baker shop. When we get closer, I can smell it more better. I shut my eyes and make 'tend I'm eating. But I keep them shut too long and I butt up 'gainst a telephone post. Mama grabs me and see if I'm hurt. I ain't bleeding or nothing and she turns me loose.

I can feel I'm getting colder and colder, and I look up to see how far we still got to go. Uptown is 'way up yonder. A half mile more, I reckon. I try to think of something. They say think and you won't get cold. I think of that poem, "Annabel Lee." I ain't been to school in so long—this bad weather—I reckon they done passed "Annabel Lee" by now. But passed it or not, I'm sure Miss Walker go'n make me recite it when I get there. That woman don't never forget nothing. I ain't never seen nobody like that in my life.

I'm still getting cold. "Annabel Lee" or no "Annabel Lee," I'm still getting cold. But I can see we getting closer. We getting there gradually.

Soon 's we turn the corner, I see a little old white lady up in front of us. She's the only lady on the street. She's all in black and she's got a long black rag over her head.

"Stop," she says.

Me and Mama stop and look at her. She must be crazy to be out in all this bad weather. Ain't got but a few other people out there, and all of them's men.

"Y'all done ate?" she says.

"Just finish," Mama says.

"Y'all must be cold then?" she says.

"We headed for the dentist," Mama says. "We'll warm up when we get there."

"What dentist?" the old lady says. "Mr. Bassett?"

"Yes, ma'am," Mama says.

"Come on in," the old lady says. "I'll telephone him and tell him y'all coming."

Me and Mama follow the old lady in the store. It's a little bitty store, and it don't have much in there. The old lady takes off her head rag and folds it up.

"Helena?" somebody calls from the back.

"Yes, Alnest?" the old lady says.

"Did you see them?"

"They're here. Standing beside me."

"Good. Now you can stay inside."

The old lady looks at Mama. Mama's waiting to hear what she brought us in here for. I'm waiting for that, too.

"I saw y'all each time you went by," she says. "I came out to catch you, but you were gone."

"We went back of town," Mama says.

"Did you eat?"

"Yes, ma'am."

The old lady looks at Mama a long time, like she's thinking Mama might be just saying that. Mama looks right back at her. The old lady looks at me to see what I have to say. I don't say nothing. I sure ain't going 'gainst my mama.

"There's food in the kitchen," she says to Mama. "I've been keeping it warm."

Mama turns right around and starts for the door.

"Just a minute," the old lady says. Mama stops. "The boy'll have to work for it. It isn't free."

"We don't take no handout," Mama says.

"I'm not handing out anything," the old lady says. "I need my garbage moved to the front. Ernest has a bad cold and can't go out there."

"James'll move it for you," Mama says.

"Not unless you eat," the old lady says. "I'm old, but I have my pride, too, you know."

Mama can see she ain't go'n beat this old lady down, so she just shakes her head.

"All right," the old lady says. "Come into the kitchen."

She leads the way with that rag in her hand. The kitchen is a little bitty old thing, too. The table and the stove just 'bout fill it up. They got a little room to the side. Somebody in there laying 'cross the bed—'cause I can see one of his feet. Must be the person she was talking to: Ernest or Alnest—something like that.

"Sit down," the old lady says to Mama. "Not you," she says to me. "You have to move the cans."

"Helena?" the man says in the other room.

"Yes, Alnest?" the old lady says.

"Are you going out there again?"

"I must show the boy where the garbage is, Alnest," the old lady says.

"Keep that shawl over your head," the old man says.

"You don't have to remind me, Alnest. Come, boy," the old lady says.

We go out in the yard. Little old back yard ain't no bigger than the store or the kitchen. But it can sleet here just like it can sleet in any big back yard. And 'fore you know it, I'm trembling.

"There," the old lady says, pointing to the cans. I pick up one of the cans and set it right back down. The can's so light, I'm go'n see what's inside of it.

"Here," the old lady says. "Leave that can alone."

I look back at her standing there in the door. She's got that black rag wrapped round her shoulders, and she's pointing one of her little old fingers at me.

"Pick it up and carry it to the front," she says. I go by her with the can, and she's looking at me all the time. I'm sure the can's empty. I'm sure she could've carried it herself—maybe both of them at the same time. "Set it on the sidewalk by the door and come back for the other one," she says.

I go and come back, and Mama looks at me when I pass her. I get the other can and take it to the front. It don't feel a bit heavier than the first one. I tell myself I ain't go'n be nobody's fool, and I'm go'n look inside this can to see just what I been hauling. First, I look up the street, then down the street. Nobody coming. Then I look over my shoulder toward the door. That little old lady done slipped up there quiet 's mouse, watching me again. Look like she knowed what I was go'n do.

"Ehh, Lord," she says. "Children, children. Come in here, boy, and go wash your hands."

I follow her in the kitchen. She points toward the bathroom, and I go in there and wash up. Little bitty old bathroom, but it's clean, clean. I don't use any of her towels; I wipe my hands on my pants legs.

When I come back in the kitchen, the old lady done dished up the food. Rice, gravy, meat—and she even got some lettuce and tomato in a saucer. She even got a glass of milk and a piece of cake there, too. It looks so good, I almost start eating 'fore I say my blessing.

"Helena?" the old man says.

"Yes, Alnest?"

"Are they eating?"

"Yes," she says.

"Good," he says. "Now you'll stay inside."

The old lady goes in there where he is and I can hear them talking. I look at Mama. She's eating slow like she's thinking. I wonder what's the matter now. I reckon she's thinking 'bout home.

The old lady comes back in the kitchen.

"I talked to Dr. Bassett's nurse," she says. "Dr. Bassett will take you as soon as you get there."

"Thank you, ma'am," Mama says.

"Perfectly all right," the old lady says. "Which one is it?"

Mama nods toward me. The old lady looks at me real sad. I look sad, too.

"You're not afraid, are you?" she says.

"No, ma'am," I say.

"That's a good boy," the old lady says. "Nothing to be afraid of. Dr. Bassett will not hurt you."

When me and Mama get through eating, we thank the old lady again.

"Helena, are they leaving?" the old man says.

"Yes, Alnest."

"Tell them I say good-bye."

"They can hear you, Alnest."

"Good-bye both mother and son," the old man says. "And may God be with you."

Me and Mama tell the old man good-bye, and we follow the old lady in the front room. Mama opens the door to go out, but she stops and comes back in the store.

"You sell salt meat?" she says.

"Yes."

"Give me two bits worth."

"That isn't very much salt meat," the old lady says.

"That's all I have," Mama says.

The old lady goes back of the counter and cuts a big piece off the chunk. Then she wraps it up and puts it in a paper bag.

"Two bits," she says.

"That looks like awful lot of meat for a quarter," Mama says.

"Two bits," the old lady says. "I've been selling salt meat behind this counter twenty-five years. I think I know what I'm doing."

"You got a scale there," Mama says.

"What?" the old lady says.

"Weigh it," Mama says.

"What?" the old lady says. "Are you telling me how to run my business?"

"Thanks very much for the food," Mama says.

"Just a minute," the old lady says.

"James," Mama says to me. I move toward the door.

"Just one minute, I said," the old lady says.

Me and Mama stop again and look at her. The old lady takes the meat out of the bag and unwraps it and cuts 'bout half of it off. Then she wraps it up again and juggs it back in the bag and gives the bag to Mama. Mama lays the quarter on the counter.

"Your kindness will never be forgotten," she says. "James," she says to me.

We go out, and the old lady comes to the door to look at us. After we go a little piece I look back, and she's still there watching us.

The sleet's coming down heavy, heavy now, and I turn up my

coat collar to keep my neck warm. My mama tells me turn it right
back down.

"You not a bum," she says. "You a man."

PROBING FOR   1. What forces have formed the mother's character? Why does she
MEANING   raise her children as she does? Was the beating James received for his refusal to kill the redbird necessary? Explain.

      2. What kind of things doesn't his mother like James to say? On
what different occasions does he repress the desire to say something to her?
Why does she make the children repress such things? What effect does
this have on them, and on James particularly?

      3. What has caused their abject poverty? What has happened to
the father? Is there any indication in the story of whether he will return?

      4. How is Auntie different from James' mother? Why is she aware
of his toothache before his mother is?

      5. What does the conversation between the boy and the preacher
in the dentist's office reveal about old and new black attitudes? Where do
the ideas of James' mother fit in?

      6. Why is James influenced by the boy rather than by the
preacher? What does the boy intend to prove by his argument about colors
and words? Is he successful? Explain.

      7. How does racial prejudice operate in the story? How is the
mother also victimized by another black? With what results?

      8. How does the old lady convince James' mother to stay and
eat? How does his mother maintain her pride? What is the effect of the
lady's kindness on James? On his mother?

      9. In her efforts to teach her son to be a man, not a bum, the
mother insists on a rigorous training. How does she communicate to James
that she cares about him at the same time? How can it be true that, at
eight years old, he knows "what she's thinking all the time"? Will this
also be true of Ty? Explain.

PROBING FOR   1. That "the sky is gray" obviously operates on a natural level.
METHOD   How does this also become symbolic? How is the coming of summer symbolic also?

      2. What limitations are placed on the author by having the story
told by an eight-year-old boy? Do you feel this narrative device is effective? Explain.

      3. What other side of James is revealed during the bus ride?
What effect does this episode have on the reader?

      4. Why is the story divided into segments?

 JAMES THURBER

The Secret Life of Walter Mitty

"We're going through!" The Commander's voice was like thin ice breaking. He wore his full-dress uniform, with the heavily braided white cap pulled down rakishly over one cold gray eye. "We can't make it, sir. It's spoiling for a hurricane, if you ask me." "I'm not asking you, Lieutenant Berg," said the Commander. "Throw on the power lights! Rev her up to 8,500! We're going through!" The pounding of the cylinders increased: ta-pocketa-pocketa-pocketa-*pocketa-pocketa*. The Commander stared at the ice forming on the pilot window. He walked over and twisted a row of complicated dials. "Switch on No. 8 auxiliary!" he shouted. "Switch on No. 8 auxiliary!" repeated Lieutenant Berg. "Full strength in No. 3 turret!" shouted the Commander. "Full strength in No. 3 turret!" The crew bending to their various tasks in the huge, hurtling eight-engined Navy hydro-plane, looked at each other and grinned. "The Old Man'll get us through," they said to one another. "The Old Man ain't afraid of Hell!" . . .

"Not so fast! You're driving too fast!" said Mrs. Mitty. "What are you driving so fast for?"

"Hmm?" said Walter Mitty. He looked at his wife, in the seat beside him, with shocked astonishment. She seemed grossly unfamiliar, like a strange woman who had yelled at him in a crowd. "You were up to fifty-five," she said. "You know I don't like to go more than forty. You were up to fifty-five." Walter Mitty drove on toward Waterbury in silence, the roaring of the SN202 through the worst storm in twenty years of Navy flying fading in the remote, intimate airways of his mind. "You're tensed up again," said Mrs. Mitty. "It's one of your days. I wish you'd let Dr. Renshaw look you over."

Walter Mitty stopped the car in front of the building where his wife went to have her hair done. "Remember to get those over-shoes while I'm having my hair done," she said. "I don't need over-shoes," said Mitty. She put her mirror back into her bag. "We've been all through that," she said, getting out of the car. "You're not a young man any longer." He raced the engine a little. "Why don't you wear your gloves? Have you lost your gloves?" Walter Mitty reached in a pocket and brought out the gloves. He put them on, but after she had turned and gone into the building and he had driven on to a red light, he took them off again. "Pick it up, brother!" snapped a cop as the light changed, and Mitty hastily pulled on his gloves and lurched ahead. He drove around the streets aimlessly for a time, and then he drove past the hospital on his way to the parking lot.

. . . "It's the millionaire banker, Wellington McMillan," said the pretty nurse. "Yes?" said Walter Mitty, removing his gloves slowly. "Who has the case?" "Dr. Renshaw and Dr. Benbow, but there are two specialists here, Dr. Remington from New York and Mr. Pritchard-Mitford from London. He flew over." A door opened down a long, cool corridor and Dr. Renshaw came out. He looked distraught and haggard. "Hello, Mitty," he said. "We're having the devil's own time with McMillan, the millionaire banker and close personal friend of Roosevelt. Obstreosis of the ductal tract. Tertiary. Wish you'd take a look at him." "Glad to," said Mitty.

In the operating room there were whispered introductions: "Dr. Remington, Dr. Mitty. Mr. Pritchard-Mitford, Dr. Mitty." "I've read your book on streptothricosis," said Pritchard-Mitford, shaking hands. "A brilliant performance, sir." "Thank you," said Walter Mitty. "Didn't know you were in the States, Mitty," grumbled Remington. "Coals to Newcastle, bringing Mitford and me up here for a tertiary." "You are very kind," said Mitty. A huge, complicated machine, connected to the operating table, with many tubes and wires, began at this moment to go pocketa-pocketa-pocketa. "The new anesthetizer is giving way!" shouted an interne. "There is no one in the East who knows how to fix it!" "Quiet, man!" said Mitty, in a low, cool voice. He sprang to the machine, which was now going pocketa-pocketa-queep-pocketa-queep. He began fingering delicately a row of glistening dials. "Give me a fountain pen!" he snapped. Someone handed him a fountain pen. He pulled a faulty piston out of the machine and inserted the pen in its place. "That will hold for ten minutes," he said. "Get on with the operation." A nurse hurried over and whispered to Renshaw, and Mitty saw the man turn pale. "Coreopsis has set in," said Renshaw nervously. "If you would take over, Mitty?" Mitty looked at him and at the craven figure of Benbow, who drank, and at the grave, uncertain faces of the two great specialists. "If you wish," he said. They slipped a white gown on him; he adjusted a mask and drew on thin gloves; nurses handed him shining . . .

"Back it up, Mac! Look out for that Buick!" Walter Mitty jammed on the brakes. "Wrong lane, Mac," said the parking-lot attendant, looking at Mitty closely. "Gee. Yeh," muttered Mitty. He began cautiously to back out of the lane marked "Exit Only." "Leave her sit there," said the attendant. "I'll put her away." Mitty got out of the car. "Hey, better leave the key." "Oh," said Mitty, handing the man the ignition key. The attendant vaulted into the car, backed it up with insolent skill, and put it where it belonged.

They're so damn cocky, thought Walter Mitty, walking along Main Street; they think they know everything. Once he had tried to take his chains off, outside New Milford, and he had got them wound around the axles. A man had had to come out in a wrecking car and unwind them, a young, grinning garageman. Since then Mrs. Mitty always made him drive to a garage to have the chains taken off. The next time, he thought, I'll wear my right arm in a sling; they won't grin at me then. I'll have my right arm in a sling and they'll see I couldn't possibly take the chains off myself. He kicked at the slush on the sidewalk. "Overshoes," he said to himself, and he began looking for a shoe store.

When he came out into the street again, with the overshoes in a box under his arm, Walter Mitty began to wonder what the other thing was his wife had told him to get. She had told him twice, before they set out from their house for Waterbury. In a way he hated these weekly trips to town—he was always getting something wrong. Kleenex, he thought, Squibb's, razor blades? No. Toothpaste, tooth-brush, bicarbonate, carborundum, initiative and referendum? He gave it up. But she would remember it. "Where's the what's-its-name?" she would ask. "Don't tell me you forgot the what's-its-name." A news-boy went by shouting something about the Waterbury trial.

. . . "Perhaps this will refresh your memory." The District Attorney suddenly thrust a heavy automatic at the quiet figure on the witness stand. "Have you ever seen this before?" Walter Mitty took the gun and examined it expertly. "This is my Webley-Vickers 50.80," he said calmly. An excited buzz ran around the courtroom. The judge rapped for order. "You are a crack shot with any sort of firearms, I believe?" said the District Attorney, insinuatingly. "Objection!" shouted Mitty's attorney. "We have shown that the defendant could not have fired the shot. We have shown that he wore his right arm in a sling on the night of the fourteenth of July." Walter Mitty raised his hand briefly and the bickering attorneys were stilled. "With any known make of gun," he said evenly, "I could have killed Gregory Fitzhurst at three hundred feet *with my left hand*." Pandemonium broke loose in the courtroom. A woman's scream rose above the bedlam and suddenly a lovely, dark-haired girl was in Walter Mitty's arms. The District Attorney struck at her savagely.

Without rising from his chair, Mitty let the man have it on the point of the chin. "You miserable cur!" . . .

"Puppy biscuit," said Walter Mitty. He stopped walking and the buildings of Waterbury rose up out of the misty countroom and surrounded him again. A woman who was passing laughed. "He said 'Puppy biscuit,' " she said to her companion. "That man said 'Puppy biscuit' to himself." Walter Mitty hurried on. He went into an A. & P., not the first one he came to but a smaller one farther up the street. "I want some biscuit for small, young dogs," he said to the clerk. "Any special brand, sir?" The greatest pistol shot in the world thought a moment. "It says 'Puppies Bark for It' on the box," said Walter Mitty.

His wife would be through at the hairdresser's in fifteen minutes, Mitty saw in looking at his watch, unless they had trouble drying it; sometimes they had trouble drying it. She didn't like to get to the hotel first; she would want him to be there waiting for her as usual. He found a big leather chair in the lobby, facing a window, and he put the overshoes and the puppy biscuit on the floor beside it. He picked up an old copy of *Liberty* and sank down into the chair. "Can Germany Conquer the World Through the Air?" Walter Mitty looked at the pictures of bombing planes and of ruined streets.
. . . "The cannonading has got the wind up in young Raleigh, sir," said the sergeant. Captain Mitty looked up at him through tousled hair. "Get him to bed," he said wearily. "With the others. I'll fly alone." "But you can't, sir," said the sergeant anxiously. "It takes two men to handle that bomber and the Archies are pounding hell out of the air. Von Richtman's circus is between here and Saulier." "Somebody's got to get that ammunition dump," said Mitty. "I'm going over. Spot of brandy?" He poured a drink for the sergeant and one for himself. War thundered and whined around the dugout and battered at the door. There was a rending of wood and splinters flew through the room. "A bit of a near thing," said Captain Mitty carelessly. "The box barrage is closing in," said the sergeant. "We only live once, Sergeant," said Mitty, with his faint, fleeting smile. "Or do we?" He poured another brandy and tossed it off. "I never see a man could hold his brandy like you, sir," said the sergeant. "Begging your pardon, sir." Captain Mitty stood up and strapped on his huge Webley-Vickers automatic. "It's forty kilometers through hell, sir," said the sergeant. Mitty finished one last brandy. "After all," he said softly, "what isn't?" The pounding of the cannon increased; there was the rat-tat-tatting of machine guns, and from somewhere came the menacing pocketa-pocketa-pocketa of the new flamethrow-

ers. Walter Mitty walked to the door of the dugout humming "Auprès de Ma Blonde." He turned and waved to the sergeant. "Cheerio!" he said. . . .

Something struck his shoulder. "I've been looking all over this hotel for you," said Mrs. Mitty. "Why do you have to hide in this old chair? How did you expect me to find you?" "Things close in," said Walter Mitty vaguely. "What?" Mrs. Mitty said. "Did you get the what's-its-name? The puppy biscuit? What's in that box?" Overshoes," said Mitty. "Couldn't you have put them on in the store?" "I was thinking," said Walter Mitty. "Does it ever occur to you that I am sometimes thinking?" She looked at him. "I'm going to take your temperature when I get you home," she said.

They went out through the revolving doors that made a faintly derisive whistling sound when you pushed them. It was two blocks to the parking lot. At the drugstore on the corner she said, "Wait here for me. I forgot something. I won't be a minute." She was more than a minute. Walter Mitty lighted a cigarette. It began to rain, rain with sleet in it. He stood up against the wall of the drugstore, smoking. . . . He put his shoulders back and his heels together. "To hell with the handkerchief," said Walter Mitty scornfully. He took one last drag on his cigarette and snapped it away. Then, with that faint, fleeting smile playing about his lips, he faced the firing squad; erect and motionless, proud and disdainful, Walter Mitty the Undefeated, inscrutable to the last.

PROBING FOR
MEANING

1. What circumstances in reality occasion each of Walter Mitty's fantasies?

2. What single aspect do his fantasies have in common? How do people react to him in reality?

3. What evidence do we have as to why Walter Mitty fantasizes? Do all people daydream as he does?

4. How does the last daydream differ from the previous ones? How significant is this?

5. How dangerous are his fantasies? Is the story to be interpreted seriously? Humorously? Explain.

PROBING FOR
METHOD

What is the author's attitude toward Mitty? Toward Mrs. Mitty? How do the details of the overshoes and the puppy biscuits contribute to your understanding of the two characters?

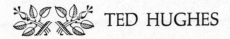 TED HUGHES

Secretary

If I should touch her she would shriek and weeping
Crawl off to nurse the terrible wound: all
Day like a starling under the bellies of bulls
She hurries among men, ducking, peeping,

Off in a whirl at the first move of a horn.
At dusk she scuttles down the gauntlet of lust
Like a clockwork mouse. Safe home at last
She mends socks with holes, shirts that are torn,

For father and brother, and a delicate supper cooks:
Goes to bed early, shuts out with the light   10
Her thirty years, and lies with buttocks tight,
Hiding her lovely eyes until day break.

PROBING FOR
MEANING

1. In each of the three verses, the poet describes the secretary at a different period of each working day. What are these periods?

2. Why would a starling "duck and peep" under the belly of a bull? In what situations does his secretary act in the same way? How does this second image tie in with the first image in this verse: "If I should touch her she would shriek and weeping/Crawl off to nurse the terrible wound: . . ."?

3. What is a "gauntlet" as mentioned in the second verse? What is the "gauntlet of lust" which the secretary must "scuttle down"?

4. What do the facts in the third verse further reveal about the secretary? How does the poet know these details?

PROBING FOR
METHOD

1. What is the poet's attitude toward the secretary? Use evidence from the poem to substantiate your answer.

2. This poem contains many words not generally thought to be "poetic." Examples include "shriek," "crawl," "bellies," etc. What do some of these words contribute to the impact of the total poem?

75

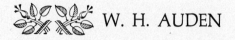 W. H. AUDEN

The Unknown Citizen

To JS/07/M/378
This Marble Monument
Is Erected by the State

He was found by the Bureau of Statistics to be
One against whom there was no official complaint,
And all the reports on his conduct agree
That, in the modern sense of an old-fashioned word, he was a
      saint,
For in everything he did he served the Greater Community.
Except for the War till the day he retired
He worked in a factory and never got fired,
But satisfied his employers, Fudge Motors Inc.
Yet he wasn't a scab or odd in his views,
For his Union reports that he paid his dues,   10
(Our report on his Union shows it was sound)
And our Social Psychology workers found
That he was popular with his mates and liked a drink.
The Press are convinced that he bought a paper every day
And that his reactions to advertisements were normal in
      every way.
Policies taken out in his name prove that he was fully in-
      sured,
And his Health-card shows he was once in hospital but left it
      cured.
Both Producers Research and High-Grade Living declare
He was fully sensible to the advantages of the Instalment
      Plan
And had everything necessary to the Modern Man,   20
A phonograph, a radio, a car and a frigidaire.
Our researchers into Public Opinion are content
That he held the proper opinions for the time of year;

When there was peace, he was for peace; when there was war
    he went.
He was married and added five children to the population,
Which our Eugenist says was the right number for a parent
    of his generation,
And our teachers report that he never interfered with their
    education.
Was he free? Was he happy? The question is absurd:
Had anything been wrong, we should certainly have heard.

PROBING FOR MEANING

1. According to the poem, what are the conditions for sainthood in the modern world?

2. What was the "Unknown Citizen" like? Did he have any distinguishing characteristics? What are the ways in which he conformed to his role in society?

3. Given the logic of the poem, why are the questions "Was he free?" and "Was he happy?" absurd?

4. Who is the "we" of the final line?

5. Do you feel that the criticisms of the man are valid? Explain.

PROBING FOR METHOD

1. What deliberate irony is suggested by the title?

2. What effect is achieved by having the poem rhyme? Does this contribute to the irony of the poem?

3. What words are used to emphasize the role of bureaucracy in contemporary life? The role of conformity?

 # THEODORE ROETHKE

Elegy for Jane

My Student, Thrown by a Horse

I remember the neckcurls, limp and damp as tendrils;
And her quick look, a sidelong pickerel smile;
And how, once startled into talk, the light syllables leaped for
    her,

And she balanced in the delight of her thought,
A wren, happy, tail into the wind,
Her song trembling the twigs and small branches.
The shade sang with her;
The leaves, their whispers turned to kissing;
And the mold sang in the bleached valleys under the rose.

Oh, when she was sad, she cast herself down into such a pure
        depth,   10
Even a father could not find her:
Scraping her cheek against straw;
Stirring the clearest water.

My sparrow, you are not here,
Waiting like a fern, making a spiny shadow.
The sides of wet stones cannot console me,
Nor the moss, wound with the last light.

If only I could nudge you from this sleep,
My maimed darling, my skittery pigeon.
Over this damp grave I speak the words of my love: 20
I, with no rights in this matter,
Neither father nor lover.

PROBING FOR   1. What characteristics of Jane does Roethke emphasize? Why
MEANING   does he also mention her depressions?
         2. What effect did Jane have on her environment?
         3. Why does the poet have "no rights in this matter"? What is
his feeling toward Jane? How would you define his "love" since he is
"neither father nor lover"?

PROBING FOR   1. An elegy is a poem on a solemn theme, often on death. In what
METHOD   way is this poem an elegy?
         2. Many images of nature are used to suggest what Jane was
like. What are they? What effect is achieved by such comparisons?
         3. What words are used to indicate sounds? What is the effect
of this emphasis on producing sounds?

Topics for Imitation

         1. Who are the most important people in your life? Is there
one person whom you understand as well as Anderson understood his
father, and Gaines, his mother? If you can think of one person whom

you would like to write about, choose one event, action or conversation through which you can best reveal that person, and write an essay in which you portray him or her through this specific moment.

2. Perhaps an important person in your experience is one you were acquainted with briefly or casually, as Podhoretz knew his English teacher; Ralbovsky, his coach; Ted Hughes, his secretary. This relationship is easier to describe than that with a person you know well, for you do not have as many details from which to select and therefore can be less concerned with limiting the topic. Your emphasis is upon creating a dominant mood about the person. Describe this individual, conveying through your choice of words your attitude toward him or her. Keep a specific audience in mind and write for that audience.

3. Discuss the tone of each of the three poems in this chapter. Do differences exist in the writers' attitudes toward their subjects? Explain, citing the language and selection of details to support your point of view.

4. Analyze the audiences of Sherwood Anderson, Norman Podhoretz and Ernest Gaines. Write an essay in which you discuss how his awareness of his audience has affected the language and tone of each of these authors.

5. Compare and contrast Sherwood Anderson's father and Ernest Gaines' mother to show their reactions to the roles society has given them as parents and to indicate how effective each is as a parent.

6. Many of the selections make statements for or against conformity to accepted norms. In this connection, discuss the extent to which conformity or nonconformity has a part in the effectiveness of a person's development. Use evidence from the selections in developing your response.

7. Social class plays a role in several of the selections: Discuss the importance of class distinctions in the main characters' lives in the Podhoretz, Gaines, Thurber and Auden selections.

8. Kennedy and Gandhi were great national leaders. Discuss the idea of leadership as these two men exhibited it, commenting on their values, their characters and their attitudes toward wealth.

9. People define winning and losing differently. Discuss the definitions of success and failure in the Anderson, Podhoretz, Ralbovsky and Gaines selections.

TWO

 PLACES

"... planet is dissimilar from planet"

"The kitchen held our lives together," Alfred Kazin says of
the kitchen in his childhood home. Places affect our lives, perhaps as much as people do. Because of their physical appearance, some places may either inspire us, as the Maine lake
does E. B. White and the Mediterranean city of Algiers does
Albert Camus, or depress us: Tom Wolfe calls Las Vegas a
"city of electronic stimulation."

We may also react to places because of our emotional associations with them, like Cleaver, in "A Day in Folsom
Prison." Tommy thinks of the candy store he manages as
"The Prison" because of his long hours there. Al Young loves
the excitement of the city and feels "Lonesome in the Country." Chad Walsh sees New York City's Port Authority
Terminal as the battleground where white armies from suburbia meet the brown and black armies from the city.

Occasionally, we may conversely leave our mark on a place,
as does Alfred Kazin's mother on her kitchen. William Stafford humorously comments on the effect California's commercialism has had on nature.

Analyze the places you have known—rooms, cities, countries. Think of the various ways in which they have affected
you. Perhaps some have left a greater impression than others.
What factors govern your reactions to place?

Organizing the Paper and Describing a Place

Since the organization of the essay will be the first technique of good writing discussed in this chapter, mentally reconstruct the author's outline as you read each essay.

Writing that gives emphasis to place is usually developed through one of two methods: use of spatial movement and exact description, or use of dominant mood description. In the former the narrator assumes the role of movie camera and attempts to give the reader as much detail about the place as possible. The narrator's comments are structured in camera-movement sequences: near-to-far, left-to-right, bottom-to-top, and so on. In the latter, the narrator selects and comments upon aspects of the place which give it a dominant mood or tone that is important to what he or she wishes to say. Which method do the writers in this chapter use?

 E. B. WHITE

Once More to the Lake

One summer, along about 1904, my father rented a camp on a lake in Maine and took us all there for the month of August. We all got ringworm from some kittens and had to rub Pond's Extract on our arms and legs night and morning, and my father rolled over in a canoe with all his clothes on; but outside of that the vacation was a success and from then on none of us ever thought there was any place in the world like that lake in Maine. We returned summer after summer—always on August 1st for one month. I have since become a salt-water man, but sometimes in summer there are days when the restlessness of the tides and the fearful cold of the sea water and the incessant wind which blows across the afternoon and into the evening make me wish for the placidity of a lake in the woods. A few weeks ago this feeling got so strong I bought myself a couple of bass hooks and a spinner and returned to the lake where we used to go, for a week's fishing and to revisit old haunts.

I took along my son, who had never had any fresh water up his nose and who had seen lily pads only from train windows. On the journey to the lake I began to wonder what it would be like. I wondered how time would have marred this unique, this holy spot— the coves and streams, the hills that the sun set behind, the camps and the paths behind the camps. I was sure the tarred road would have found it out and I wondered in what other ways it would be desolated. It is strange how much you can remember about places like that once you allow your mind to return into the grooves which lead back. You remember one thing, and that suddenly reminds you of another thing. I guess I remembered clearest of all the early mornings, when the lake was cool and motionless, remembered how the bedroom smelled of the lumber it was made of and of the wet woods whose scent entered through the screen. The partitions in the camp were thin and did not extend clear to the top of the rooms, and as I was always the first up I would dress softly so as not to wake the others, and sneak out into the sweet outdoors and start out in the canoe, keeping close along the shore in the long shadows of the pines. I remembered being very careful never to rub my paddle against the gunwale for fear of disturbing the stillness of the cathedral.

The lake had never been what you would call a wild lake. There were cottages sprinkled around the shores, and it was in farming country although the shores of the lake were quite heavily wooded. Some of the cottages were owned by nearby farmers, and you would live at the shore and eat your meals at the farmhouse. That's what our family did. But although it wasn't wild, it was a fairly large and undisturbed lake and there were places in it which, to a child at least, seemed infinitely remote and primeval.

I was right about the tar: it led to within half a mile of the shore. But when I got back there, with my boy, and we settled into a camp near a farmhouse and into the kind of summertime I had known, I could tell that it was going to be pretty much the same as it had been before—I knew it, lying in bed the first morning, smelling the bedroom, and hearing the boy sneak quietly out and go off along the shore in a boat. I began to sustain the illusion that he was I, and therefore, by simple transposition, that I was my father. This sensation persisted, kept cropping up all the time we were there. It was not an entirely new feeling, but in this setting it grew much stronger. I seemed to be living a dual existence. I would be in the middle of some simple act, I would be picking up a bait box or laying down a table fork, or I would be saying something, and suddenly it would be not I but my father who was saying the words or making the gesture. It gave me a creepy sensation.

We went fishing the first morning. I felt the same damp moss covering the worms in the bait can, and saw the dragonfly alight on the tip of my rod as it hovered a few inches from the surface of the water. It was the arrival of this fly that convinced me beyond any doubt that everything was as it always had been, that the years were a mirage and there had been no years. The small waves were the same, chucking the rowboat under the chin as we fished at anchor, and the boat was the same boat, the same color green and the ribs broken in the same places, and under the floor-boards the same freshwater leavings and débris—the dead helgramite,[1] the wisps of moss, the rusty discarded fishhook, the dried blood from yesterday's catch. We stared silently at the tips of our rods, at the dragonflies that came and went. I lowered the tip of mine into the water, tentatively, pensively dislodging the fly, which darted two feet away, poised, darted two feet back, and came to rest again a little farther up the rod. There had been no years between the ducking of this dragonfly and the other one—the one that was part of memory. I looked at the boy, who was silently watching his fly, and it was my hands that held his rod, my eyes watching. I felt dizzy and didn't know which rod I was at the end of.

We caught two bass, hauling them in briskly as though they were mackerel, pulling them over the side of the boat in a businesslike manner without any landing net, and stunning them with a blow on the back of the head. When we got back for a swim before lunch, the lake was exactly where we had left it, the same number of inches from the dock, and there was only the merest suggestion of a breeze. This seemed an utterly enchanted sea, this lake you could leave to its own devices for a few hours and come back to, and find that it had not stirred, this constant and trustworthy body of water. In the shallows, the dark, water-soaked sticks and twigs, smooth and old, were undulating in clusters on the bottom against the clean ribbed sand, and the track of the mussel was plain. A school of minnows swam by, each minnow with its small individual shadow, doubling the attendance, so clear and sharp in the sunlight. Some of the other campers were in swimming, along the shore, one of them with a cake of soap, and the water felt thin and clear and unsubstantial. Over the years there had been this person with the cake of soap, this cultist, and here he was. There had been no years.

Up to the farmhouse to dinner through the teeming, dusty field, the road under our sneakers was only a two-track road. The middle track was missing, the one with the marks of the hooves and the splotches of dried, flaky manure. There had always been three tracks to choose from in choosing which track to walk in; now the choice was narrowed down to two. For a moment I missed terribly the middle alternative. But the way led past the tennis court, and something about the way it lay there in the sun reassured me; the tape had

---

[1] The nymph of the May-fly, used as bait.

loosened along the backline, the alleys were green with plantains and other weeds, and the net (installed in June and removed in September) sagged in the dry noon, and the whole place steamed with midday heat and hunger and emptiness. There was a choice of pie for dessert, and one was blueberry and one was apple, and the waitresses were the same country girls, there having been no passage of time, only the illusion of it as in a dropped curtain—the waitresses were still fifteen; their hair had been washed, that was the only difference—they had been to the movies and seen the pretty girls with the clean hair.

Summertime, oh summertime, pattern of life indelible, the fade-proof lake, the woods unshatterable, the pasture with the sweet fern and the juniper forever and ever, summer without end; this was the background, and the life along the shore was the design, the cottages with their innocent and tranquil design, their tiny docks with the flagpole and the American flag floating against the white clouds in the blue sky, the little paths over the roots of the trees leading from camp to camp and the paths leading back to the outhouses and the can of lime for sprinkling, and at the souvenir counters at the store the miniature birch-bark canoes and the post cards that showed things looking a little better than they looked. This was the American family at play, escaping the city heat, wondering whether the newcomers in the camp at the head of the cove were "common" or "nice," wondering whether it was true that the people who drove up for Sunday dinner at the farmhouse were turned away because there wasn't enough chicken.

It seemed to me, as I kept remembering all this, that those times and those summers had been infinitely precious and worth saving. There had been jollity and peace and goodness. The arriving (at the beginning of August) had been so big a business in itself, at the railway station the farm wagon drawn up, the first smell of the pine-laden air, the first glimpse of the smiling farmer, and the great importance of the trunks and your father's enormous authority in such matters, and the feel of the wagon under you for the long ten-mile haul, and at the top of the last long hill catching the first view of the lake after eleven months of not seeing this cherished body of water. The shouts and cries of the other campers when they saw you, and the trunks to be unpacked, to give up their rich burden. (Arriving was less exciting nowadays, when you sneaked up in your car and parked it under a tree near the camp and took out the bags and in five minutes it was all over, no fuss, no loud wonderful fuss about trunks.)

Peace and goodness and jollity. The only thing that was wrong now, really, was the sound of the place, an unfamiliar nervous

sound of the outboard motors. This was the note that jarred, the one
thing that would sometimes break the illusion and set the years
moving. In those other summertimes all motors were inboard; and
when they were at a little distance, the noise they made was a
sedative, an ingredient of summer sleep. They were one-cylinder and
two-cylinder engines, and some were make-and-break and some were
jump-spark,[2] but they all made a sleepy sound across the lake. The
one-lungers throbbed and fluttered and the twin-cylinder ones purred
and purred, and that was a quiet sound too. But now the campers all
had outboards. In the daytime, in the hot mornings, these motors
made a petulant, irritable sound; at night, in the still evening when
the afterglow lit the water, they whined about one's ears like mos-
quitoes. My boy loved our rented outboard, and his great desire was
to achieve singlehanded mastery over it, and authority, and he soon
learned the trick of choking it a little (but not too much), and the
adjustment of the needle valve. Watching him I would remember the
things you could do with the old one-cylinder engine with the heavy
flywheel, how you could have it eating out of your hand if you got
really close to it spiritually. Motor boats in those days didn't have
clutches, and you would make a landing by shutting off the motor at
the proper time and coasting in with a dead rudder. But there was a
way of reversing them, if you learned the trick, by cutting the switch
and putting it on again exactly on the final dying revolution of the
flywheel, so that it would kick back against compression and begin
reversing. Approaching a dock in a strong following breeze, it was
difficult to slow up sufficiently by the ordinary coasting method, and
if a boy felt he had complete mastery over his motor, he was tempted
to keep it running beyond its time and then reverse it a few feet from
the dock. It took a cool nerve, because if you threw the switch a
twentieth of a second too soon you would catch the flywheel when it
still had speed enough to go up past center, and the boat would leap
ahead, charging bull-fashion at the dock.

We had a good week at the camp. The bass were biting well
and the sun shone endlessly, day after day. We would be tired at
night and lie down in the accumulated heat of the little bedrooms
after the long hot day and the breeze would stir almost imperceptibly
outside and the smell of the swamp drift in through the rusty screens.
Sleep would come easily and in the morning the red squirrel would be
on the roof, tapping out his gay routine. I kept remembering everything, lying in bed in the mornings—the small steamboat that had a
long rounded stern like the lip of a Ubangi, and how quietly she ran
on the moonlight sails; when the older boys played their mandolins
and the girls sang and we ate doughnuts dipped in sugar, and how

[2] Methods of ignition timing.

sweet the music was on the water in the shining night, and what it had felt like to think about girls then. After breakfast we would go up to the store and the things were in the same place—the minnows in a bottle, the plugs and spinners disarranged and pawed over by the youngsters from the boys' camp, the fig newtons and the Beeman's gum. Outside, the road was tarred and cars stood in front of the store. Inside, all was just as it had always been, except there was more Coca-Cola and not so much Moxie and root beer and birch beer and sarsaparilla. We would walk out with a bottle of pop apiece and sometimes the pop would backfire up our noses and hurt. We explored the streams, quietly, where the turtles slid off the sunny logs and dug their way into the soft bottom; and we lay on the town wharf and fed worms to the tame bass. Everywhere we went I had trouble making out which was I, the one walking at my side. the one walking in my pants.

One afternoon while we were there at that lake a thunderstorm came up. It was like the revival of an old melodrama that I had seen long ago with childish awe. The second-act climax of the drama of the electrical disturbance over a lake in America had not changed in any important respect. This was the big scene, still the big scene. The whole thing was so familiar, the first feeling of oppression and heat and a general air around camp of not wanting to go very far away. In midafternoon (it was all the same) a curious darkening of the sky, and a lull in everything that had made life tick; and then the way the boats suddenly swung the other way at their moorings with the coming of a breeze out of the new quarter, and the premonitory rumble. Then the kettle drum, then the snare, then the bass drum and cymbals, then crackling light against the dark, and the gods grinning and licking their chops in the hills. Afterward the calm, the rain steadily rustling in the calm lake, the return of light and hope and spirits, and the campers running out in joy and relief to go swimming in the rain, their bright cries perpetuating the deathless joke about how they were getting simply drenched, and the children screaming with delight at the new sensation of bathing in the rain, and the joke about getting drenched linking the generations in a strong indestructible chain. And the comedian who waded in carrying an umbrella.

When the others went swimming my son said he was going in too. He pulled his dripping trunks from the line where they had hung all through the shower, and wrung them out. Languidly, and with no thought of going in, I watched him, his hard little body, skinny and bare, saw him wince slightly as he pulled up around his vitals the small, soggy, icy garment. As he buckled the swollen belt suddenly my groin felt the chill of death.

PROBING FOR   1. White describes the Maine lake as a "holy spot." What details
MEANING   from the essay defend this description?

       2. What particular features distinguish this lake from others?

       3. "I seemed to be living a dual existence." What does the author mean by this? What importance does this statement have for the essay?

       4. "Arriving was less exciting nowadays." What other differences does the author discover between his childhood and adult visits to the lake?

       5. What does the last sentence mean? Does it have any connection with the rest of the essay?

PROBING FOR   1. White describes the reflection of the tall pines on the surface
METHOD   of the lake as a "cathedral." What other comparisons does he make in describing the lake?

       2. Did White have to limit his topic? What might his broader topic have been? What sentence might be his "thesis sentence"?

       3. What attitude does White convey toward his subject? Cite language and detail in your answer.

       4. Does White at any point in the essay foreshadow the last sentence? Does he prepare us for it in any way?

Organizing the Paper

ILLUS-
TRATION   *What framework is evident in White's essay?*   White first gives us some background on his visits to the lake, and also a general description of the lake, before developing the main idea of his essay: the "dual existence" experiences. His outline might have looked like the following:

    I. Introduction (paragraphs 1 to 3)
       A. Background (paragraph 1)
          1. Childhood trips to the lake
          2. Decision to return
       B. Current trip to the lake (paragraph 2)
       C. General description of the lake (paragraph 3)

   II. "Dual Existence" Experiences (paragraphs 4 to 11)
       A. Introduction (paragraph 4)
       B. Fishing (paragraphs 5 and 6)
       C. Dinner at the farmhouse (paragraph 7)
       D. The "American family at play" (paragraph 8)
       E. The arriving (paragraph 9)
       F. Unfamiliar sound (paragraph 10)
       G. Conclusion (paragraph 11)
          1. Sleeping
          2. Waking
          3. Visiting the store
          4. Exploring

  III. Conclusion (paragraphs 12 and 13)
       A. The thunderstorm (paragraph 12)
       B. Final realization of meaning of experience at lake (paragraph 13)

INDUCTION   *Principles of organizing a paper.*   Remember the poet who tried sixty-six words before finding the right one? Good writing results from much effort. One important step in writing an essay, which is time-consuming but very helpful, is developing the outline. The well-developed outline is essential because it helps the writer to focus sharply on a subject by eliminating wandering from the subject, repeating earlier points and neglecting major aspects of the topic.

There are at least two ways of approaching the organization of an essay through outlining. The more common method is to list all aspects of a topic, arrange them in an appropriate sequence and proceed to write. Many writers find that a second method works better, since they do not know what they want to say until they actually begin writing. These writers prefer to make their outlines after they have written a first draft. With all their ideas down, they then sort them into logical outline sequence. After completing the outline, they write a final draft.

IMITATION   *Procedures to follow in organizing your paper.*

A. Write your thesis sentence at the top of the page, making sure it is phrased as clearly as possible.

B. To make an outline under the first method: (1) list all of the ideas which occur to you in thinking about your topic. (2) Once you have made an extensive list, rearrange the items into headings and sub-headings. Your headings will form the major points which will later constitute the body of your paper. (3) Group all the other items under the major headings, eliminating those which, on second thought, obviously do not fit in. Your sub-headings should develop your headings, just as your headings develop your paper topic. (4) Check to see that each division is distinct from the others to avoid overlapping. (5) Determine if any major points have been omitted. Once you have followed these steps, you are ready to begin writing.

C. In the second method of outlining, begin with a first draft of your topic. Next, make an outline based on the draft, with each paragraph topic a heading and each example supporting the topic a sub-heading. Scrutinize your outline carefully. Does each heading belong? Are the points arranged in a logical order? What other points can you now think of to include? Once you have answered these questions and made the necessary adjustments, you are ready to begin the final draft.

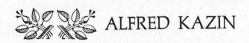 ALFRED KAZIN

The Kitchen

In Brownsville tenements the kitchen is always the largest room and the center of the household. As a child I felt that we lived in a kitchen to which four other rooms were annexed. My mother, a "home" dressmaker, had her workshop in the kitchen. She told me once that she had begun dressmaking in Poland at thirteen; as far back as I can remember, she was always making dresses for the local women. She had an innate sense of design, a quick eye for all the subtleties in the latest fashions, even when she despised them, and great boldness. For three or four dollars she would study the fashion magazines with a customer, go with the customer to the remnants store on Belmont Avenue to pick out the material, argue the owner down—all remnants stores, for some reason, were supposed to be shady, as if the owners dealt in stolen goods—and then for days would patiently fit and baste and sew and fit again. Our apartment was always full of women in their housedresses sitting around the kitchen table waiting for a fitting. My little bedroom next to the kitchen was the fitting room. The sewing machine, an old nut-brown Singer with golden scrolls painted along the black arm and engraved along the two tiers of little drawers massed with needles and thread on each side of the treadle, stood next to the window and the great coal-black stove which up to my last year in college was our main source of heat. By December the two outer bedrooms were closed off, and used to chill bottles of milk and cream, cold borscht and jellied calves' feet.

The kitchen held our lives together. My mother worked in it all day long, we ate in it almost all meals except the Passover *seder*, I did my homework and first writing at the kitchen table, and in winter I often had a bed made up for me on three kitchen chairs near the stove. On the wall just over the table hung a long horizontal mirror that sloped to a ship's prow at each end and was lined in cherry wood. It took up the whole wall, and drew every object in the kitchen to itself. The walls were a fiercely stippled whitewash, so often re-whitened by my father in slack seasons that the paint looked as if it had been squeezed and cracked into the walls. A large electric bulb hung down in the center of the kitchen at the end of a chain that had been hooked into the ceiling; the old gas ring and key still jutted out of the wall like antlers. In the corner next to the toilet was the sink at which we washed, and the square tub in which my mother did our clothes. Above it, tacked to the shelf on which were pleasantly ranged square, blue-bordered white sugar and spice jars, hung calendars from the Public National Bank on Pitkin Avenue and the Minsker Progressive Branch of the Workman's Circle; receipts for the payment of insurance premiums and household bills on a spindle: two little boxes engraved with Hebrew letters. One of these was for the poor, the other to buy back the Land of Israel. Each spring a bearded little man would suddenly appear in our kitchen, salute us with a hurried Hebrew blessing, empty the boxes (sometimes with a sidelong look of disdain if they were not full), hurriedly bless us again for remembering our less fortunate Jewish brothers and sisters, and so take his departure until the next spring after vainly trying to persuade my mother to take still another box. We did occasionally remember to drop coins in the boxes, but this was usually only on the dreaded morning of "mid-terms" and final examinations, because my mother thought it would bring me luck. She was extremely superstitious, but embarrassed about it, and always laughed at herself whenever, on the morning of an examination, she counseled me to leave the house on my right foot. "I know it's silly," her smile seemed to say, "but what harm can it do? It may calm God down."

The kitchen gave a special character to our lives—my mother's character. All my memories of that kitchen are dominated by the nearness of my mother sitting all day long at her sewing machine, by the clacking of the treadle against the linoleum floor, by the patient twist of her right shoulder as she automatically pushed at the wheel with one hand or lifted the foot to free the needle where it had got stuck in a thick piece of material. The kitchen was her life. Year by year, as I began to take in her fantastic capacity for labor and her anxious zeal, I realized it was ourselves she kept stitched together. I can never remember a time when she was not working. She worked because the law of her life was work, work and anxiety; she worked because she would have found life meaningless without work. She read almost no English; she could read the Yiddish paper, but never felt she had time to. We were always talking of time when I would teach her how to read, but somehow there was never time. When I awoke in the morning she was already at her machine, or in the great morning crowd of housewives at the grocery getting fresh rolls for breakfast. When I returned from school she was at her machine, or conferring over *McCall's* with some neighborhood woman who had come in pointing hopefully to an illustration—"Mrs. Kazin! Mrs. Kazin! Make me a dress like it shows here in the picture!" When my father came home from work she had somehow mysteriously interrupted herself to make supper for us and, the dishes cleared and washed, was back at her machine. When I went to bed at night, often she was still there, pounding away at the treadle, hunched over the wheel, her hands steering a piece of gauze under the needle with a finesse that always contrasted sharply with her swollen hands and broken nails. Her left hand had been pierced through when as a girl she had worked in the infamous Triangle Shirtwaist Factory on the East Side. A needle had gone straight through the palm, severing a large vein. They had sewn it up for her so clumsily that a tuft of flesh always lay folded over the palm.

The kitchen was the great machine that set our lives running; it whirred down a little only on Saturdays and holy days. From my mother's kitchen I gained my first picture of life as a white, overheated, starkly lit workshop redolent with Jewish cooking, crowded with women in housedresses, strewn with fashion magazines, patterns, dress material, spools of thread—and at whose center, so lashed to her machine that bolts of energy seemed to dance out of her hands and feet as she worked, my mother stamped the treadle hard against the floor, hard, hard, and silently, grimly at war, beat out the first rhythm of the world for me.

Every sound from the street roared and trembled at our windows—a mother feeding her child on the doorstep, the screech of the trolley cars on Rockaway Avenue, the eternal smash of a handball against the wall of our house, the clatter of *"der Italyéner's"* cart packed with watermelons, the sing-song of the old-clothes men walking Chester Street, the cries *"Arbes! Arbes! Kinder! Kinder! Heyse gute árbes!"* All day long people streamed into our apartment as a matter of course—"customers," upstairs neighbors, downstairs neighbors, women who would stop in for a half-hour's talk, salesmen, relatives, insurance agents. Usually they came in without ringing the bell—everyone knew my mother was always at home. I would hear the front door opening, the wind whistling through our front hall, and then some familiar face would appear in our kitchen with the same bland, matter-of-fact inquiring look: no need to stand on ceremony; my mother and her kitchen were available to everyone all day long.

At night the kitchen contracted around the blaze of light on the cloth, the patterns, the ironing board where the iron had burned a black border around the tear in the muslin cover; the finished dresses looked so frilly as they jostled on their wire hangers after all the work my mother had put into them. And then I would get that strangely ominous smell of tension from the dress fabrics and the burn in the cover of the ironing board—as if each piece of cloth and paper crushed with light under the naked bulb might suddenly go up in flames. Whenever I pass some small tailoring shop still lit up at night and see the owner hunched over his steam press; whenever in some poorer neighborhood of the city I see through a window some small crowded kitchen naked under the harsh light glittering in the ceiling, I still smell that fiery breath, that warning of imminent fire. I was always holding my breath. What I must have felt most about ourselves, I see now, was that we ourselves were like kindling—that all the hard-pressed pieces of ourselves and all the hard-used objects in that kitchen were like so many slivers of wood that might go up in flames if we came too near the white-blazing filaments in that naked bulb. Our tension itself was fire, we ourselves were forever burning— to live, to get down the foreboding in our souls, to make good.

Twice a year, on the anniversaries of her parents' deaths, my mother placed on top of the ice-box an ordinary kitchen glass packed with wax, the *yortsayt*, and lit the candle in it. Sitting at the kitchen table over my homework, I would look across the threshold to that mourning-glass, and sense that for my mother the distance from our kitchen to *der heym*, from life to death, was only a flame's length away. Poor as we were, it was not poverty that drove my mother so hard; it was loneliness—some endless, bitter brooding over all those left behind, dead or dying or soon to die; a loneliness locked up in her kitchen that dwelt every day on the hazardousness of life and the nearness of death, but still kept struggling in the lock, trying to get us through by endless labor.

With us, life started up again only on the last shore. There seemed to be no middle ground between despair and the fury of our ambition. Whenever my mother spoke of her hopes for us, it was with such unbelievingness that the likes of us would ever come to anything, such abashed hope and readiness for pain, that I finally came to see in the flame burning on top of the ice-box death itself burning away the bones of poor Jews, burning out in us everything but courage, the blind resolution to live. In the light of that mourning-candle, there were ranged around me how many dead and dying—how many eras of pain, of exile, of dispersion, of cringing before the powers of this world!

It was always at dusk that my mother's loneliness came home most to me. Painfully alert to every shift in the light at her window, she would suddenly confess her fatigue by removing her pince-nez, and then wearily pushing aside the great mound of fabrics on her machine, would stare at the street as if to warm herself in the last of the sun. "How sad it is!" I once heard her say. "It grips me! It grips me!" Twilight was the bottommost part of the day, the chillest and loneliest time for her. Always so near to her moods, I knew she was fighting some deep inner dread, struggling against the returning tide of darkness along the streets that invariably assailed her heart with the same foreboding—"Where? Where now? Where is the day taking us now?"

Yet one good look at the street would revive her. I see her now, perched against the windowsill, with her face against the glass, her eyes almost asleep in enjoyment, just as she starts up with the guilty cry—"What foolishness is this in me!"—and goes to the stove to prepare supper for us; a moment, only a moment, watching the evening crowd of women gathering at the grocery for fresh bread and milk. But between my mother's pent-up face at the window and the winter sun dying in the fabrics—"Alfred see how beautiful!"—she has drawn for me one single line of sentience. . . .

PROBING FOR   1. What is the most outstanding feature of the kitchen? Why does
MEANING   Kazin use this feature to explain that "the kitchen held our lives together"?

     2. How is the physical appearance of the kitchen affected by the time of day? What changes take place in his mother's mood as evening approaches?

     3. What characteristics of Jewish life are brought out in the essay?

     4. In the past, as this essay illustrates, the kitchen was the focal point of family life. Is it still today? Has it been replaced by any other room? Discuss.

PROBING FOR   1. Kazin uses many detailed descriptions to create a feeling of pic-
METHOD   toral accuracy. For example, notice his detailed description of the sewing machine in the first paragraph. Find other examples of extensive use of detail. How do these details help achieve the author's purpose for the essay?

     2. Kazin uses many metaphors in which the kitchen or objects in it are compared to intangible features of the family's life. Cite some examples of these metaphors and discuss their effectiveness.

     3. How has Kazin organized his essay? What are his main points? His supporting points?

     4. How does the language in the final paragraph give the reader an indication that the essay is being concluded?

Describing a Place

ILLUS-   *How does Kazin aid the reader in visualizing his mother's kitchen?*
TRATION Kazin first considers the room in reference to the other rooms in the apartment: the kitchen is the center of the household to which the other rooms are annexed. He then describes the kitchen itself. At one wall is the table around which most of the family's activities occur. He proceeds to the other important wall of the kitchen which contains a window. On either side of this window are the most significant objects in the room—a sewing machine and a coal stove.

     In paragraph 2, having established a dominant impression of the room, Kazin adds other details. On the wall near the table hangs a "long horizontal mirror that sloped to a ship's prow at each end and was lined in cherry wood." He focuses briefly on the white of the walls and moves then to the center of the room where hangs an electric bulb and proceeds finally to a corner with a sink and wash tub. Above the former is a shelf from which family mementos and bills are hung and which holds two boxes for Hebrew charities. In a later paragraph, Kazin describes the neighborhood beyond the kitchen, returning in the final paragraphs to the kitchen at night. The remaining sections of the essay express his reactions to this place.

     Kazin's spatial description moves logically from large to small, from inner to outer, from left to right, to aid us in seeing and understanding his family's kitchen.

INDUCTION   *Principles of spatial cohesion.*   There are various methods by which the headings in an outline may be arranged in the development of a topic. Usually the subject suggests its own method of arrangement. In describing a place, for example, the writer follows a spatial pattern. That is, he arranges his description in an order which enables the reader to easily visualize the area described. He paints a picture with words.

Analogy can be a useful device for describing a place. An "analogy" is an extended comparison of two objects, places or ideas which, although dissimilar, have important points in common. For example, Kazin's comparison in his line "The kitchen was the great machine that set our lives running," if extended to a paragraph or an entire essay, would have been an analogy rather than a metaphor. By comparing the kitchen to a machine, Kazin tells us something about his kitchen that a direct statement ("The kitchen was the most important room in the house") cannot tell us as well. An extended comparison or analogy is often used to describe a complicated or unfamiliar area or object, or to achieve a unified description.

IMITATION   *Procedures to follow in describing a place.*

A. Examine the place that you wish to describe. What is the main impression of the place which you wish to convey to your reader?

B. Observe which details must be included to convey that main impression. What details could be omitted without distortion or blurring?

C. Determine how best to present your description. The following are two useful patterns of organization:

  1. Begin with an overall impression and then add contributing details as Kazin does in establishing the kitchen as the center of his apartment before describing the room itself.

  2. Begin with details and conclude with an overall impression. This method achieves a dramatic effect.

D. Next, determine which method to use in presenting your details: left to right, inner to outer, front to back, top to bottom, or large to small.

E. Would an analogy be useful? Does your apartment building look like a castle fortress with its moat (of grass), bridge (of concrete), towers (of chimneys), balconies (porches)? Does your car give you the comfort of a womb—by protecting you from the outside world, keeping you warm, letting you dream? Is the bar where you work like a church with an altar (bar), pews (stools), candles (sparkling glasses), stained-glass windows (reflections in the mirror of colorful liquors), congregation (customers), confessional priest (bartender)? Don't strain for a comparison, but if one fits well, use it. Also, use metaphors and similes, as Kazin does, to help the reader visualize your place. Both short and long comparisons are effective description devices.

 ELDRIDGE CLEAVER

A Day in Folsom Prison

Folsom Prison, September 19, 1965

My day begins officially at 7:00, when all inmates are required to get out of bed and stand before their cell doors to be counted by guards who walk along the tier saying, "1, 2, 3 . . ." However, I never remain in bed until 7. I'm usually up by 5:30. The first thing I do is make up my bed. Then I pick up all my books, newspapers, etc., off the floor of my cell and spread them over my bed to clear the floor for calisthenics. In my cell, I have a little stool on which I lay a large plywood board, about 2½ by 3 feet, which I use as a typing and writing table. At night, I load this makeshift table down with books and papers, and when I read at night I spill things all over the floor. When I leave my cell, I set this board, loaded down, on my bed, so that if a guard comes into my cell to search it, he will not knock the board off the stool, as has happened before. Still in the nude, the way I sleep, I go through my routine: kneebends, butterflies, touching my toes, squats, windmills. I continue for about half an hour.

Sometimes, if I have something I want to write or type so that I can mail it that morning, I forego my calisthenics. But this is unusual. (We are required, if we want our mail to go out on a certain day, to have it in the mailbox by about 8:00. When we leave our cells at 7:30 to go to breakfast, we pass right by the mailbox and drop in our mail on the way to mess hall.)

Usually, by the time I finish my calisthenics, the trustee (we call him tiertender, or keyman) comes by and fills my little bucket with hot water. We don't have hot running water ourselves. Each cell has a small sink with a cold-water tap, a bed, a locker, a shelf or two along the wall, and a commode. The trustee has a big bucket, with a long spout like the ones people use to water their flowers, only without the sprinkler. He pokes the spout through the bars and pours you about a gallon of hot water. My cell door doesn't have bars on it; it is a solid slab of steel with fifty-eight holes in it about the size of a half dollar, and a slot in the center, at eye level, about an inch wide and five inches long. The trustee sticks the spout through one of the little holes and pours my hot water, and in the evenings the guard slides my mail in to me through the slot. Through the same slot the convicts pass newspapers, books, candy, and cigarettes to one another.

When the guard has mail for me he stops at the cell door and calls my name, and I recite my number—A29498—to verify that I am the right Cleaver. When I get mail I avert my eyes so I can't see who it's from. Then I sit down on my bed and peep at it real slowly, like a poker player peeping at his cards. I can feel when I've got a letter from you, and when I peep up on your name on the envelope I let out a big yell. It's like having four aces. But if the letter is not from you, it's like having two deuces, a three, a four, and a five, all in scrambled suits. A bum kick. Nothing. What is worse is when the guard passes my door without pausing. I can hear his keys jingling. If he stops at my door the keys sound like Christmas bells ringing, but if he keeps going they just sound like—keys.

I live in the honor block. In the other blocks, the fronts of the cells consist of nothing but bars. When I first moved into the honor block, I didn't like it at all. The cells seemed made for a dungeon. The heavy steel doors slammed shut with a clang of finality that chilled my soul. The first time that door closed on me I had the same wild, hysterical sensation I'd felt years ago at San Quentin when they first locked me in solitary. For the briefest moment I felt like yelling out for help, and it seemed that in no circumstances would I be able to endure that cell. All in that split second I felt like calling out to the guards, pleading with them to let me out of the cell, begging them to let me go, promising them that I would be a good boy in the future.

But just as quickly as the feeling came, it went, dissolved, and I felt at peace with myself. I felt that I could endure anything, everything, even the test of being broken on the rack. I've been in every type of cell they have in the prisons of California, and the door to my present cell seems the most cruel and ugly of all. However, I have grown to like this door. When I go out of my cell, I can hardly wait to get back in, to slam that cumbersome door, and hear the sharp click as the trustee snaps the lock behind me. The trustees keep the keys to the cells of the honor block all day, relinquishing them at night, and to get into your cell, all you have to do is round up the trustee in charge of your tier. Once inside my cell, I feel safe: I don't have to watch the other convicts any more or the guards in the gun towers. If you live in a cell with nothing but bars on the front, you cannot afford to relax; someone can walk along the tier and throw a Molotov cocktail in on you before you know it, something I've seen happen in San Quentin. Whenever I live in one of those barred cells, I keep a blanket within easy reach in case of emergency, to smother a fire if need be. Paranoia? Yes, but it's the least one can do for oneself. In my present cell, with its impregnable door, I don't worry about sabotage—although if someone wanted to badly enough, they could figure something out.

Well . . . after I've finished my calisthenics and the hot water has arrived, I take me a bird (jailbird) bath in the little sink. It's usually about 6:00 by then. From then until 7:30, when we are let out for breakfast, I clean up my cell and try to catch a little news over the radio. Radio?—each cell has a pair of earphones!—with only two channels on it. The programs are monitored from the radio room. The radio schedule is made up by the radio committee, of which I am a member.

At 7:30, breakfast. From the mess hall, every day except Saturday, my day off, I go straight to the bakery, change into my white working clothes, and that's me until about noon. From noon, I am "free" until 3:20, the evening mandatory lockup, when we are required, again, to stand before our cell doors and be counted. There is another count at 6:30 P.M.—three times every day without fail.

When I'm through working in the bakery, I have the choice of (1) going to my cell; (2) staying in the dining room to watch TV; (3) going down to the library; or (4) going out to the yard to walk around, sit in the sun, lift weights, play some funny game—like checkers, chess, marbles, horseshoes, handball, baseball, shuffleboard, beating on the punching bag, basketball, talk, TV, paddle-tennis, watching the other convicts who are watching other convicts. When I first came to Folsom, I was astonished to see the old grizzled cons playing marbles. The marble players of Folsom are legendary throughout the prison system: I first heard about them years ago. There is a sense of ultimate defeat about them. Some guy might boast about how he is going to get out next time and stay out, and someone will put him down by saying he'll soon be back, playing marbles like a hasbeen, a neverwas, blasted back into childhood by a crushing defeat to his final dream. The marble players have the game down to an art, and they play all day long, fanatically absorbed in what they are doing.

If I have a cell partner who knows the game, I play him chess now and then, maybe a game each night. I have a chess set of my own and sometimes when I feel like doing nothing else, I take out a little envelope in which I keep a collection of chess problems clipped from newspapers, and run off one or two. But I have never been able to give all my time to one of these games. I am seldom able to play a game of chess out on the yard. Whenever I go out on the yard these days, I'm usually on my way to the library.

On the yard there is a little shack off to one corner which is the office of the Inmates Advisory Council (IAC). Sometimes I visit the shack to shoot the bull and get the latest drawings (news). And sometimes I go out to the weight-lifting area, strip down to a pair of trunks, and push a little iron for a while and soak up the sun.

At 3:20, lockup. Stand for count. After count, off to the evening meal. Back to the cell. Stand for count at 6:30. After the 6:30 count, we are all let out of our cells, one tier at a time, for showers, to exchange dirty socks and towels for clean ones, a haircut, then back to the cell. I duck this crush by taking my showers in the bakery. At night, I only go to exchange my linen. In the honor block, we are allowed to come out after 6:30 count every Saturday, Sunday, and Wednesday night to watch TV until 10:00, before we are locked up for the night. The only time I went out for TV was to dig the broads on Shindig and Hollywood-A-Go-Go, but those programs don't come on anymore. We recently got the rule changed so that, on TV nights, those in the honor block can type until 10:00. It used to be that no typing was allowed after 8:00. I am very pleased to be able to get in that extra typing time: I can write you more letters.

On Thursday I go out of my cell after the 6:30 count to attend the weekly IAC meetings. These meetings adjourn promptly at 9:00. On Saturday mornings, my off day, I usually attend the meetings of the Gavel Club, but this past Saturday I was in the middle of my last letter to you and I stole away to my cell. I enjoyed it so much that I am tempted to put the Gavel Club down, but I hope that I don't because that's where I'm gaining some valuable experience and technique in public speaking.

On the average I spend approximately seventeen hours a day in my cell. I enjoy the solitude. The only drawback is that I am unable to get the type of reading material I want, and there is hardly anyone with a level head to talk to.

There are quite a few guys here who write. Seems that every convict wants to. Some of them have managed to sell a piece here and there. They have a writers' workshop which meets in the library under the wing of our librarian. I've never had a desire to belong to this workshop, partly because of my dislike for the attitude of the librarian and partly because of the phony, funny-style convicts. Mostly, I suppose, it's because the members of the workshop are all white and all sick when it comes to color. They're not all sick, but they're not for real. They're fair-weather types, not even as lukewarm as good white liberals, and they conform to the Mississippi atmosphere prevalent here in Folsom. Blacks and whites do not fraternize together in comfort here. Harry Golden's concept of vertical integration and horizontal segregation about covers it. The whites want to talk with you out on the yard or at work, standing up, but they shun you when it comes to sitting down. For instance, when we line up for chow, the lines leading into the mess halls are integrated. But once inside the mess hall, blacks sit at tables by themselves and whites sit with themselves or with the Mexicans.

There's this one Jewish stud out of New York who fell out of Frisco. He thinks he is another Lenny Bruce. In point of fact he is funny and very glib, and I dig rapping (talking) with him. He's a hype but he is very down with the current scene. Says that he lived in North Beach and all that, and that he has this chick who writes him who is a member of the DuBois Club in Frisco. Well, this cat is well read and we exchange reading material. He says that at home he has every copy of *The Realist* published up to the time of his fall. *The Evergreen Review* kills him. We communicate pretty well and I know that stud is not a racist, but he is a conformist—which in my book is worse, more dangerous, than an out-and-out foe. The other day we were talking about the Free Speech Movement. He was reading a book by Paul Goodman, *Growing Up Absurd*, which he had with him. We were very hung up talking and then it was time for lunch. We got in line and continued our conversation. He was trying to convince me that the whole FSM was predicated on the writings of Paul Goodman, and that he had heard, with his own ears, Mario Savio say as much. Then all of a sudden I noticed this cat grow leery and start looking all around. He made me nervous. I thought maybe someone was trying to sneak up on us with a knife or something. When he kept doing this, I asked him what the f- - - was the matter with him. He turned real red and said that he "just remembered" that he had to talk to another fellow. I dug right away what the kick was, so I said, "later," and he split. I'm used to such scenes, having a 400-year heritage of learning to roll with that type of punch. I saw him in the mess hall looking very pushed out of shape. I had to laugh at him. I felt that he was probably thinking that if the whites put the blacks in the gas chambers they might grab him too if he was with me. That thought tickled me a little as I watched him peeping around like a ferret. One of his points of indignation is that, he says, he will never forgive Israel for kidnaping and killing Eichmann, and he gets mad at me because I take Israel's side, just to keep the conversation alive. Too much agreement kills a chat. What really bugs him is when I say that there are many blacks who, if they were in the position, would do a little rounding up of the Eichmann types in America. A few days later he told me, "You saw through me the other day, didn't you?"

"I see through you every day," I told him. He looked as if he expected or wanted me to hit him or something. I told him that he was good for nothing but to be somebody's jailhouse wife and he laughed, then launched into a Lenny Bruce–type monologue.

My own reaction is to have as little as possible to do with the whites. I have no respect for a duck who runs up to me on the yard all buddy-buddy, and then feels obliged not to sit down with me. It's not that I'm dying to sit with him either, but there is a principle involved which cuts me deeply.

Talk about hypocrisy: you should see the library. We are allowed to order, from the state library, only non-fiction and law books. Of the law books, we can only order books containing court opinion. We can get any decision of the California District Court of Appeals, the California Supreme Court, the U.S. District Courts, the Circuit Courts, and the U.S. Supreme Court. But books of an explanatory nature are prohibited. Many convicts who do not have lawyers are forced to act *in propria persona*. They do all right. But it would be much easier if they could get books that showed them how properly to plead their cause, how to prepare their petitions and briefs. This is a perpetual sore point with the Folsom Prison Bar Association, as we call ourselves.

All of the novels one *needs* to read are unavailable, and the librarian won't let you send for them. I asked him once if he had read a certain book.

"Oh, yes!" he exclaimed.

"What did you think of it?" I asked.

"Absolutely marvelous!" he said.

"How about letting me send to the state library for it?" I asked.

"No."

Books that one wants to read—so bad that it is a taste in the mouth, like Calvin C. Hernton's *Sex and Racism in America*—he won't let you have.

"The warden says 'no sex,' " is his perpetual squelch.

There is a book written by a New York judge which gives case histories of prostitutes. The authors explore why white prostitutes, some of them from the deepest South, had Negroes for pimps, and I wanted to reread it.

"No sex," said the librarian. He is indifferent to the fact that it is a matter of life and death to me! I don't know how he justifies this because you can go over to the inmate canteen and buy all the prurient pot-boiling anti-literature that has ever been written. But everything that "is happening" today is verboten. I've been dying to read Norman Mailer's *An American Dream*, but that too is prohibited. You can have *Reader's Digest*, but *Playboy*?—not a chance. I have long wanted to file suit in Federal Court for the right to receive *Playboy* magazine. Do you think Hugh Hefner would finance such an action? I think some very nice ideas would be liberated.

The library does have a selection of very solid material, things done from ten years ago all the way back to the Bible. But it is unsatisfactory to a stud who is trying to function in the last half of the twentieth century. Go down there and try to find Hemingway,

Mailer, Camus, Sartre, Baldwin, Henry Miller, Terry Southern, Julian Mayfield, Bellow, William Burroughs, Allen Ginsberg, Herbert Gold, Robert Gover, J. O. Killens, etc.—no action. They also have this sick thing going when it comes to books by and about Negroes. Robert F. Williams' book, *Negroes with Guns*, is not allowed any more. I ordered it from the state library before it was too popular around here. I devoured it and let a few friends read it, before the librarian dug it and put it on the blacklist. Once I ordered two books from the inmate canteen with my own money. When they arrived here from the company, the librarian impounded them, placing them on my "property" the same as they did my notebooks.

I want to devote my time to reading and writing, with everything else secondary, but I can't do that in prison. I have to keep my eyes open at all times or I won't make it. There is always some madness going on, and whether you like it or not you're involved. There is no choice in the matter: you cannot sit and wait for things to come to you. So I engage in all kinds of petty intrigue which I've found necessary to survival. It consumes a lot of time and energy. But it is necessary.

PROBING FOR
MEANING

1. Why does Cleaver choose to relate the chronology of his day in describing Folsom Prison to his lawyer (the "you" of the essay)?

2. Cleaver writes of prison life with great restraint or understatement. In which paragraphs can you "read between the lines" and imagine he must feel or think more than he says? Are there situations in which he expresses himself or his emotions fully? Why does he vary his degree of honesty?

3. How would you characterize Cleaver from this essay? How is he different from the other convicts?

4. What is his reaction to Folsom Prison? Why does he choose these particular details of prison life to describe?

5. To what does "Harry Golden's concept of vertical integration and horizontal segregation" refer? Some conditions of Folsom which Cleaver describes characterize prison society but not the world beyond the walls. For example, censorship of mails, radio programs and reading material applies only to prison. Does the concept of "vertical integration and horizontal segregation" pertain to society as well? Explain.

PROBING FOR
METHOD

1. This essay depicts the author's attitude toward place even though it gives very little exact detail about place. You actually know very little about what the prison looks like. Instead Cleaver uses selection of details and choice of words to convey the feeling of being in prison. What examples of careful selection of language and detail can you cite?

2. At what points in the essay does Cleaver use spatial description? Why has he elected to describe these parts of Folsom Prison and not others?

3. Cleaver's writing is designed to give emphasis to the claustro-phobic prison atmosphere. Notice, for example, his fifth paragraph. What specific aspects of his style underscore the closed-in feeling?

4. What word would you use to describe the tone of this essay? What elements of Cleaver's style give support to tone? How does his audience affect his tone? Who is his audience?

5. This essay begins with a chronological organization but moves from that to a detailed discussion of important problems. At what point does this shift occur? Is it smooth? What would have happened to the essay had Cleaver continued to write in strict chronological order?

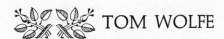 TOM WOLFE

Las Vegas (What?) Las Vegas (Can't hear you! Too noisy) Las Vegas!!!!

Hernia, hernia, hernia, hernia, hernia, hernia, hernia, hernia, hernia, hernia, hernia, hernia, HERNia; hernia, HERNia, hernia, hernia, hernia, hernia, HERNia, HERNia, HERNia; hernia, hernia, hernia, hernia, hernia, hernia, hernia, eight is the point, the point is eight, hernia, hernia, HERNia; hernia, hernia, hernia, hernia, all right, hernia, hernia, hernia, hernia, hard eight, hernia, hernia, hernia, HERNia, hernia, hernia, hernia, HERNia, hernia, hernia, hernia, HERNia, hernia, hernia, hernia, hernia

"What is all this *hernia hernia* stuff?"

This was Raymond talking to the wavy-haired fellow with the stick, the dealer, at the craps table about 3:45 Sunday morning. The stickman had no idea what this big wiseacre was talking about, but he resented the tone. He gave Raymond that patient arch of the eyebrows known as a Red Hook brushoff, which is supposed to convey some such thought as, I am a very tough but cool guy, as you can tell by the way I carry my eyeballs low in the pouches, and if this wasn't such a high-class joint we would take wiseacres like you out back and beat you into jellied madrilene.

At this point, however, Raymond was immune to subtle looks.

The stickman tried to get the game going again, but every time he would start up his singsong, by easing the words out through the nose, which seems to be the style among craps dealers in Las Vegas—"All right, a new shooter . . . eight is the point, the point is eight" and so on—Raymond would start droning along with him in exactly the same tone of voice, "Hernia, hernia, hernia, hernia, HERNia, HERNia, hernia; hernia, hernia, hernia."

Everybody at the craps table was staring in consternation to think that anybody would try to needle a tough, hip, elite *soldat* like a Las Vegas craps dealer. The gold-lamé odalisques of Los Angeles were staring. The Western sports, fifty-eight-year-old men who wear Texas string ties, were staring. The old babes at the slot machines, holding Dixie Cups full of nickles, were staring at the craps tables, but cranking away the whole time.

Raymond, who is thirty-four years old and works as an engineer in Phoenix, is big but not terrifying. He has the sort of thatchwork hair that grows so low all along the forehead there is no logical place to part it, but he tries anyway. He has a huge, prognathous jaw, but it is as smooth, soft and round as a melon, so that Raymond's total effect is that of an Episcopal divinity student.

The guards were wonderful. They were dressed in cowboy uniforms like Bruce Cabot in *Sundown* and they wore sheriff's stars.

"Mister, is there something we can do for you?"

"The expression is 'Sir,' " said Raymond. "You said 'Mister.' The expression is 'Sir.' How's your old Cosa Nostra?"

Amazingly, the casino guards were easing Raymond out peaceably, without putting a hand on him. I had never seen the fellow before, but possibly because I had been following his progress for the last five minutes, he turned to me and said, "Hey, do you have a car? This wild stuff is starting again."

The gist of it was that he had left his car somewhere and he wanted to ride up the Strip to the Stardust, one of the big hotel-casinos. I am describing this big goof Raymond not because he is a typical Las Vegas tourist, although he has some typical symptoms, but because he is a good example of the marvelous impact Las Vegas has on the senses. Raymond's senses were at a high pitch of excitation, the only trouble being that he was going off his nut. He had been up since Thursday afternoon, and it was now about 3:45 A.M. Sunday. He had an envelope full of pep pills—amphetamine—in his left coat pocket and an envelope full of Equanils—meprobamate—in his right pocket, or were the Equanils in the left and the pep pills in the right? He could tell by looking, but he wasn't going to look any more. He didn't care to see how many were left.

He had been rolling up and down the incredible electric-sign gauntlet of Las Vegas' Strip, U.S. Route 91, where the neon and the par lamps—bubbling, spiraling, rocketing, and exploding in sunbursts ten stories high out in the middle of the desert—celebrate one-story casinos. He had been gambling and drinking and eating now and again at the buffet tables the casinos keep heaped with food day and night, but mostly hopping himself up with good old amphetamine, cooling himself down with meprobamate, then hooking down more alcohol, until now, after sixty hours, he was slipping into the symptoms of toxic schizophrenia.

He was also enjoying what the prophets of hallucinogen call "consciousness expansion." The man was psychedelic. He was beginning to isolate the components of Las Vegas' unique bombardment of the senses. He was quite right about this *hernia hernia* stuff. Every casino in Las Vegas is, among the other things, a room full of craps tables with dealers who keep up a running singsong that sounds as though they are saying "hernia, hernia, hernia, hernia, hernia" and so on. There they are day and night, easing a running commentary through their nostrils. What they have to say contains next to no useful instruction. Its underlying message is, We are the initiates, riding the crest of chance. That the accumulated sound comes out "hernia" is merely an unfortunate phonetic coincidence. Actually, it is part of something rare and rather grand: a combination of baroque stimuli that brings to mind the bronze gongs, no larger than a blue plate, that Louis XIV, his ruff collars larded with the lint of the foul Old City of Byzantium, personally hunted out in the bazaars of Asia Minor to provide exotic acoustics for his new palace outside Paris.

The sounds of the craps dealer will be in, let's say, the middle register. In the lower register will be the sound of the old babes at the slot machines. Men play the slots too, of course, but one of the indelible images of Las Vegas is that of the old babes at the row upon row of slot machines. There they are at six o'clock Sunday morning no less than at three o'clock Tuesday afternoon. Some of them pack their old hummocky shanks into Capri pants, but many of them just put on the old print dress, the same one day after day, and the old hob-heeled shoes, looking like they might be going out to buy eggs in Tupelo, Mississippi. They have a Dixie Cup full of nickles or dimes in the left hand and an Iron Boy work glove on the right hand to keep the calluses from getting sore. Every time they pull the handle, the machine makes a sound much like the sound a cash register makes before the bell rings, then the slot pictures start clattering up from left to right, the oranges, lemons, plums, cherries, bells, bars, buckaroos—the figure of a cowboy riding a bucking bronco. The whole sound keeps churning up over and over again in eccentric series all over the place, like one of those random-sound radio symphonies by John Cage. You can hear it at any hour of the day or night all over Las Vegas. You can walk down Fremont Street at dawn and hear it without even walking in a door, that and the spins of the wheels of fortune, a boring and not very popular sort of simplified roulette, as the tabs flap to a stop. As an overtone, or at times simply as a loud sound, comes the babble of the casino crowds, with an occasional shriek from the craps tables, or, anywhere from 4 P.M. to 6 A.M., the sound of brass instruments or electrified string instruments from the cocktail-lounge shows.

The crowd and band sounds are not very extraordinary, of course. But Las Vegas' Muzak is. Muzak pervades Las Vegas from the time you walk into the airport upon landing to the last time you leave the casinos. It is piped out to the swimming pool. It is in the drugstores. It is as if there were a communal fear that someone, somewhere in Las Vegas, was going to be left with a totally vacant minute on his hands.

Las Vegas has succeeded in wiring an entire city with this electronic stimulation, day and night, out in the middle of the desert. In the automobile I rented, the radio could not be turned off, no matter which dial you went after. I drove for days in a happy burble of Action Checkpoint News, "Monkey No. 9," "Donna, Donna, the Prima Donna," and picking-and-singing jingles for the Frontier Bank and the Fremont Hotel.

One can see the magnitude of the achievement. Las Vegas takes what in other American towns is but a quixotic inflammation of the senses for some poor salary mule in the brief interval between the flagstone rambler and the automatic elevator downtown and magnifies it, foliates it, embellishes it into an institution.

For example, Las Vegas is the only town in the world whose skyline is made up neither of buildings, like New York, nor of trees, like Wilbraham, Massachusetts, but signs. One can look at Las Vegas from a mile away on Route 91 and see no buildings, no trees, only signs. But such signs! They tower. They revolve, they oscillate, they soar in shapes before which the existing vocabulary of art history is helpless. I can only attempt to supply names—Boomerang Modern, Palette Curvilinear, Flash Gordon Ming-Alert Spiral, McDonald's Hamburger Parabola, Mint Casino Elliptical, Miami Beach Kidney. Las Vegas' sign makers work so far out beyond the frontiers of conventional studio art that they have no names themselves for the forms they create. Vaughan Cannon, one of those tall, blond Westerners, the builders of places like Las Vegas and Los Angeles, whose eyes seem to have been bleached by the sun, is in the back shop of the Young Electric Sign Company out on East Charleston Boulevard with Herman Boernge, one of his designers, looking at the model they have prepared for the Lucky Strike Casino sign, and Cannon points to where the sign's two great curving faces meet to form a narrow vertical face and says:

"Well, here we are again—what do we call that?"

"I don't know," says Boernge. "It's sort of a nose effect. Call it a nose."

Okay, a nose, but it rises sixteen stories high above a two-story building. In Las Vegas no farseeing entrepreneur buys a sign to fit a building he owns. He rebuilds the building to support the biggest sign he can get up the money for and, if necessary, changes the name. The Lucky Strike Casino today is the Lucky Casino, which fits better when recorded in sixteen stories of flaming peach and incandescent yellow in the middle of the Mojave Desert. In the Young Electric Sign Co. era signs have become the architecture of Las Vegas, and the most whimsical, Yale-seminar-frenzied devices of the two late geniuses of Baroque Modern, Frank Lloyd Wright and Eero Saarinen, seem rather stuffy business, like a jest at a faculty meeting, compared to it. Men like Boernge, Kermit Wayne, Ben Mitchem and Jack Larsen, formerly an artist for Walt Disney, are the designer-sculptor geniuses of Las Vegas, but their motifs have been carried faithfully throughout the town by lesser men, for gasoline stations, motels, funeral parlors, churches, public buildings, flophouses and sauna baths.

Then there is a stimulus that is both visual and sexual—the Las Vegas buttocks décolletage. This is a form of sexually provocative dress seen more and more in the United States, but avoided like Broadway message-embroidered ("Kiss Me, I'm Cold") underwear in the fashion pages, so that the euphemisms have not been established and I have no choice but clinical terms. To achieve buttocks décolletage a woman wears bikini-style shorts that cut across the round fatty masses of the buttocks rather than cupping them from below, so that the outer-lower edges of these fatty masses, or "cheeks," are exposed. I am in the cocktail lounge of the Hacienda Hotel, talking to managing director Dick Taylor about the great success his place has had in attracting family and tour groups, and all around me the waitresses are bobbing on their high heels, bare legs and décolletage-bare backsides, set off by pelvis-length lingerie of an uncertain denomination. I stare, but I am new here. At the White Cross Rexall drugstore on the Strip a pregnant brunette walks in off the street wearing black shorts with buttocks décolletage aft and illusion-of-cloth nylon lingerie hanging fore, and not even the old mom's-pie pensioners up near the door are staring. They just crank away at the slot machines. On the streets of Las Vegas, not only the show girls, of which the town has about two hundred fifty, bona fide, in residence, but girls of every sort, including, especially, Las Vegas' little high-school buds, who adorn what locals seeking roots in the sand call "our city of churches and schools," have taken up the chic of wearing buttocks décolletage step-ins under flesh-tight slacks, with the outline of the undergarment showing through fashionably. Others go them one better. They achieve the effect of having been dipped once, briefly, in Helenca stretch nylon. More and more they look like those wonderful old girls out of Flash Gordon who were wrapped just once over in Baghdad pantaloons of clear polyethylene with only Flash Gordon between them and the insane red-eyed assaults of the minions of Ming. It is as if all the hip young suburban gals of America named Lana, Deborah and Sandra, who gather wherever the arc lights shine and the studs steady their coiffures in the plate-glass reflection, have convened in Las Vegas with their bouffant hair above and anatomically stretch-pant-swathed little bottoms below, here on the new American frontier. But exactly!

PROBING FOR
MEANING

1. Since Wolfe admits Raymond isn't a typical Las Vegas tourist, why does the author dramatize his escapades in the city in introducing the essay?

2. What does the inside of a Las Vegas casino look like? Sound like? Why are so many people described when Wolfe's purpose is to describe the city?

3. Why does "Muzak" permeate Las Vegas from airport to casinos twenty-four hours a day, according to the author? What does this detail add to his description?

4. "Signs have become the architecture of Las Vegas," says Wolfe. What examples support this statement?

5. Why does Wolfe call Las Vegas "the new American frontier"? How does the "buttocks décolletage" substantiate this description of the city? What other aspects of the city further support his point?

6. At what junctures in the essay does Wolfe discuss people's motivation in coming to Las Vegas and behaving as they do?

PROBING FOR
METHOD

1. What do you think of Wolfe's title? Of his introduction?

2. Wolfe uses many words and phrases from the Middle East and the Orient such as "gold odalisques," "larded with the lint of the foul Old City of Byzantium," the "bazaars of Asia Minor," "Baghdad pantaloons," "minions of Ming." What extra dimension do these images add to his description of Las Vegas?

3. What tone does Wolfe employ in describing Las Vegas? Cite words, phrases and selection of detail in supporting your answer.

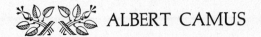 ALBERT CAMUS

Summer in Algiers

to Jacques Heurgon

The loves we share with towns are often secret ones. Cities like Paris, Prague and even Florence are closed in upon themselves and thus restrict the world peculiar to them. But Algiers, like other privileged places such as coastal towns, lies open to the sky like a mouth or like a wound. What you can love in Algiers is what everybody lives off: the sea visible at every corner, a certain weight of sunlight, the beauty of the race. And, as always, this generosity and lack of modesty also hold a more secret flavour. In Paris, you can feel nostalgic for space and for the beating of wings. Here, at least, man has everything he needs, and, thus assured of his desires, can measure up his wealth.

You doubtless need to spend a long time in Algiers to understand how desiccating an excess of nature's blessings can be. There is nothing here for people seeking knowledge, education or self-improvement. This land contains no lessons. It neither promises nor reveals. It is content to give, but does so profusely. Everything here is revealed to the naked eye, and is known the very moment it is enjoyed. Its pleasures have no remedies and its joys remain without hope. What it demands are clear-sighted souls, that is to say those without consolation. It asks us to make an act of lucidity as we make an act of faith. Strange country, which gives the men it nourishes both their wretchedness and their greatness! It is not surprising that the sensual wealth heaped on the man of feeling in this country should coincide with the most extreme deprivation. There is no truth that does not carry its bitterness within itself. Why then should it be surprising if I never love the face of this country more than in the midst of its poorest inhabitants?

Throughout their youth, men find here a life which matches their beauty. Then, afterwards, come decline and forgetfulness. They have wagered on the flesh, but they knew that they would lose. In Algiers, everything is a refuge and an occasion for triumphs for those who are young and alive: the bay, the sun, the games marked out in red and white on the terraces over towards the sea, the flowers and

109

stadia, the cool-legged girls. But for the man who has lost his youth there is nothing to hang on to, and no place where melancholy can escape from itself. Elsewhere, the terraces in Italy, the cloisters of Europe or the shape of the hills in Provence, are all places where man can flee from his humanity and be gently saved from himself. But everything here demands solitude and young men's blood. Goethe on his deathbed called for light and this is a historic remark. In Belcourt and Bab-el-Oued, the old men sitting at the back of cafés listen to young men with brilliantined hair boasting of their exploits.

It is the summer which grants us these beginnings and ends in Algiers. During these months, the town is deserted. But the poor and the sky are always with us. With the first, we go down together towards the port and its human treasures: the gentle warmth of the water and the brown bodies of the women. In the evening, crammed with these riches, they go back to the oilskin cloth and oil-lamp that are the only background that they know.

In Algiers, you don't say "to go swimming" but "to dive in for a swim." I won't insist. People bathe in the port and rest on the buoys. When you go close to a buoy on which a pretty girl is already sitting, you shout to your friends: "I tell you it's a seagull." These are healthy pleasures. They obviously constitute the ideal for these young men, since most of them continue to live like this during the winter, and each day at noon strip themselves bare in the sun for a frugal lunch. Not that they have read the boring sermons of our nudists, those protestants of the body (there is a way of systematizing the body which is as infuriating as systems for the soul). But they "like being in the sun." We shall never give enough importance to what this custom represents for our time. For the first time in two thousand years, the body has been shown naked on the beaches. For twenty centuries, men have tried to impose decency on the insolence and simplicity of the Greeks, to play down the flesh and complicate our clothes. Today, reaching back over this history, the young men sprinting on the Mediterranean beaches rediscover the magnificent gestures of the athletes of Delos. And by thus living close to the body, and living by the body, we learn that it has its own nuances, its life, and, to venture an absurdity, its own psychology.[1] The evolution of the

---

[1] May I be so foolish as to say that I do not like the way Gide exalts the body? He asks it to hold back his desire in order to make it more intense. He thus brings himself close to those who, in the slang of brothels, are termed weirdies or kinkies. Christianity also seeks to suspend desire. But, more naturally, sees this a mortification. My friend Vincent, who is a cooper and junior breast-stroke champion, has an even clearer view of things. He drinks when he is thirsty, if he wants a woman tries to sleep with her, and would marry her if he loved her (this hasn't happened yet). Then he always says: "That's better" —an energetic summary of the apology one could write for satiety.

body, like that of the mind, has its history, its reversals, its gains and its losses. With only this nuance: colour. When you go to swim in the port during summer, you notice that everybody's skin is changing at the same time from white to gold, then to brown, and, finally, to a tobacco colour which represents the final stage which the body can manage in this quest for transformation. The Kasbah's pattern of white cubes dominates the whole port. When you are at water level, people's bodies form a bronzed frieze against the glaring white background of the Arab town. And, as you move into the month of August and the sun grows stronger, the white of the houses becomes more blinding and skins take on a darker glow. How then can you fail to identify yourself with this dialogue between stone and flesh which matches the seasons and the sun? You spend the whole morning diving in the sea, with garlands of laughter among spouts of water, in long paddling trips around red and black cargo vessels (the ones from Norway smell of all kinds of wood, the ones from Germany reek of oil, the ones going from port to port along the coast smell of wine and old casks). When the sun is brimming over from every corner of the sky, the orange-coloured canoe laden with sunburnt bodies brings us back in a mad race. And when, in a sudden pause in the rhythmic stroke of the fruit-coloured blades of the double paddle, we glide smoothly into the harbour, how can I help but know that I am carrying across the smooth waters a bronzed cargo of gods in whom I recognize my brothers?

But, at the other end of the town, the summer already offers us the contrast of its other wealth: I mean its silences and boredom. These silences do not always have the same quality, according to whether they are born of shadow or of sun. There is the silence of noon on Government Square. In the shade of the trees that grow each side, Arabs sell penny glasses of iced lemonade, perfumed with orange blossom. Their cry of "cool, cool" echoes across the empty square. When it fades away, silence falls again under the sun: in the merchant's pitcher, the ice moves and I can hear it tinkling. There reigns the silence of the siesta. In the streets round the docks, in front of the squalid barbers' shops, you can measure the silence by the melodious buzzing of the flies behind the hollow reed curtains. Elsewhere, in the Moorish cafés in the Kasbah, it is men's bodies which are silent, which cannot drag themselves away, leave the glass of tea, and rediscover time through the pounding of their own pulse. But there is, above all, the silence of the summer evenings.

Is it because these brief moments when day swings over into night are peopled with signs and secret calls that Algiers is linked so closely to them in my heart? When I have been away from this country for some time, I imagine its dusks as promises of happiness. On the hills looking down over the town, there are paths among the mastic-trees and olive-trees. And it is towards them that my heart then turns. I can see sheaves of blackbirds rising up against the green horizon. In the sky, suddenly emptied of its sun, something releases its hold. A whole small people of red clouds stretches up until it melts into the air. Almost immediately afterwards, there appears the first star that had been forming and growing harder in the thickness of the heavens. And then, sudden and all-consuming, night. What is so unique in these fleeting evenings of Algiers that it releases so many things in me? They leave a sweetness on my lips, but before I have time to weary of it, it has already vanished into darkness. Is this the secret of its persistence? The tenderness of this country is furtive and overwhelming. But once we feel it, then our heart at least surrenders. On the Padovani beach, the dance-hall is open every day. And, in this immense rectangular box which stands open to the sea all along one side, the penniless youth of the district come to dance until evening. Often, I would wait there for one particular moment. In the daytime, the dance-hall is protected by a sloping wooden roof. When the sun has gone in, this is removed. The hall is then filled with a strange green light, born of the double shell of the sky and sea. When you sit a long way from the windows, you can see only the sky, and, like puppets in a shadow-theatre, the faces of the dancers floating past one after another. Sometimes the musicians play a waltz and the dark profiles then revolve like cut-out figures placed on a record player. Night comes quickly then, and, with it, the lights. But I shall never be able to describe the secret enchantment of this subtle moment. What I do remember is a magnificent, tall girl who had danced all one afternoon. She was wearing a necklace of jasmine on her close-fitting blue dress, which was damp with sweat right down the back. She was laughing and throwing back her head as she danced. When she passed in front of the tables, she left behind her a mingled scent of flowers and flesh. When evening came, I could no longer see her body pressed against her partner, but the white of her jasmine and the black of her hair were revolving one after the other against the sky, and when she threw back her full throat I could hear her laugh and see her partner's silhouette lean suddenly forward. It is to evenings such as these that I owe my idea of innocence. And I am learning that these beings charged with violence cannot be separated from the sky in which their desires revolve.

In the local cinemas in Algiers, there are often mint pastilles on sale with red letters engraved upon them expressing everything needed for the birth of love: (1) questions: "When will you marry me?"; "Do you love me?"; (2) replies: "Madly"; "Next spring." After having prepared the ground, you pass them to your neighbour who replies in the same vein or simply plays the fool. In Belcourt, there have been marriages arranged like this and whole lives decided by an exchange of mint-flavoured sweets. And this gives a good picture of the childlike people of this country.

The sign of youth is perhaps a magnificent vocation for easy pleasures. But, above all, it lies in a haste to live that borders on extravagance. In Belcourt, as in Bab-el-Oeud, people marry young. They start work very early, and exhaust the range of human experience in ten years. A workman of thirty has already played all his cards. He waits for the end with his wife and children around him. His delights have been swift and merciless. So has his life. And you then understand why he should have been born of this country where everything is given to be taken away. In this abundance and profusion, life follows the curve of the great passions, sudden, demanding, generous. It is not to be built up but to be burned away. Reflection or self-improvement are quite irrelevant. The notion of hell, for example, is here nothing more than an amusing joke. Only the very virtuous are allowed such fancies. And I believe that virtue is a meaningless word throughout the whole of Algeria. Not that these men lack principles. They have their code of morality, which is very well defined. You "don't let your mother down." You see to it that your wife is respected in the street. You show consideration to pregnant women. You don't attack an enemy two to one, because "that's dirty." If anyone fails to observe these elementary rules, "He's not a man" and that's all there is to it. This seems to me just and strong. There are still many of us who observe the highway code, the only disinterested one I know. But at the same time the shopkeepers' ethic is unknown. I have always seen the faces around me take on an expression of pity when a man goes by between two policemen. And, before finding out whether the man was a thief, a patricide, or simply an eccentric, people said: "Poor fellow," or again, with a touch of admiration: "He's a pirate."

There are peoples born for pride and for life. It is they who nourish the most singular vocation for boredom. It is also they who look upon death with most repulsion. Apart from sensual delights, the Algerians' amusements are idiotic. For years now the entertainment of the over-thirty age group has been fully catered for by a bowling club, by friendly society dinners, cheap cinemas and communal celebrations. Sundays in Algiers are of the gloomiest. How could this mindless people disguise the deep horror of its life with myths? In Algiers, everything associated with death is either ridiculous or detestable. These people have neither religion nor idols and die alone after having lived in a crowd. I know nowhere more hideous than the cemetery of the Boulevard Bru, which stands facing one of the most beautiful landscapes in the world. A fearful sadness rises from the black setting where, in aesthetic horror piled on aesthetic horror, death reveals its true face. "Everything fades away," say the heart-shaped ex-votos, "except memory." And they all insist upon that ridiculous eternity which the heart of those who loved us provides at so low a cost. The same phrases serve all forms of despair. They address the corpse and call it "thou": "Our memory will never abandon thee,"—a gloomy pretence by means of which one lends a body and desires to what is at best a black liquid. Elsewhere, in the midst of a stupefying display of flowers and marble birds, you find this reckless vow: "Never shall thy grave lack flowers." But you are quickly reassured: the words are carved around a gilded stucco bouquet, a great time-saver for the living (like those flowers termed everlasting which owe their pompous name to the gratitude of those who still jump on moving buses). Since one must move with the times, the classical warbler is sometimes replaced by a breath-taking pearl aeroplane, piloted by a simpering angel who, in defiance of all logic, has been provided with a magnificent pair of wings.

How can one nevertheless explain that these images of death never cut themselves off from life? Here, values are closely linked together. The favourite joke of the Algerian undertakers, when they have no one in the hearse, is to shout: "Like a ride, honey?" to the pretty girls they meet on the way. This may well have symbolic, if somewhat tasteless, implications. It can also seem blasphemous to acknowledge the news of someone's death by winking your left eye and saying: "Poor chap, he won't sing any more." Or, like that woman from Oran who had never loved her husband: "God gave him to me, God has taken him away." But when all is said and done, I don't see what is sacred about death, and I am, on the contrary, very aware of the difference between fear and respect. Everything here breathes the horror of dying in a country which is an invitation to life. And yet it is under the very walls of this cemetery that the young men of Belcourt arrange their meetings, and the girls let themselves be kissed and fondled.

I fully realize that such a people cannot be accepted by everyone. Here, intelligence occupies nothing like the place it does in Italy. This race is uninterested in the mind. It worships and admires the body. From this it derives its strength, its naïve cynicism,[1] and a puerile vanity that leads it to be severely criticized. People frequently criticize it for its "mentality," that is to say for a particular mode of life and set of values. And it is true that a certain intensity of life involves some injustice. Here, nevertheless, is a people with no past, no tradition, and yet which is not lacking in poetry. But it is a poetry whose hard and sensual quality I know very well, a poetry that is far from tenderness, even from the tenderness of the Algerian sky, the

[1] See note on page 116.

only poetry which in fact moves me and makes me one with myself. The opposite of a civilized people is a creative one. These barbarians lounging on the beaches give me the unreasoned hope that, perhaps without knowing it, they are modelling the face of a culture where man's greatness will finally discover its true visage. This people, plunged wholly in the present, lives with neither myths nor consolation. It has placed all its goods on this earth and hence remains defenceless against death. The gifts of physical beauty have been heaped upon it. And, with them, that strange greed which always accompanies this futureless wealth. Everything that people do in Algiers indicates a disgust for stability and a lack of regard for the future. People hasten to live, and if an art were to be born here it would conform to that hatred of permanence which led the Dorians to carve their first column out of wood. And yet it is true that one can find a certain moderation as well as a constant excess in the strained and violent face of this people, in this summer sky emptied of tenderness, beneath which all truths can be told and on which no deceitful divinity has traced the signs of hope or of redemption. Between this sky and the faces looking up to it there is nothing on which to hang a mythology, a literature, an ethic or a religion; only stones, flesh, stars and those truths which the hand can touch.

A man who can feel his links with one hand, his love for a few men, who knows that there is always a place where his heart will find its resting place, already owns many certainties in his life. And yet, certainly, this can be insufficient. But everything, at certain moments, yearns for that land of the soul. "Yes, it is there that we must return." What is strange in finding here on earth the union for which Plotinus yearned? Unity expresses itself here in terms of sun and sea. The heart feels it through a certain taste of flesh which constitutes its bitterness and greatness. I learn that there is no superhuman happiness, no eternity outside the curve of the days. These paltry and essential goods, these relative truths, are the only ones that can move me. I have not enough soul to understand the other, "ideal" ones. Not that we should behave as beasts, but I can see no point in the happiness of angels. All I know is that this sky will last longer than I shall. And what can I call eternity except what will continue after my death? What I am expressing here is not the creature's self-satisfaction with its own condition. It is something quite different. It is not always easy to be a man, even less to be a man who is pure. But to be pure means rediscovering that country of the soul where the throbbing of our blood mingles with the violent pulsations of the afternoon sun. It is a well-known fact that we always recognize our homeland when we are about to lose it. Those whose self-torments are too great

are those whom their homeland rejects. I have no desire here to be
brutal or to appear exaggerated. But what in fact denies me in this life
is first of all what kills me. Everything that exalts life at the same time
increases its absurdity. In the summer of Algiers, I learn that only one
thing is more tragic than suffering, and that is the life of a happy
man. But this can also be the path to a greater life, since it can teach
us not to cheat.

Many people, in fact, affect a love of life in order to avoid
love itself. They try to enjoy themselves and "make experiments." But
this is an intellectual attitude. You need a rare vocation to become a
sensualist. A man lives out his life without the help of his mind, with
its triumphs and defeats, its simultaneous loneliness and companionship. I think that we can often feel a secret shame at the sight of these
men from Belcourt who work, defend their wives and children, often
without a word of reproach. I certainly have no illusions. There is not
much love in the lives that I am describing. I should rather say that
there is no longer very much. But at least they have eluded nothing.
There are words which I have never really understood, like that of
sin. I nevertheless believe that these men never sinned against life.
For if there is a sin against life, it lies perhaps less in despairing of it
than in hoping for another life and evading the implacable grandeur
of the one we have. These men have not cheated. They were gods of
the summer at twenty in their thirst for life, and they are still gods
today, stripped of all hope. I have seen two of them die. They were
full of horror, but silent. It is better like that. From the mass of evils
swarming in Pandora's box, the Greeks brought out hope as the very
last, as the most terrible of all. I know of no more moving symbol.
But hope, contrary to popular belief, is tantamount to resignation.
And living means not being resigned.

This at least is the bitter lesson of summers in Algiers. But
already the season is trembling and summer dips away. The first
September rains, after so much violence and tension, come like the
first tears shed by a liberated land, as if for a few days this country
were bathed in tenderness. Yet at the same time the carob trees are
casting the scent of love over the whole of Algeria. In the evening,
after the rain, the whole earth lies with its belly moistened by an
almond-flavoured seed, and after yielding to the sun throughout the
summer lies at rest. And once again this scent lays its blessing upon
the nuptials between man and the earth, and raises in us the only
truly virile love that this world holds: one which is generous and will
die.

Note: Here, as an illustration, is the account of a fight over-
heard in Bab-el-Oued and reproduced word for word. (The narrator
does not always speak the language of Musette's Cagayous. This is not

surprising. The Cagayous' language is often a literary one, that is to say a reconstruction. Members of the "underworld" do not always use slang. They use slang expressions, which is different. The Algerian uses a typical vocabulary and a special syntax. But it is by their introduction into French that these creations find their flavour.)

So then Coco comes on forward and tells him: "Just hold it a minute now, hold it." Up comes the other fellow and says: "Now what?" Then Coco says to him: "I'll be letting you have it." "*You'll* be letting *me* have it?" Then he puts his hand behind his back, but that was it. So then Coco says to him: "Now keep your hands in front, because I'll be having your 45 and you'll be biting the dust all the same."

So the other one kept his hand in front. And Coco gave him one, just one, not two, just one. The other man was on the deck, going "Ow, Ow." Then everybody came. And the bundle was on. One of them went up to Coco, then two then three. But I said to him: "Here, you're going to hit my brother, are you?" "What do you mean, he's your brother?" "If it's not my brother then he's as good as." Then I thumped him. Coco was thumping, I was thumping, Lucien was thumping. I'd got one of them in the corner and was giving him the head. Then the law arrived. They put the chains on us, you know. Red with shame, I was, going all the way through Bab-el-Oued. In front of the *Gentlemen's Bar* there were some of my pals and some little girls as well. Red with shame, I was. But afterwards, Lucien's father told us: "You were right to do it."

PROBING FOR
MEANING

1. What are the things one can love in Algiers? Why is the city also "desiccating"? How is the city contrasted with noncoastal, interior cities like Paris?

2. Why is Algiers "privileged" because it lies open to the sky like a "mouth" or a "wound"? How does the city's sensual wealth coincide with extreme deprivation?

3. Why is life for the young in Algiers? What do the aged do? In what way have the aged "wagered on the flesh"?

4. What is the psychology of the body? How is this a contradiction in terms?

5. What characteristics of the people are emphasized?

6. Briefly describe the code of ethics of the people of Algiers. Why is virtue a meaningless word?

7. Why can the inhabitants believe in neither myths nor consolation? What is their feeling about death?

8. Why does Camus believe that the men of Algiers have never sinned against life? How is hope "tantamount to resignation"?

9. What is the "bitter lesson" of summers in Algiers?

1. In what way is the essay a development of opposites? How does Camus use contrast to present Algiers?

2. What colors are emphasized in Camus' description of Algiers? What is the "dialogue between stone and flesh"?

3. How does Camus' word selection underscore his enchantment with dusk in Algiers?

4. Why has Camus chosen the example of the street fight presented in the footnote to illustrate the naïve cynicism of the people?

5. What do the following words means? Use each in a sentence of your own.

desiccating
frieze
nuances
paltry
pastilles
puerile
satiety
squalid

 ERNEST HEMINGWAY

Soldier's Home

Krebs went to the war from a Methodist college in Kansas. There is a picture which shows him among his fraternity brothers, all of them wearing exactly the same height and style collar. He enlisted in the Marines in 1917 and did not return to the United States until the second division returned from the Rhine in the summer of 1919.

There is a picture which shows him on the Rhine with two German girls and another corporal. Krebs and the corporal look too big for their uniforms. The German girls are not beautiful. The Rhine does not show in the picture.

By the time Krebs returned to his home town in Oklahoma the greeting of heroes was over. He came back much too late. The men from the town who had been drafted had all been welcomed elaborately on their return. There had been a great deal of hysteria. Now the reaction had set in. People seemed to think it was rather ridiculous for Krebs to be getting back so late, years after the war was over.

At first Krebs, who had been at Belleau Wood, Soissons, the Champagne, St. Mihiel and in the Argonne did not want to talk about the war at all. Later he felt the need to talk but no one wanted to hear about it. His town had heard too many atrocity stories to be thrilled by actualities. Krebs found that to be listened to at all he had to lie, and after he had done this twice he, too, had a reaction against the war and against talking about it. A distaste for everything that had happened to him in the war set in because of the lies he had told. All of the times that had been able to make him feel cool and clear inside himself when he thought of them; the times so long back when he had done the one thing, the only thing for a man to do, easily and naturally, when he might have done something else, now lost their cool, valuable quality and then were lost themselves.

His lies were quite unimportant lies and consisted in attributing to himself things other men had seen, done or heard of, and stating as facts certain apocryphal incidents familiar to all soldiers. Even his lies were not sensational at the pool room. His acquaintances, who had heard detailed accounts of German women found chained to machine guns in the Argonne forest and who could not comprehend, or were barred by their patriotism from interest in, any German machine gunners who were not chained, were not thrilled by his stories.

Krebs acquired the nausea in regard to experience that is the result of untruth or exaggeration, and when he occasionally met another man who had really been a soldier and they talked a few minutes in the dressing room at a dance he fell into the easy pose of the old soldier among other soldiers: that he had been badly, sickeningly frightened all the time. In this way he lost everything.

During this time, it was late summer, he was sleeping late in bed, getting up to walk down town to the library to get a book, eating lunch at home, reading on the front porch until he became bored and then walking down through the town to spend the hottest hours of the day in the cool dark of the pool room. He loved to play pool.

In the evening he practised on his clarinet, strolled down town, read and went to bed. He was still a hero to his two young sisters. His mother would have given him breakfast in bed if he had wanted it. She often came in when he was in bed and asked him to tell her about the war, but her attention always wandered. His father was non-committal.

Before Krebs went away to the war he had never been allowed to drive the family motor car. His father was in the real estate business and always wanted the car to be at his command when he required it to take clients out into the country to show them a piece of farm property. The car always stood outside the First National Bank building where his father had an office on the second floor. Now, after the war, it was still the same car.

Nothing was changed in the town except that the young girls

had grown up. But they lived in such a complicated world of already
defined alliances and shifting feuds that Krebs did not feel the energy
or the courage to break into it. He liked to look at them, though.
There were so many good-looking young girls. Most of them had
their hair cut short. When he went away only little girls wore their
hair like that or girls that were fast. They all wore sweaters and shirt
waists with round Dutch collars. It was a pattern. He liked to look at
them from the front porch as they walked on the other side of the
street. He liked to watch them walking under the shade of the trees.
He liked the round Dutch collars above their sweaters. He liked their
silk stockings and flat shoes. He liked their bobbed hair and the way
they walked.

When he was in town their appeal to him was not very
strong. He did not like them when he saw them in the Greek's ice
cream parlor. He did not want them themselves really. They were too
complicated. There was someting else. Vaguely he wanted a girl but
he did not want to have to work to get her. He would have liked to
have a girl but he did not want to have to spend a long time getting
her. He did not want to get into the intrigue and the politics. He did
not want to have to do any courting. He did not want to tell any more
lies. It wasn't worth it.

He did not want any consequences. He did not want any
consequences ever again. He wanted to live along without consequences. Besides he did not really need a girl. The army had taught
him that. It was all right to pose as though you had to have a girl.
Nearly everybody did that. But it wasn't true. You did not need a girl.
That was the funny thing. First a fellow boasted how girls mean
nothing to him, that he never thought of them, that they could not
touch him. Then a fellow boasted that he could not get along without
girls, that he had to have them all the time, that he could not go to
sleep without them.

That was all a lie. It was all a lie both ways. You did not need
a girl unless you thought about them. He learned that in the army.
Then sooner or later you always got one. When you were really ripe
for a girl you always got one. You did not have to think about it.
Sooner or later it would come. He had learned that in the army.

Now he would have liked a girl if she had come to him and
not wanted to talk. But here at home it was all too complicated. He
knew he could never get through it all again. It was not worth the
trouble. That was the thing about French girls and German girls.
There was not all this talking. You couldn't talk much and you did
not need to talk. It was simple and you were friends. He thought
about France and then he began to think about Germany. On the
whole he had liked Germany better. He did not want to leave Ger-

many. He did not want to come home. Still, he had come home. He sat on the front porch.

He liked the girls that were walking along the other side of the street. He liked the look of them much better than the French girls or the German girls. But the world they were in was not the world he was in. He would like to have one of them. But it was not worth it. They were such a nice pattern. He liked the pattern. It was exciting. But he would not go through all the talking. He did not want one badly enough. He liked to look at them all, though. It was not worth it. Not now when things were getting good again.

He sat there on the porch reading a book on the war. It was a history and he was reading about all the engagements he had been in. It was the most interesting reading he had ever done. He wished there were more maps. He looked forward with a good feeling to reading all the really good histories when they would come out with good detail maps. Now he was really learning about the war. He had been a good soldier. That made a difference.

One morning after he had been home about a month his mother came into his bedroom and sat on the bed. She smoothed her apron.

"I had a talk with your father last night, Harold," she said, "and he is willing for you to take the car out in the evenings."

"Yeah?" said Krebs, who was not fully awake. "Take the car out? Yeah?"

"Yes. Your father has felt for some time that you should be able to take the car out in the evenings whenever you wished but we only talked it over last night."

"I'll bet you made him," Krebs said.

"No. It was your father's suggestion that we talk the matter over."

"Yeah. I'll bet you made him," Krebs sat up in bed.

"Will you come down to breakfast, Harold?" his mother said.

"As soon as I get my clothes on," Krebs said.

His mother went out of the room and he could hear her frying something downstairs while he washed, shaved and dressed to go down into the dining-room for breakfast. While he was eating breakfast his sister brought in the mail.

"Well, Hare," she said. "You old sleepy-head. What do you ever get up for?"

Krebs looked at her. He liked her. She was his best sister.

"Have you got the paper?" he asked.

She handed him *The Kansas City Star* and he shucked off its brown wrapper and opened it to the sporting page. He folded *The*

Star open and propped it against the water pitcher with his cereal dish to steady it, so he could read while he ate.

"Harold," his mother stood in the kitchen doorway, "Harold, please don't muss up the paper. Your father can't read his *Star* if it's been mussed."

"I won't muss it," Krebs said.

His sister sat down at the table and watched him while he read.

"We're playing indoor over at school this afternoon," she said. "I'm going to pitch."

"Good," said Krebs. "How's the old wing?"

"I can pitch better than lots of the boys. I tell them all you taught me. The other girls aren't much good."

"Yeah?" said Krebs.

"I tell them all you're my beau. Aren't you my beau, Hare?"

"You bet."

"Couldn't your brother really be your beau just because he's your brother?"

"I don't know."

"Sure you know. Couldn't you be my beau, Hare, if I was old enough and if you wanted to?"

"Sure. You're my girl now."

"Am I really your girl?"

"Sure."

"Do you love me?"

"Uh, huh."

"Will you love me always?"

"Sure."

"Will you come over and watch me play indoor?"

"Maybe."

"Aw, Hare, you don't love me. If you loved me, you'd want to come over and watch me play indoor."

Krebs' mother came into the dining-room from the kitchen. She carried a plate with two fried eggs and some crisp bacon on it and a plate of buckwheat cakes.

"You run along, Helen," she said. "I want to talk to Harold."

She put the eggs and bacon down in front of him and brought in a jug of maple syrup for the buckwheat cakes. Then she sat down across the table from Krebs.

"I wish you'd put down the paper a minute, Harold," she said.

Krebs took down the paper and folded it.

"Have you decided what you are going to do yet, Harold?" his mother said, taking off her glasses.

"No," said Krebs.

"Don't you think it's about time?" His mother did not say this in a mean way. She seemed worried.

"I hadn't thought about it," Krebs said.

"God has some work for every one to do," his mother said. "There can be no idle hands in His Kingdom."

"I'm not in His Kingdom," Krebs said.

"We are all of us in His Kingdom."

Krebs felt embarrassed and resentful as always.

"I've worried about you so much, Harold," his mother went on. "I know the temptations you must have been exposed to. I know how weak men are. I know what your own dear grandfather, my own father, told us about the Civil War and I have prayed for you. I pray for you all day long, Harold."

Krebs looked at the bacon fat hardening on his plate.

"Your father is worried, too," his mother went on. "He thinks you have lost your ambition, that you haven't got a definite aim in life. Charley Simmons, who is just your age, has a good job and is going to be married. The boys are all settling down; they're all determined to get somewhere; you can see that boys like Charley Simmons are on their way to being really a credit to the community."

Krebs said nothing.

"Don't look that way, Harold," his mother said. "You know we love you and I want to tell you for your own good how matters stand. Your father does not want to hamper your freedom. He thinks you should be allowed to drive the car. If you want to take some of the nice girls out riding with you, we are only too pleased. We want you to enjoy yourself. But you are going to have to settle down to work, Harold. Your father doesn't care what you start in at. All work is honorable as he says. But you've got to make a start at something. He asked me to speak to you this morning and then you can stop in and see him at his office."

"Is that all?" Krebs said.

"Yes. Don't you love your mother, dear boy?"

"No," Krebs said.

His mother looked at him across the table. Her eyes were shiny. She started crying.

"I don't love anybody," Krebs said.

It wasn't any good. He couldn't tell her, he couldn't make her see it. It was silly to have said it. He had only hurt her. He went over and took hold of her arm. She was crying with her head in her hands.

"I didn't mean it," he said. "I was just angry at something. I didn't mean I didn't love you."

His mother went on crying. Krebs put his arm on her shoulder.

"Can't you believe me, mother?"

His mother shook her head.

"Please, please, mother. Please believe me."

"All right," his mother said chokily. She looked up at him. "I believe you, Harold."

Krebs kissed her hair. She put her face up to him.

"I'm your mother," she said. "I held you next to my heart when you were a tiny baby."

Krebs felt sick and vaguely nauseated.

"I know, Mummy," he said. "I'll try and be a good boy for you."

"Would you kneel and pray with me, Harold?" his mother asked.

They knelt down beside the dining-room table and Krebs's mother prayed.

"Now, you pray, Harold," she said.

"I can't," Krebs said.

"Try, Harold."

"I can't."

"Do you want me to pray for you?"

"Yes."

So his mother prayed for him and then they stood up and Krebs kissed his mother and went out of the house. He had tried so to keep his life from being complicated. Still, none of it had touched him. He had felt sorry for his mother and she had made him lie. He would go to Kansas City and get a job and she would feel all right about it. There would be one more scene maybe before he got away. He would not go down to his father's office. He would miss that one. He wanted his life to go smoothly. It had just gotten going that way. Well, that was all over now, anyway. He would go over to the schoolyard and watch Helen play indoor baseball.

PROBING FOR
MEANING

1. Characterize Harold Krebs. What aspects of his personality are emphasized? Is there anything particularly unusual about him?

2. What were his experiences before the war? What did he experience during the war? What is his daily routine after he returns from the war?

3. What does Krebs initially feel about his war experiences? Why is this feeling changed when he returns home? What is the effect on Krebs of lying about his war experiences?

4. Why does Krebs not want an emotional involvement with a female? What kind of relationship does he want?

5. Describe Krebs' relationship with his sister. What are his feelings toward his parents? How do his parents treat him?

6. What are Krebs' religious beliefs? What is revealed about his

religious beliefs and his relationship with his parents during the scene at breakfast in which he and his mother kneel and pray?

7. What are Krebs' plans for the future? How is the meaning of the story revealed by these plans? Do you think that he will become a "credit to the community" as his parents wish?

8. Although Hemingway does not directly describe Krebs' home town, he indirectly conveys a sense of the place. What details contribute to our understanding of this Oklahoma town? How would you summarize Hemingway's attitude toward it? Is Krebs' attitude similar to or different from the author's? If Krebs had returned to a different home, would his life after the war have been different? Explain. How typical is his home town?

PROBING FOR
METHOD
1. What is the effect of the repetition of sentence structure throughout the story? Give examples of this use of repetition. Is the author able to keep the story interesting even though he rarely varies the sentence structure? Explain.

2. Describe the method of narration of the story.

3. What is the significance of the photograph showing Krebs and another corporal with two German girls? Why does the author include this seemingly irrelevant detail?

4. Krebs enjoys girl watching from his front porch but the same girls he watches have no appeal for him when he is in the town. How does the author use this contrast to present an insight into Krebs?

5. What irony is implied in the title of the story?

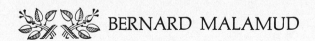 BERNARD MALAMUD

The Prison

Though he tried not to think of it, at twenty-nine Tommy Castelli's life was a screaming bore. It wasn't just Rosa or the store they tended for profits counted in pennies, or the unendurably slow hours and endless drivel that went with selling candy, cigarettes, and soda water; it was this sick-in-the-stomach feeling of being trapped in old mistakes, even some he had made before Rosa changed Tony into Tommy. He had been as Tony a kid of many dreams and schemes, especially getting out of this tenement-crowded, kid-squawking neighborhood, with its lousy poverty, but everything had fouled up against him before he could. When he was sixteen he quit the vocational school where they were making him into a shoemaker, and began to hang out with the gray-hatted, thick-soled-shoe boys, who had the spare time and the mazuma and showed it in fat wonderful rolls down in the cellar clubs to all who would look, and everybody did, popeyed. They were the ones who had bought the silver caffe espresso urn and later the television, and they arranged the pizza parties and had the girls down; but it was getting in with them and their cars, leading to the holdup of a liquor store, that had started all the present trouble. Lucky for him the coal-and-ice man who was their landlord knew the leader in the district, and they arranged something so nobody bothered him after that. Then before he knew what was going on—he had been frightened sick by the whole mess—there was his father cooking up a deal with Rosa Agnello's old man that Tony would marry her and the father-in-law would, out of his savings, open a candy store for him to make an honest living. He wouldn't spit on a candy store, and Rosa was too plain and lank a chick for his personal taste, so he beat it off to Texas and bummed around in too much space, and when he came back everybody said it was for Rosa and the candy store, and it was all arranged again and he, without saying no, was in it.

That was how he had landed on Prince Street in the Village, working from eight in the morning to almost midnight every day, except for an hour off each afternoon when he went upstairs to sleep, and on Tuesdays, when the store was closed and he slept some more and went at night alone to the movies. He was too tired always for schemes now, but once he tried to make a little cash on the side by secretly taking in punchboards some syndicate was distributing in the neighborhood, on which he collected a nice cut and in this way saved fifty-five bucks that Rosa didn't know about; but then the syndicate was written up by a newspaper, and the punchboards all disappeared. Another time, when Rosa was at her mother's house, he took a chance and let them put in a slot machine that could guarantee a nice piece of change if he kept it long enough. He knew of course he couldn't hide it from her, so when she came and screamed when she saw it, he was ready and patient, for once not yelling back when she yelled, and he explained it was not the same as gambling because anybody who played it got a roll of mints every time he put in a nickel. Also the machine would supply them a few extra dollars cash they could use to buy television so he could see the fights without going to a bar; but Rosa wouldn't let up screaming, and later her father came in shouting that he was a criminal and chopped the machine apart with a plumber's hammer. The next day the cops raided for slot machines and gave out summonses wherever they found them, and though Tommy's place was practically the only candy store in the neighborhood that didn't have one, he felt bad about the machine for a long time.

Mornings had been his best time of day because Rosa stayed upstairs cleaning, and since few people came into the store till noon, he could sit around alone, a toothpick in his teeth, looking over the *News* and *Mirror* on the fountain counter, or maybe gab with one of the old cellar-club guys who had happened to come by for a pack of butts, about a horse that was running that day or how the numbers were paying lately; or just sit there, drinking coffee and thinking how far away he could get on the fifty-five he had stashed away in the cellar. Generally the mornings were this way, but after the slot machine, usually the whole day stank and he along with it. Time rotted in him, and all he could think of the whole morning, was going to sleep in the afternoon, and he would wake up with the sour remembrance of the long night in the store ahead of him, while everybody else was doing as he damn pleased. He cursed the candy store and Rosa, and cursed, from its beginning, his unhappy life.

It was on one of these bad mornings that a ten-year-old girl from around the block came in and asked for two rolls of colored tissue paper, one red and one yellow. He wanted to tell her to go to hell and stop bothering, but instead went with bad grace to the rear, where Rosa, whose bright idea it was to keep the stuff, had put it. He went from force of habit, for the girl had been coming in every Monday since the summer for the same thing, because her rock-faced mother, who looked as if she arranged her own widowhood, took care of some small kids after school and gave them the paper to cut out dolls and such things. The girl, whose name he didn't know, re-sembled her mother, except her features were not quite so sharp and she had very light skin with dark eyes; but she was a plain kid and would be more so at twenty. He had noticed, when he went to get the paper, that she always hung back as if afraid to go where it was dark, though he kept the comics there and most of the other kids had to be slapped away from them; and that when he brought her the tissue paper her skin seemed to grow whiter and her eyes shone. She always handed him two hot dimes and went out without glancing back.

It happened that Rosa, who trusted nobody, had just hung a mirror on the back wall, and as Tommy opened the drawer to get the girl her paper this Monday morning that he felt so bad, he looked up and saw in the glass something that made it seem as if he were dreaming. The girl had disappeared, but he saw a white hand reach into the candy case for a chocolate bar and for another, then she came forth from behind the counter and stood there, innocently waiting for him. He felt at first like grabbing her by the neck and socking till she threw up, but he had been caught, as he sometimes was, by his thought of how his Uncle Dom, years ago before he went away, used to take with him Tony alone of all the kids, when he went crabbing to Sheepshead Bay. Once they went at night and threw the baited wire traps into the water and after a while pulled them up and they had this green lobster in one, and just then this fat-faced cop came along and said they had to throw it back unless it was nine inches. Dom said it was nine inches, but the cop said not to be a wise guy so Dom measured it and it was ten, and they laughed about that lobster all night. Then he remembered how he had felt after Dom was gone, and tears filled his eyes. He found himself thinking about the way his life had turned out, and then about this girl, moved that she was so young and a thief. He felt he ought to do something for her, warn her to cut it out before she got trapped and fouled up her life before it got started. His urge to do this was strong, but when he went forward she looked up frightened because he had taken so long. The fear in her eyes bothered him and he didn't say anything. She thrust out the dimes, grabbed at the tissue rolls and ran out of the store.

He had to sit down. He kept trying to make the desire to speak to her go away, but it came back stronger than ever. He asked himself what difference does it make if she swipes candy—so she swipes it; and the role of reformer was strange and distasteful to him, yet he could not convince himself that what he felt he must do was unimportant. But he worried he would not know what to say to her. Always he had trouble speaking right, stumbled over words, especially in new situations. He was afraid he would sound like a jerk and she would not take him seriously. He had to tell her in a sure way so that even if it scared her, she would understand he had done it to set her straight. He mentioned her to no one but often thought about her, always looking around whenever he went outside to raise the awning or wash the window, to see if any of the girls playing in the street was her, but they never were. The following Monday, an hour after opening the store he had smoked a full pack of butts. He thought he had found what he wanted to say but was afraid for some reason she wouldn't come in, or if she did, this time she would be afraid to take the candy. He wasn't sure he wanted that to happen until he had said what he had to say. But at about eleven, while he was reading the *News*, she appeared, asking for the tissue paper, her eyes shining so he had to look away. He knew she meant to steal. Going to the rear he slowly opened the drawer, keeping his head lowered as he sneaked a look into the glass and saw her slide behind the counter. His heart beat hard and his feet felt nailed to the floor. He tried to remember what he had intended to do, but his mind was like a dark, empty room so he let her, in the end, slip away and stood tongue-tied, the dimes burning his palm.

Afterwards, he told himself that he hadn't spoken to her because it was while she still had the candy on her, and she would have been scared worse than he wanted. When he went upstairs, instead of sleeping, he sat at the kitchen window, looking out into the back yard. He blamed himself for being too soft, too chicken, but then he thought, no there was a better way to do it. He would do it indirectly, slip her a hint he knew, and he was pretty sure that would stop her. Sometime after, he would explain to her why it was good she had stopped. So next time he cleaned out this candy platter she helped herself from, thinking she might get wise he was on to her, but she seemed not to, only hesitated with her hand before she took two candy bars from the next plate and dropped them into the black patent leather purse she always had with her. The time after that he cleaned out the whole top shelf, and still she was not suspicious, and reached down to the next and took something different. One Monday he put some loose change, nickels and dimes, on the candy plate, but she left them there, only taking the candy, which bothered him a little. Rosa asked him what he was mooning about so much and why was he eating chocolate lately. He didn't answer her, and she began to look suspiciously at the women who came in, not excluding the little girls; and he would have been glad to rap her in the teeth, but it didn't matter as long as she didn't know what he had on his mind. At the same time he figured he would have to do something sure soon, or it would get harder for the girl to stop her stealing. He had to be strong about it. Then he thought of a plan that satisfied him. He would leave two bars on the plate and put in the wrapper of one a note she could read when she was alone. He tried out on paper many messages to her, and the one that seemed best he cleanly printed on a strip of cardboard and slipped it under the wrapper of one chocolate bar. It said, "Don't do this any more or you will suffer your whole life." He puzzled whether to sign it A Friend or Your Friend and finally chose Your Friend.

This was Friday, and he could not hold his impatience for Monday. But on Monday she did not appear. He waited for a long time, until Rose came down, then he had to go up and the girl still hadn't come. He was greatly disappointed because she had never failed to come before. He lay on the bed, his shoes on, staring at the ceiling. He felt hurt, the sucker she had played him for and was now finished with because she probably had another on her hook. The more he thought about it the worse he felt. He worked up a splitting headache that kept him from sleeping, then he suddenly slept and woke without it. But he had awaked depressed, saddened. He thought about Dom getting out of jail and going away God knows where. He wondered whether he would ever meet up with him somewhere, if he took the fifty-five bucks and left. Then he remembered Dom was a pretty old guy now, and he might not know him if they did meet. He thought about life. You never really got what you wanted. No matter how hard you tried you made mistakes and couldn't get past them. You could never see the sky outside or the ocean because you were in a prison, except nobody called it a prison, and if you did they didn't know what you were talking about, or they said they didn't. A pall settled on him. He lay motionless, without thought or sympathy for himself or anybody.

But when he finally went downstairs, ironically amused that Rosa had allowed him so long a time without bitching, there were people in the store and he could hear her screeching. Shoving his way through the crowd he saw in one sickening look that she had caught the girl with the candy bars and was shaking her so hard the kid's head bounced back and forth like a balloon on a stick. With a curse he tore her away from the girl, whose sickly face showed the depth of her fright.

"Whatsamatter," he shouted at Rosa, "you want her blood?"

"She's a thief," cried Rosa.

"Shut your face."

To stop her yowling he slapped her across her mouth, but it was a harder crack than he had intended. Rosa fell back with a gasp. She did not cry but looked around dazedly at everybody, and tried to smile, and everybody there could see her teeth were flecked with blood.

"Go home," Tommy ordered the girl, but then there was a movement near the door and her mother came into the store.

"What happened?" she said.

"She stole my candy," Rosa cried.

"I let her take it," said Tommy.

Rosa stared at him as if she had been hit again, then with mouth distorted began to sob.

"One was for you, Mother," said the girl.

Her mother socked her hard across the face. "You little thief, this time you'll get your hands burned good."

She pawed at the girl, grabbed her arm and yanked it. The girl, like a grotesque dancer, half ran, half fell forward, but at the door she managed to turn her white face and thrust out at him her red tongue.

1. Malamud portrays two different stages in the life of the central character. What were the characteristics of Tony's life as opposed to Tommy's? Why does Tommy keep thinking of his Uncle Dom?

2. Why did Tommy return from Texas? What does this point out about him?

3. What is your reaction to Rosa? To what extent is she to blame for Tommy's conception of life as a prison?

4. What function does the little girl have in the story? Why is Tommy so upset about her? Why doesn't he confront her? Is Tommy

naïve in thinking that he could influence her? Why does she react to him
as she does at the end?

5. What is Malamud's attitude toward Tommy? Compare Malamud's attitude to your own.

PROBING FOR   1. From whose point of view is the story told—the author's or
METHOD   Tony's? What effect does this narrative point of view achieve?

2. Describe the introduction to the story. How does the opening
set the tone for the entire story?

3. What details does Malamud include to create a claustrophobic
atmosphere for the reader as well as for Tommy?

 CHAD WALSH

Port Authority Terminal: 9 a.m. Monday

From buses beached like an invasion fleet
They fill the waiting room with striding feet.

Their faces, white, and void of hate or pity,
Move on tall bodies toward the conquered city.

Among the lesser breeds of black and brown
They board their taxis with an absent frown,

Each to his concrete citadel,
To rule the city and to buy and sell.

At five o'clock they ride the buses back,
Leaving their Irish to guard the brown and black.   10

At six a drink, at seven dinner's served.
At ten or twelve, depressed, undressed, unnerved,

They mount their wives, dismount, they doze and dream
Apocalyptic Negroes in a stream

Of moving torches, marching from the slums,
Beating a band of garbage pails for drums,

Marching, with school-age children in their arms,
Advancing on the suburbs and the farms,

To integrate the schools and burn the houses . . .
The normal morning comes, the clock arouses   20

Junior and senior executive alike.
Back on the bus, and down the usual pike.

From buses beached like an invasion fleet
They fill the waiting room with striding feet.

PROBING FOR
MEANING

1. To whom does "they" refer in line 2? Why might the poet describe their faces as "void of hate or pity" and as wearing "an absent frown"?

2. What part do the various ethnic groups found in every large city play in this poem? What relationship do the commuters have with the Irish? With the "brown and black"?

3. What comment is the poet making about the lives of the commuters at home in suburbia? What does the dream sequence reveal?

PROBING FOR
METHOD

1. What words convey the image of the commuters as soldiers and New York as a battlefield? Why does the poet feel that this is an appropriate metaphor?

2. What effect does the rhyme structure have on the meaning of the poem?

3. What effect is achieved by having the poem's last two lines repeat the opening couplet?

 AL YOUNG

Lonesome in the Country

How much of me is sandwiches radio beer?
How much pizza traffic & neon messages?
I take thoughtful journeys to supermarkets,
philosophize about the newest good movie,
camp out at magazine racks & on floors,
catch humanity leering back in laundromats,
invent shortcuts by the quarter hour

There's meaning to all this itemization
& I'd do well to look for it in woodpiles
or in hills & springs or trees in the woods

10

instead of staying in the shack all the time
imagining too much
                falling asleep in old chairs

All that childhood I spent in farmhouses
& still cant tell one bush from another—
Straight wilderness would wipe me out
faster than cancer from cigarette smoke

Meantime my friends are out all day long
stomping thru the woods all big-eyed
& that's me walking the road afternoons   20
head in a book
           all that hilly sweetness wasting

PROBING FOR MEANING

1. "There's meaning to all this itemization." What itemizing does the poet do? What meaning is in it?

2. Why is his stay in the country "lonesome"? Why would "straight wilderness" wipe him out "faster than cancer from cigarette smoke"?

3. Why does he walk in the road reading a book instead of going with his friends into the "hilly sweetness"? What is the author's attitude toward himself? Toward his friends?

PROBING FOR METHOD

Much of the language is informal with the prose quality of literal statement instead of imagery. What makes it a poem? Is it a poem?

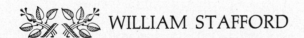 WILLIAM STAFFORD

The Star in the Hills

A star hit in the hills behind our house
up where the grass turns brown touching the sky.

Meteors have hit the world before, but this was near,
and since TV; few saw, but many felt the shock.
The state of California owns that land
(and out from shore three miles), and any stars
that come will be roped off and viewed on week days 8 to 5.

A guard who took the oath of loyalty and denied
any police record told me this:
"If you don't have a police record yet   10
you could take the oath and get a job
if California should be hit by another star."

"I'd promise to be loyal to California
and to guard any stars that hit it," I said,
"or any place three miles out from shore,
unless the star was bigger than the state—
in which case I'd be loyal to it."

But he said no exceptions were allowed,
and he leaned against the state-owned meteor
so calm and puffed a cork-tip cigarette   20
that I looked down and traced with my foot in the dust
and thought again and said, "OK—any star."

PROBING FOR   1. What happens to the star after it reaches the earth? What is
    MEANING   the meaning of the fact that "few saw, but many felt the shock" in light
of the poet's statement that it was "since TV"? Why does California
"own" the meteor? How does the state evidence its ownership?
            2. Why must the guard pledge loyalty to the state? Why are
there "no exceptions" allowed?
            3. What is the poem saying about loyalty to meteors? What
is the significance of the narrator's statement that he will not take
the oath of loyalty to "any star"?
            4. To what extent is it important that the location of the poem is
California? Could it be any other state?

PROBING FOR   1. What is the tone of the poem? In this regard, how would you
    METHOD   describe the narrator's attitude throughout the poem?
            2. What features of the guard does the poet emphasize? Can the
reader picture the guard's appearance from this description?
            3. How would you characterize the style of the poem? Is the dia-
logue between the guard and the narrator realistically presented?

Topics for Imitation

            1. Has a place affected you as the lake did White, as his
mother's kitchen did Kazin, or as Folsom Prison did Cleaver? Describe
this place, using spatial cohesion, trying also to convey your reaction
to it.

2. Write a visual description of a place that you know well. Use spatial order to help your reader see it as you do or once did. Decide the spatial pattern that you wish to use before beginning. Use analogy if an extended comparison is appropriate.

3. Discuss the various descriptions of city life found in the selections of this chapter. How does the tone differ from author to author?

4. Places often affect people's behavior. Discuss the influence of the lake, Folsom Prison, Las Vegas and Krebs' home town on the characters in the appropriate selections. How might these or similar places affect people in general?

5. People's behavior also affects place. To what extent have the kitchen, Las Vegas, the candy store in "The Prison" and the country in "Lonesome in the Country" been shaped by personal or cultural behavior or attitudes?

6. In "Summer in Algiers" Camus says that civilization thwarts human creativity through the physical and psychological confinement it imposes. Discuss Camus' assertion in terms of the Cleaver, Wolfe, Hemingway, Malamud and Stafford selections.

7. Discuss the responses to nature of White, Camus, Young and Stafford. Account as much as possible for the differences in their attitudes.

8. In "Once More to the Lake," "The Kitchen" and "Summer in Algiers" place evokes an important insight for the author or a character. Discuss the interaction between person and place that made the insight possible.

THREE

EVENTS AND EXPERIENCES

"... first snow and kiss and fight"

When Alex Haley finally discovered who his African forbears were, he wept. As he says in his essay in this chapter, "If you really knew the odyssey of us millions of black Americans, if you really knew how we came in the seeds of our forefathers, captured, driven, beaten, inspected, bought, branded, chained in foul ships, if you really knew, you needed weeping . . ."

Alex Haley's search for his "furthest-back person, the African" was an intensely emotional personal experience which he felt was also of value to other black Americans: "Back home, I knew that what I must write, really, was our black saga, where any individual's past is the essence of the millions'."

In this chapter you will encounter other writers who write of their experiences because of their value for others. Adrienne Rich, the poet, writes of her ambivalent reactions to motherhood; Anthony Burgess, an Englishman, evaluates a year lived in America; and Joyce Maynard analyzes her elementary school days in Oyster River. Dee Brown, in telling the story of Chief Joseph of the Nez Percé tribe, reminds us of our capacity for evil as a nation and Hana Wehle, a survivor of Auschwitz, dramatizes an experience in the death camp in which the greatest atrocities in human history were enacted.

The poems and short stories communicate still other experiences, like growing old ("The Sojourner"), parting from a loved one ("My Life Closed Twice") and watching a friend suffer ("The Burning").

Developing the Paragraph and Narrating and Evaluating an Event

A discussion of paragraphing will be included in this chapter as another technique of good writing. You should also become aware of the introductions and conclusions to the essays as models for your own first and final paragraphs.

As you read the essays narrating events and experiences, analyze the methods the writers have used to enable the reader to participate in the event and to inform him of its significance for him.

 JOYCE MAYNARD

The Lion Tamers

I watch them every year, the six-year-olds, buying lunch boxes and snap-on bow ties and jeweled barrettes, swinging on their mothers' arms as they approach the school on registration day or walking ahead a little, stiff in new clothes. Putting their feet on the shoe salesman's metal foot measurer, eying the patent leather and ending up with sturdy brown tie oxfords, sitting rigid in the barber's chair, heads balanced on white-sheeted bodies like cherries on cupcakes, as the barber snips away the kindergarten hair for the new grown-up cut, striding past the five-year-olds with looks of knowing pity (ah, youth) they enter elementary school, feigning reluctance—with scuffing heels and dying TV cowboy groans shared in the cloakroom, but filled with hope and anticipation of all the mysteries waiting in the cafeteria and the water fountain and the paper closet, and in the pages of the textbooks on the teachers' desks. With pink erasers and a sheath of sharpened pencils, they file in so really bravely, as if to tame lions, or at least subdue the alphabet. And instead, I long to warn them, watching this green young crop pass by each year, seeing them enter a red-brick, smelly-staircase world of bathroom passes and penmanship drills, gongs and red x's, and an unexpected snap to the teacher's slingshot voice (so slack and giving, when she met the mothers). I want to tell them about the back pages in the teacher's record book, of going to the principal's office or staying behind an extra year. Quickly they learn how little use they'll have for lion-taming apparatus. They are, themselves, about to meet the tamer.

I can barely remember it now, but I know that I once felt that first-day eagerness too. Something happened, though, between that one pony-tail-tossing, skirt-flouncing, hand-waving ("*I* know the answer—call on *me*") day and the first day of all the other years I spent in public school. It wasn't just homework and the struggle to get up at seven every morning, it was the *kind* of homework assignments we were given and the prospect of just what it was that we were rousing ourselves for—the systematic breaking down, work-book page by workbook page, drill after drill, of all the joy we started out with. I don't think I'm exaggerating when I say that, with very few exceptions, what they did to (not *for*) us in elementary school was not unlike what I would sometimes do to my cats: dress them up in doll clothes because they looked cute that way.

We were forever being organized into activities that, I suspect, looked good on paper and in school board reports. New programs took over and disappeared as approaches to child education changed. One year we would go without marks, on the theory that marks were a "poor motivating factor," "an unnatural pressure," and my laboriously researched science and social studies reports would come back with a check mark or a check plus inside the margin. Another year every activity became a competition, with posters tacked up on the walls showing who was ahead that week, our failures and our glories bared to all the class. Our days were filled with electrical gimmicks, film strips and movies and overhead projectors and tapes and supplementary TV shows, and in junior high, when we went audio-visual, a power failure would have been reason enough to close down the school.

But though the educational jargon changed, the school's basic attitude remained constant. Anything too different (too bad or too exceptional), anything that meant making another column in the record book, was frowned upon. A lone recorder, in a field of squeaking flutophones, a reader of Dickens, while the class was laboring page by page (out loud, pace set by the slowest oral readers) with the adventures of the Marshall family and their dog Ranger, a ten-page story when the teacher had asked for a two-pager—they all met with suspicion. Getting straight A's was fine with the school as long as one pursued the steady, earnest, unspectacular course. But to complete a piece of work well, without having followed the prescribed steps— that seemed a threat to the school, proof that we could progress without it. Vanity rears its head everywhere, even in the classroom, but surely extra guards against it should be put up there. I remember an English teacher who wouldn't grant me an A until second term, an indication, for whoever cared about that sort of thing, that under her tutelage I had *improved.* Every composition was supposed to have evolved from three progressively refined rough drafts. I moved in just the opposite direction for the school's benefit: I wrote my "final drafts" the first time around, then deliberately aged them a bit with earnest-looking smudges and erasures.

Kids who have gone through elementary school at the bottom of their class might argue here that it *was* the smart ones who got special attention—independent study groups, free time to spend acting in plays and writing novels (we were always starting autobiographies) and researching "Special Reports"—all the things that kept our groups self-perpetuating, with the children lucky enough to start out on top forever in the teachers' good graces, and those who didn't start there always drilling on decimals and workbook extra-work pages. But Oyster River was an exemplary democratic school and showed exemplary concern for slow students—the under-achievers— and virtuously left the quick and bright to swim for themselves, or tread water endlessly.

It always seemed to me as a Group One member, that there was little individual chance to shine. It was as if the school had just discovered the division of labor concept, and oh, how we divided it. Book reports, math problems, maps for history and even art projects—we did them all in committee. Once we were supposed to write a short story that way, pooling our resources of Descriptive Adjectives and Figures of Speech to come up with an adventure that read like one of those typing-book sentences ("A quick brown fox . . ."), where every letter of the alphabet is represented. Our group drawings had the look of movie magazine composites that show the ideal star, with Paul Newman's eyes, Brando's lips, Steve McQueen's hair. Most people loved group work—the kids because working together meant not working very hard, tossing your penny in the till and leaving it for someone else to count, the teachers because committee projects prepared us for community work (getting along with the group, leadership abilities . . .) and, more important, I think, to some of them, they required a lot less marking time than individual projects did. The finished product didn't matter so much—in fact, anything too usual seemed only to rock our jointly rowed canoe.

The school day was for me, and for most of us, I think, a mixture of humiliation and boredom. Teachers would use their students for the entertainment of the class. Within the first few days of the new term, someone quickly becomes the class jester, someone is the class genius, the "brain" who, the teacher, with doubtful modesty, reminds us often, probably has a much higher IQ than she. Some student is the troublemaker black sheep (the one who always makes her sigh), the one who will be singled out as the culprit when the whole class seems like a stock exchange of note passing, while all the others stare at him, looking shocked.

Although their existence is denied now, in this modern, psychologically enlightened age, teachers' pets are still very much around, sometimes in the form of the girl with super-neat penmanship and Breck-clean hair, sometimes in the person of the dependable Brain, who always gets called on when the superintendent is visiting the class. Teachers, I came to see, could be intimidated by a class, coerced or conned into liking the students who were popular among the kids, and it was hard not to miss, too, that many teachers were not above using unpopular students to gain acceptance with the majority. They had an instinct, teachers did, for who was well-liked and who wasn't; they learned all the right nicknames and turned away, when they could, if one of their favorites was doing the kind of thing that brought a 3 in conduct. We saw it all, like underlings watching the graft operations of ambitious politicians, powerless to do anything about it.

That was what made us most vulnerable: our powerlessness. Kids don't generally speak up or argue their case. No one is a child long enough, I suppose, or articulate enough, while he is one, to become a spokesman for his very real, and often oppressed, minority group. And then when we outgrow childhood, we no longer care, and feel, in fact, that if *we* went through it all, so should the next generation. Children are *expected* to be adversaries of school and teachers, so often, in the choosing up of sides, parents will side with the school. Nobody expects children to like school; therefore it's no surprise when they don't. What should be a surprise is that they dislike it for many good reasons.

It would be inaccurate to say I hated school. I had a good time sometimes, usually when I was liked, and therefore on top. And with all the other clean-haired girls who had neat penmanship and did their homework, I took advantage of my situation. When I was on the other side of the teacher's favor though, I realized that my sun-basking days had always depended on there being someone in the shade. That was the system—climbing up on one another's heads, putting someone down so one's own stature could be elevated. Elementary school was a club that not only reinforced the class system but created it—a system in which the stutterer and the boy who can't hit a baseball start out, and remain, right at the bottom, a system where being in the middle—not too high or low—is best of all.

I had imagined, innocently, on my first day at school, that once the kids saw how smart I was, they'd all be my friends. I see similar hopes on the faces I watch heading to the front every September—all the loved children, tops in their parents' eyes, off to be "re-evaluated" in a world where only one of thirty can be favorite, each child unaware, still, that he is not the only person in the universe, and about to discover that the best means of survival is to blend in (adapting to the group, it's called), to go from being one to being one in a crowd of many, many others.

PROBING FOR
MEANING

1. With what "lion-taming apparatus" do children begin first grade? How do they instead become "the tamed"?

2. What fault does Maynard find with the innovative programs attempted in her own elementary school?

3. She accuses teachers and students of playing games with each other. How effectively does she analyze the dynamics of the classroom in your opinion?

4. Maynard speaks of the powerlessness of children throughout the essay. Why do teachers and administration enforce this powerlessness?

5. "Elementary school was a club that not only reinforced the class system but created it." In how many instances does the author prove this to be true?

6. What suggestions does she give of what an ideal school would be like?

PROBING FOR
METHOD

1. Discuss the author's use of comparisons—similes and metaphors. How effective are they in each context?

2. How in her conclusion does Maynard allude to her introduction? Why would a writer build such a "frame" around her essay?

3. Has Maynard effectively limited her topic? Why or why not?

4. How would you describe her tone? Through which method does she convey her attitude: words, selection of details, or outright statements? Cite examples.

5. To what extent does she use chronological development in recounting this experience?

Developing the Paragraph

ILLUS-
TRATION

How does Maynard structure her paragraphs? Each paragraph develops one major aspect of her topic. In her first paragraph, the author asserts the topic itself: that while children anticipate beginning school, they are going to be disappointed.

Paragraph 2 introduces us to the author's own experiences in school which she will use throughout the essay to substantiate why children shouldn't expect much of their education.

Paragraph 3 discusses the organization of school activities. "Anything too different . . . was frowned upon," the author claims in the next paragraph.

In paragraph 5, she supports her previous statement with the example of smart students who aren't given the help they need. In paragraph 6 she complains that all work is done in committees.

She maintains in the next two paragraphs that teachers humiliate or flatter students for their own ends. Paragraph 9 concludes that students are powerless.

Schools are clubs reinforcing the class system is her final shot. In her last paragraph she refers again to "all the loved children" ready to begin school who will be disillusioned.

In each paragraph Maynard employs a technique used by many good writers which is to express the main idea concretely in one sentence somewhere in the paragraph, usually in the beginning or concluding sentence. Notice, for example, that the last two sentences of paragraph 1 summarize the idea of that paragraph. And in paragraph 2, the second sentence is a "topic" sentence.

The first sentence of paragraph 3 introduces the topic of the paragraph just as the second sentence does in the following paragraph. Which sentences in the remaining paragraphs summarize the topics of those units?

Maynard has developed the main idea of each paragraph in various ways throughout the essay. The sentences in paragraph 1, for example, contrast details of kids' expectations with reality. In paragraph 2, her sentences analyze her topic sentence; that is, they explain, by breaking the process into parts, what was wrong with school.

Paragraphs 3 and 4 use examples to support the main idea as do paragraphs 6 and 8. Paragraphs 5 and 11 again use contrast, while "reasons why" supplies the technique for development of paragraphs 6 and 9. Other techniques are classification (paragraph 7) and cause and effect (paragraph 10).

Paragraphs 1 and 11 fulfill special functions. The author's first paragraph introduces the essay by (1) interesting the reader in the material through an entertaining description of six-year-olds preparing for school and (2) indicating by the end of the paragraph what the essay is to be about.

Her last paragraph contains a note of finality, indicating the essay has been concluded. By referring to the ideas of the introduction, she erects a "frame" around the essay, thus underlining its unity while at the same time concluding it.

INDUCTION   *Principles of paragraph development.*   The basic structure of the paragraph is similar to that of the essay as a whole. Like the essay, the paragraph limits itself to one topic capable of expansion within a limited space.

Also, just as the essay outline follows a certain method of development, so must the sentences in the paragraph develop the topic logically. Furthermore, the first paragraph of the essay introduces the subject, and correspondingly, the first sentence of the paragraph often is an introduction or "topic" sentence. Finally, in long paragraphs, the last sentence may act as a conclusion.

A simplified method of forming good paragraphs with effective topic sentences involves the use of the essay outline. Each of the major headings when stated in sentence form may be used as the topic sentence of a paragraph. The development of each paragraph involves explaining the point in the topic sentence.

A frequent method of paragraph development is to give examples which illustrate the topic sentence. Other ways in which paragraphs may be expanded include the use of details as well as adopting those methods which apply to the essay as a whole: spatial order, chronological order, contrast and comparison, cause and effect and analysis.

In writing your essay, two paragraphs which may present difficulty are the introduction and the conclusion. The former has a two-fold function: to interest the reader in the essay and to give him some idea of its purpose. The first sentence is important in capturing the reader's attention. If framed as a question, it will arouse the reader's curiosity. If composed as a startling statement, it will intrigue him. Your first paragraph is a "come on" and should give just enough information on your topic to compel the reader's interest.

The conclusion to a short essay should not simply summarize the paper; only in long essays where the reader might forget earlier points is the summary conclusion effective. The conclusion should present to the reader aspects of your subject about which he might think further. It should leave an impact just as dramatic as an effective introduction. Most importantly, it should leave no doubt in the reader's mind that the thoughts on the paper have been brought together with some degree of finality.

IMITATION   *Procedures to follow in developing paragraphs.*

A. Write each major heading in your outline in sentence form.

B. Use each sentence as the topic sentence of a paragraph in your paper.

C. Once you have the topic sentence formulated for each paragraph, use the sub-headings in your outline to develop the rest of the paragraph. Develop your paragraph logically; that is, arrange the sentences in an effective pattern.

1. If the paragraph describes a place, follow the spatial pattern described in Chapter II.

2. If it narrates an event, develop a chronological arrangement.

3. Often sentences in a paragraph simply add supporting details. These details can be arranged so that less important details precede more important ones or vice versa.

4. For the more complicated methods of paragraph develop-

ment, see Chapter IV for cause-and-effect development and Chapter V for contrast and comparison.

D. No rules have been formulated for the length of paragraphs, but some guidelines are useful:

1. A heading from your outline which can be explained in a sentence or two is not worth a separate paragraph. You should join it to either the preceding or following paragraph if possible, or simply delete it.

2. Some headings may need to be divided into two or more paragraphs if the subject requires more than five or six well-developed sentences. In this case, each sub-heading should be written in sentence form and serve as a topic sentence for a second (or third) paragraph.

E. Use your "thesis" sentence in developing your introduction. Your introduction should fulfill two purposes: it should be interesting, and it should be informative.

F. The conclusion should not simply summarize the essay, but neither should it develop a new topic. The best conclusion stresses a particular aspect of the topic for the readers to think about on their own. Also, its tone of finality should clearly indicate that the essay is being concluded.

Analyze the introductions and conclusions to several of the essays you have read in Chapters I and II. How have the authors developed their introductions? Have they interested you in their subject matter? What other techniques might the authors have used? For example, how could Anderson have introduced his account through an anecdote? On the other hand, what shocking statement might Wolfe have used instead of his anecdotal approach?

How do Anderson and Podhoretz achieve a note of finality in their conclusions? Do their conclusions include summaries of the essay? Have they stressed what the readers should further think about on their own? What other methods of concluding can you discern in the first two chapters? How is a note of finality achieved in each case?

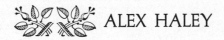 ALEX HALEY

My Furthest-Back Person—"The African"

My Grandma Cynthia Murray Palmer lived in Henning, Tenn. (pop. 500), about 50 miles north of Memphis. Each summer as I grew up there, we would be visited by several women relatives who were mostly around Grandma's age, such as my Great Aunt Liz

Murray who taught in Oklahoma, and Great Aunt Till Merriwether from Jackson, Tenn., or their considerably younger niece, Cousin Georgia Anderson from Kansas City, Kan., and some others. Always after the supper dishes had been washed, they would go out to take seats and talk in the rocking chairs on the front porch, and I would scrunch down, listening, behind Grandma's squeaky chair, with the dusk deepening into night and the lightning bugs flicking on and off above the now shadowy honeysuckles. Most often they talked about our family—the story had been passed down for generations—until the whistling blur of lights of the southbound Panama Limited train *whooshing* through Henning at 9:05 P.M. signaled our bedtime.

So much of their talking of people, places and events I didn't understand: For instance, what was an "Ol' Massa," and "Ol' Missus" or a "plantation"? But early I gathered that white folks had done lots of bad things to our folks, though I couldn't figure out why. I guessed that all that they talked about had happened a long time ago, as now or then Grandma or another, speaking of someone in the past, would excitedly thrust a finger toward me, exclaiming, "Wasn't big as *this* young 'un!" And it would astound me that anyone as old and gray-haired as they could relate to my age. But in time my head began both a recording and picturing of the more graphic scenes they would describe, just as I also visualized David killing Goliath with his slingshot, Old Pharaoh's army drowning, Noah and his ark, Jesus feeding that big multitude with nothing but five loaves and two fishes, and other wonders that I heard in my Sunday school lessons at our New Hope Methodist Church.

The furthest-back person Grandma and the others talked of—always in tones of awe, I noticed—they would call "The African." They said that some ship brought him to a place that they pronounced " 'Naplis." They said that then some "Mas' John Waller" bought him for his plantation in "Spot-sylvania County, Va." This African kept on escaping, the fourth time trying to kill the "hateful po' cracker" slave-catcher, who gave him the punishment choice of castration or of losing one foot. This African took a foot being chopped off with an ax against a tree stump, they said, and he was about to die. But his life was saved by "Mas' John's" brother— "Mas' William Waller," a doctor, who was so furious about what had happened that he bought the African for himself and gave him the name "Toby."

Crippling about, working in "Mas' William's" house and yard, the African in time met and mated with "the big house cook named Bell," and there was born a girl named Kizzy. As she grew up her African daddy often showed her different kinds of things, telling her what they were in his native tongue. Pointing at a banjo, for example, the African uttered, *"ko"*; or pointing at a river near the plantation, he would say, *"Kamby Bolong."* Many of his strange words started with a *"k"* sound, and the little, growing Kizzy learned gradually that they identified different things.

When addressed by other slaves as "Toby," the master's name for him, the African said angrily that his name was *"Kin-tay."* And as he gradually learned English, he told young Kizzy some things about himself—for instance, that he was not far from his village, chopping wood to make himself a drum, when four men had surprised, overwhelmed, and kidnapped him.

So Kizzy's head held much about her African daddy when at age 16 she was sold away onto a much smaller plantation in North Carolina. Her new "Mas' Tom Lea" fathered her first child, a boy she named George. And Kizzy told her boy all about his African grandfather. George grew up to be such a gamecock fighter that he was called "Chicken George," and people would come from all over and "bet big money" on his cockfights. He mated with Matilda, another of Lea's slaves; they had seven children, and he told them the stories and strange sounds of their African great-grandfather. And one of those children, Tom, became a blacksmith who was bought away by a "Mas' Murray" for his tobacco plantation in Alamance County, N.C.

Tom mated there with Irene, a weaver on the plantation. She also bore seven children, and Tom now told them all about their African great-great-grandfather, the faithfully passed-down knowledge of his sounds and stories having become by now the family's prideful treasure.

The youngest of that second set of seven children was a girl, Cynthia, who became my maternal Grandma (which today I can only see as fated). Anyway, all of this is how I was growing up in Henning at Grandma's, listening from behind her rocking chair as she and the other visiting old women talked of that African (never then comprehended as *my* great-great-great-great-grandfather) who said his name was *"Kin-tay,"* and said *"ko"* for banjo, *"Kamby Bolong"* for river, and a jumble of other *"k"*-beginning sounds that Grandma privately muttered, most often while making beds or cooking, and who also said that near his village he was kidnapped while chopping wood to make himself a drum.

The story had become nearly as fixed in my head as in Grandma's by the time Dad and Mama moved me and my two younger brothers, George and Julius, away from Henning to be with them at the small black agricultural and mechanical college in Normal, Ala., where Dad taught.

To compress my next 25 years: When I was 17 Dad let me enlist as a mess boy in the U.S. Coast Guard. I became a ship's cook out in the South Pacific during World War II, and at night down by my bunk I began trying to write sea adventure stories; mailing them off to magazines and collecting rejection slips for eight years before some editors began purchasing and publishing occasional stories. By 1949 the Coast Guard had made me its first "journalist"; finally with 20 years' service, I retired at the age of 37, determined to make a full time career of writing. I wrote mostly magazine articles; my first book was "The Autobiography of Malcolm X."

Then one Saturday in 1965 I happened to be walking past the National Archives building in Washington. Across the interim years I had thought of Grandma's old stories—otherwise I can't think what diverted me up the Archives' steps. And when a main reading room desk attendant asked if he could help me, I wouldn't have dreamed of admitting to him some curiosity hanging on from boyhood about my slave forebears. I kind of bumbled that I was interested in census records of Alamance County, North Carolina, just after the Civil War.

The microfilm rolls were delivered, and I turned them through the machine with a building sense of intrigue, viewing in different census takers' penmanship an endless parade of names. After about a dozen microfilmed rolls, I was beginning to tire, when in utter astonishment I looked upon the names of Grandma's parents: Tom Murray, Irene Murray . . . older sisters of Grandma's as well— every one of them a name that I'd heard countless times on her front porch.

It wasn't that I hadn't believed Grandma. You just *didn't* not believe my Grandma. It was simply so uncanny actually seeing those names in print and in official U.S. Government records.

During the next several months I was back in Washington whenever possible, in the Archives, the Library of Congress, the Daughters of the American Revolution Library. (Whenever black attendants understood the idea of my search, documents I requested reached me with miraculous speed.) In one source or another during 1966 I was able to document at least the highlights of the cherished family story. I would have given anything to have told Grandma, but, sadly, in 1949 she had gone. So I went and told the only survivor of those Henning front-porch storytellers: Cousin Georgia Anderson, now in her 80's in Kansas City, Kan. Wrinkled, bent, not well herself, she was so overjoyed, repeating to me the old stories and sounds; they were like Henning echoes: "Yeah, boy, that African say his name was '*Kin-tay*'; he say the banjo was '*ko*,' an' the river '*Kamby Bolong*,' an' he was off choppin' some wood to make his drum when they grabbed 'im!" Cousin Georgia grew so excited we had to stop her, calm her down, "You go'head, boy! Your grandma an' all of 'em—they up there watching what you do!"

That week I flew to London on a magazine assignment. Since by now I was steeped in the old, in the past, scarcely a tour guide missed me—I was awed at so many historical places and treasures I'd heard of and read of. I came upon the Rosetta stone in the British Museum, marveling anew at how Jean Champollion, the French archaeologist, had miraculously deciphered its ancient demotic and hieroglyphic texts . . .

The thrill of that just kept hanging around in my head. I was on a jet returning to New York when a thought hit me. Those strange, unknown-tongue sounds, always part of our family's old story . . . they were obviously bits of our original African *"Kin-tay's"* native tongue. What specific tongue? Could I somehow find out?

Back in New York, I began making visits to the United Nations Headquarters lobby; it wasn't hard to spot Africans. I'd stop any I could, asking if my bits of phonetic sounds held any meaning for them. A couple of dozen Africans quickly looked at me, listened, and took off—understandably dubious about some Tennesseean's accent alleging "African" sounds.

My research assistant, George Sims (we grew up together in Henning), brought me some names of ranking scholars of African linguistics. One was particularly intriguing: a Belgian- and English-educated Dr. Jan Vansina; he had spent his early career living in West African villages, studying and tape-recording countless oral histories that were narrated by certain very old African men; he had written a standard textbook, "The Oral Tradition."

So I flew to the University of Wisconsin to see Dr. Vansina. In his living room I told him every bit of the family story in the fullest detail that I could remember it. Then, intensely, he queried me about the story's relay across the generations, about the gibberish of *"k"* sounds Grandma had fiercely muttered to herself while doing her housework, with my brothers and me giggling beyond her hearing at what we had dubbed "Grandma's noises."

Dr. Vansina, his manner very serious, finally said, "These sounds your family has kept sound very probably of the tongue called 'Mandinka.'"

I'd never heard of any "Mandinka." Grandma just told of the African saying *"ko"* for banjo, or *"Kamby Bolong"* for a Virginia river.

Among Mandinka stringed instruments, Dr. Vansina said, one of the oldest was the *"kora."*

"Bolong," he said, was clearly Mandinka for "river." Preceded by *"Kamby,"* it very likely meant "Gambia River."

Dr. Vansina telephoned an eminent Africanist colleague, Dr. Philip Curtin. He said that the phonetic *"Kin-tay"* was correctly spelled *"Kinte,"* a very old clan that had originated in Old Mali. The

Kinte men traditionally were blacksmiths, and the women were potters and weavers.

I knew I must get to the Gambia River.

The first native Gambian I could locate in the U.S. was named Ebou Manga, then a junior attending Hamilton College in upstate Clinton, N.Y. He and I flew to Dakar, Senegal, then took a smaller plane to Yundum Airport, and rode in a van to Gambia's capital, Bathurst. Ebou and his father assembled eight Gambia government officials. I told them Grandma's stories, every detail I could remember, as they listened intently, then reacted. " '*Kamby Bolong*' of course is Gambia River!" I heard. "But more clue is your forefather's saying his name was '*Kinte*.' " Then they told me something I would never even have fantasized—that in places in the back country lived very old men, commonly called *griots,* who could tell centuries of the histories of certain very old family clans. As for *Kintes,* they pointed out to me on a map some family villages, Kinte-Kundah, and Kinte-Kundah Janneh-Ya, for instance.

The Gambian officials said they would try to help me. I returned to New York dazed. It is embarrassing to me now, but despite Grandma's stories, I'd never been concerned much with Africa, and I had the routine images of African people living mostly in exotic jungles. But a compulsion now laid hold of me to learn all I could, and I began devouring books about Africa, especially about the slave trade. Then one Thursday's mail contained a letter from one of the Gambian officials, inviting me to return there.

Monday I was back in Bathurst. It galvanized me when the officials said that a *griot* had been located who told the *Kinte* clan history—his name was Kebba Kanga Fofana. To reach him, I discovered, required a modified safari: renting a launch to get upriver, two land vehicles to carry supplies by a roundabout land route, and employing finally 14 people, including three interpreters and four musicians, since a *griot* would not speak the revered clan histories without background music.

The boat Baddibu vibrated upriver, with me acutely tense: Were these Africans maybe viewing me as but another of the pith-helmets? After about two hours, we put in at James Island, for me to see the ruins of the once British-operated James Fort. Here two centuries of slave ships had loaded thousands of cargoes of Gambian tribespeople. The crumbling stones, the deeply oxidized swivel cannon, even some remnant links of chain seemed all but impossible to believe. Then we continued upriver to the left-bank village of Albreda, and there put ashore to continue on foot to Juffure, village of the *griot.* Once more we stopped, for me to see *toubob kolong,* "the white man's well," now almost filled in, in a swampy area with abundant, tall, saw-toothed grass. It was dug two centuries ago to "17 men's height deep" to insure survival drinking water for long-driven, famishing coffles of slaves.

Walking on, I kept wishing that Grandma could hear how her stories had led me to the "*Kamby Bolong.*" (Our surviving storyteller Cousin Georgia died in a Kansas City hospital during this same morning, I would learn later.) Finally, Juffure village's playing children, sighting us, flashed an alert. The 70-odd people came rushing from their circular, thatch-roofed, mud-walled huts, with goats bounding up and about, and parrots squawking from up in the palms. I sensed him in advance somehow, the small man amid them, wearing a pillbox cap and an off-white robe—the *griot*. Then the interpreters went to him, as the villagers thronged around me.

And it hit me like a gale wind: every one of them, the whole crowd, was *jet black*. An enormous sense of guilt swept me—a sense of being some kind of hybrid . . . a sense of being impure among the pure. It was an awful sensation.

The old *griot* stepped away from my interpreters and the crowd quickly swarmed around him—all of them buzzing. An interpreter named A. B. C. Salla came to me; he whispered: "Why they stare at you so, they have never seen here a black American." And that hit me: I was symbolizing for them twenty-five millions of us they had never seen. What did they think of me—of us?

Then abruptly the old *griot* was briskly walking toward me. His eyes boring into mine, he spoke in Mandinka, as if instinctively I should understand—and A. B. C. Salla translated:

"Yes . . . we have been told by the forefathers . . . that many of us from this place are in exile . . . in that place called America . . . and in other places."

I suppose I physically wavered, and they thought it was the heat; rustling whispers went through the crowd, and a man brought me a low stool. Now the whispering hushed—the musicians had softly begun playing *kora* and *balafon*, and a canvas sling lawn seat was taken by the *griot*, Kebba Kanga Fofana, aged 73 "rains" (one rainy season each year). He seemed to gather himself into a physical rigidity, and he began speaking the *Kinte* clan's ancestral oral history; it came rolling from his mouth across the next hours . . . 17th- and 18th-century *Kinte* lineage details, predominantly what men took wives; the children they "begot," in the order of their births; those children's mates and children.

Events frequently were dated by some proximate singular physical occurrence. It was as if some ancient scroll were printed indelibly within the *griot's* brain. Each few sentences or so, he would pause for an interpreter's translation to me. I distill here the essence:

The *Kinte* clan began in Old Mali, the men generally black-smiths ". . . who conquered fire," and the women potters and weavers. One large branch of the clan moved to Mauretania from where one son of the clan, Kairaba Kunta Kinte, a Moslem Marabout holy man, entered Gambia. He lived first in the village of Pakali N'Ding; he moved next to Jiffarong village; ". . . and then he came here, into our own village of Juffure."

In Juffure, Kairaba Kunta Kinte took his first wife, ". . . a Mandinka maiden, whose name was Sireng. By her, he begot two sons, whose names were Janneh and Saloum. Then he got a second wife, Yaisa. By her, he begot a son, Omoro."

The three sons became men in Juffure. Janneh and Saloum went off and found a new village, Kinte-Kundah Janneh-Ya. "And then Omoro, the youngest son, when he had 30 rains, took as a wife a maiden, Binta Kebba.

"And by her, he begot four sons—Kunta, Lamin, Suwadu, and Madi . . ."

Sometimes, a "begotten," after his naming, would be accompanied by some later-occurring detail, perhaps as ". . . in time of big water (flood), he slew a water buffalo." Having named those four sons, now the *griot* stated such a detail.

"About the time the king's soldiers came, the eldest of these four sons, Kunta, when he had about 16 rains, went away from this village, to chop wood to make a drum . . . and he was never seen again . . ."

Goose-pimples the size of lemons seemed to pop all over me. In my knapsack were my cumulative notebooks, the first of them including how in my boyhood, my Grandma, Cousin Georgia and the others told of the African "*Kin-tay*" who always said he was kidnapped near his village—while chopping wood to make a drum . . .

I showed the interpreter, he showed and told the *griot*, who excitedly told the people; they grew very agitated. Abruptly then they formed a human ring, encircling me, dancing and chanting. Perhaps a dozen of the women carrying their infant babies rushed in toward me, thrusting the infants into my arms conveying, I would later learn, "the laying on of hands . . . through this flesh which is us, we are you, and you are us." The men hurried me into their mosque, their Arabic praying later being translated outside: "Thanks be to Allah for returning the long lost from among us." Direct descendants of Kunta Kinte's blood brothers were hastened, some of them from nearby villages, for a family portrait to be taken with me, surrounded by actual ancestral sixth cousins. More symbolic acts filled the remaining day.

When they would let me leave, for some reason I wanted to

go away over the African land. Dazed, silent in the bumping Land
Rover, I heard the cutting staccato of talking drums. Then when we
sighted the next village, its people came thronging to meet us. They
were all—little naked ones to wizened elders—waving, beaming; amid
a cacophony of crying out; and then my ears identified their words:
"*Meester Kinte! Meester Kinte!*"

Let me tell you something: I am a man. But I remember the
sob surging up from my feet, flinging up my hands before my face
and bawling as I had not done since I was a baby . . . the jet-black
Africans were jostling, staring . . . I didn't care, with the feelings
surging. If you really knew the odyssey of us millions of black
Americans, if you really knew how we came in the seeds of our
forefathers, captured, driven, beaten, inspected, bought, branded,
chained in foul ships, if you really knew, you needed weeping . . .

Back home, I knew that what I must write, really, was our
black saga, where any individual's past is the essence of the millions'.
Now flat broke, I went to some editors I knew, describing the
Gambian miracle, and my desire to pursue the research; Doubleday
contracted to publish, and Reader's Digest to condense the projected
book; then I had advances to travel further.

What ship brought Kinte to Grandma's " 'Naplis" (Annapolis,
Md., obviously)? The old *griot's* time reference to "king's soldiers"
sent me flying to London. Feverish searching at last identified, in
British Parliament records, "Colonel O'Hare's Forces," dispatched in
mid-1767 to protect the then British-held James Fort whose ruins I'd
visited. So Kunta Kinte was down in some ship probably sailing later
that summer from the Gambia River to Annapolis.

Now I feel it was fated that I had taught myself to write in
the U.S. Coast Guard. For the sea dramas I had concentrated on had
given me years of experience searching among yellowing old U.S.
maritime records. So now in English 18th Century marine records I
finally tracked ships reporting themselves in and out to the Com-
mandant of the Gambia River's James Fort. And then early one
afternoon I found that a Lord Ligonier under a Captain Thomas
Davies had sailed on the Sabbath of July 5, 1767. Her cargo: 3,265
elephants' teeth, 3,700 pounds of beeswax, 800 pounds of cotton, 32
ounces of Gambian gold, and 140 slaves; her destination: "Annapolis."

That night I recrossed the Atlantic. In the Library of Con-
gress the Lord Ligonier's arrival was one brief line in "Shipping In
The Port of Annapolis—1748–1775." I located the author, Vaughan
W. Brown in his Baltimore brokerage office. He drove to Historic
Annapolis, the city's historical society, and found me further documen-
tation of her arrival on Sept. 29, 1767. (Exactly two centuries later,

Sept. 29, 1967, standing, staring seaward from an Annapolis pier, again I knew tears.) More help came in the Maryland Hall of Records. Archivist Phebe Jacobsen found the Lord Ligonier's arriving customs declaration listing, "98 Negroes"—so in her 86-day crossing, 42 Gambians had died, one among the survivors being 16-year-old Kunta Kinte. Then the microfilmed Oct. 1, 1767, Maryland Gazette contained, on page two, an announcement to prospective buyers from the ship's agents, Daniel of St. Thos. Jenifer and John Ridout (the Governor's secretary): "from the River GAMBIA, in AFRICA . . . a cargo of choice, healthy SLAVES . . ."

PROBING FOR   1. What role does oral history play in Haley's search for his
MEANING   African past, both in America and Africa? What written records aided him?

2. Haley says "any individual's past is the essence of the millions'" in the black saga. What then would be the general history of the blacks from Africa to the present day based on Haley's discoveries of his own past? What role do white people play in this history according to Haley?

3. Why did Haley feel "impure" in Africa? Why was he different from the Africans? What was their attitude toward him?

4. What incidents moved Haley to tears? Why?

5. For what reasons did the author embark on his search for his African past? Of what benefit was the experience for him?

PROBING FOR   1. Why does Haley repeat the elements of the African's story so
METHOD   many times? What effect is he trying to achieve?

2. What does Haley accomplish by comparing his historical search to his seeing an artifact of European civilization, the Rosetta Stone, in the British Museum?

3. What attitude does Haley adopt toward his material?

4. There are two levels of events in the essay: Haley's search and the African's abduction and enslavement. Which is told in consecutive chronological order and which is not? Why?

Evaluating an Event

ILLUS-   *How does Haley narrate and evaluate his search for the African?* He
TRATION   follows the most simple pattern possible for relating an event to an audience: he begins his account at the beginning of the event and proceeds chronologically to the end.

He introduces his narrative with his childhood experiences listening to his grandmother's family stories and then relates the most important tale—that of the furthest-back person, "The African." He then describes step by step his unraveling of the historical facts behind Kunta Kinte's cature and transport to America. He ends the essay very dramatically with his discovery of the final piece of the puzzle: a newspaper account of the arrival in America of the cargo ship carrying the African.

A clear sense of this chronological organization can be obtained from the topic sentences of his paragraphs in which he inserts chronological markers. For example, in paragraph 4 the phrase "in time" indicates a passing of time from paragraph 3. The word "gradually" in the second sentence of paragraph 5 denotes the further passing of time. Notice these time markers in each paragraph, usually in the topic sentence.

Haley is not simply writing a personal diary in this account. Rather, as he says, he is writing the "black saga, where any individual's past is the essence of the millions'." Throughout his account, one can sense, behind Haley's own story, the story of all black Americans. In the first three paragraphs, for instance, he dramatizes very effectively the oral nature of American black history; whereas white history has been carefully recorded, black history exists, if at all, in the stories handed down from generation to generation by word of mouth. In the third paragraph, he also emphasizes the courage of the native Africans, a quality which, in Kunta Kinte's insistence on preserving his African heritage, survived their subsequent enslavement.

In his account of piecing the history together, Haley reveals to us the very exacting (and expensive) research methods necessary for such a search. He also educates us about African culture through his description of the *griot* and his role. At the same time, he reveals his emotional reactions to his discoveries, emotions all black Americans must share.

Haley, then, has not simply related a personal story for whatever personal value it has but has instead chosen a narrative for its informational and emotional value for his readers as well.

INDUCTION   *Principles of narrating and evaluating events and experiences.*

1. In recreating an event that took place in time, a writer wants the reader to experience the event with him. The most useful organization to follow is a chronological pattern: narrate the stages in the order in which they occurred, thus enabling the reader to participate in the pattern of events.

2. A second narrative method is the flashback, in which the outcome of the event is referred to in the introduction and then the sequence of events is begun in the first paragraph of the body.

3. The account should have informational value for the reader: the subject should have a broader appeal than something included in a diary or in a letter to a friend. Like all essays, the purpose of narrative must be to inform. The subject should therefore be chosen for its informational or expository value. This information and evaluation is included as the narrative progresses.

IMITATION   *Procedures to follow in narrating and evaluating an event.*

1. Choose an event you have witnessed or an experience you have had that has informational value for a reader. For example, Joyce Maynard evaluates her experience in elementary school and thereby writes

a valuable critique on our educational system. Haley's narrative informs us of missing segments of black history. You may have attended a church encounter group or an Indianapolis 500 race or visited Europe. Your topic might include the mechanics and effects of the encounter group, the types of people who attend automobile races or the differences between European and American trains. Don't, of course, impart too many different types of information. Here, as always, limit yourself to a specific topic.

2. Organize your outline to establish a chronological pattern.

3. Insert words or phrases in your topic sentences as "time markers" to indicate where in the sequence of events each paragraph belongs.

4. Impart your information to the reader as you narrate your experience.

 ANTHONY BURGESS

Is America Falling Apart?

I am back in Bracciano, a castellated town about 13 miles north of Rome, after a year in New Jersey. I find the Italian Government still unstable, gasoline more expensive than anywhere in the world, butchers and bank clerks and tobacconists (which also means salt-sellers) ready to go on strike at the drop of a *cappello*, neo-Fascists at their dirty work, the hammer and sickle painted on the rumps of public statues, a thousand-lire note (officially worth about $1.63) shrunk to the slightness of a dollar bill.

Nevertheless, it's delightful to be back. People are underpaid but they go through an act of liking their work, the open markets are luscious with esculent color, the community is more important than the state, the human condition is humorously accepted. The *tramontana* blows viciously today, and there's no central heating to turn on, but it will be pleasant when the wind drops. The two television channels are inadequate, but next Wednesday's rerun of an old Western, with Gary Cooper coming into a saloon saying "*Ciao, ragazzi,*" is something to look forward to. Manifold consumption isn't important here. The quality of life has nothing to do with the quantity of brand names. What matters is talk, family, cheap wine in the open air, the wresting of minimal sweetness out of the long-known bitterness of living. I was spoiled in New Jersey. The Italian for *spoiled* is *viziato*, cognate with *vitiated*, which has to do with vice.

Spoiled? Well, yes. I never had to shiver by a fire that wouldn't draw, or go without canned kraut juice or wild rice. America made me develop new appetites in order to make proper use of the supermarket. A character in Evelyn Waugh's *Put Out More Flags* said that the difference between prewar and postwar life was that, prewar, if one thing went wrong the day was ruined; postwar, if one thing went right the day would be made. America is a prewar country, psychologically unprepared for one thing to go wrong. Now everything seems to be going wrong. Hence the neurosis, despair, the Kafka feeling that the whole marvelous fabric of American life is coming apart at the seams. Italy is used to everything going wrong. This is what the human condition is about.

Let me stay for a while on this subject of consumption. American individualism, on the face of it an admirable philosophy, wishes to manifest itself in independence of the community. You don't share things in common; you have your own things. A family's strength is signalized by its possessions. Herein lies a paradox. For the desire for possessions must eventually mean dependence on possessions. Freedom is slavery. Once let the acquisitive instinct burgeon (enough flour for the winter, not just for the week), and there are ruggedly individual forces only too ready to make it come to full and monstrous blossom. New appetites are invented; what to the European are bizarre luxuries become, to the American, plain necessities.

During my year's stay in New Jersey I let my appetites flower into full Americanism except for one thing. I did not possess an automobile. This self-elected deprivation was a way into the nastier side of the consumer society. Where private ownership prevails, public amenities decay or are prevented from coming into being. The wretched run-down rail services of America are something I try, vainly, to forget. The nightmare of filth, outside and in, that enfolds the trip from Springfield, Mass., to Grand Central Station would not be accepted in backward Europe. But far worse is the nightmare of travel in and around Los Angeles, where public transport does not exist and people are literally choking to death in their exhaust fumes. This is part of the price of the metaphysic of individual ownership.

But if the car owner can ignore the lack of public transport, he can hardly ignore the decay of services in general. His car needs mechanics, and mechanics grow more expensive and less efficient. The gadgets in the home are cheaper to replace than repair. The more efficiently self-contained the home, primary fortress of independence, seems to be, the more dependent it is on the great impersonal corporations, as well as a diminishing army of servitors. Skills at the lowest level have to be wooed slavishly and exorbitantly rewarded. Plumbers will not come. Nor, at the higher level, will doctors. And doctors and dentists, in a nation committed to maiming itself with sugar and cholesterol, know their scarcity value and behave accordingly.

Americans are at last realizing that the acquisition of goods is not the whole of life. Consumption, on one level, is turning insipid, especially as the quality of the artifacts themselves seems to be deteriorating. Planned obsolescence is not conducive to pride in workmanship. On another level, consumption is turning sour. There is a growing guilt about the masses of discarded junk—rusting automobiles and refrigerators and washing machines and dehumidifiers—that it is uneconomical to recycle. Indestructible plastic hasn't even the grace to undergo chemical change. America, the world's biggest consumer, is the world's biggest polluter. Awareness of this is a kind of redemptive grace, but it doesn't appreciably lead to repentance and a revolution in consumer habits. Citizens of Los Angeles are horrified by that daily pall of golden smog, but they don't noticeably clamor for a decrease in the number of owner-vehicles. There is no worse neurosis than that which derives from a consciousness of guilt and an inability to reform.

America is anachronistic in so many ways, and not least in its clinging to a belief—now known to be unviable—in the capacity of the individual citizen to do everything for himself. Americans are admirable in their distrust of the corporate state—they have fought both Fascism and Communism—but they forget that there is a use for everything, even the loathesome bureaucratic machine. America needs a measure of socialization, as Britain needed it. Things—especially those we need most—don't always pay their way, and it is here that the state must enter, dismissing the profit element. Part of the present American neurosis, again, springs from awareness of this but inability to do anything about practical implementation. Perhaps only a country full of bombed cities feels capable of this kind of social revolution.

It would be supererogatory for me to list those areas in which thoughtful Americans feel that collapse is coming. It is enough for me to concentrate on what, during my New Jersey stay, impinged on my own life. Education, for instance, since I have a 6-year-old son to be brought up. America has always despised its teachers and, as a consequence, it has been granted the teachers it deserves. The quality of first-grade education that my son received, in a New Jersey town noted for the excellence of its public schools, could not, I suppose, be faulted on the level of dogged conscientiousness. The principal had read all the right pedagogic books, and was ready to quote these in the footnotes to his circular exhortations to parents. The teachers worked rigidly from the approved rigidly programed primers, ensuring that school textbook publication remains the big business it is.

But there seemed to be no spark; no daring, no madness, no readiness to engage the individual child's mind as anything other than raw material for statistical reductions. The fear of being unorthodox is rooted in the American teacher's soul: you can be fired for treading the path of experimental enterprise. In England, teachers cannot be fired, except for raping girl students and getting boy students drunk. In consequence, there is the kind of security that breeds eccentric genius, the capacity for firing mad enthusiasms.

I know that American technical genius, and most of all the moon landings, seems to give the lie to too summary a condemnation of the educational system, but there is more to education than the segmental equipping of the mind. There is that transmission of the value of the past as a force still miraculously fertile and moving— mostly absent from American education at all levels.

Of course, America was built on a rejection of the past. Even the basic Christianity which was brought to the continent in 1620 was of a novel and bizarre kind that would have nothing to do with the great rank river of belief that produced Dante and Michelangelo. America as a nation has never been able to settle to a common belief more sophisticated than the dangerous naïveté of the Declaration of Independence. "Life, liberty and the pursuit of happiness," indeed. And now America, filling in the vacuum left by the liquefied British Empire, has the task of telling the rest of the world that there's something better than Communism. The something better can only be money-making and consumption for its own sake. In the name of this ghastly creed the jungles must be defoliated.

No wonder the guilt of the thoughtful Americans I met in Princeton and New York and, indeed, all over the Union tended to express itself as an extravagant masochism, a desire for flagellation. Americans want to take on all the blame they can find, gluttons for punishment. "What do Europeans really think of us?" is a common question at parties. The expected answer is: "They think you're a load of decadent, gross-lipped, potbellied, callous, overbearing neoimperialists." Then the head can be bowed and the chest smitten: "*Nostra culpa, nostra maxima culpa. . . .*" But the fact is that such an answer, however much desired, would not be an honest one. Europeans think more highly of Americans now than they ever did. Let me try to explain why.

When Europe, after millennia of war, rapine, slavery, famine, intolerance, had sunk to the level of a sewer, America became the golden dream, the Eden where innocence could be recovered. Original sin was the monopoly of that dirty continent over there; in America man could glow in an aura of natural goodness, driven along his shining path by divine reason. The Declaration of Independence itself is a monument to reason. Progress was possible, and the wrongs committed against the Indians, the wildlife, the land itself, could be explained away in terms of the rational control of environment necessary for the building of a New Jerusalem. Right and wrong made up the moral dichotomy; evil—that great eternal inextirpable entity—had no place in America.

At last, with the Vietnam war and especially the Mylai horror, Americans are beginning to realize that they are subject to original sin as much as Europeans are. Some things—the massive crime figures, for instance—can now be explained only in terms of absolute evil. Europe, which has long known about evil and learned to live with it (*live* is *evil* spelled backwards), is now grimly pleased to find that America is becoming like Europe. America is no longer Europe's daughter nor her rich stepmother: she is Europe's sister. The agony that America is undergoing is not to be associated with breakdown so much as with the parturition of self-knowledge.

It has been assumed by many that the youth of America has been in the vanguard of the discovery of both the disease and the cure. The various copping out movements, however, from the Beats on, have committed the gross error of assuming that original sin rested with their elders, their rulers, and that they themselves could manifest their essential innocence by building little neo-Edens. The drug culture could confirm that the paradisal vision was available to all who sought it. But instant ecstasy has to be purchased, like any other commodity, and, in economic terms, that passive life of pure being involves parasitism. Practically all of the crime I encountered in New York—directly or through report—was a preying of the opium-eaters on the working community. There has to be a snake in paradise. You can't escape the heritage of human evil by building communes, usually on an agronomic ignorance that, intended to be a rejection of inherited knowledge, that suspect property of the elders, does violence to life. The American young are well-meaning but misguided, and must not themselves be taken as guides.

The guides, as always, lie among the writers and artists. And Americans ought to note that, however things may seem to be falling apart, arts and the humane scholarship are flourishing here, as they are not, for instance, in England. I'm not suggesting that Bellow, Mailer, Roth and the rest have the task of finding a solution to the American mess, but they can at least clarify its nature and show how it relates to the human condition in general. Literature, that most directly human of the arts, often reacts magnificently to an ambience of unease or apparent breakdown. The Elizabethans, to whose era we look back as to an irrecoverable Golden Age, were far more conscious than modern Americans of the chaos and corruption and incompetence of the state. Shakespeare's period was one of poverty, unemployment, ghastly inflation, violence in the streets. Twenty-six years after his death there was a bloody civil war, followed by a dictatorship of religious fanatics, followed by a calm respite in which the seeds of a revolution were sown. England survived. America will survive.

I'm not suggesting that Americans sit back and wait for a transient period of mistrust and despair to resolve itself, like a disease, through the unconscious healing forces which lie deep in organic nature. Man, as Thornton Wilder showed in *The Skin of Our Teeth*, always comes through—though sometimes only just. Americans living here and now have a right to an improvement in the quality of their lives, and they themselves, not the remote governors, must do something about it. It is not right that men and women should fear to go on the streets at night, and that they should sometimes fear the police as much as the criminals, both of whom sometimes look like mirror images of each other. I have had too much evidence, in my year in New Jersey, of the police behaving like the "Fascist pigs" of the revolutionary press. There are too many guns about, and the disarming of the police should be a natural aspect of the disarming of the entire citizenry.

American politics, at both the state and the Federal levels, is too much concerned with the protection of large fortunes, America being the only example in history of a genuine timocracy. The wealth qualification for the aspiring politician is taken for granted; a governmental system dedicated to the promotion of personal wealth in a few selected areas will never act for the public good. The time has come, nevertheless, for citizens to demand, from their government, a measure of socialization—the provision of amenities for the many, of which adequate state pensions and sickness benefits, as well as nationalized transport, should be priorities.

As for those remoter solutions to the American nightmare— only an aspect, after all, of the human nightmare—an Englishman must be diffident about suggesting that America made her biggest mistake in becoming America—meaning a revolutionary republic based on a romantic view of human nature. To reject a limited monarchy in favor of an absolute one (which is, after all, what the American Presidency is) argues a trust in the disinterestedness of an elected ruler which is, of course, no more than a reflection of belief in the innate goodness of man—so long as he happens to be American man. The American Constitution is out of date. Republics tend to corruption. Canada and Australia have their own problems, but they are happier countries than America.

This *Angst* about America coming apart at the seams, which apparently is shared by nearly 50 per cent of the entire American population, is something to rejoice about. A sense of sin is always admirable, though it must not be allowed to become neurotic. If electric systems break down and gadgets disintegrate, it doesn't matter much. There is always wine to be drunk by candlelight, uniced. If America's position as a world power collapses, and the Union dissolves into independent states, there is still the life of the family or the individual to be lived. England has survived her own dissolution as an imperial power, and Englishmen seem to be happy enough. But I ask the reader to note that I, an Englishman, no longer live in England, and I can't spend more than six months at a stretch in Italy—or any other European country, for that matter. I home to America as to a country more stimulating than depressing. The future of mankind is being worked out there on a scale typically American— vast, dramatic, almost apocalyptical. I brave the brutality and the guilt in order to be in on the scene. I shall be back.

PROBING FOR
MEANING

1. What contrast does Burgess develop between New Jersey and Bracciano, Italy? What does he find wrong in Italy? Why, however, does he enjoy his return?

2. What is the similarity between America and a prewar European country? What is the "Kafka feeling" Burgess sees in American life?

3. What paradox is involved in the coexistence of American individualism and consumerism? What is the effect of private ownership on public transportation? On public services in general?

4. Why is "consumption turning sour" in American life? In this regard, why has the recognition that consumption leads to pollution caused "neurosis" in Americans? How is this neurosis connected to the anachronistic belief in doing everything for oneself? What does Burgess suggest as a solution?

5. What criticisms does Burgess make of the American educational system? How does he suggest that the problems are a result of our national character and form of government?

6. Why does Burgess feel that the term "extravagant masochism" characterizes Americans? What do Europeans think of America? Why?

7. What effect did involvement in Vietnam and the incident at Mylai have on the national consciousness?

8. What criticisms of American youth does Burgess develop? What are the "misguided assumptions" of American youth? Why does Burgess look to artists and writers as guides? Explain.

9. What further criticisms of American police, politics and tend-

encies toward violence does Burgess state? Do you agree with his criticisms? Explain.

10. Why, after criticizing America to such an extent, does Burgess
want to return? What are his reasons for optimism concerning America?
What does he find when he contemplates America's sense of sin?

PROBING FOR
METHOD

1. Why does Burgess begin his essay on America with a description of a small town north of Rome?

2. Is there a logical structure to the essay? Explain. How well does
Burgess develop his ideas?

3. What is the tone of the essay? To what extent is Burgess an
objective observer of the American scene?

4. The number of difficult words in this essay suggests that Burgess is writing for a sophisticated audience. Familiarize yourself with the
following words. Use each in a sentence of your own. Think of a less for-
mal synonym for each.

amenities	metaphysic
anachronistic	millennia
Angst	obsolescence
burgeon	paradox
castellated	parturition
cognate	pedagogic
dichotomy	rapine
exorbitantly	servitors
flagellation	supererogatory
inextirpable	timocracy
insipid	tramontana

 ADRIENNE RICH

Anger and Tenderness

> . . . *to understand is always an ascending movement; that is why*
> *comprehension ought always to be concrete. (one is never got out*
> *of the cave, one comes out of it.)*
> —*Simone Weil,* First and Last Notebooks

Entry from my journal, November 1960
My children cause me the most exquisite suffering of which I

have any experience. It is the suffering of ambivalence: the murderous alternation between bitter resentment and raw-edged nerves, and blissful gratification and tenderness. Sometimes I seem to myself, in my feelings toward these tiny guiltless beings, a monster of selfishness and intolerance. Their voices wear away at my nerves, their constant needs, above all their need for simplicity and patience, fill me with despair at my own failures, despair too at my fate, which is to serve a function for which I was not fitted. And I am weak sometimes from held-in rage. There are times when I feel only death will free us from one another, when I envy the barren woman who has the luxury of her regrets but lives a life of privacy and freedom.*

And yet at other times I am melted with the sense of their helpless, charming and quite irresistible beauty—their ability to go on loving and trusting—their staunchness and decency and unselfconsciousness. *I love them.* But it's in the enormity and inevitability of this love that the sufferings lie.

April 1961
A blissful love for my children engulfs me from time to time and seems almost to suffice—the aesthetic pleasure I have in these little, changing creatures, the sense of being loved, however dependently, the sense too that I'm not an utterly unnatural and shrewish mother—much though I am!

May 1965
To suffer with and for and against a child—maternally, egotistically, neurotically, sometimes with a sense of helplessness, sometimes with the illusion of learning wisdom—but always, everywhere, in body and soul, *with* that child—because that child is a piece of oneself.

To be caught up in waves of love and hate, jealousy even of the child's childhood; hope and fear for its maturity; longing to be free of responsibility, tied by every fibre of one's being.

That curious primitive reaction of protectiveness, the beast defending her cub, when anyone attacks or criticizes him—And yet no one more hard on him than I!

September 1965
Degradation of anger. Anger at a child. How shall I learn to absorb the violence and make explicit only the caring? Exhaustion of anger. Victory of will, too dearly bought—far too dearly!

March 1966
Perhaps one is a monster—an anti-woman—something driven and without recourse to the normal and appealing consolations of love, motherhood, joy in others . . .

* The term "barren woman" was easy for me to use, unexamined, fifteen years ago. . . . [I]t seems to me now a term both tendentious and meaningless, based on a view of women which sees motherhood as our only positive definition.

Unexamined assumptions: First, that a "natural" mother is a person without further identity, one who can find her chief gratification in being all day with small children, living at a pace tuned to theirs; that the isolation of mothers and children together in the home must be taken for granted; that maternal love is, and should be, quite literally selfless; that children and mothers are the "causes" of each other's suffering. I was haunted by the stereotype of the mother whose love is "unconditional"; and by the visual and literary images of motherhood as a singleminded identity. If I knew parts of myself existed that would never cohere to those images, weren't those parts then abnormal, monstrous? And—as my eldest son, now aged twenty-one, remarked on reading the above passages: "You seemed to feel you ought to love us all the time. But there *is* no human relationship where you love the other person at every moment." Yes, I tried to explain to him, but women—above all, mothers—have been supposed to love that way.

From the fifties and early sixties, I remember a cycle. It began when I had picked up a book or began trying to write a letter, or even found myself on the telephone with someone toward whom my voice betrayed eagerness, a rush of sympathetic energy. The child (or children) might be absorbed in busyness, in his own dreamworld; but as soon as he felt me gliding into a world which did not include him, he would come to pull at my hand, ask for help, punch at the typewriter keys. And I would feel his wants at such a moment as fraudulent, as an attempt moreover to defraud me of living even for fifteen minutes as myself. My anger would rise; I would feel the futility of any attempt to salvage myself, and also the inequality between us: my needs always balanced against those of a child, and always losing. I could love so much better, I told myself, after even a quarter-hour of selfishness, of peace, of detachment from my children. A few minutes! But it was as if an invisible thread would pull taut between us and break, to the child's sense of inconsolable abandonment, if I moved—not even physically, but in spirit—into a realm beyond our tightly circumscribed life together. It was as if my placenta had begun to refuse him oxygen. Like so many women, I waited with impatience for the moment when their father would return from work, when for an hour or two at least the circle drawn around mother and children would grow looser, the intensity between us slacken, because there was another adult in the house.

I did not understand that this circle, this magnetic field in which we lived, was not a natural phenomenon.

Intellectually, I must have known it. But the emotion-charged, tradition-heavy form in which I found myself cast as the Mother seemed, then, as ineluctable as the tides. And, because of this form—

this microcosm in which my children and I formed a tiny, private emotional cluster, and in which (in bad weather or when someone was ill) we sometimes passed days at a time without seeing another adult except for their father—there *was* authentic need underlying my child's invented claims upon me when I seemed to be wandering away from him. He was reassuring himself that warmth, tenderness, continuity, solidity were still there for him, in my person. My singularity, my uniqueness in the world as *his mother*—perhaps more dimly also as Woman—evoked a need vaster than any single human being could satisfy, except by loving continuously, unconditionally, from dawn to dark, and often in the middle of the night.

2

In a living room in 1975, I spent an evening with a group of women poets, some of whom had children. One had brought hers along, and they slept or played in adjoining rooms. We talked of poetry, and also of infanticide, of the case of a local woman, the mother of eight, who had been in severe depression since the birth of her third child, and who had recently murdered and decapitated her two youngest, on her suburban front lawn. Several women in the group, feeling a direct connection with her desperation, had signed a letter to the local newspaper protesting the way her act was perceived by the press and handled by the community mental health system. Every woman in that room who had children, every poet, could identify with her. We spoke of the wells of anger that her story cleft open in us. We spoke of our own moments of murderous anger at our children, because there was no one and nothing else on which to discharge anger. We spoke in the sometimes tentative, sometimes rising, sometimes bitterly witty, unrhetorical tones and language of women who had met together over our common work, poetry, and who found another common ground in an unacceptable, but undeniable anger. The words are being spoken now, are being written down; the taboos are being broken, the masks of motherhood are cracking through.

For centuries no one talked of these feelings. I became a mother in the family-centered, consumer-oriented, Freudian-American world of the 1950s. My husband spoke eagerly of the children we would have; my parents-in-law awaited the birth of their grandchild. I had no idea of what *I* wanted, what *I* could or could not choose. I only knew that to have a child was to assume adult womanhood to the full, to prove myself, to be "like other women."

To be "like other women" had been a problem for me. From

the age of thirteen or fourteen, I had felt I was only acting the part of a feminine creature. At the age of sixteen my fingers were almost constantly ink-stained. The lipstick and high heels of the era were difficult-to-manage disguises. In 1945 I was writing poetry seriously, and had a fantasy of going to postwar Europe as a journalist, sleeping among the ruins in bombed cities, recording the rebirth of civilization after the fall of the Nazis. But also, like every other girl I knew, I spent hours trying to apply lipstick more adroitly, straightening the wandering seams of stockings, talking about "boys." There were two different compartments, already, to my life. But writing poetry, and my fantasies of travel and self-sufficiency, seemed more real to me; I felt that as an incipient "real woman" I was a fake. Particularly was I paralyzed when I encountered young children. I think I felt men could be—wished to be—conned into thinking I was truly "feminine"; a child, I suspected, could see through me like a shot. This sense of acting a part created a curious sense of guilt, even though it was a part demanded for survival.

I have a very clear, keen memory of myself the day after I was married: I was sweeping a floor. Probably the floor did not really need to be swept; probably I simply did not know what else to do with myself. But as I swept that floor I thought: "Now I am a woman. This is an age-old action, this is what women have always done." I felt I was bending to some ancient form, too ancient to question. *This is what women have always done.*

As soon as I was visibly and clearly pregnant, I felt, for the first time in my adolescent and adult life, not-guilty. The atmosphere of approval in which I was bathed—even by strangers on the street, it seemed—was like an aura I carried with me, in which doubts, fears, misgivings, met with absolute denial. *This is what women have always done.*

Two days before my first son was born, I broke out in a rash which was tentatively diagnosed as measles, and was admitted to a hospital for contagious diseases to await the onset of labor. I felt for the first time a great deal of conscious fear, and guilt toward my unborn child, for having "failed" him with my body in this way. In rooms near mine were patients with polio; no one was allowed to enter my room except in a hospital gown and mask. If during pregnancy I had felt in any vague command of my situation, I felt now totally dependent on my obstetrician, a huge, vigorous, paternal man, abounding with optimism and assurance, and given to pinching my cheek. I had gone through a healthy pregnancy, but as if tranquilized or sleep-walking. I had taken a sewing class in which I produced an unsightly and ill-cut maternity jacket which I never wore; I had made curtains for the baby's room, collected baby clothes, blotted out as much as possible the woman I had been a few months earlier. My second book of poems was in press, but I had stopped writing poetry, and read little except household magazines and books on child-care. I felt myself perceived by the world simply as a pregnant woman, and it seemed easier, less disturbing, to perceive myself so. After my child was born the "measles" were diagnosed as an allergic reaction to pregnancy.

Within two years, I was pregnant again, and writing in a notebook:

November 1956
Whether it's the extreme lassitude of early pregnancy or something more fundamental, I don't know; but of late I've felt, toward poetry,—both reading and writing it—nothing but boredom and indifference. Especially toward my own and that of my immediate contemporaries. When I receive a letter soliciting mss., or someone alludes to my "career," I have a strong sense of wanting to deny all responsibility for and interest in that person who writes —or who wrote.

If there is going to be a real break in my writing life, this is as good a time for it as any. I have been dissatisfied with myself, my work, for a long time.

My husband was a sensitive, affectionate man who wanted children and who—unusual in the professional, academic world of the fifties—was willing to "help." But it was clearly understood that this "help" was an act of generosity; that *his* work, *his* professional life, was the real work in the family; in fact, this was for years not even an issue between us. I understood that my struggles as a writer were a kind of luxury, a peculiarity of mine; my work brought in almost no money: it even cost money, when I hired a household helper to allow me a few hours a week to write. "Whatever I ask he tries to give me," I wrote in March 1958, "but always the initiative has to be mine." I experienced my depressions, bursts of anger, sense of entrapment, as burdens my husband was forced to bear because he loved me; I felt grateful to be loved in spite of bringing him those burdens.

But I was struggling to bring my life into focus. I had never really given up on poetry, nor on gaining some control over my existence. The life of a Cambridge tenement backyard swarming with children, the repetitious cycles of laundry, the night-wakings, the interrupted moments of peace or of engagement with ideas, the ludicrous dinner parties at which young wives, some with advanced degrees, all seriously and intelligently dedicated to their children's welfare and their husbands' careers, attempted to reproduce the amenities of Brahmin Boston, amid French recipes and the pretense of effortlessness—above all, the ultimate lack of seriousness with which women were regarded in that world—all of this defied analysis at that time, but I *knew* I had to remake my own life. I did not then understand that we—the women of that academic community—as in so many middle-class communities of the period—were expected to fill both the part of the Victorian Lady of Leisure, the Angel in the House, and also of the Victorian cook, scullery maid, laundress, governess, and nurse. I only sensed that there were false distractions sucking at me, and I wanted desperately to strip my life down to what was essential.

June 1958
These months I've been all a tangle of irritations deepening to anger: bitterness, disillusion with society and with myself; beating out at the world, rejecting out of hand. What, if anything, has been positive? Perhaps the attempt to remake my life, to save it from mere drift and the passage of time . . .

The work that is before me is serious and difficult and not at all clear even as to plan. Discipline of mind and spirit, uniqueness of expression, ordering of daily existence, the most effective functioning of the human self—these are the chief things I wish to achieve. So far the only beginning I've been able to make is to waste less time. That is what some of the rejection has been all about.

By July of 1958 I was again pregnant. The new life of my third—and, as I determined, my last—child, was a kind of turning for me. I had learned that my body was not under my control; I had not intended to bear a third child. I knew now better than I had ever known what another pregnancy, another new infant, meant for my body and spirit. Yet, I did not think of having an abortion. In a sense, my third son was more actively chosen than either of his brothers; by the time I knew I was pregnant with him, I was not sleepwalking any more.

August 1958 (Vermont)
I write this as the early rays of the sun light up our hillside and eastern windows. Rose with [the baby] at 5:30 A.M. and have fed him and breakfasted. This is one of the few mornings on which I haven't felt terrible mental depression and physical exhaustion.
    . . . I have to acknowledge to myself that I would not have chosen to have more children, that I was beginning to look to a time, not too far off, when I should again be free, no longer so physically tired, pursuing a more or less intellectual and creative life. . . . The *only* way I can develop now is through much harder, more continuous, connected work than my present life

makes possible. Another child means postponing this for some years longer—and years at my age are significant, not to be tossed lightly away.

And yet, somehow, something, call it Nature or that affirming fatalism of the human creature, makes me aware of the inevitable as already part of me, not to be contended against so much as brought to bear as an additional weapon against drift, stagnation and spiritual death. (For it is really death that I have been fearing —the crumbling to death of that scarcely-born physiognomy which my whole life has been a battle to give birth to—a recognizable, autonomous self, a creation in poetry and in life.)

If more effort has to be made then I will make it. If more despair has to be lived through, I think I can anticipate it correctly and live through it.

Meanwhile, in a curious and unanticipated way, we really do welcome the birth of our child.

There was, of course, an economic as well as a spiritual margin which allowed me to think of a third child's birth not as my own death-warrant but as an "additional weapon against death." My body, despite recurrent flares of arthritis, was a healthy one; I had good prenatal care; we were not living on the edge of malnutrition; I knew that all my children would be fed, clothed, breathe fresh air; in fact it did not occur to me that it could be otherwise. But, in another sense, beyond that physical margin, I knew I was fighting for my life through, against, and with the lives of my children, though very little else was clear to me. I had been trying to give birth to myself; and in some grim, dim way I was determined to use even pregnancy and parturition in that process.

Before my third child was born I decided to have no more children, to be sterilized. (Nothing is removed from a woman's body during this operation; ovulation and menstruation continue. Yet the language suggests a cutting- or burning-away of her essential womanhood, just as the old word "barren" suggests a woman eternally empty and lacking.) My husband, although he supported my decision, asked whether I was sure it would not leave me feeling "less feminine." In order to have the operation at all, I had to present a letter, counter-signed by my husband, assuring the committee of physicians who approved such operations that I had already produced three children, and stating my reasons for having no more. Since I had had rheumatoid arthritis for some years, I could give a reason acceptable to the male panel who sat on my case; my own judgment would not have been acceptable. When I awoke from the operation, twenty-four hours after my child's birth, a young nurse looked at my chart and remarked coldly: "Had yourself spayed, did you?"

The first great birth-control crusader, Margaret Sanger, remarks that of the hundreds of women who wrote to her pleading for contraceptive information in the early part of the twentieth century, all spoke of wanting the health and strength to be better mothers to the children they already had; or of wanting to be physically affectionate to their husbands without dread of conceiving. None was refusing motherhood altogether, or asking for an easy life. These women—mostly poor, many still in their teens, all with several children—simply felt they could no longer do "right" by their families, whom they expected to go on serving and rearing. Yet there always has been, and there remains, intense fear of the suggestion that women shall have the final say as to how our bodies are to be used. It is as if the suffering of the mother, the primary identification of woman *as* the mother—were so necessary to the emotional grounding of human society that the mitigation, or removal, of that suffering, that identification, must be fought at every level, including the level of refusing to question it at all.

PROBING FOR
MEANING

1. What is the nature of the ambivalence that Rich feels toward her children in her journal entries? What are the emotions she experiences?

2. What are the "unexamined assumptions" made in the journal entries that the author can now view from a different perspective? Do you feel these assumptions were valid? Explain.

3. How does Rich characterize her children's relationship with their mother? Does she question their need for unconditional love?

4. How has her perspective toward children and motherhood changed by the poets' meeting in 1975?

5. How did conditions in the 1950's contribute to Rich's ambivalence toward the feminine role during her childhood and the years prior to her marriage? Why was she "paralyzed" by young children during this time?

6. Why does she experience guilt about her failure to adjust to her role? How does marriage and pregnancy relieve this guilt?

7. Characterize her husband's attitude. What is shown by *her* attitude toward her husband in the early years of their marriage? How does the academic world also contribute to the role confusion Rich experiences?

8. How does Rich view her poetry at different times in her life? What does this changing attitude reveal?

9. What change in perspective has occurred by the birth of her third child? What does she mean when she writes that this birth was an "additional weapon against death"?

10. Why does she decide to be sterilized? What is revealed by the reactions of her husband, the male panel and the nurse and by the necessity of obtaining permission?

11. What were the reasons women had for obtaining contraceptive information from Margaret Sanger? What is their connection with Rich's desire to be sterilized? What does Rich suggest as the reason for the primary identification of woman as mother?

PROBING FOR
METHOD

1. What is the effect of the journal entries? Why would the author choose to present the entries rather than simply to describe her feelings during this period? Why are the entries taken from different years?

2. What effect is achieved by isolating the following sentence in a separate paragraph? "I did not understand that this circle, this magnetic field in which we lived, was not a natural phenomenon."

3. Is "Anger and Tenderness" a good title? Explain.

4. How do the journal entries contribute to the organization of the essay? Generally, what is the pattern of development of the essay?

5. Is there a contrast between the writing styles of the journal entries and the rest of the essay? Explain.

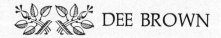 DEE BROWN

The Flight of the Nez Percés

The whites told only one side. Told it to please themselves. Told much that is not true. Only his own best deeds, only the worst deeds of the Indians, has the white man told.

—YELLOW WOLF OF THE NEZ PERCÉS

The earth was created by the assistance of the sun, and it should be left as it was. . . . The country was made without lines of demarcation, and it is no man's business to divide it. . . . I see the whites all over the country gaining wealth, and see their desire to give us lands which are worthless. . . . The earth and myself are of one mind. The measure of the land and the measure of our bodies are the same. Say to us if you can say it, that you were sent by the Creative Power to talk to us. Perhaps you think the Creator sent you here to dispose of us as you see fit. If I thought you were sent by the Creator I might be induced to think you had a right to dispose of me. Do not misunderstand me, but understand me fully with reference to my affection for the land. I never said the land

was mine to do with it as I chose. The one who has the right to dispose of it is the one who has created it. I claim a right to live on my land, and accord you the privilege to live on yours.
　　　　　—HEINMOT TOOYALAKET (CHIEF JOSEPH) OF THE NEZ PERCÉS

In September, 1805, when Lewis and Clark came down off the Rockies on their westward journey, the entire exploring party was half-famished and ill with dysentery—too weak to defend themselves. They were in the country of the Nez Percés, so named by French trappers, who observed some of these Indians wearing dentalium shells in their noses. Had the Nez Percés chosen to do so, they could have put an end to the Lewis and Clark expedition there on the banks of Clearwater River, and seized their wealth of horses. Instead the Nez Percés welcomed the white Americans, supplied them with food, and looked after the explorers' horses for several months while they continued by canoe to the Pacific shore.

Thus began a long friendship between the Nez Percés and white Americans. For seventy years the tribe boasted that no Nez Percé had ever killed a white man. But white men's greed for land and gold finally broke the friendship.

In 1855 Governor Isaac Stevens of Washington Territory invited the Nez Percés to a peace council. "He said there were a great many white people in the country, and many more would come; that he wanted the land marked out so that the Indians and white men could be separated. If they were to live in peace it was necessary, he said, that the Indians should have a country set apart for them, and in that country they must stay."

Tuekakas, a chief known as Old Joseph by the white men, told Governor Stevens that no man owned any part of the earth, and a man could not sell what he did not own.

The governor could not comprehend such an attitude. He urged Old Joseph to sign the treaty and receive presents of blankets. "Take away your paper," the chief replied. "I will not touch it with my hand."

Aleiya, who was called Lawyer by the white men, signed the treaty, and so did several other Nez Percés, but Old Joseph took his people back to their home in Wallowa Valley, a green country of winding waters, wide meadows, mountain forests, and a clear blue lake. Old Joseph's band of Nez Percés raised fine horses and cattle, lived in fine lodges, and when they needed anything from the white men they traded their livestock.

Only a few years after the first treaty signing, government men were swarming around the Nez Percés again, wanting more land. Old Joseph warned his people to take no presents from them, not even one blanket. "After a while," he said, "they will claim that you have accepted pay for your country."[1]

In 1863 a new treaty was presented to the Nez Percés. It took away the Wallowa Valley and three-fourths of the remainder of their land, leaving them only a small reservation in what is now Idaho. Old Joseph refused to attend the treaty signing, but Lawyer and several other chiefs—none of whom had ever lived in the Valley of Winding Waters—signed away their people's lands. The "thief treaty," Old Joseph called it, and he was so offended that he tore up the Bible a white missionary had given him to convert him to Christianity. To let the white men know he still claimed the Wallowa Valley, he planted poles all around the boundaries of the land where his people lived.

Not long after that, Old Joseph died (1871), and the chief-tainship of the band passed to his son, Heinmot Tooyalaket (Young Joseph), who was then about thirty years old. When government officials came to order the Nez Percés to leave the Wallowa Valley and go to Lapwai reservation, Young Joseph refused to listen. "Neither Lawyer nor any other chief had authority to sell this land," he said. "It has always belonged to my people. It came unclouded to them from our fathers, and we will defend this land as long as a drop of Indian blood warms the hearts of our men."[2] He petitioned the Great Father, Ulysses Grant, to let his people stay where they had always lived, and on June 16, 1873, the President issued an executive order withdrawing Wallowa Valley from settlement by white men.

In a short time a group of commissioners arrived to begin organization of a new Indian agency in the valley. One of them mentioned the advantages of schools for Joseph's people. Joseph replied that the Nez Percés did not want the white man's schools.

"Why do you not want schools?" the commissioner asked.

"They will teach us to have churches," Joseph answered.

"Do you not want churches?"

"No, we do not want churches."

"Why do you not want churches?"

"They will teach us to quarrel about God," Joseph said. "We do not want to learn that. We may quarrel with men sometimes about things on this earth, but we never quarrel about God. We do not want to learn that."[3]

Meanwhile, white settlers were encroaching upon the valley, with their eyes on the Nez Percé land. Gold was found in nearby mountains. The goldseekers stole the Indians' horses, and stockmen

---

[1] Chief Joseph. "An Indian's Views of Indian Affairs." *North American Review*, Vol. 128, 1879, p. 417.

[2] *Ibid.*, p. 418.

[3] U.S. Commissioner of Indian Affairs. Annual Report, 1873, p. 527.

stole their cattle, branding them so the Indians could not claim them back. White politicians journeyed to Washington, telling lies about the Nez Percés. They charged the Indians with being a threat to the peace and with stealing the settlers' livestock. This was the reverse of the truth, but as Joseph said, "We had no friend who would plead our cause before the law council."[4]

Two years after the Great Father promised Wallowa Valley to Joseph's people forever, he issued a new proclamation, reopening the valley to white settlement. The Nez Percés were given "a reasonable time" to move to the Lapwai reservation. Joseph had no intention of giving up the valley of his fathers, but in 1877 the government sent the One-Armed-Soldier-Chief, General Howard, to clear all Nez Percés out of the Wallowa area.

In the four years that had passed since Oliver Otis Howard treated Cochise and the Apaches with justice, he had learned that the Army was not tolerant of "Indian lovers." He came now to the Northwest country, determined to restore his standing with the military by carrying out his orders swiftly and to the letter. Privately he told trusted friends that "it is a great mistake to take from Joseph and his band of Nez Percé Indians that valley." But in May, 1877, he summoned Joseph to Lapwai for a council which was to set the date they must surrender their land.

To accompany him to Lapwai, Joseph chose White Bird, Looking Glass, his brother Ollokot, and the Wallowa prophet Toohoolhoolzote. The prophet was a tall, thick-necked, very ugly Indian with a gift for eloquent rebuttal. "A fugitive from hell," was the way one white man described him. At the opening of the council, which was held in a building across from the Fort Lapwai guardhouse, Joseph presented Toohoolhoolzote as spokesman for the Wallowa Nez Percés.

"Part of the Nez Percés gave up their land," the prophet said. "We never did. The earth is part of our body, and we never gave up the earth."

"You know very well that the government has set apart a reservation, and that the Indians must go on it," Howard declared.

"What person pretended to divide the land and put us on it?" Toohoolhoolzote demanded.

"I am the man. I stand here for the President." Howard was beginning to lose his temper. "My orders are plain and will be executed."

The prophet continued prodding the One-Armed-Soldier-Chief, asking him how the land could belong to white men if it had come down to the Nez Percés from their fathers. "We came from the

[4] Chief Joseph, p. 419.

earth, and our bodies must go back to the earth, our mother," he said.

"I don't want to offend your religion," Howard replied testily, "but you must talk about practicable things. Twenty times over I hear that the earth is your mother and about chieftainship from the earth. I want to hear it no more, but come to business at once."

"Who can tell me what I must do in my own country?" Toohoolhoolzote retorted.[5]

The argument continued until Howard felt he must demonstrate his power. He ordered the prophet arrested and taken to the guardhouse, and then he bluntly informed Joseph that the Nez Percés had thirty days in which to move from the Wallowa Valley to the Lapwai reservation.

"My people have always been the friends of white men," Joseph said. "Why are you in such a hurry? I cannot get ready to move in thirty days. Our stock is scattered, and Snake River is very high. Let us wait until fall, then the river will be low."

"If you let the time run over one day," Howard replied harshly, "the soldiers will be there to drive you onto the reservation, and all your cattle and horses outside of the reservation at that time will fall into the hands of the white men."

Joseph knew now that he had no alternative. To defend the valley with less than a hundred warriors was impossible. When he and his subchiefs returned home they found soldiers already there. They held a council and decided to gather their stock immediately for the move to Lapwai. "The white men were many and we could not hold our own with them. We were like deer. They were like grizzly bears. We had a small country. Their country was large. We were contented to let things remain as the Great Spirit made them. They were not, and would change the rivers and mountains if they did not suit them."[6]

Even before they started the long march, some of the warriors began talking of war rather than be driven like dogs from the land where they were born. Toohoolhoolzote, released from prison, declared that blood alone would wash out the disgrace the One-Armed-Soldier-Chief had put upon him. Joseph, however, continued to counsel peace.

To meet General Howard's deadline, they had to leave much of their livestock in the valley, and when they came to Snake River the stream was swirling with melted snow from the mountains. Miraculously they got their women and children across on buffalo-

---

[5] U.S. Secretary of War. Annual Report, 1877, p. 594. McWhorter, Lucullus V. *Yellow Wolf: His Own Story.* Caldwell, Idaho, 1940, p. 39.
[6] Chief Joseph, pp. 420, 423.

hide rafts without serious accident, but while they were engaged in this task a party of white men came and stole some of their cattle from the waiting herd. Then, when they hurriedly tried to swim their livestock across the river, many animals were lost to the swift-flowing current.

More embittered than ever, the chiefs demanded that Joseph halt the march in Rocky Canyon and hold a council. Toohoolhoolzote, White Bird, and Ollokot spoke for war. Joseph told them it was "better to live at peace than to begin a war and lie dead." The others called him a coward, but he refused to back down.

While they were camped in the canyon, a small band of warriors slipped away one night, and when they returned the Nez Percés could no longer claim that they had never killed a white man. The warriors had killed eleven, in revenge for the theft of their stock and for being driven from their valley.

Like many another peace-loving Indian chief, Joseph was now trapped between the pressures of the white men and the fury of his desperate people. He chose to stay with his people. "I would have given my own life," he said, "if I could have undone the killing of white men by my people. I blame my young men and I blame the white men. . . . I would have taken my people to the buffalo country [Montana] without fighting, if possible. . . . We moved over to White Bird Creek, sixteen miles away, and there encamped, intending to collect our stock before leaving; but the soldiers attacked us, and the first battle was fought."[7]

Although outnumbered two to one, the Nez Percés drew Howard's soldiers into a trap at White Bird Canyon on June 17, turning the attackers' flank, killing a third of them, and routing the remainder. Ten days later the One-Armed-Soldier-Chief brought up heavy reinforcements to do battle again, but the Nez Percés slipped away across the mountains. In a succession of shrewd military actions, Joseph outmaneuvered the pursuing soldiers, severely punished an advance detachment, and then raced to the Clearwater, where Chief Looking Glass was waiting with more warriors.

The combined force of Nez Percés now numbered 250 warriors, with 450 noncombatants, their baggage, and two thousand horses. At White Bird Canyon they had captured several rifles and a good supply of ammunition.

After withdrawing beyond the Clearwater (where their fathers had welcomed Lewis and Clark as the forerunners of white civilization), Joseph called a council of chiefs. They all knew they could never return to the Valley of Winding Waters or go without punishment to Lapwai. Only one course was left to them—flight to

7 *Ibid.*, p. 425.

Canada. Sitting Bull of the Sioux had fled to the Grandmother's land, and the American soldiers dared not go there to kill him. If the Nez Percés could reach the Lolo Trail and cross the Bitterroot Mountains, they might be able to escape to Canada.

Because they were accustomed to crossing the Bitterroots to hunt in Montana, the Nez Percés quickly outdistanced Howard's baggage-laden army. On July 25 they were filing down the canyon near the mouth of Lolo Creek when their scouts sighted soldiers ahead. The Bluecoats were constructing a log barricade at a narrow place in the pass.

Under a white flag, Joseph, Looking Glass, and White Bird rode down to the barricade, dismounted calmly, and shook hands with the commanding officer, Captain Charles Rawn. The chiefs noted that there were about two hundred soldiers in the camp.

"We are going by you without fighting, if you will let us," Joseph said to the captain, "but we are going by you anyhow."[8]

Rawn told Joseph that they could pass only if they gave up their arms. White Bird replied that their warriors would never do that.

Knowing that General Howard was approaching from the west and that another large force under Colonel John Gibbon was marching from the east, Captain Rawn decided to stall for time. He suggested that they meet again the next day to discuss arrangements for passage. To this the chiefs agreed, but after two more days of fruitless parleying, the Nez Percé leaders decided they could wait no longer.

Early on the morning of July 28, Looking Glass moved the warriors into a screening line among the trees on the upper slope of the canyon. At the same time, Joseph led the noncombatants and livestock up a gulch, climbed to the top of a mountain, and was well around the canyon barricade before Captain Rawn discovered what the Nez Percés were doing. The captain went in pursuit of the Indians, but after a few skirmishes with Joseph's rearguard warriors he decided not to risk a real fight and returned to his now useless barricade.

Believing that they had escaped from Howard, and unaware of Gibbon's approaching army, the chiefs decided to move south to the familiar hunting country of the Big Hole. There they could rest their ponies and hunt wild game. If the white men would leave them alone, perhaps they would not have to go to the Grandmother's land and join Sitting Bull.

On the night of August 9, the One Who Limps (Colonel Gibbon) brought up a mixed column of local volunteers and mounted

[8] *Ibid.*, p. 426.

infantrymen and concealed them on a hillside overlooking the Nez
Percé camp on Big Hole River. As dawn approached, the volunteers
asked Gibbon if they should take prisoners during the attack. Gibbon
replied that he wanted no Indian prisoners, male or female. The night
air was cold, and the men warmed themselves by drinking whiskey.
At first daylight several were drunk when Gibbon gave the command
to attack. The infantry line began firing volleys, and then charged the
Nez Percé tepees.

Fifteen-year-old Kowtoliks was asleep when he heard the
rattle of rifle fire. "I jumped from my blankets and ran about thirty
feet and threw myself on hands and knees, and kept going. An old
woman, Patsikonmi, came from the teepee and did the same thing—
bent down on knees and hands. She was to my left, and was shot in
the breast. I heard the bullet strike. She said to me, 'You better not
stay here. Be going. I'm shot.' Then she died. Of course I ran for my
life and hid in the bushes. The soldiers seemed shooting everywhere.
Through tepees and wherever they saw Indians. I saw little children
killed and men fall before bullets coming like rain."[9]

Another teen-age boy, Black Eagle, was awakened by bullets
passing through his family tepee. In his fright he ran and jumped into
the river, but the water was too cold. He came out and helped save
the horses by driving them up a hill and out of sight of the soldiers.

The Indians, meanwhile, had recovered from the shock of the
surprise attack. While Joseph directed the rescue of the noncombatants, White Bird deployed the warriors for a counterattack. "Fight!
Shoot them down!" he shouted. "We can shoot as well as any of
these soldiers."[10] The marksmanship of the Nez Percés, in fact, was
superior to that of Gibbon's men. "We now mixed those soldiers
badly," Yellow Wolf said. "Scared, they ran back across the river.
They acted as if drinking. We thought some got killed by being
drunk."

When the soldiers tried to set up a howitzer, the Nez Percés
swarmed over the gun crew, seized the cannon, and wrecked it. A
warrior fixed his rifle sights on Colonel Gibbon and made him the
One Who Limps Twice.

By this time Joseph had the camp in motion, and while a
handful of warriors kept Gibbon's soldiers pinned down behind a
makeshift barricade of logs and boulders, the Nez Percés resumed
flight. They turned southward and away from Canada, because they
believed it was the only way left to shake off their pursuers. The
warriors had killed thirty soldiers and wounded at least forty. But in
Gibbon's merciless dawn attack, eighty Nez Percés had died, more

9 McWhorter, p. 144.
10 Shields, G. D. *Battle of the Big Hole.* Chicago, 1889, pp. 51–52.

than two-thirds of them women and children, their bodies riddled with bullets, their heads smashed in by bootheels and gunstocks. "The air was heavy with sorrow," Yellow Wolf said. "Some soldiers acted with crazy minds."[11]

The Nez Percé rear guard probably could have starved out Gibbon's barricaded soldiers and killed them all had not General Howard come to the rescue with a fresh force of cavalrymen. Withdrawing hurriedly, the warriors overtook Joseph to warn him that the One-Armed-Soldier-Chief was on their trail again.

"We retreated as rapidly as we could," Joseph said. "After six days General Howard came close to us, and we went out and attacked him, and captured nearly all his horses and mules."[12] Actually the captured livestock were mostly mules, but they were pack animals which had been carrying Howard's supplies and ammunition. Leaving the soldiers floundering in their rear, the Indians crossed Targhee Pass into Yellowstone Park on August 22.

Only five years earlier the Great Council in Washington had made the Yellowstone area into the country's first national park, and in that summer of 1877 the first adventuresome American tourists were admiring its natural wonders. Among them was none other than the Great Warrior Sherman, who had come out West on an inspection tour to find out how fewer than three hundred Nez Percé warriors, burdened with their women and children, could make fools out of the entire Army of the Northwest.

When Sherman learned that the fleeing Indians were crossing Yellowstone Park almost within view of his luxurious camp, he began issuing urgent orders to fort commanders in all directions to put a network of soldiers around these impudent warriors. Nearest at hand was the Seventh Cavalry, which had been brought back to strength during the year since Custer led it to disaster on the Little Bighorn. Eager to vindicate the regiment's honor by a victory over any Indians willing to fight, the Seventh moved southwestward toward the Yellowstone. During the first week in September Nez Percé scouts and Seventh Cavalry scouts sighted each other's columns almost daily. By clever maneuvering, the Indians shook loose from the Seventh after a skirmish at Canyon Creek, and headed north for Canada. They had no way of knowing, of course, that the Great Warrior Sherman had ordered Bear Coat Miles in a forced march from Fort Keogh, on a course that would cut across their path.

On September 23, after fighting rearguard actions almost daily, the Nez Percés forded the Missouri River at Cow Island Landing. During the next three days scouts reported no sign of soldiers

[11] McWhorter, pp. 120, 132.
[12] Chief Joseph, p. 427.

anywhere. On the twenty-ninth, hunters located a small buffalo herd. As they were short of food and ammunition and their horses were badly worn from the fast pace, the chiefs decided to camp in the Bear Paw Mountains. Next day, after filling their empty stomachs on buffalo meat, they would try to reach the Canadian border in one more long march.

"We knew General Howard was more than two suns back on our trail," Yellow Wolf said. "It was nothing hard to keep ahead of him."[13]

Next morning, however, two scouts came galloping from the south, shouting, "Soldiers! Soldiers!" While the camp was preparing to move out, another scout appeared on a distant bluff, waving a blanket signal—*Enemies right on us! Soon the attack!*

It was a cavalry charge ordered by Bear Coat Miles, whose Indian scouts a few hours earlier had picked up the trail of the Nez Percés. Riding with the charging cavalry were the thirty Sioux and Cheyenne scouts who had been bought by the Bluecoats at Fort Robinson, the young warriors who had turned their backs on their people by putting on soldier uniforms—an action which had precipitated the assassination of Crazy Horse.

The thunder of six hundred galloping horses made the earth tremble, but White Bird calmly posted his warriors in front of the camp. As the first wave of pony soldiers swept down upon them, the Nez Percé warriors opened with deadly accurate fire. In a matter of seconds they killed twenty-four soldiers, wounded forty-two others, and stopped the charge in a wild scramble of plunging horses and unsaddled troopers.

"We fought at close range," Chief Joseph said, "not more than twenty steps apart, and drove the soldiers back upon their main line, leaving their dead in our hands. We secured their arms and ammunition. We lost, the first day and night, eighteen men and three women." Among the dead were Joseph's brother Ollokot and the tough old prophet Toohoolhoolzote.

When darkness fell the Nez Percés tried to slip away to the north, but Bear Coat had put a cordon of soldiers completely around their camp. The warriors spent the night digging entrenchments, expecting another attack at daylight.

Instead of attacking, however, Bear Coat sent a messenger out with a white flag. The messenger brought a demand for Joseph to surrender and save the lives of his people. Joseph sent back a reply: he would think about it and let General Miles know his decision soon. Snow had begun to fall, and the warriors were hopeful that a blizzard might provide an escape screen to Canada.

[13] McWhorter, p. 204.

Later in the day, some of Miles's Sioux scouts rode out under another truce flag. Joseph walked across the battlefield to meet them. "They said they believed that General Miles was sincere and really wanted peace. I walked on to General Miles's tent."

For the next two days Joseph was a prisoner, held by Bear Coat in violation of the flag of truce. During this time Miles brought up artillery and resumed the attack, but the Nez Percé warriors held their ground, and Joseph refused to surrender while he was a prisoner. On both days a bitter cold wind flung showers of snow over the battlefield.

On the third day, Joseph's warriors managed to get him free. They captured one of Miles's officers and threatened to kill him unless the general released their chief. That same day, however, General Howard and his lumbering army arrived to reinforce Miles, and Joseph knew that his dwindling band of warriors was doomed. When Miles sent truce messengers to arrange a battlefield council, Joseph went to hear the general's surrender terms. They were simple and direct: "If you will come out and give up your arms," Miles said, "I will spare your lives and send you to your reservation."[14]

Returning to his besieged camp, Joseph called his chiefs together for the last time. Looking Glass and White Bird wanted to fight on, to the death if necessary. They had struggled for thirteen hundred miles; they could not quit now. Joseph reluctantly agreed to postpone his decision. That afternoon in the final skirmish of the four-day siege, a sharpshooter's bullet struck Looking Glass in the left forehead and killed him instantly.

"On the fifth day," Joseph said, "I went to General Miles and gave up my gun." He also made an eloquent surrender speech, which was recorded in the English translation by Lieutenant Charles Erskine Scott Wood,* and in time it became the most quoted of all American Indian speeches:

Tell General Howard I know his heart. What he told me before I have in my heart. I am tired of fighting. Our chiefs are killed. Looking Glass is dead. Toohoolhoolzote is dead. The old men are all dead. It is the young men who say yes or no. He who led on the young men [Ollokot] is dead. It is cold and we have no blankets. The little children are freezing to death. My people, some of them, have run away to the hills, and have no blankets, no

---

[14] Chief Joseph, pp. 425, 428.

* Lieutenant Wood left the Army not long afterward to become a lawyer and an author of satirical poems and essays. His experiences with Chief Joseph and the Nez Percés influenced his later life; he became an ardent fighter for social justice and a defender of the dispossessed.

food; no one knows where they are—perhaps freezing to death. I want to have time to look for my children and see how many of them I can find. Maybe I shall find them among the dead. Hear me, my chiefs! I am tired; my heart is sick and sad. From where the sun now stands I will fight no more forever.[15]

After dark, while the surrender arrangements were under way, White Bird and a band of unyielding warriors crept through ravines in small groups and started running on foot for the Canadian border. On the second day they were across, and on the third day they saw mounted Indians in the distance. One of the approaching Indians made a sign: *What Indians are you?*

Nez Percé, they replied, and asked: *Who are you?*

Sioux, was the answer.

The next day Sitting Bull took the fugitive Nez Percés into his Canadian village.[16]

For Chief Joseph and the others, however, there was to be no freedom. Instead of conducting them to Lapwai, as Bear Coat Miles had promised, the Army shipped them like cattle to Fort Leavenworth, Kansas. There, on a swampy bottomland, they were confined as prisoners of war. After almost a hundred died, they were transferred to a barren plain in the Indian Territory. As had happened to the Modocs, the Nez Percés sickened and died—of malaria and heartbreak.

Bureaucrats and Christian gentlemen visited them frequently, uttering words of sympathy and writing endless reports to various organizations. Joseph was allowed to visit Washington, where he met all the great chiefs of government. "They all say they are my friends," he said, "and that I shall have justice, but while their mouths all talk right I do not understand why nothing is done for my people. . . . General Miles promised that we might return to our own country. I believed General Miles, or *I never would have surrendered*."

He then made an impassioned appeal for justice: "I have heard talk and talk, but nothing is done. Good words do not last long unless they amount to something. Words do not pay for my dead people. They do not pay for my country, now overrun by white men. . . . Good words will not give my people good health and stop them from dying. Good words will not get my people a home where they can live in peace and take care of themselves. I am tired of talk that comes to nothing. It makes my heart sick when I remember all the good words and broken promises. . . . You might as well expect the rivers to run backward as that any man who was born a free man

15 U.S. Secretary of War. Report, 1877, p. 630.
16 Chief Joseph, p. 432.

should be contented when penned up and denied liberty to go where he pleases. . . . I have asked some of the great white chiefs where they get their authority to say to the Indian that he shall stay in one place, while he sees white men going where they please. They cannot tell me.

"Let me be a free man—free to travel, free to stop, free to work, free to trade where I choose, free to choose my own teachers, free to follow the religion of my fathers, free to think and talk and act for myself—and I will obey every law, or submit to the penalty."[17]

But no one listened. They sent Joseph back to Indian Territory, and there he remained until 1885. In that year, only 287 captive Nez Percés were still alive, most of them too young to remember their previous life of freedom, or too old and sick and broken in spirit to threaten the mighty power of the United States. Some of the survivors were permitted to return to their people's reservation at Lapwai. Chief Joseph and about 150 others were considered too dangerous to be penned up with other Nez Percés, whom they might influence. The government shipped them to Nespelem on the Colville Reservation in Washington, and there they lived out their lives in exile. When Joseph died on September 21, 1904, the agency physician reported the cause of death as "a broken heart."

PROBING FOR MEANING

1. What difference in perspective exists between the Nez Percés and the white Americans regarding the possession of land? Why is this central to the Nez Percés' problems? How does the discovery of gold intensify the problem?

2. Describe young Joseph. What type of leader is he? Why does he resist the idea of schools for his people?

3. Describe Oliver Otis Howard. How did he treat the Apaches? With what result? What change occurs in his dealings with the Nez Percés?

4. When ordered to leave the Wallowa Valley, why does Joseph decide not to fight? What pressures are placed on him when some of his warriors first kill white men?

5. What occurs at Lolo Creek? How did you react to the soldiers' behavior during this encounter? Similarly, how did you feel when the soldiers made Joseph a prisoner after sending out a truce flag?

6. What finally precipitates Joseph's surrender? How are he and his tribe treated after he surrenders?

7. Does the essay affect your view of the treatment of American Indians by the U.S. government? In what perspective does the essay place recent Indian land claims?

[17] *Ibid.*

1. What is the effect of the introduction? What does this first en-counter between Lewis and Clark and the Nez Percés establish?

2. Is the essay written objectively? Are both the Indian and gov-ernment viewpoints given fair treatment? Explain.

3. How would you characterize the style of the essay? The lan-guage that describes the action?

4. What qualities are present in Joseph's surrender speech that would make it the most quoted of all American Indian speeches?

 HANA WEHLE

Birkenau-Auschwitz, July 1944

Introduction

This article is an English translation of a witness statement which I wrote under my then name Hana Roubíčková, shortly after the war, to be included in the first documentary book on Auschwitz, *Továrna na Smrt* (*The Death Factory*), by Ota Kraus and Erich Schön-Kulka, published in Prague in 1946 by ČIN Publishers.

The authors introduced my statement as follows: "Hana Roubíčková from Prague, prisoner number 71,584, has given us the following account of those who survived the months of March and July, 1944."

A short explanation will familiarize the reader with the hap-penings leading to the events referred to in my statement: The camp Birkenau B/II/b was that part of the Auschwitz concentration camp which was known as the "Czech Family Camp." Its first inmates were 5000 Jewish men, women and children who arrived there on Septem-ber 7 and 9, 1943, in two transports from the concentration camp Terezín (Theresienstadt) in Czechoslovakia. Unlike all preceding transports, these two were not subjected to the notorious selection upon arrival in which the fit were thumbed to the right and life but the unfit to the left and death in the gas chambers. Instead, under a new scheme ordered by the General Reich Security Authority in Berlin, the inmates were to be kept in this camp in a sort of isolation or quarantine of six months duration, after which period those who were still alive would be liquidated or, as it was called euphemistically, "subjected to Special Treatment." In line with this plan, the night of the 8th of March 1944, the surviving 4000 men, women and children from the September transports were gassed, while the survivors from two subsequent transports from Terezin which had arrived in this camp in December 1943—including myself—were to be spared for another three months, until their "quarantine" would be over by the 20th of June. However, when the end of that period arrived, the camp population—which in the meantime had been augmented by about 7500 prisoners who had arrived from Terezin in May 1944—was not liquidated in its entirety; what happened instead, is described in my statement.

After March 8th, our camp was like a cemetery. The roads and blocks were half empty, but at every turn we saw the faces of our murdered comrades. Their jobs had been taken over by persons who came with our convoy. We all knew that in three months time we too would have been in the camp half a year and that when this period was up we too would be on our way to the gas chambers.

Another transport arrived from Terezin in May. The camp elder, an old Auschwitz inmate, a convicted murderer, who was entrusted by the SS commander with the camp supervision, immediately assigned a number of the newcomers to various camp functions declaring that he wanted to have trained people in those spots by the time the people from our transports would go to their deaths in July.

We worked so as not to have to think about our fate, but everything seemed utterly senseless. Why should we improve conditions in the camp? For whom? They made us work merely to fill in time until July! We counted the months, weeks, days. Spring came, but we prisoners saw nothing but sand, barbed wire and a patch of blue sky. It was to be our last spring. And we were counting our days . . . .

Everybody in the camp got more and more tense. Every evening we stood outside our blocks far into the night, looking towards the crematoria. The leaping flames shot upwards through the heavy pall of smoke, striking at the sky like some desperate accusing finger. The stench of cremated bones was wafted towards us. A few days more, and we too would be swallowed up in that voracious chimney. And the starry sky would look down just as indifferently at yet another mass murder.

It was a Saturday evening. Suddenly the Rapportfuhrer, the SS officer in charge, appeared in our camp. This was something unusual. Was he bringing our sentence of death? No! He was merely giving an apparently unimportant piece of news: All men and women between the ages of sixteen and forty were to have a "medical check-up" by the head SS doctor, Mengele, to see if they were fit enough to be sent out on working convoys; the remainder were to stay in the camp. Naturally, nobody believed him. In vain did he try to persuade us that now, in the fifth year of the war, Germany needed workers from among our ranks. No, we thought to ourselves, we know very well that this is another of those fake convoys to Heydebreck; we are not fools, and we know perfectly well why they are playing this little game with us—they want first to get all the healthy, relatively strong people out of the camp so as to avoid any chance of unrest, since those remaining, mothers with children, the old and the feeble, are certain not to offer any resistance.

That night, nobody slept in our camp; shadowy figures could be seen creeping from block to block. We were planning a revolt. We refused to go to our death! Or if we did, we would at least see to it that we took some of those monsters along with us! We meant it in deadly earnest, but deep in our hearts we knew all too well that we could never hope to come out of it alive. They would send us to our death when we were least expecting it. They had always been one step ahead of us! Our revolt evaporated.

The next day, we paraded for the medical check-up; the men in the morning, and the women in the afternoon. I knew that Dr. Mengele would find me fit, but I did not feel happy about it. The whole thing was mere play-acting. We were all going to the gas chambers, but separated from each other, first the young and then the old. They would not even allow us to make our last journey alongside our mothers.

It was a Sunday morning, July 1, 1944; the entire population of the camp was out on the camp road. Our men were marching away in fives. We were all keyed up with excitement. Would they wheel to the right, into the men's quarantine camp B/II/a, like our comrades in March, or were they really going to the train?

They were going to the left! We held our breath. After a short while, which seemed an eternity, the prisoners in the men's camp B/II/d signaled to us that our men were at the disinfection block changing into striped prison uniforms. Still a spark of hope, then! Would they really go to work?

At noon we all stood on the camp road, staring in the direction of the waiting stock-cars. We remained like this for two hours. Finally the procession of blue-and-white-striped comrades appeared on the ramp. But we would only believe it when we saw them getting into the cattle-cars with our own eyes. We strained our eyes. Yes, they were our men! They were alive, they were really going to work somewhere! It was a miracle, we young people were not going to have to die! We wildly kissed and embraced each other, drunk with happiness. We were going to live, we were going to live. . . .

It was not until later that we realized that only about 3,000 of our 10,000 were going to live. Our fathers and mothers, our sick and weak comrades, our children opening like flowers—all of them would go to the gas chambers. It was hard indeed to say good-bye. We knew that we should never see them again.

Mothers who were recognized as being fit for work had to choose between leaving the camp without their children or dying with their children. The majority chose the gas chamber. As we the young and healthy passed through the camp gates, we were overwhelmed by the sensations of guilt and joy. Here in this camp we had lived through indescribable horrors, we had seen many of our friends die, we had ourselves waited for death. And now we were leaving behind our nearest and dearest, our parents and children—but we might go on to live.

Two days later, dressed in uniforms of sackcloth, together with our spoons and blankets constituting our entire luggage, we got into the cattle trucks, each truckload being guarded by two SS men with rifles. The train slowly gathered speed. We passed the family camp where we had lived, but it was already empty; all our dear ones had been taken to the gas chambers two days before. Tomorrow, or in a few days time, new prisoners would arrive and in the course of time they too would be destroyed.

But we did not wish to think of the past. We were glad to be alive and unafraid of the future. After all, no other camp could possibly be so terrible as this camp of death, and the war was bound to be over some day! We watched the tall crematorium chimneys disappearing farther and farther behind us until they were completely out of sight. We breathed a profound sigh of relief, confident that we had escaped those chimneys once and for all.

PROBING FOR MEANING

1. In this essay the attitudes of the prisoners in a concentration camp are described. How did they endure each day despite the ominous presence of the crematoria?

2. Why did the prisoners not revolt?

3. What are some examples of the "play-acting" between guards and prisoners in their interactions with each other? Why did this "play-acting" go on when both sides knew what usually happened to the prisoners?

4. Why were those who survived "overwhelmed by the sensations of guilt and joy"? Should they have been ambivalent?

5. To what extent is this an experience that should be shared with all Jews as Haley feels his search for his African ancestry should be shared with all blacks? To what extent do both experiences have an appeal that is universal as well?

PROBING FOR
METHOD

1. What is the tone of the essay? To what extent is it similar to Eldridge Cleaver's tone in "A Day in Folsom Prison" (Chapter II)? Why would similarities exist?

2. Notice that Wehle uses the plural pronoun "we" almost exclusively. What effect does she create by not using the first person singular pronoun "I"?

 CARSON McCULLERS

The Sojourner

The twilight border between sleep and waking was a Roman one this morning: splashing fountains and arched, narrow streets, the golden lavish city of blossoms and age-soft stone. Sometimes in this semiconsciousness he sojourned again in Paris, or German war rubble, or a Swiss skiing and a snow hotel. Sometimes, also, in a fallow Georgia field at hunting dawn. Rome it was this morning in the yearless region of dreams.

John Ferris awoke in a room in a New York hotel. He had the feeling that something unpleasant was awaiting him—what it was, he did not know. The feeling, submerged by matinal necessities, lingered even after he had dressed and gone downstairs. It was a cloudless autumn day and the pale sunlight sliced between the pastel skyscrapers. Ferris went into the next-door drugstore and sat at the end booth next to the window glass that overlooked the sidewalk. He ordered an American breakfast with scrambled eggs and sausage.

Ferris had come from Paris to his father's funeral which had taken place the week before in his home town in Georgia. The shock of death had made him aware of youth already passed. His hair was receding and the veins in his now naked temples were pulsing and prominent and his body was spare except for an incipient belly bulge. Ferris had loved his father and the bond between them had once been extraordinarily close—but the years had somehow unraveled this filial devotion; the death, expected for a long time, had left him with an unforeseen dismay. He had stayed as long as possible to be near his mother and brothers at home. His plane for Paris was to leave the next morning.

Ferris pulled out his address book to verify a number. He turned the pages with growing attentiveness. Names and addresses from New York, the capitals of Europe, a few faint ones from his home state in the South. Faded, printed names, sprawled drunken ones. Betty Wills: a random love, married now. Charlie Williams: wounded in the Hürtgen Forest, unheard of since. Grand old Williams—did he live or die? Don Walker: a B.T.O. in television, getting rich. Henry Green: hit the skids after the war, in a sanitarium now, they say. Cozie Hall: he had heard that she was dead. Heedless, laughing Cozie—it was strange to think that she too, silly girl, could die. As Ferris closed the address book, he suffered a sense of hazard, transience, almost of fear.

It was then that his body jerked suddenly. He was staring out of the window when there, on the sidewalk, passing by, was his ex-wife. Elizabeth passed quite close to him, walking slowly. He could not understand the wild quiver of his heart, nor the following sense of recklessness and grace that lingered after she was gone.

Quickly Ferris paid his check and rushed out to the sidewalk. Elizabeth stood on the corner waiting to cross Fifth Avenue. He hurried toward her meaning to speak, but the lights changed and she crossed the street before he reached her. Ferris followed. On the other side he could easily have overtaken her, but he found himself lagging unaccountably. Her fair hair was plainly rolled, and as he watched her Ferris recalled that once his father had remarked that Elizabeth had a "beautiful carriage." She turned at the next corner and Ferris followed, although by now his intention to overtake her had disappeared. Ferris questioned the bodily disturbance that the sight of Elizabeth aroused in him, the dampness of his hands, the hard heartstrokes.

It was eight years since Ferris had last seen his ex-wife. He knew that long ago she had married again. And there were children. During recent years he had seldom thought of her. But at first, after the divorce, the loss had almost destroyed him. Then after the anodyne of time, he had loved again, and then again. Jeannine, she was now. Certainly his love for his ex-wife was long since past. So why the unhinged body, the shaken mind? He knew only that his clouded heart was oddly dissonant with the sunny, candid autumn day. Ferris wheeled suddenly and, walking with long strides, almost running, hurried back to the hotel.

Ferris poured himself a drink, although it was not yet eleven o'clock. He sprawled out in an armchair like a man exhausted, nursing his glass of bourbon and water. He had a full day ahead of him as he was leaving by plane the next morning for Paris. He checked over his obligations: take luggage to Air France, lunch with his boss, buy shoes and an overcoat. And something—wasn't there something else? Ferris finished his drink and opened the telephone directory.

His decision to call his ex-wife was impulsive. The number was under Bailey, the husband's name, and he called before he had much time for self-debate. He and Elizabeth had exchanged cards at Christmastime, and Ferris had sent a carving set when he received the announcement of her wedding. There was no reason *not* to call. But as he waited, listening to the ring at the other end, misgiving fretted him.

Elizabeth answered; her familiar voice was a fresh shock to him. Twice he had to repeat his name, but when he was identified, she sounded glad. He explained he was only in town for that day. They had a theater engagement, she said—but she wondered if he would come by for an early dinner. Ferris said he would be delighted.

As he went from one engagement to another, he was still bothered at odd moments by the feeling that something necessary was forgotten. Ferris bathed and changed in the late afternoon, often thinking about Jeannine: he would be with her the following night. "Jeannine," he would say, "I happened to run into my ex-wife when I was in New York. Had dinner with her. And her husband, of course. It was strange seeing her after all these years."

Elizabeth lived in the East Fifties, and as Ferris taxied uptown he glimpsed at intersections the lingering sunset, but by the time he reached his destination it was already autumn dark. The place was a building with a marquee and a doorman, and the apartment was on the seventh floor.

"Come in, Mr. Ferris."

Braced for Elizabeth or even the unimagined husband, Ferris was astonished by the freckled red-haired child; he had known of the children, but his mind had failed somehow to acknowledge them. Surprise made him step back awkwardly.

"This is our apartment," the child said politely. "Aren't you Mr. Ferris? I'm Billy. Come in."

In the living room beyond the hall, the husband provided another surprise; he too had not been acknowledged emotionally. Bailey was a lumbering red-haired man with a deliberate manner. He rose and extended a welcoming hand.

"I'm Bill Bailey. Glad to see you. Elizabeth will be in, in a minute. She's finishing dressing."

The last words struck a gliding series of vibrations, memories of the other years. Fair Elizabeth, rosy and naked before her bath. Half-dressed before the mirror of her dressing table, brushing her fine, chestnut hair. Sweet, casual intimacy, the soft-fleshed loveliness indisputably possessed. Ferris shrank from the unbidden memories and compelled himself to meet Bill Bailey's gaze.

"Billy, will you please bring that tray of drinks from the kitchen table?"

The child obeyed promptly, and when he was gone Ferris remarked conversationally, "Fine boy you have there."

"We think so."

Flat silence until the child returned with a tray of glasses and a cocktail shaker of Martinis. With the priming drinks they pumped up conversation: Russia, they spoke of, and the New York rain-making, and the apartment situation in Manhattan and Paris.

"Mr. Ferris is flying all the way across the ocean tomorrow," Bailey said to the little boy who was perched on the arm of his chair, quiet and well behaved. "I bet you would like to be a stowaway in his suitcase."

Billy pushed back his limp bangs. "I want to fly in an airplane and be a newspaperman like Mr. Ferris." He added with sudden assurance, "That's what I would like to do when I am big."

Bailey said, "I thought you wanted to be a doctor."

"I do!" said Billy. "I would like to be both. I want to be a atom-bomb scientist too."

Elizabeth came in carrying in her arms a baby girl.

"Oh, John!" she said. She settled the baby in the father's lap. "It's grand to see you. I'm awfully glad you could come."

The little girl sat demurely on Bailey's knees. She wore a pale pink crepe de Chine frock, smocked around the yoke with rose, and a matching silk hair ribbon tying back her pale soft curls. Her skin was summer tanned and her brown eyes flecked with gold and laughing. When she reached up and fingered her father's horn-rimmed glasses, he took them off and let her look through them a moment. "How's my old Candy?"

Elizabeth was very beautiful, more beautiful perhaps than he had ever realized. Her straight clean hair was shining. Her face was softer, glowing and serene. It was a madonna loveliness, dependent on the family ambiance.

"You've hardly changed at all," Elizabeth said, "but it has been a long time."

"Eight years." His hand touched his thinning hair self-consciously while further amenities were exchanged.

Ferris felt himself suddenly a spectator—an interloper among these Baileys. Why had he come? He suffered. His own life seemed so solitary, a fragile column supporting nothing amidst the wreckage of the years. He felt he could not bear much longer to stay in the family room.

He glanced at his watch. "You're going to the theater?"

"It's a shame," Elizabeth said, "but we've had this engagement for more than a month. But surely, John, you'll be staying home one of these days before long. You're not going to be an expatriate, are you?"

"Expatriate," Ferris repeated. "I don't much like the word."

"What's a better word?" she asked.

He thought for a moment. "Sojourner might do."

Ferris glanced again at his watch, and again Elizabeth apologized. "If only we had known ahead of time—"

"I just had this day in town. I came home unexpectedly. You see, Papa died last week."

"Papa Ferris is dead?"

"Yes, at Johns Hopkins. He had been sick there nearly a year. The funeral was down home in Georgia."

"Oh, I'm so sorry, John. Papa Ferris was always one of my favorite people."

The little boy moved from behind the chair so that he could look into his mother's face. He asked, "Who is dead?"

Ferris was oblivious to apprehension; he was thinking of his father's death. He saw again the outstretched body on the quilted silk within the coffin. The corpse flesh was bizarrely rouged and the familiar hands lay massive and joined above a spread of funeral roses. The memory closed and Ferris awakened to Elizabeth's calm voice.

"Mr. Ferris's father, Billy. A really grand person. Somebody you didn't know."

"But why did you call him *Papa* Ferris?"

Bailey and Elizabeth exchanged a trapped look. It was Bailey who answered the questioning child. "A long time ago," he said, "your mother and Mr. Ferris were once married. Before you were born—a long time ago."

"Mr. Ferris?"

The little boy stared at Ferris, amazed and unbelieving. And Ferris's eyes, as he returned the gaze, were somehow unbelieving too. Was it indeed true that at one time he had called this stranger, Elizabeth, Little Butterduck during nights of love, that they had lived together, shared perhaps a thousand days and nights and—finally— endured in the misery of sudden solitude the fiber by fiber (jealousy, alcohol and money quarrels) destruction of the fabric of married love?

Bailey said to the children, "It's somebody's suppertime. Come on now."

"But Daddy! Mama and Mr. Ferris—I—"

Billy's everlasting eyes—perplexed and with a glimmer of hostility—reminded Ferris of the gaze of another child. It was the young son of Jeannine—a boy of seven with a shadowed little face and knobby knees whom Ferris avoided and usually forgot.

"Quick march!" Bailey gently turned Billy toward the door. "Say good night now, son."

"Good night, Mr. Ferris." He added resentfully, "I thought I was staying up for the cake."

"You can come in afterward for the cake," Elizabeth said. "Run along now with Daddy for your supper."

Ferris and Elizabeth were alone. The weight of the situation descended on those first moments of silence. Ferris asked permission to pour himself another drink and Elizabeth set the cocktail shaker on the table at his side. He looked at the grand piano and noticed the music on the rack.

"Do you still play as beautifully as you used to?"

"I still enjoy it."

"Please play, Elizabeth."

Elizabeth arose immediately. Her readiness to perform when asked had always been one of her amiabilities; she never hung back, apologized. Now as she approached the piano there was the added readiness of relief.

She began with a Bach prelude and fugue. The prelude was as gaily iridescent as a prism in a morning room. The first voice of the fugue, an announcement pure and solitary, was repeated intermingling with a second voice, and again repeated within an elaborated frame, the multiple music, horizontal and serene, flowed with unhurried majesty. The principal melody was woven with two other voices, embellished with countless ingenuities—now dominant, again submerged, it had the sublimity of a single thing that does not fear surrender to the whole. Toward the end, the density of the material gathered for the last enriched insistence on the dominant first motif and with a chorded final statement the fugue ended. Ferris rested his head on the chair back and closed his eyes. In the following silence a clear, high voice came from the room down the hall.

"Daddy, how *could* Mama and Mr. Ferris—" A door was closed.

The piano began again—what was this music? Unplaced, familiar, the limpid melody had lain a long while dormant in his heart. Now it spoke to him of another time, another place—it was the music Elizabeth used to play. The delicate air summoned a wilderness of memory. Ferris was lost in the riot of past longings, conflicts, ambivalent desires. Strange that the music, catalyst for this tumultuous anarchy, was so serene and clear. The singing melody was broken off by the appearance of the maid.

"Miz Bailey, dinner is out on the table now."

Even after Ferris was seated at the table between his host and hostess, the unfinished music still overcast his mood. He was a little drunk.

"*L'improvisation de la vie humaine,*" he said. "There's nothing that makes you so aware of the improvisation of human existence as a song unfinished. Or an old address book."

"Address book?" repeated Bailey. Then he stopped, noncommittal and polite.

"You're still the same old boy, Johnny," Elizabeth said with a trace of the old tenderness.

It was a Southern dinner that evening, and the dishes were his old favorites. They had fried chicken and corn pudding and rich, glazed candied sweet potatoes. During the meal Elizabeth kept alive a conversation when the silences were overlong. And it came about that Ferris was led to speak of Jeannine.

"I first knew Jeannine last autumn—about this time of the year—in Italy. She's a singer and she had an engagement in Rome. I expect we will be married soon."

The words seemed so true, inevitable, that Ferris did not at first acknowledge to himself the lie. He and Jeannine had never in that year spoken of marriage. And indeed, she was still married—to a White Russian money-changer in Paris from whom she had been separated for five years. But it was too late to correct the lie. Already Elizabeth was saying: "This really makes me glad to know. Congratulations, Johnny."

He tried to make amends with truth. "The Roman autumn is so beautiful. Balmy and blossoming." He added, "Jeannine has a little boy of six. A curious trilingual little fellow. We go to the Tuileries sometimes."

A lie again. He had taken the boy once to the gardens. The sallow foreign child in shorts that bared his spindly legs had sailed his boat in the concrete pond and ridden the pony. The child had wanted to go in to the puppet show. But there was not time, for Ferris had an engagement at the Scribe Hotel. He had promised they would go to the guignol another afternoon. Only once had he taken Valentin to the Tuileries.

There was a stir. The maid brought in a white-frosted cake with pink candles. The children entered in their night clothes. Ferris still did not understand.

"Happy birthday, John," Elizabeth said. "Blow out the candles."

Ferris recognized his birthday date. The candles blew out lingeringly and there was the smell of burning wax. Ferris was thirty-eight years old. The veins in his temples darkened and pulsed visibly.

"It's time you started for the theater."

Ferris thanked Elizabeth for the birthday dinner and said the appropriate good-byes. The whole family saw him to the door.

A high, thin moon shone above the jagged, dark skyscrapers. The streets were windy, cold. Ferris hurried to Third Avenue and hailed a cab. He gazed at the nocturnal city with the deliberate attentiveness of departure and perhaps farewell. He was alone. He longed for flight-time and the coming journey.

The next day he looked down on the city from the air, burnished in sunlight, toylike, precise. Then America was left behind and there was only the Atlantic and the distant European shore. The ocean was milky pale and placid beneath the clouds. Ferris dozed most of the day. Toward dark he was thinking of Elizabeth and the visit of the previous evening. He thought of Elizabeth among her family with longing, gentle envy and inexplicable regret. He sought the melody, the unfinished air, that had so moved him. The cadence, some unrelated tones, were all that remained; the melody itself evaded him. He had found instead the first voice of the fugue that Elizabeth had played—it came to him, inverted mockingly and in a minor key. Suspended above the ocean the anxieties of transience and solitude no longer troubled him and he thought of his father's death with equanimity. During the dinner hour the plane reached the shore of France.

At midnight Ferris was in a taxi crossing Paris. It was a clouded night and mist wreathed the lights of the Place de la Concorde. The midnight bistros gleamed on the wet pavements. As always after a transocean flight the change of continents was too sudden. New York at morning, this midnight Paris. Ferris glimpsed the disorder of his life: the succession of cities, of transitory loves; and time, the sinister glissando of the years, time always.

"*Vite! Vite!*" he called in terror. "*Dépêchez-vous.*"

Valentin opened the door to him. The little boy wore pajamas and an outgrown red robe. His grey eyes were shadowed and, as Ferris passed into the flat, they flickered momentarily.

"*J'attends Maman.*"

Jeannine was singing in a night club. She would not be home before another hour. Valentin returned to a drawing, squatting with his crayons over the paper on the floor. Ferris looked down at the drawing—it was a banjo player with notes and wavy lines inside a comic-strip balloon.

"We will go again to the Tuileries."

The child looked up and Ferris drew him closer to his knees. The melody, the unfinished music that Elizabeth had played, came to him suddenly. Unsought, the load of memory jettisoned—this time bringing only recognition and sudden joy.

"Monsieur Jean," the child said, "did you see him?"

Confused, Ferris thought only of another child—the freckled, family-loved boy. "See who, Valentin?"

"Your dead papa in Georgia." The child added, "Was he okay?"

Ferris spoke with rapid urgency: "We will go often to the Tuileries. Ride the pony and we will go into the guignol. We will see the puppet show and never be in a hurry any more."

"Monsieur Jean," Valentin said. "The guignol is now closed."

Again, the terror, the acknowledgment of wasted years and death. Valentin, responsive and confident, still nestled in his arms. His cheek touched the soft cheek and felt the brush of the delicate eyelashes. With inner desperation he pressed the child close—as though an emotion as protean as his love could dominate the pulse of time.

PROBING FOR MEANING

1. His father's death has caused Ferris to evaluate his own life. What is your impression of the way he is living? What reaction does he have to the names and addresses in his address book?

2. Elizabeth is described in considerable detail. What is she like? Whose fault does it seem to be that they divorced?

3. What is the difference in connotation between "sojourner" and "expatriate"?

4. What reaction does Ferris have to his visit with the Baileys? What prompts him to lie to Elizabeth? Do you think that the visit will change his relationship with Jeannine and Valentin?

5. What insight does Ferris have while in the taxi crossing Paris? What is the connection between this insight and Ferris' behavior with Valentin? Explain the meaning of the last sentence of the story.

PROBING FOR METHOD

1. What effect does the author create through the descriptions of the first paragraph? How would you characterize the style of sentences such as, "Rome it was this morning in the yearless region of dreams," and "It was a cloudless autumn day and the pale sunlight sliced between the pastel skyscrapers"?

2. How is the narration handled? Does the reader learn the inner thoughts of anyone besides Ferris? What effect is created by this narrative point of view?

3. Why does the author describe the musical interlude in so much depth? Why is it important that Elizabeth plays a fugue (a musical com-

position in which two opposite themes are interwoven)? What symbolism is involved in the fact that Ferris can recall the fugue but that the second piece which Elizabeth played evades his memory?

4. Many of the difficult words in the story are central to the writer's themes. Determine the meanings of the following words. Organize them into groups reflecting different themes in the story.

ambiance	guignol
amiabilities	incipient
anodyne	limpid
bistros	matinal
cadence	motif
dissonant	protean
equanimity	sojourner
expatriate	sublimity
filial	transience
fugue	transitory
glissando	

 JACK CADY

The Burning

Sunlight gleamed as Singleton and I walked down the hill to the charred wreckage of what had been a truck. Gates was dead, and the breeze lifted sooty material that mixed with the valley smells of weeds, flowers, and diesel stink. Manny was in jail. Nothing more could be done for Gates, but now Manny was sitting in his own fire, burning because he was kind, because he was gentle.

Traffic was moving as usual on the long slopes; only an occasional car slowed, its occupants looking over the scene of last night's fire. The truck drivers would know all about the trouble, and they did not want to see. Besides, there was a hill to climb on either side of the valley. They could not afford to lose speed. I knew that by now the word of the burning had spread at least a hundred miles. As far as Lexington, drivers would be leaning against counters listening, with wildness spreading in them. Singleton and I had not slept through the long night. We revisited the scene because we felt it was the final thing we could do for both men.

Close-up the sunlight played on bright runs of metal where someone had pulled the cab apart hoping to recover enough of Gates's remains for burial. An oil fire, when the oil is pouring on a man, doesn't leave much. Only the frame and other heavy structural members of the truck remained.

"If he had only been knocked out or killed before the fire got to him . . ." We were both thinking the words. Either might have said them.

"His company's sending an investigator," Singleton told me. "But since we're here, let's go over it. They'll be sure to ask."

"Are you going to pull?"

"No." He shook his head and ran his hand across his face. "No. Next week maybe or the week after. I'm not steady. I called for three drivers. That's one for your rig too."

"Thanks. I've got vacation coming. I'm taking it."

The road surface along the wreck was blackened, and the asphalt waved and sagged. It was a bad spot. The state should have put up signs. Forty-seven feet of power and payload; now it seemed little there in the ditch, its unimportance turning my stomach. I wanted to retch. I felt lonely and useless.

We walked to the far hill to look at the tire marks. Narrow little lines which swung wide across the other lane and then back in, suddenly breaking and spinning up the roadway. Heavy black lines were laid beside them where the driver of the car being passed had ridden his brakes and then gone on up the hill. Coming down were the marks Gates made, and they showed that he had done what a trucker is supposed to do. He had avoided at all costs. The marks ran off the road.

I never knew him. Manny, tall, sandy-haired, and laughing, was my good friend, but I did not know Gates. I did not know until later that Singleton knew him.

We had picked Gates up twenty miles back on the narrow two-lane that ran through the Kentucky hills. We rode behind him figuring to pass when he got a chance to let us around. It was early, around 3 A.M., but there was still heavy vacation-season traffic. Manny was out front behind Gates. My rig was second behind him, and Singleton was behind me. Our three freights were grossing less than fifty thousand so we could go.

Gates's tanker must have scaled at around sixty thousand. Even with that weight you can usually go, but his gas-powered tractor was too light.

It slowed us to be laying back, but there was no reason to dog it. He was making the best time he could. He topped the hill by June's Stop and ran fast after he crested on the long slope down. He had Manny by maybe two hundred yards because Manny had signaled into June's.

When he signaled I checked my mirrors. Singleton kept pulling so I kept pulling. When he saw us coming on, Manny canceled the signal and went over the top behind Gates. It allowed enough of a lag for Gates to get out front, and it kept Manny from being killed.

We took the hill fast. You have to climb out the other side. I was a quarter mile back, running at forty-five and gaining speed, when I saw the headlights of the little car swing into the lane ahead of Gates's tanker. The driver had incorrectly estimated the truck's speed or the car's passing power.

It was quick and not bad at first. The tanker went into the ditch. The car cut back in, broke traction, and spun directly up the roadway. It came to a stop next to Manny's rig, almost brushing against his drive axle and not even bending sheet metal, a fluke. The car it had passed went onto the shoulder and recovered. The driver took it on up the hill to get away from the wreck and involvement.

Manny was closer. He had perhaps a second more to anticipate the wreck. He had stopped quicker than I believed possible. It was about a minute before the fire started. I was running with my extinguisher when I saw it, and knew I would be too late.

"I wish he'd exploded," Singleton said. He kicked up dust along the roadway. He was too old for this, and he was beat-out and shaken. The calmness of resignation was trying to take him, and I hoped it would. I wondered to myself if those clear eyes that had looked down a million and a half miles of road had ever looked at anything like this.

"Exploded? Yes, either that or got out."

"He was hurt. I think he was hurt bad." He looked at me almost helplessly. "No sense wishing; let's go back up."

After the wreck Singleton had backed his rig over the narrow two-lane, following the gradual bend of the road in the dark. He had taken the two girls from the small car into his cab.

I had stayed a little longer until Gates's burning got really bad. Then I brought the little car in, feeling the way I feel in any car: naked, unprotected, and nearly blind. I was shaking from weakness. The road was blocked above. There was no oncoming beyond the pot flares. The cop with the flashlight had arrived ten or fifteen minutes after the wreck. Behind me the fire rose against the summer blackness and blanketed the valley with the acrid smell of number-two diesel. Because of the distance, Manny's rig seemed almost in the middle of the fire and silhouetted against the burning, though I knew he had stopped nearly fifty yards up the roadway. My own rig was pulled in behind him; its markers stood pale beside the bigger glow. As I was about to go past the cop, he waved me over.

"Where you taking it?"

"Just to the top," I told him. "The girls were pretty shaken up. Don't worry, they won't go anywhere."

"Think they need an ambulance?" He paused, uncertain. "Christ," he said. "Will that other cruiser ever get here?"

"What about Manny?" I asked.

"In there." He nodded to where Manny sat in the cruiser. The lights were out inside. He could not be seen. "I'll take a statement at the top. You'll see him at the top."

I wanted to call to Manny, but there was nothing I could do. I took the car on to June's Stop. Rigs were starting to pile in, even stacking up along the roadway. Cars were parked around and between them, blacked out and gleaming small and dull in the lights from the truck markets. Most of the guys had cut their engines. It would be a long wait.

Singleton's truck was down by the restaurant. Inside around the counter, which formed a kind of box, drivers were sitting and talking. A few were standing around. They were excited and walked back and forth. I wanted coffee, needed it, but I could not go in. At least not then. A driver came up behind me.

"You Wakefield?" he asked. He meant did I drive for Wakefield. My name is Arnold.

I told him yes.

"Your buddy took the girls to Number Twelve. He said to come."

"As if we didn't have enough trouble . . ."

"He's got the door open." The guy grinned. He was short with a light build and was in too good a mood. I disliked him right away. "Listen," he said. "They say there's going to be a shakedown."

"Who says?"

"Who knows? That's just the word. If you left anything back there, you'd better get it out. Check it with June."

He means guns and pills. A lot of companies require them in spite of the law. A lot of guys carry them on their own, the guns I mean. Pills are Benzedrine, Bennies, or a stronger kind called footballs. Only drivers who don't know any better use them to stay awake or get high on.

"I've got it right here," I told him, and patted my side pocket. "I'll hang onto it myself."

"Your funeral," he said, grinning. He gave me a sick feeling.

He was a guy with nose trouble, one who spreads his manure up and down the road, a show-off to impress waitresses. "Thanks," I said, and turned to go to the motel room.

"Hey," he yelled, "what do you think will happen to him?"

"You figure it out." I went over to the motel, found Twelve, and went inside.

The room had twin beds. Singleton was sitting on one, facing the two girls on the other. One was kind of curled up. The other was leaning forward still crying. Vassar, I thought. No, nothing like that on 25 South; University of Kentucky likely, but the same sorry type. I edged down beside Singleton. "Why do you bother?" I asked him. "To hell with them." The girl bawling looked up hard for a moment and started bawling worse.

"I had room," she bawled.

We were all under a strain. The diesel smell was bad, but the other smell that I would never forget had been worse. Even away from the fire I seemed still to smell it.

"You thought you had room!" I yelled at her.

"No, really. I was all right. I had room." She was convinced, almost righteous. At some other time she might have been pretty. Both were twenty or twenty-one. The curled-up one was sort of mousy-looking. The one who was bawling was tall with long hair. I thought of her as a thing.

"No—really," I yelled at her; "you had no room, but keep lying to yourself. Pretty soon that'll make everything OK."

"Leave it, Arn," Singleton told me. "You're not doing any good."

He went to the sink to wet a towel, bringing it to the girl. "Wipe your face," he told her. Then he turned to me. "Did you bring their car?"

"I brought it—just a minute. You can have them in just a minute." I was still blind angry. "Old, young, men, women, we've seen too many of their kind. I just want to say it once." I looked directly at her. "How much have you driven?"

For a moment it didn't take; then she understood.

"Five years."

"Not years. Miles."

"Why—I guess—I don't know. Five years."

"Five thousand a year? Ten thousand? That would be plenty; you haven't driven that much. Five years times ten is fifty thousand. That's six to eight months' work for those guys down there. *You had no room!*" I bit it out at her. She just looked confused, and I felt weak. "I'm ready to leave it now," I told Singleton. "I should have known. Remember, we've got a friend down there."

"I've got two."

He looked different than ever before. He sat slouched on the bed and leaned forward a little. His hands were in his lap, and the lines and creases in his face were shadowed in the half-light from the floor lamp.

"Who was he?" I asked.

He looked at me. I realized with a shock that he had been fighting back tears, but his eyes were gray and clear as always. The silver hair that had been crossed with dark streaks as long as I had known him now seemed a dull gray. The hands in his lap were steady. He reached into a pocket.

"Get coffee." He looked at the girls. "Get two apiece for everybody."

"Who was it, Singleton?"

"Get the coffee. We'll talk later." He looked at the girl who was curled up. "She's not good."

"Shock?"

"Real light. If it was going to get worse, I think it would have. Maybe you'd better bring June." He got up again and tried to straighten the curled-up girl. He asked her to turn on her back. She looked OK. She tried to fight him. "Help him," I told the one who had been bawling.

The restaurant was better than a hundred yards off. A hillbilly voice was deviling a truck song. June was in the kitchen. I told her I needed help, and she came right away. Business is one thing, people are another. She has always been that way. She brought a Silex with her, and we walked back across the lot. In the distance there was the sound of two sirens crossing against each other.

"The other police car."

"That and a fire truck," she told me.

June is a fine woman, once very pretty but now careless of her appearance and too heavy. It is always sad and a little strange to see a nice-looking woman allow herself to slide. There must be reasons, but not the kind that bear thinking about. She had a good hand with people, a good way. She ran a straight business. When we came to the room, she asked us to leave and started mothering the girls. We went outside with the coffee and sat on the step.

"I'm sorry," I told him. "I shouldn't have blown up, but for a minute I could have killed them. I hate every fool like them."

"It's their road too."

"I know."

"Everybody makes mistakes. You—me—nobody has perfect judgment."

"But not like that."

"No. No, we're not like that, but she won't ever be again either. She has to live with that."

I understood a little more about him. He was good in his judgments. It was suddenly not a matter for us to forgive. There was the law. It had nothing to do with us.

"Manny never held those brakes against you," he told me.

Once I had checked his truck for him, and he had a failure. I wanted to say that it was different.

We sat listening to the muffled sounds from the room behind us. Soon, off at the downhill corner of the lot, headlights appeared coming from the wreck. The state car cruised across the lot. It stopped at the end of the motel row. Singleton stood up and motioned to him. The car moved toward us, rolling in gently. The cop got out. Manny was sitting in the back seat. He was slumped over and quiet. When the cop slammed the door, he did not look up.

He was an older cop, too old to be riding a cruiser. In the darkness and excitement there had been no way to tell much about him. He was tired and walked to us unofficially. We made room for him on the step. He sat between us, letdown, his hands shaking with either fatigue or nervousness.

"Charles," he said to Singleton, "who was he?"

"You'd better have some coffee," Singleton told him. He reached over and put his hand on the cop's shoulder. I poured coffee from the Silex, and he drank it fast.

"Gates," said Singleton. "Island Oil. When Haber went broke, I pulled tanks for two years." He stopped as if reflecting. "He was pretty good. I broke him in."

The cop pointed to the car. "Him?"

"Manley, Johnny Manley."

"You're taking him in," I said. "What's the charge?"

"I don't know," the cop told me. "I wouldn't even know what would stick. His rig's half out in one lane. If you're going to say I need a charge, then I'll take him in for obstructing the road."

"I didn't mean that. I'm not trying to push you. I just wanted to see how you felt."

"Then ask straight out. I don't know what I think myself till I get the whole story."

Singleton walked to the car. He leaned through the window to call softly to Manny. Manny did not move, and Singleton leaned against the car for a little while as the cop and I sat and watched. A couple of drivers came by, curious but respectfully silent, and the cop ran them off. June came out with a chair and sat beside the steps. The two girls came out and stood quietly. I looked at them. They were both young, pretty, and in the present circumstances useless and destructively ignorant. I could no longer hate them.

"Is that him?" one of them whispered.

"Yes." I felt like whispering myself. It seemed wrong to be talking about him when he was no more than ten yards off, but I doubted that he was listening to anyone. He was looking down, his long body slumped forward and his hair astray. His face, which was never very good-looking, was drawn tight around his fixed eyes, and his hands were not visible. Perhaps he held them in his lap.

"They can't prove nothing," the cop said. "I bet he gets off." He stood up. "Let's get it over with; we've wasted time."

Singleton came back then. "Tell me," the cop said to him.

"He won't be driving again. I don't know what the law will do, but I know what Manny can't do. He won't take another one out. You can take her statement on the accident"—he pointed at one of the girls—"and his"—he pointed at me. "I was just over the crest—couldn't see it very well. What I can tell you about is afterward, but"—he turned to the girls—"I want to tell you something first because maybe you ought to know. I've known that man yonder seven, eight years. He's a quiet guy. Doesn't say much; really not hard to get to know. He likes people, has patience with them. Sometimes you think he'd be more sociable if he just knew how to start." He hesitated as if searching for words.

"I don't know exactly how to tell it. Instead of talking, he does nice things. Always has extra equipment to spare if the scales are open and the ICC's checking, or maybe puts a bag of apples in your cab before you leave out. Kid stuff—yes, that's it, kid stuff a lot of the time. Sometimes guys don't understand and joke him.

"When he finally got married, it was to a girl who started the whole thing, not him. She was wild. Silly, you know, not especially bad but not the best either. She worked at a stop in Tennessee and quit work after she married instead of going back like she planned. The guy has something. He did good for that girl. I don't know what's going to happen to them now, and it's none of our business I guess, but I just thought you ought to know."

He turned back to the cop. "I came over the crest and saw Manny's and Arnie's stoplights and saw Arnie's trailer jump and pitch sideways till he corrected and got it stopped. I pulled in behind them, and they were both already out and running. Before I got there, I saw the fire. He could tell you more about how it started." He looked at me. I was thinking about it. I nodded for him to go on because it was very real to me, still happening. I wondered if maybe I could get out of having to describe it. I knew there would have to be a corroborative statement, so as Singleton told it I thought along with him.

He did a good job of the telling. He had gotten there only a minute or so after Manny and I were on the scene. Manny jumped from his cab, dodged around the car with the girls in it, and ran to the wreck. I took only enough time to grab my extinguisher. When I got there, Manny was on top of the wreck trying to pull Gates out and holding the door up at the same time.

The tanker had gone in hitting the ditch fast but stretching out the way you want to try to hit a ditch. It had made no motion to jackknife. The ditch had been too deep, and instead it had lain over on its side. All along there—for that matter, all through those hills—the roadside is usually an outcropping of limestone, slate, and coal. In the cuts and even in the valleys there is rock. Until the truck was pulled off, there would be no way to know. It was likely that the tank and maybe his saddle tank had been opened up on an outcrop of rock. There was a little flicker of fire forward of the cab. Gasoline, I had thought, but it did not grow quick like gasoline. The diesel from his tank was running down the ditch and muffled it some at first.

I went for it with the extinguisher, but it was growing and the extinguisher was a popgun. Manny started yelling to come help him, and I whirled and climbed up over the jutting wheel. Singleton was suddenly there, grabbing me, boosting me up. I took the cab door and held it up, and Gates started to yell.

Manny had him under the shoulders pulling hard, had him about halfway out, but he was hung up. I believe Gates's leg was pinched or held by the wheel. Otherwise Manny would not have gotten him out that far. Manny knew though. He knelt down beside him staring into the wrecked cab.

The fire was getting big behind me, building with a roar. It was flowing down the ditch but gaining backward over the surface rapidly. I gave Manny a little shove and closed the door over Gates's head so we could both reach him through the window. He was a small chunky man—hard to grasp. We got him under the arms and pulled hard, and he screamed again. The heat was close now. I was terrified, confused. We could not pull harder. There was no way to get him out.

Then I was suddenly alone. Manny jumped down, stumbling against Singleton, who tried to climb up and was driven back, his face lined and desperate in the fire glow. Manny disappeared running into the darkness. Where I was above the cab, the air was getting unbearably hot. The fire had not yet worked in under the wreck. I tugged hopelessly until I could no longer bear the heat and jumped down and rolled away. Singleton helped me up and pulled me back just as the screams changed from hurt to fear; high, weeping, desperate and unbelieving cries as the heat but not the fire got to him.

I was held in horrified disbelief of what was happening. Outside the cab and in front of it were heavy oil flames. Gates, his head and neck and one hand outside the window, was leaning back away from them, screaming another kind of cry because the fire that had been getting close had arrived. The muscles of his neck and face were cast bronze in the fire glow, and his mouth was a wide black circle issuing cries. His eyes were closed tight, and his straining hand tried to pull himself away.

Then there was a noise, and he fell back and disappeared into the fire, quietly sinking to cremation with no further sound, and we turned to look behind us. Manny was standing helplessly, his pistol dropping from his shaking hand to the ground, and then he too was falling to the ground, covering his eyes with his hands and rolling on his side away from us.

"If I'd known, I wouldn't have stopped him," Singleton told the cop. "Of all the men I know, he's the only one who could have done that much."

He hesitated, running his hand through his graying hair. "I didn't help, you understand—didn't help." He looked pleading. "Nothing I could do, no use—Arn didn't help. Only Manny."

The girls and June were sobbing. The sky to the eastward was coming alive with light. The cop who was too old to be riding a cruiser looked blanched and even older in the beginning dawn. I felt as I had once felt at sea after battling an all-night storm. Only Singleton seemed capable of further speech, his almost ancient features passive but alive.

He looked at the patrol car where Manny still slumped. "They can't prove he killed a man. There's nothing to prove it with. They can't even prove the bullet didn't miss, and in a way that's the worst thing that can happen. You see, I know him. You think maybe he'll change after a while—maybe it will dull down and let him live normal. It won't. I sat with him before you came and did what I could, and it was nothing. Do they electrocute in this state or use gas? If they were kind, the way he is kind, they'd do one or the other."

PROBING FOR MEANING

1. Characterize Arnie. What kind of person is he? What is his reaction to what has happened? Why is he so mad at the two girls? When is he able to control his hatred?

2. Characterize Singleton. Why does he react differently from Arnie to the events?

3. How are two relatively minor characters, June and the policeman, described? What do their characterizations contribute to the meaning of the story?

4. What differences between truckers and drivers of passenger

cars are emphasized? In this regard, why are truckers such a close-knit group? What does the reader learn about their lives?

5. How is Manny described? Why does Singleton relate some of the details of Manny's life? What was Manny's crime? How do you feel about it? Should he be prosecuted?

6. What does Singleton mean when he states that the death penalty would be a "kind" fate for Manny? What does the story say about death? What will be the effect of Gates' death on those who will continue living?

PROBING FOR
METHOD

1. The narrator, Arnie, introduces the characters and speaks about the incident in retrospect, yet the reader learns the details gradually and doesn't know the entire story until the end. What effect is achieved by having the story unfold slowly?

2. What evidence of foreshadowing can you find in the story? Is the foreshadowing misleading? In what way?

3. How is the actual burning of Gates described? Is this incident described effectively?

4. What examples can you find of the idiosyncratic style of speaking of truckers? Does this add anything to the story? Why or why not?

 ADRIENNE RICH

Trying to Talk with a Man

Out in this desert we are testing bombs,

that's why we came here.

Sometimes I feel an underground river
forcing its way between deformed cliffs
an acute angle of understanding
moving itself like a locus of the sun
into this condemned scenery.

What we've had to give up to get here—
whole LP collections, films we starred in
playing in the neighborhoods, bakery windows   10

full of dry, chocolate-filled Jewish cookies,
the language of love-letters, of suicide notes,
afternoons on the riverbank
pretending to be children

Coming out to this desert
we meant to change the face of
driving among dull green succulents
walking at noon in the ghost town
surrounded by a silence

that sounds like the silence of the place   20
except that it came with us
and is familiar
and everything we were saying until now
was an effort to blot it out—
Coming out here we are up against it

Out here I feel more helpless
with you than without you
You mention the danger
and list the equipment
we talk of people caring for each other   30
in emergencies—laceration, thirst—
but you look at me like an emergency

Your dry heat feels like power
your eyes are stars of a different magnitude
they reflect lights that spell out: EXIT
when you get up and pace the floor

talking of the danger
as if it were not ourselves
as if we were testing anything else.

PROBING FOR   1. At what point do you realize the poem is meant symbolically
MEANING   and not as a literal journey to a desert testing site? What is actually happening in the poem?
     2. What do the things they've "had to give up to get here" represent?
     3. In what sense did the "silence of the place" come with them? Why is conversation often an attempt to blot out silence? Why are they "up against it" in the desert?

4. Why does she feel more helpless with him than without him? Why does she say he looks at her "like an emergency"?

5. How do their reactions to their conversations differ? Do they succeed in the purpose of their journey?

PROBING FOR   1. What is the speaker's mood at the beginning of the poem? Does
METHOD   her mood fluctuate at all?

2. What function does the title play?

3. The poem is based on an extended metaphor, that of the desert testing site. How many images in the poem actually form part of this metaphor? What do they mean in each case?

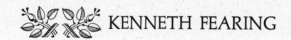 KENNETH FEARING

American Rhapsody (2)

First you bite your fingernails. And then you comb your hair
      again. And then you wait. And wait.
(They say, you know, that first you lie. And then you steal,
      they say. And then, they say, you kill.)

Then the doorbell rings. Then Peg drops in. And Bill. And
      Jane. And Doc.
And first you talk, and smoke, and hear the news and have a
      drink. Then you walk down the stairs.
And you dine, then, and go to a show after that, perhaps, and
      after that a night spot, and after that come home
      again, and climb the stairs again, and again go to bed.

But first Peg argues, and Doc replies. First you dance the
      same dance and you drink the same drink you always
      drank before.
And the piano builds a roof of notes above the world.
And the trumpet weaves a dome of music through space. And
      the drum makes a ceiling over space and time and
      night.

And then the table-wit. And then the check. Then home again
    to bed.
But first, the stairs   10
And do you know, baby, as you climb the stairs, do you still
    feel as you felt back there?
Do you feel again as you felt this morning? And the night
    before? And then the night before that?

(They say, you know, that first you hear voices. And then
    you have visions, they say. Then, they say, you kick
    and scream and rave.)
Or do you feel: What is one more night in a lifetime of
    nights?
What is one more death, or friendship, or divorce out of two,
    or three? Or four? Or five?
One more face among so many, many faces, one more life
    among so many million lives?

But first, baby, as you climb and count the stairs (and they
    total the same) did you, sometime or somewhere,
    have a different idea?
Is this, baby, what you were born to feel, and do, and be?

PROBING FOR   1. Why does the poet insist on listing every action he and his
MEANING   friends take? What actions are they? What is the poet's attitude toward
them?

2. Who is the "you" of the poem?

3. What philosophy of life does the poet feel he and his friends
share? What "different idea" might he be referring to near the end of the
poem?

4. What is the significance of the title?

PROBING FOR   1. Why are some actions placed between parentheses? Of what
METHOD   particular significance are these actions?

2. Why does the poet twice indicate that it is time to go to bed
and then flash back to an earlier part of the evening?

3. What is the order of the questions that the poet asks? How
does this development build emphasis?

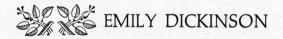 EMILY DICKINSON

My Life Closed Twice Before Its Close

My life closed twice before its close—
It yet remains to see
If Immortality unveil
A third event to me

So huge, so hopeless to conceive
As these that twice befell.
Parting is all we know of heaven,
And all we need of hell.

PROBING FOR MEANING

1. What are the two meanings of "close" in the title and the first line? How do you explain the first two events signified by "twice"?
2. To what does "it" in line 2 refer?
3. What is the "third event"? Why is it "hopeless to conceive"?
4. What do the final two lines mean?

PROBING FOR METHOD

1. Notice the economy of words used by Dickinson. Discuss how this economy is achieved.
2. What connection is there between the words "closed," "see," "unveil" and "conceive"? Explain.

Topics for Imitation

1. Most writers of narratives choose events and experiences that are of informational value to their readers. As Alex Haley says of his search for his African ancestor, "Back home, I knew that what I must write, really, was our black saga, where any individual's past is the essence of the millions'." If you have witnessed an event or had an experience that other people can learn from, relate that event in chronological order, including whatever information you obtained from that experience that will be of value to your reader.

2. Choose an experience you have had—dating, school, camping, traveling, Vietnam—and form a conclusion about that experience which can be of value to other people. For example, you might conclude about dating that dating many different types of people is an education in itself. Using this conclusion as a thesis statement, organize your outline and form topic sentences for your paragraphs from this thesis statement. Use your own experience to supply details and examples in developing your paragraphs. Use Joyce Maynard's essay as a model; for example, use analysis rather than chronological order.

3. "The Sojourner" and "Trying to Talk with a Man" dramatize the man-woman relationship. Examine an aspect of this relationship that the selections have in common. How do they differ?

4. Death is an experience shared by the author of "Birkenau-Auschwitz," the main characters in "The Sojourner" and "The Burning" and the poet in "My Life Closed Twice." How do their reactions to death vary?

5. Past experiences—their own or others'—play an important role in the essays of Haley, Brown and Wehle. What has motivated the writer in each case to write about historical figures or events? Does the fact that each essay is concerned with an ethnic group have any relevance to the writer's purpose?

6. Experiences with the educational system are primarily negative according to Maynard and Burgess. What are the negative features of our school system according to these writers? To what extent are your own educational experiences similar or different?

7. Frustration resulting from unexpressed creativity is an experience common to Rich in "Anger and Tenderness" and Fearing in "American Rhapsody (2)." Why is their creativity suppressed and to what extent do you empathize with their predicament? Is the suppression necessary in each case?

8. Discuss the individual's confrontation with the group in the Maynard, Burgess, Cady and Fearing selections.

9. Discuss the experience of motherhood considering Elizabeth in "The Sojourner" and Adrienne Rich.

FOUR

 EMOTIONS

"to each his world is private"

While we experience our emotions individually, as members
of a society we often have feelings which others share. Social
forces influence us just as do individual people, places and
experiences. For example, the writers in this chapter, many
of them psychologists and sociologists, believe that factors in
our society cause all Americans to feel at times lonely,
apathetic, violent, and maritally and/or sexually frustrated.

The writers attempt to explain the societal causes of these
emotions we share with one another, hoping thereby to ease
our isolation and to search for solutions. Bertrand Russell is
concerned with "what conditions seem on the whole to make
for happiness in marriage and what for unhappiness." Herbert
Gold tries "to work out an explanation for the upsurge in
violence in contemporary America." "Hate is not the opposite
of love; apathy is," says Rollo May in delineating the causes
and effects of apathy. Suzanne Gordon, like Gold and May,
believes that "life in America has exploded." She maintains
that "loneliness is one main ingredient in the fallout" and
searches for the origins of the problem of loneliness in her
essay. Finally, Nora Ephron, speaking of the sexual fantasies
even liberated women have, says, "The movement may manage to clean up the mess in society, but I don't know whether
it can ever clean up the mess in our minds."

The short stories and poems in this chapter dramatize the
effects of these communal emotions on individuals, particularly on children. James Dickey and Ann Petry show the
effects of society's problems on lovers; Gary Gildner, how our

215

society perpetuates violence in the young; Tillie Olsen, the effects of poverty on children; and Howard Nemerov, the effects of society's confusion on the education of the young.

Analyzing Causes and Effects and Achieving Coherence

The writers in this chapter not only analyze our emotional states in their various manifestations, but they also seek to explain their causes. The organization of their essays, therefore, follows a cause-and-effect pattern. Look for the causal relationship in each essay.

The second technique of effective writing to be studied here is the unifying of various parts of your essay through connecting devices. As you read, ask yourself how the writers have connected the ideas in their words, phrases, sentences and paragraphs.

 BERTRAND RUSSELL

Marriage

I propose to discuss marriage without reference to children, merely as a relation between men and women. Marriage differs, of course, from other sex relations by the fact that it is a legal institution. It is also in most communities a religious institution, but it is the legal aspect which is essential. The legal institution merely embodies a practice which exists not only among primitive men but among apes and various other animals. Animals practice what is virtually marriage, whenever the cooperation of the male is necessary to the rearing of the young. As a rule, animal marriages are monogamic, and according to some authorities this is the case in particular amongst the anthropoid apes. It seems, if these authorities are to be believed, that these fortunate animals are not faced with the problems that beset human communities, since the male, once married, ceases to be attracted to any other female, and the female, once married, ceases to be attractive to any other male. Among the anthropoid apes, therefore, although they do not have the assistance of religion, sin is unknown, since instinct suffices to produce virtue. There is some evidence that among the lowest races of savages a similar state of affairs exists. Bushmen are said to be strictly monogamous, and I understand that the Tasmanians (now extinct) were invariably faithful to their wives. Even in civilized mankind faint traces of monogamic instinct can sometimes be perceived. Considering the influence of habit over behavior, it is perhaps surprising that the hold of monogamy on instinct is not stronger than it is. This, however, is an example of the mental peculiarity of human beings, from which spring both their vices and their intelligence, namely the power of imagination to break up habits and initiate new lines of conduct.

It seems probable that what first broke up primitive monogamy was the intrusion of the economic motive. This motive, wherever it has any influence upon sexual behavior, is invariably disastrous, since it substitutes relations of slavery or purchase for relations based upon instinct. In early agricultural and pastoral communities both wives and children were an economic asset to a man. The wives worked for him, and the children, after the age of five or six, began to be useful in the fields or in tending beasts. Consequently the most powerful men aimed at having as many wives as possible. Polygamy can seldom be the general practice of a community, since there is not as a rule a great excess of females; it is the prerogative of chiefs and rich men. Numerous wives and children form a valuable property, and will therefore enhance the already privileged position of their owners. Thus the primary function of a wife comes to be that of a lucrative domestic animal, and her sexual function becomes subordinated. At this level of civilization it is as a rule easy for a man to divorce his wife, though he must in that case restore to her family any dowry that she may have brought. It is, however, in general impossible for a wife to divorce her husband.

The attitude of most semi-civilized communities towards adultery is of a piece with this outlook. At a very low level of civilization adultery is sometimes tolerated. The Samoans, we are told, when they have to go upon a journey, fully expect their wives to console themselves for their absence.* At a slightly higher level, however, adultery in women is punished with death or at best with very severe penalties. Mungo Park's account of Mumbo Jumbo used to be well known when I was young, but I have been pained in recent years to find highbrow Americans alluding to Mumbo Jumbo as a god of the Congo. He was in fact neither a god nor connected with the Congo. He was a pretense demon invented by the men of the upper

* Margaret Mead, "Coming of Age in Samoa," 1928, p. 104ff.

Niger to terrify women who had sinned. Mungo Park's account of him so inevitably suggests a Voltairean view as to the origins of religion that it has tended to be discreetly suppressed by modern anthropologists, who cannot bear the intrusion of rational scoundrelism into the doings of savages. A man who had intercourse with another man's wife was, of course, also a criminal, but a man who had intercourse with an unmarried woman did not incur any blame unless he diminished her value in the marriage market.

With the coming of Christianity this outlook was changed. The part of religion in marriage was very greatly augmented, and infractions of the marriage law came to be blamed on grounds of taboo rather than of property. To have intercourse with another man's wife remained, of course, an offense against that man, but to have any intercourse outside marriage was an offense against God, and this, in the view of the Church, was a far graver matter. For the same reason divorce, which had previously been granted to men on easy terms, was declared inadmissible. Marriage became a sacrament and therefore lifelong.

Was this a gain or a loss to human happiness? It is very hard to say. Among peasants the life of married women has always been a very hard one, and on the whole it has been hardest among the least civilized peasants. Among most barbarous peoples a woman is old at twenty-five, and cannot hope at that age to retain any traces of beauty. The view of women as a domestic animal was no doubt very pleasant for men, but for women it meant a life of nothing but toil and hardship. Christianity, while in some ways it made the position of women worse, especially in the well-to-do classes, did at least recognize their theological equality with men, and refused to regard them as absolutely the property of their husbands. A married woman had not, of course, the right to leave her husband for another man, but she could leave him for a life of religion. And on the whole progress towards a better status for women was easier, in the great bulk of the population, from the Christian than from the pre-Christian standpoint.

When we look round the world at the present day and ask ourselves what conditions seem on the whole to make for happiness in marriage and what for unhappiness, we are driven to a somewhat curious conclusion, that the more civilized people become the less capable they seem of lifelong happiness with one partner. Irish peasants, although until recent times marriages were decided by the parents, were said by those who ought to know them to be on the whole happy and virtuous in their conjugal life. In general, marriage is easiest where people are least differentiated. When a man differs little from other men, and a woman differs little from other women, there is no particular reason to regret not having married some one else. But people with multifarious tastes and pursuits and interests will tend to desire congeniality in their partners, and to feel dissatisfied when they find that they have secured less of it than they might have obtained. The Church, which tends to view marriage solely from the point of view of sex, sees no reason why one partner should not do just as well as another, and can therefore uphold the indissolubility of marriage without realizing the hardship that this often involves.

Another condition which makes for happiness in marriage is paucity of unowned women and absence of social occasions when husbands meet other women. If there is no possibility of sexual relations with any women other than one's wife, most men will make the best of the situation and, except in abnormally bad cases, will find it quite tolerable. The same thing applies to wives, especially if they never imagine that marriage should bring much happiness. That is to say, a marriage is likely to be what is called happy if neither party ever expected to get much happiness out of it.

Fixity of social custom, for the same reason, tends to prevent what are called unhappy marriages. If the bonds of marriage are recognized as final and irrevocable, there is no stimulus to the imagination to wander outside and consider that a more ecstatic happiness might have been possible. In order to secure domestic peace where this state of mind exists, it is only necessary that neither the husband nor the wife should fall outrageously below the commonly recognized standard of decent behavior, whatever this may be.

Among civilized people in the modern world none of these conditions for what is called happiness exist, and accordingly one finds that very few marriages after the first few years are happy. Some of the causes of unhappiness are bound up with civilization, but others would disappear if men and women were more civilized than they are. Let us begin with the latter. Of these the most important is bad sexual education, which is a far commoner thing among the well-to-do than it can ever be among peasants. Peasant children early become accustomed to what are called the facts of life, which they can observe not only among human beings but among animals. They are thus saved from both ignorance and fastidiousness. The carefully educated children of the well-to-do, on the contrary, are shielded from all practical knowledge of sexual matters, and even the most modern parents, who teach children out of books, do not give them that sense of practical familiarity which the peasant child early acquires. The triumph of Christian teaching is when a man and woman marry without either having had previous sexual experience. In nine cases out of ten where this occurs, the results are unfortunate. Sexual behavior among human beings is not instinctive, so that the inexperienced bride and bridegroom, who are probably quite unaware of this fact, find themselves overwhelmed with shame and discomfort. It is little better when the woman alone is innocent but the man has acquired his knowledge from prostitutes. Most men do not realize that a process of wooing is necessary after marriage, and many well-brought-up women do not realize what harm they do to marriage by remaining reserved and physically aloof. All this could be put right by better sexual education, and is in fact very much better with the generation now young than it was with their parents and grand-parents. There used to be a widespread belief among women that they were morally superior to men on the ground that they had less pleasure in sex. This attitude made frank companionship between husbands and wives impossible. It was, of course, in itself quite unjustifiable, since failure to enjoy sex, so far from being virtuous, is a mere physiological or psychological deficiency, like a failure to enjoy food, which also a hundred years ago was expected of elegant females.

Other modern causes of unhappiness in marriage are, how-ever, not so easily disposed of. I think that uninhibited civilized people, whether men or women, are generally polygamous in their instincts. They may fall deeply in love and be for some years entirely absorbed in one person, but sooner or later sexual familiarity dulls the edge of passion, and then they begin to look elsewhere for a revival of the old thrill. It is, of course, possible to control this impulse in the interests of morality, but it's very difficult to prevent the impulse from existing. With the growth of women's freedom there has come a much greater opportunity for conjugal infidelity than existed in former times. The opportunity gives rise to the thought, the thought gives rise to the desire, and in the absence of religious scruples the desire gives rise to the act.

Women's emancipation has in various ways made marriage more difficult. In old days the wife had to adapt herself to the husband, but the husband did not have to adapt himself to the wife. Nowadays many wives, on grounds of woman's right to her own individuality and her own career, are unwilling to adapt themselves to their husbands beyond a point, while men who still hanker after the old tradition of masculine domination see no reason why they should do all the adapting. This trouble arises especially in connection with infidelity. In the old days the husband was occasionally unfaithful, but as a rule his wife did not know of it. If she did, he confessed that he had sinned and made her believe that he was penitent. She, on the other hand, was usually virtuous. If she was not, and the fact came to her husband's knowledge, the marriage broke up. Where, as happens in many modern marriages, mutual faithfulness is not demanded, the instinct of jealousy nevertheless survives, and often proves fatal to the persistence of any deeply rooted intimacy even where no overt quarrels occur.

There is another difficulty in the way of modern marriage, which is felt especially by those who are most conscious of the value of love. Love can flourish only as long as it is free and spontaneous; it tends to be killed by the thought that it is a duty. To say that it is your duty to love so-and-so is the surest way to cause you to hate him or her. Marriage as a combination of love with legal bonds thus falls between two stools. Shelley says:

> I never was attached to that great sect
> Whose doctrine is, that each one should select
> Out of the crowd a mistress or a friend,
> And all the rest, though fair and wise, commend
> To cold oblivion, though it is in the code
> Of modern morals, and the beaten road
> Which those poor slaves with weary footsteps tread,
> Who travel to their home among the dead
> By the broad highway of the world, and so
> With one chained friend, perhaps a jealous foe,
> The dreariest and the longest journey go.

There can be no doubt that to close one's mind on marriage against all the approaches of love from elsewhere is to diminish receptivity and sympathy and the opportunities of valuable human contacts. It is to do violence to something which, from the most idealistic standpoint, is in itself desirable. And like every kind of restrictive morality it tends to promote what one may call a policeman's outlook upon the whole of human life—the outlook, that is to say, which is always looking for an opportunity to forbid something.

For all these reasons, many of which are bound up with things undoubtedly good, marriage has become difficult, and if it is not to be a barrier to happiness it must be conceived in a somewhat new way. One solution often suggested, and actually tried on a large scale in America, is easy divorce. I hold, of course, as every humane person must, that divorce should be granted on more grounds than are admitted in the English law, but I do not recognize in easy divorce a solution of the troubles of marriage. Where a marriage is childless, divorce may be often the right solution, even when both parties are doing their best to behave decently; but where there are children the stability of marriage is to my mind a matter of considerable importance. I think that where a marriage is fruitful and both parties to it are reasonable and decent the expectation ought to be that it will be lifelong, but not that it will exclude other sex relations. A marriage which begins with passionate love and leads to children who are desired and loved ought to produce so deep a tie between a man and woman that they will feel something infinitely precious in their companionship, even after sexual passion has decayed, and even if either or both feels sexual passion for someone else. This mellowing of marriage has been prevented by jealousy, but jealousy, though it is an instinctive emotion, is one which can be controlled if it is recognized as bad, and not supposed to be the expression of a just moral indignation. A companionship which has lasted for many years and through many deeply felt events has a richness of content which cannot belong to the first days of love, however delightful these may be. And any person who appreciates what time can do to enhance values will not lightly throw away such companionship for the sake of new love.

It is therefore possible for a civilized man and woman to be happy in marriage, although if this is to be the case a number of conditions must be fulfilled. There must be a feeling of complete equality on both sides; there must be no interference with mutual freedom; there must be the most complete physical and mental intimacy; and there must be a certain similarity in regard to standards of values. (It is fatal, for example, if one values only money while the other values only good work.) Given all these conditions, I believe marriage to be the best and most important relation that can exist between two human beings. If it has not often been realized hitherto, that is chiefly because husband and wife have regarded themselves as each other's policeman. If marriage is to achieve its possibilities, husbands and wives must learn to understand that whatever the law may say, in their private lives they must be free.

PROBING FOR MEANING

1. Why do apes and savages practice monogamy while civilized man does not?

2. What influence did economic factors have on primitive monogamy historically? On adultery?

3. What influence did Christianity have on monogamy? On the role of women?

4. What causes does Russell cite for the success of monogamy under Christianity?

5. According to Russell, what are the causes of unhappy marriages in our contemporary, highly civilized world?

6. Why is divorce not the answer in Russell's view? Why does he believe in marriage? Under what conditions does he believe marriage can succeed?

7. Do you agree that marriage should be continued as an institution of society? Do you agree with Russell's conditions for its continuance? Would you propose other solutions to the problem?

1. What tone does Russell adopt in his essay? Does he maintain the same tone throughout? Explain.

2. Describe the level of audience for whom Russell is writing as nearly as you can after studying carefully his style.

3. What pattern of organization does he use in the essay?

4. Russell typically makes an assertion and then illustrates it or comments about it, sometimes for the next several paragraphs. Find a place in the essay where he states a major idea and then uses the immediately following paragraphs to expand and illustrate that one idea.

5. In what way does the final paragraph sound final? What aspects of its tone and message qualify it to serve as conclusion?

Analyzing Causes and Effects

How does Bertrand Russell organize a cause-and-effect essay? In "Marriage" Russell is concerned with the decreasing degree of happiness which, he believes, the institution of marriage affords to Western man. This subject lends itself naturally to an exploration of the causes of the effect of marital unhappiness.

Since marriage was once relatively successful, Russell begins his essay with an initial cause-and-effect relationship: the causes of the success of monogamy in primitive and Christian societies. After establishing the causes of the earlier success of marriage, he then analyzes the causes for its present failure.

His conclusion reverses his earlier pattern of causal analysis of a given effect by suggesting, instead, what forces, if put into motion, could become the cause of a future effect: the renewed success of marriage.

His essay organization might be outlined like this:

I. Cause-and-Effect Relationship A
A. Effect: Monogamy is practiced successfully by primitive man.
B. Causes:
1. Men and women who are defined by their roles are not distinguishable from others of their sex and therefore no incentive exists to change or add partners.
2. No social occasions occur at which to meet other potential partners.
3. Fixity of social custom makes divorce unheard-of.

II. Cause-and-Effect Relationship B
A. Effect: In our civilized world, monogamy isn't fulfilling.
B. Causes:
1. Sexual education, despite high degree of civilization, is inadequate.
2. Man's inherent polygamous instincts are no longer inhibited by society.
3. Women have become emancipated and more expectant.
4. Love cannot flourish in a legalistic atmosphere.

III. Cause-and-Effect Relationship C
A. Desired effect: Marriage as an institution gives fulfillment to each partner.
B. Causes which must be implemented if effect is to be achieved:
1. Each partner recognizes equality of other.
2. Mutual freedom is allowed.
3. Complete physical and mental intimacy exists.
4. Standards of values are similar.

INDUCTION   *Principles of cause-and-effect development.* As indicated in previous chapters, the subject about which you are writing usually suggests a particular method of organization. For example, when describing a place, spatial cohesion is the logical method of development; when relating events, chronological order is often followed.

A third common method of development ensues when you analyze the causes of a particular situation. This cause-and-effect technique either presents an effect and then proceeds to analyze the causes, or prophesies effects which could result from existing forces.

In analyzing the causes of an effect, you must be careful to establish that the causes you suggest actually did create the effect. For example, would it be fair to say that the easing of divorce laws leads to the disintegration of marriage?

Also, you must include all major causes of an effect. Women's emancipation, for example, could not be considered the only cause of marital unhappiness.

IMITATION   *Procedures to follow in developing a cause-and-effect essay.*

A. Analyze your topic. Does it suggest a cause-and-effect organization? In other words, are you interested in determining why a situation has come about or, on the other hand, what effect an existing situation might cause?

B. Check your analysis of the causes of your effect to make sure that you have not been illogical either in assigning as causes factors which did not contribute to the effect or in omitting important causes.

C. The simplest approach to the cause-and-effect essay is to begin with a description of the effect and then discuss the causes. If Russell had simplified his approach, for example, his outline might have been:

I. Introduction: Effect—lack of fulfillment in modern marriage.

II. Causes of the above effect:
A. Inadequate sexual education.
B. Polygamy as a natural instinct of man.
C. Emancipation of women.
D. Unnaturalness of legal tie between lovers.

III. Conclusion: Marriage must be reformulated if it is to succeed.

For the beginning writer, this simplified approach is suggested.

 ROLLO MAY

Our Schizoid World

Cassandra: Apollo was the seer who set me this work. . . .
Chorus: Were you already ecstatic in the skill of God?
Cassandra: Yes; even then I read my city's destinies.
                    —*from* Agamemnon, *by Aeschylus*

The striking thing about love and will in our day is that, whereas in the past they were always held up to us as the *answer* to life's predicaments, they have now themselves become the *problem*. It is always true that love and will become more difficult in a transitional age; and ours is an era of radical transition. The old myths and symbols by which we oriented ourselves are gone, anxiety is rampant; we cling to each other and try to persuade ourselves that what we feel is love; we do not will because we are afraid that if we choose one thing or one person we'll lose the other, and we are too insecure to take that chance. The bottom then drops out of the conjunctive emotions and processes—of which love and will are the two foremost examples. The individual is forced to turn inward; he becomes obsessed with the new form of the problem of identity, namely, Even-if-I-know-who-I-am, I-have-no-significance. I am unable to influence others. The next step is apathy. And the step following that is violence. For no human being can stand the perpetually numbing experience of his own powerlessness.

So great was the emphasis on love as the resolution to life's predicament that people's self-esteem ascended or fell depending on whether or not they had achieved it. Those who believed they had found it indulged in self-righteousness, confident in their visible proof of salvation as the Calvinist's wealth used to be tangible evidence of his being numbered among the elect. Those who failed to find it felt not simply bereft to a greater or lesser extent, but, on a deeper and more damaging inner level, their self-esteem was undermined. They felt marked as a new species of pariah, and would confess in psychotherapy that they awoke in the small hours of the morning not necessarily especially lonely or unhappy but plagued with the gnawing conviction that they had somehow missed the great secret of life.

And all the while, with rising divorce rates, the increasing banalization of love in literature and art, and the fact that sex for many people has become more meaningless as it is more available, this "love" has seemed tremendously elusive if not an outright illusion. Some members of the new political left came to the conclusion that love is destroyed by the very nature of our bourgeois society, and the reforms they proposed had the specific purpose of making "a world in which love is more possible."[1]

In such a contradictory situation, the sexual form of love—lowest common denominator on the ladder of salvation—understandably became our preoccupation; for sex, as rooted in man's inescapable biology, seems always dependable to give at least a facsimile of love. But sex, too, has become Western man's test and burden more than his salvation. The books which roll off the presses on technique in love and sex, while still best-sellers for a few weeks, have a hollow ring: for most people seem to be aware on some scarcely articulated level that the frantic quality with which we pursue technique as our way to salvation is in direct proportion to the degree to which we have lost sight of the salvation we are seeking. It is an old and ironic habit of human beings to run faster when we have lost our way; and we grasp more fiercely at research, statistics, and technical aids in sex when we have lost the values and meaning of love. Whatever merits or failings the Kinsey studies and the Masters-Johnson research have in their own right, they are symptomatic of a culture in which the personal meaning of love has been progressively lost. Love had been assumed to be a motivating force, a power which could be relied upon to push us onward in life. But the great shift in our day indicates that the motivating force itself is now called into question. Love has become a problem to itself.

So self-contradictory, indeed, has love become that some of those studying family life have concluded that "love" is simply the name for the way more powerful members of the family control other members. Love, Ronald Laing maintains, is a cover for violence.

The same can be said about will. We inherited from our Victorian forefathers the belief that the only real problem in life was to decide rationally *what* to do—and then *will* would stand ready as the "faculty" for making us do it. Now it is no longer a matter of deciding what to do, but of *deciding how to decide. The very basis of will itself is thrown into question.*

Is will an illusion? Many psychologists and psychotherapists, from Freud down, have argued that it is. The terms "will power" and "free will," so necessary in the vocabulary of our fathers, have all but

[1] Carl Oglesby, in *A Prophetic Minority*, by Jack Newfield (New York: New American Library, 1966), p. 19.

dropped completely out of any contemporary, sophisticated discussion; or the words are used in derision. People go to therapists to find substitutes for their lost will: to learn how to get the "unconscious" to direct their lives, or to learn the latest conditioning technique to enable them to behave, or to use new drugs to release some motive for living. Or to learn the latest method of "releasing affect," unaware that affect is not something you strive for in itself but a by-product of the way you give yourself to a life situation. And the question is, What are they going to use the situation *for*? In his study of will, Leslie Farber asserts that in this failure of will lies the central pathology of our day, and that our time should be called the "age of the disordered will."[2]

In such an age of radical transition, the individual is driven back into his own consciousness. When the foundations of love and will have been shaken and all but destroyed, we cannot escape the necessity of pushing below the surface and searching within our own consciousness and within the "collective unarticulated consciousness" of our society for the sources of love and will. I use the term "source" as the French speak of the "source" of a river—the springs from which the water originally comes. If we can find the sources from which love and will spring, we may be able to discover the new forms which these essential experiences need in order to become viable in the new age into which we are moving. In this sense, our quest, like every such exploration, is a moral quest, for we are seeking the bases on which a morality for a new age can be founded. Every sensitive person finds himself in Stephen Dedalus' position: "I go forth . . . to forge in the smithy of my soul the uncreated conscience of my race."

My term "schizoid," in the title of this chapter, means *out of touch; avoiding close relationships; the inability to feel.* I do not use the term as a reference to psychopathology, but rather as a general condition of our culture and the tendencies of people which make it up. Anthony Storr, describing it more from the point of view of individual psychopathology, holds that the schizoid person is cold, aloof, superior, detached. This may erupt in violent aggression. All of which, says Storr, is a complex mask for a repressed longing for love. The detachment of the schizoid is a defense against hostility and has its source in a distortion of love and trust in infancy which renders him forever fearing actual love "because it threatens his very existence."[3]

[2] Leslie Farber, *The Ways of the Will* (New York: Basic Books, 1965), p. 48.
[3] Anthony Storr, *Human Aggression* (New York: Atheneum, 1968), p. 85.

I agree with Storr as far as he goes, but I am contending that the schizoid condition is a general tendency in our transitional age, and that the "helplessness and disregard" in infancy to which Storr refers comes not just from parents but from almost every aspect of our culture. The parents are themselves helpless and unwitting expressions of their culture. The schizoid man is the natural product of the technological man. It is one way to live and is increasingly utilized—and it may explode into violence. In its "normal" sense, the schizoid does not require repression. Whether the schizoid character state later breaks down into a schizophrenic-like state in any given case, only the future can decide. But this is much less apt to happen, as in the case with many patients, if the individual can frankly admit and confront the schizoid characteristic of his present state. Anthony Storr goes on to indicate that the schizoid character has a "conviction of being unlovable, and a feeling of being attacked and humiliated by criticism."[4]

While I value Storr's description, there is one point where it breaks down. This is in his citing Freud, Descartes, Schopenhauer, and Beethoven as examples of the schizoid. "In the case of Descartes and Schopenhauer, it is their very alienation from love which has given birth to their philosophies." And with Beethoven,

> In compensation for his disappointment with, and resentment of, actual human beings, Beethoven imagined an ideal world of love and friendship. . . . His music, perhaps more obviously than that of any other composer, displays considerable aggression in the sense of power, forcefulness and strength. It is easy to imagine that, had he not been able to sublimate his hostility in his music, he might well have succumbed to a paranoid psychosis.[5]

Storr's dilemma is that if these men are seen as psychopathological and then had assumedly been "cured," we would not have had their creations. Thus, I believe it must be admitted that the schizoid state can be a constructive way of dealing with profoundly difficult situations. Whereas other cultures pushed schizoid persons toward being creative, our culture pushes people toward becoming more detached and mechanical.

In centering upon the problems of love and will, I do not forget the positive characteristics of our time and the potentialities for individual fulfillment. It is an obvious fact that when an age is torn loose from its moorings and everyone is to some degree thrown on his own, more people can take steps to find and realize themselves.

[4] *Ibid.*
[5] *Ibid.*, p. 88.

. . .

Earlier, I quoted Leslie Farber's assertion that our period should be called the "age of disordered will." But what underlies this disordered will?

I shall take my own leap in proposing an answer. I believe it is a state of feelinglessness, the despairing possibility that nothing matters, a condition very close to apathy. Pamela H. Johnson, after reporting the murders on the moors of England, found herself unable to shake loose her conviction that "We may be approaching the state which the psychologists call affectlessness."[6] If apathy or affectlessness is a dominant mood emerging in our day, we can understand on a deeper level why love and will have become so difficult.

What some of us were nonplussed to find in our patients in the 1950's has, in its predictive fashion, during the last few years, emerged as an overt issue gravely troubling our whole society. I wish to quote from my book, *Man's Search for Himself*, written in 1952 and published the following year:

> It may sound surprising when I say, on the basis of my own clinical practice as well as that of my psychological and psychiatric colleagues, that the chief problem of people in the middle decade of the twentieth century is *emptiness*.[7]
>
> While one might laugh at the meaningless boredom of people a decade or two ago, the emptiness has for many now moved from the state of boredom to a state of futility and despair which holds promise of dangers.[8]
>
> . . . The human being cannot live in a condition of emptiness for very long: if he is not growing *toward* something, he does not merely stagnate; the pent-up potentialities turn into morbidity and despair, and eventually into destructive activities.[9]
>
> The *feeling* of emptiness or vacuity . . . generally comes from people's feeling that they are *powerless* to do anything effective about their lives or the world they live in. Inner vacuousness is the long-term, accumulated result of a person's particular conviction about himself, namely his conviction that he cannot act as an entity in directing his own life, or change other people's attitudes toward him, or effectually influence the world around him. Thus he gets the deep sense of despair and futility which so many people in

[6] P. H. Johnson, *On Iniquity: Reflections Arising out of the Moors Murder Trial* (New York, Scribners).

[7] Rollo May, *Man's Search for Himself* (New York: W. W. Norton & Co., 1953), p. 14. The problem which seemed to me to be emerging in a new and unique form I first called the patients' "emptiness," not an entirely well-chosen phrase. I meant by it a state closely allied to apathy.

[8] *Ibid.*, p. 24.

[9] *Ibid.*

our day have. And soon, since what he wants and what he feels can make no real difference, he gives up wanting and feeling.[10]

. . . Apathy and lack of feeling are also defenses against anxiety. When a person continually faces dangers he is powerless to overcome, his final line of defense is at last to avoid even feeling the dangers.[11]

It was not until the mid-60's that this problem erupted in the form of several incidents that shook us to the very foundations. Our "emptiness" had been turning into despair and destructiveness, violence and assassination; it is now undeniable that these go hand in hand with apathy. "For more than half an hour, 38 respectable, law-abiding citizens in Queens," reported *The New York Times* in March, 1964, "watched a killer stalk and stab a woman in three separate attacks in Kew Gardens."[12] In April of the same year, the *Times* said, in an impassioned editorial about another event in which a crowd urged a deranged youth who was clinging to a hotel ledge to jump, calling him "chicken" and "yellow": "Are they any different from the wild-eyed Romans watching and cheering as men and beasts tore each other apart in the Colosseum? . . . Does the attitude of that Albany mob bespeak a way of life for many Americans? . . . If so, the bell tolls for all of us."[13] In May of that year, a *Times* article was headed "Rape Victim's Screams Draw 40 But No One Acts."[14] A number of similar events occurred during the next months which awakened us from our apathy long enough to realize how apathetic we had become, and how much modern city existence had developed in us the habit of uninvolvement and unfeeling detachment.

I am aware how easy it is to exaggerate specific events, and I have no wish to overstate my case. Nevertheless, I do believe that there is in our society a definite trend toward a state of affectlessness as an attitude toward life, a character state. The anomie about which intellectuals had speculated earlier seemed now to emerge with a hideous reality on our very streets and in our very subways.

What shall we call this state reported by so many of our contemporaries—estrangement, playing it cool, alienation, withdrawal of feeling, indifference, anomie, depersonalization? Each one of these terms expresses a part of the condition to which I refer—a condition in which men and women find themselves experiencing a distance between themselves and the objects which used to excite their affec-

[10] *Ibid.,* pp. 24–25.
[11] *Ibid.,* p. 25.
[12] *The New York Times,* March 27, 1964.
[13] *Ibid.,* April 16, 1964.
[14] *Ibid.,* May 6, 1964.

tion and their will.[15] I wish to leave open for the moment what the sources of this are. When I use the term "apathy," despite its limiting connotations, it is because its literal meaning is the closest to what I am describing: "want of feeling; lack of passion, emotion or excitement, indifference." Apathy and the schizoid world go hand in hand as cause and effect of each other.

Apathy is particularly important because of its close relation to love and will. Hate is not the opposite of love; apathy is. The opposite of will is not indecision—which actually may represent the struggle of the *effort* to decide, as in William James—but being uninvolved, detached, unrelated to the significant events. Then the issue of will never can arise. The interrelation of love and will inheres in the fact that both terms describe a person in the process of reaching out, moving toward the world, seeking to affect others or the inanimate world, and opening himself to be affected; molding, forming, relating to the world or requiring that it relate to him. This is why love and will are so difficult in an age of transition, when all the familiar mooring places are gone. The blocking of the ways in which we affect others and are affected by them is the essential disorder of both love and will. Apathy, or a-pathos, is a withdrawal of feeling; it may begin as playing it cool, a studied practice of being unconcerned and unaffected. "I did not want to get involved," was the consistent response of the thirty-eight citizens of Kew Gardens when they were questioned as to why they had not acted. Apathy, operating like Freud's "death instinct," is a gradual letting go of involvement until one finds that life itself has gone by.

Viewing the society freshly, students often have a clearer insight into this than older adults—though they tend, in oversimplified fashion, to blame it on the institutions. "We have just not been given any passionate sense of the excitement of intellectual life around here," said the editor of the Columbia *Spectator*.[16] A student columnist in *The Michigan Daily* wrote, "This institution has dismally failed to inculcate, in most of its undergraduates at least, anything approaching an intellectual appetite." He spoke of the drift "toward something worse than mediocrity—and that is absolute indifference. An indifference towards perhaps even life itself."[17] "We

[15] Keniston, in *The Uncommitted*, speaking of this anomie, writes: "Our age inspires scant enthusiasm. In the industrial West, and increasingly now in the uncommitted nations, ardor is lacking; instead men talk of their growing distance from each other, from their social order, from their work and play, and from the values and heroes which in a perhaps romanticized past seem to have given order, meaning, and coherence to their lives."

[16] James H. Billington, "The Humanistic Heartbeat Has Failed," *Life Magazine*, p. 32.

[17] *Ibid.*

were all divided up into punches on an IBM card," a Berkeley student
remarked. "We decided to punch back in the riots of 1964, but the
real revolution around here will come when we decide to burn com-
puter cards as well as draft cards."[18]

There is a dialectical relationship between apathy and violence. To live in apathy provokes violence; and, in incidents like those
cited above, violence promotes apathy. Violence is the ultimate destructive substitute which surges in to fill the vacuum where there is
no relatedness.[19] There are degrees of violence, from the relatively
normal shock effect of many forms of modern art, through pornography and obscenity—which achieve their desired reaction through
violence to our forms of life—to the extreme pathology of assassinations and the murders of the moors. When inward life dries up, when
feeling decreases and apathy increases, when one cannot affect or
even genuinely *touch* another person, violence flares up as a daimonic
necessity for contact, a mad drive forcing touch in the most direct
way possible.[20] This is one aspect of the well-known relationship
between sexual feelings and crimes of violence. To inflict pain and
torture at least proves that one can affect somebody. In the alienated
state of mass communication, the average citizen knows dozens of TV
personalities who come smiling into his living room of an evening—
but he *himself is never known.* In this state of alienation and
anonymity, painful for anyone to bear, the average person may well
have fantasies which hover on the edge of real pathology. The mood
of the anonymous person is, if I cannot affect or touch anybody, I can
at least shock you into some feeling, force you into some passion
through wounds and pain; I shall at least make sure we both feel
something, and I shall force you to see me and know that I also am
here! Many a child or adolescent has forced the group to take
cognizance of him by destructive behavior; and though he is condemned, at least the community notices him. To be actively hated is
almost as good as to be actively liked; it breaks down the utterly
unbearable situation of anonymity and aloneness.

But having seen the serious affects of apathy, we need now to
turn to the fact of its necessity; and, in its "normal schizoid" form,
how it can be turned into a consecutive function. Our tragic paradox

---

[18] *Ibid.*

[19] "Public apathy," says Dr. Karl Menninger, "is itself a manifestation
of aggression." Karl Menninger at a conference of the Medical Correctional Association on violence, covered by *The New York Times,* April 12, 1964.

[20] The vast need of our society for touch and the revolt against its
prohibition are shown in the growth of all the forms of touch therapy, from
Esalen on down to the group therapy in the next room. These rightly reflect the
need, but they are in error in their anti-intellectual bias and in the grandiose
aims which they assert for what is essentially a corrective measure. They are also
in error in their failure to see that this is an aspect of the whole society which
must be changed, and changed on a deeper level involving the whole man.

is that in contemporary history, we *have* to protect ourselves by some kind of apathy. "Apathy is a curious state," remarks Harry Stack Sullivan, "It is a way used to survive defeat without material damage, although if it endures too long one is damaged by the passage of time. Apathy seems to me to be a miracle of protection by which a personality in utter fiasco rests until it can do something else."[21] The longer the situation goes unmet, the more apathy is prolonged; and it sooner or later becomes a character state. This affectlessness is a shrinking-up in the winds of continuous demands, a freezing in the face of hyperstimuli, letting the current go by since one fears he would be overwhelmed if he responded to it. No one who has ever ridden the subway at rush hour, with its cacophonous din and hordes of anonymous humanity, will be surprised at this.

It is not difficult to appreciate how people living in a schizoid age have to protect themselves from tremendous overstimulation—protect themselves from the barrage of words and noise over radio and TV, protect themselves from the assembly line demands of collectivized industry and gigantic factory-modeled multiversities. In a world where numbers inexorably take over as our means of identification, like flowing lava threatening to suffocate and fossilize all breathing life in its path; in a world where "normality" is defined as keeping your cool; where sex is so available that the only way to preserve any inner center is to learn to have intercourse without committing yourself—in such a schizoid world, which young people experience more directly since they have not had time to build up the defenses which dull the senses of their elders, it is not surprising that will and love have become increasingly problematic and even, as some people believe, impossible of achievement.

But what of the constructive use of this schizoid situation? We have seen how Cézanne could turn his schizoid personality into a way of expressing the most significant forms of modern life, and could stand against the debilitating tendencies in our society by means of his art. We have seen that the schizoid stand is necessary, now we shall inquire how, in its healthy dimensions, it can also be turned to good. The constructive schizoid person stands against the spiritual emptiness of encroaching technology and does not let himself be emptied by it. He lives and works with the machine without becoming a machine. He finds it necessary to remain detached enough to get meaning from the experience, but in doing so to protect his own inner life from impoverishment.

Dr. Bruno Bettelheim finds the same supremacy of the aloof person—whom I would call schizoid—in his experiences in the concentration camps during World War II.

---

[21] Harry Stack Sullivan, *The Psychiatric Interview* (New York: W. W. Norton & Co., 1954), p. 184.

According to psychoanalytic convictions then current . . . aloof-
ness from other persons and emotional distance from the world
were viewed as weakness of character. My comments . . . on the
admirable way in which a group of what I call "anointed persons"
behaved in the concentration camps suggest how struck I was with
these very aloof persons. They were very much out of contact with
their unconscious but nevertheless retained their old personality
structure, stuck to their values in the face of extreme hardships,
and as persons were hardly touched by the camp experience. . . .
These very persons who, according to existing psychoanalytic
theory, should have had weak personalities apt to readily disintegrate, turned out to be heroic leaders, mainly because of the
strength of their character.[22]

Indeed, studies have shown that the persons who survive
most effectively in space ships, and who can adjust to the sensory
deprivation necessary for such a life—our comrades of the twenty-
first century—are those who can detach and withdraw into themselves. "There are reasons to believe," writes Arthur J. Brodbeck after
summarizing the evidence," that it may well be the schizoid personality that will be best able to endure the requirements of extended
space travel."[23] They preserve the inner world which the very
hyperstimuli of our age would take away. These introverts can continue to exist despite the overpowering stimuli or lack of it, for they
have learned to develop a "constructive" schizoid attitude toward life.
Since we must live in the world as we find it, this distinguishing of
the constructively schizoid attitude is an important part of our problem.

Apathy is the withdrawal of will and love, a statement that
they "don't matter," a suspension of commitment. It is necessary in
times of stress and turmoil; and the present great quantity of stimuli
is a form of stress. But apathy, now in contrast to the "normal"
schizoid attitude, leads to emptiness and makes one less able to
defend oneself, less able to survive. However understandable the state
we are describing by the term apathy is, it is also essential that we
seek to find a new basis for the love and will which have been its chief
casualties.

PROBING FOR
MEANING

1. In paragraph 1, May introduces the causes and effects of "the
problem of love and will." What are the causes of both the inability to love
and the lack of will in our culture? What effects result from the lack of
love and will?

[22] Bruno Bettelheim, *The Informed Heart* (Glencoe, Ill.: The Free Press,
1960), pp. 20–21.
[23] Arthur J. Brodbeck, "Placing Aesthetic Developments in Social Context: A Program of Value Analysis," *Journal of Social Issues* (January, 1964), 17.

2. What evidence in paragraph 2 does the author give that people can no longer feel love?

3. Why does May believe that sex as well as love "has become Western man's test and burden more than his salvation"? Why does May say that the books on sexual techniques all "have a hollow ring"? Do you agree? Explain.

4. The problem of will, May states, is "no longer a matter of deciding what to do, but of deciding how to decide." What does this statement mean?

5. How does May believe our troubled society can restore the possibilities of love and will?

6. Why does May use the word "schizoid" to describe modern man? Do you agree with his description? Explain. What term does he use synonymously with "schizoid"?

7. What examples of the schizoid personality at work does May give?

8. May says, "Hate is not the opposite of love; apathy is." Explain. To what extent do you agree?

9. May states, "There is a dialectical relationship between apathy and violence." What relationship does he establish?

10. May admits that "we have to protect ourselves by some kind of apathy." Apathy, then, can also be positive. Describe the author's notion of constructive apathy. What examples does he give of the need for a healthy, schizoid attitude? Where does he draw the line between healthy and unhealthy apathy?

PROBING FOR METHOD

1. How has May organized his cause-and-effect essay? Point out paragraphs that might mark heading shifts in his outline.

2. What words and phrases in his second paragraph provide distinct bridges from the first?

3. How is the third paragraph tied to the second? Point out examples of good cohesion in other paragraph sequences throughout the essay.

4. Study the second to the last paragraph carefully. What holds all of the sentences together? Point out words and phrases that provide the necessary cohesion.

Achieving Coherence

ILLUSTRATION

What methods has May used to achieve coherence in his essay? The most obvious way in which May connects the various parts of his essay is through his repetition of words and phrases that are related to his topic. For example, the phrase "love and will" occurs in the first, second and fourth sentences of the essay, clearly tying the sentences of the introductory paragraph together. The second, third and fourth paragraphs, furthermore, are related to the introduction through the repetition of the word "love" just as the fifth and sixth paragraphs are connected through the use of the word "will." Paragraphs 7 and 11 use the phrase "love and will" again, bringing the first half of the essay neatly together.

The other key word used to unify the parts of the essay is "schizoid," which is first used in paragraph 8. "Schizoid" and its various synonyms—apathetic, affectless, and so on—are used throughout the last half of the essay to achieve coherence among the paragraphs. In paragraph 18, "apathy" and "love and will" are brought together to explain May's main point throughout: that apathy is an effect of the inability to love and will. Finally, in the conclusion, "apathy" and "love and will" are brought together once again to underline May's central point in the essay.

May uses other cohesive devices in the essay. Notice his use of the word "such" in the topic sentences of paragraphs 3 and 7 to refer back to the previous paragraph, thus linking the two paragraphs. In paragraphs 15, 17 and 19, he uses "this" as either a demonstrative pronoun or adjective to link the subject matter of the two paragraphs.

Sentences within paragraphs are also linked together as we have seen by May's repetition of the phrase "love and will" in his introduction. Other connective methods in the first paragraph include the use of words marking the chronology of the emotional stages he is describing: "The *next* step is apathy. And the step *following that* is violence."

Phrases and clauses within a sentence must also be linked. Again, in the introduction, notice the method of linking the parts of the third sentence: May uses a parallel form for each clause, beginning with the word "we."

Conjunctions, of course, are the most obvious linking device for any writer. Notice May's use of the conjunctions "as," "but" and "and" in the second paragraph. What precise connections do they achieve between words, phrases and sentences? How do they differ from each other?

INDUCTION   *Principles of cohesion.*   Connectives are words and phrases that build bridges between ideas, enabling the reader to understand how the parts of the essay relate to one another. If connections are not established, the reader may doubt the unity of the paper. Connections must be formed between words, phrases, clauses, sentences and paragraphs.

The simplest and most effective method of achieving cohesion lies in the use of conjunctions. Conjunctions may show equality in relationships (*and, also, furthermore, another, in addition to*); contrast (*or, but, however, nevertheless, in spite of*); cause and effect (*therefore, consequently, as a result of, because, so*); or chronology (*now, then, afterwards, finally*).

Another cohesive device is the repetition of key words or phrases within a sentence, within a paragraph and throughout the essay. These key words and phrases emanate from the central idea of your essay—your thesis sentence—just as May's repetition of "schizoid" comes from the main idea of his essay.

A third cohesive device is the use of demonstrative pronouns and adjectives. These "demonstrate" very clearly connections between thoughts.

"A book that I have read is . . . This book is . . . This (book) is . . ."

Precision in choosing connectives is important; do not use *and* when you mean *therefore*, for example, since the relationship established by one word is different from that established by the other.

Each sentence should contain some connective device relating it to the preceding sentences. The topic sentence of each paragraph is the most important place for the insertion of cohesive words and phrases, for this sentence must establish a clear relationship between the paragraph it introduces and the key elements of the preceding paragraph. Looking back at Alex Haley's essay in Chapter III, for example, notice that each of his topic sentences contains a transitional word establishing how that paragraph fits into the chronological order of the essay.

IMITATION   *Procedures to follow in establishing cohesion.*

A. In order to clearly establish a connection between the parts of your essay, you must first determine what the connections are. After forming your thesis sentence, your outline, your topic sentences and, finally, your paragraphs, you have gone through several steps in the process of determining these connections.

B. You are now ready for a more refined stage in the process: the insertion of cohesive devices to indicate these connections to the reader. The devices should be inserted at the following points:

Point of Connection	*Connecting Devices*
1. Between words	conjunctions, demonstrative adjectives
2. Between phrases	conjunctions, demonstrative adjectives, repetition of key words
3. Between clauses	conjunctions, repetition of key words and phrases, demonstrative pronouns and adjectives
4. Between sentences	all of the above
5. Between paragraphs	all of the above
6. Throughout the essay	repetition of key words and phrases

C. If you find that overall cohesion does not exist, then your paper lacks unity and you must revise your draft. The insertion of cohesive devices is a final check on the consistency and unity of your topic.

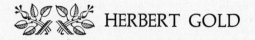 HERBERT GOLD

"Let's Kill the First Red-Haired Man We See . . ."

1

A group of amiable artists and rock musicians came together a summer ago to plan a grand free outdoor festival of their joyful crafts in San Francisco, but a man who called himself Mother John appeared at their meetings and said he'd tear them apart, he'd burn them down: "I ain't rational and I'll wipe you out."

"What's your last name, sir?"

"Motherf—— John from Out-of-Town."

The insurance went up and the folks got scared. There were ten or twenty or thirty of these mothers, or maybe the same one with ten, twenty, or thirty faces, but they were all talking about burning, ripping, exploding, and such. The festival in the park was canceled.

Why did the mothers threaten? They wanted to hurt. *Why?* Well, maybe they were fascist right-wing third-world meth-freak Maoist hippie deviationist paranoids, or maybe they were just out-people wanting in, fearing that someone might find fun and profit in the festival. They really don't know or can't say. They are rebels without a pause.

The man who commits random violence always thinks his attack is justified, of course. "He gave a me a lotta lip"—the true-life explanation, folks, for shooting a fellow shopper. Or: "I just don't like guys who smile to themselves." But we know that the gesture is in excess of the provocation. Maybe logically we can't explain it, but a lotta lip isn't reason enough to kill in a busy department store during the January White Sale.

In my novel *The Great American Jackpot*, a young man named Al Dooley robs a bank because he's lonely and seeks meaning. Well, there are other reasons, even good ones. But *he* doesn't really know them, and to the world, too, his action seems eccentric, unpredictable, irrational. He is strung out and strange to himself, and a menace to others. He wants to greet reality with an answering blow. I think him a frequent American.

Traditional violence usually had a clear aim. The man with the stick hit the other man to grab his goods, land, or woman. Contemporary random violence has murky origins—killing without hatred, rape without lust, war against phantom enemies. It hits first because otherwise someone might hit back. Causeless violence? No, but action far in excess of cause, similar to methedrine speed in excess of organic velocity.

On the Lower East Side of New York, for example, a fertile plantation area for the Mother Johns of this world, speed freaks, motorcyclists, disaffected workers, chafing neighborhood nationality groups, blacks, cops and mimeograph Maoists, all are battling each other in some weird parody of the troubadour games of murder. "Okay, world," they seem to be saying, toeing the earth shyly, "here we go with a free outdoor X-rated movie. And bring the kiddies to the slaughter."

This is a violent country.

Everyone who walks the streets of America knows it. If you can't walk, you read the newspapers. If you can't read, you see it on television. The subtle mining of violence under the surface control of America goes beyond anything a law-and-order manipulation of police authority can resolve.

For a time I accepted a wry, half-paranoid suspicion that my own person (horn-rimmed novelist, nosy face) invited attack. I've gradually come to realize that I'm no worse than others, but just being alive invites attack. For example:

I was walking in a heavy rain. The street was deserted. A man came toward me in black-militant drag, boots, leather, beret, and his lips moving, discussing with invisible enemies. But I was visible. Our eyes met. I stopped for a moment to let him by and he glared at me. "Hi," I said weakly.

"Man, I don't see it like that," he said. "I'm gonna *kill* you."

But there was no action. There was only the wish to murder.

And there is also, oddly enough—this is often ignored—the reciprocal wish to have violence done. I know a girl, a very pretty actress, who has been raped twice. Does she invite it? Well, she undresses at night, with shades up, and when she hears a sound at the window, she goes to open the door to see what's happening. And I was standing on the street near the San Francisco Art Museum when I saw an old acquaintance, the girl friend of a friend, and I jokingly went up to her and said, "Hey, chick, you want to do something really filthy?"

She paused and looked up into my face with a welcoming smile: "What?" Then her face darkened with disappointment. "Oh," she said, "it's Herb. I didn't recognize you at first." She later explained that she was kind of upset that day and bored and—oh, you know, looking for something to do. I realized an odd fact about rapists and molesters. They are offering a product which not many women want to buy—*but some do.*

There is no lack, of course, of the traditional kinds of violence—between colors, races, generations, classes.

My wife and I were strolling in Berkeley after a party. A group of cops was hassling a couple in an old station wagon decorated with hippie, love and peace insignia. The five policemen were teasing the kids, looking for drugs, it seemed, or maybe just *looking.* A boy of high school age, long hair, blue jeans, called out, "They don't have a search warrant! You don't have to let them!"

It was careless of him to incite the police.

One huge cop went lazily moving toward the kid. The kid started to run, very fast—ahah, he'll get away. The cop thumped after him. We kept walking in response to the other cops' jerking thumbs: *Keep moving.* But in the direction of the kid. He slipped and fell, bounced to his feet and kept running, but the cop was close now. Suddenly, to our amazement, we heard a thud of feet. *All* the five cops had abandoned the car and were chasing this boy who had yelled at them. They passed us, grinning, clutching clubs, some with hands on their pistols. They rounded the corner and I heard the boy scream, "I surrender!" He stood with hands up, trembling. The first cop to reach him cracked him on the head with his club and sent him staggering and bleeding. The others gathered around as a small Saturday-night crowd appeared. He gave them his papers. He was okay. He was even white. A couple of Berkeley ladies, spinsters or schoolteachers or grandmothers, were standing nearby. The cop who had hit him said, "Okay, kid, go home now."

They didn't arrest him. They had made their investigation, administered justice, and dismissed the case, all in one swift comment of billy club on skull. He was bleeding from the nose. He was vomiting. He needed to see a doctor. The ladies soothed him and led him away.

The cops were pleased that they had made another request for polite attention to one's elders. But they had also created another cop-hating radical, ready to kill. And not just the boy, of course, but the ladies and me, too.

2

While trying to work out an explanation for the upsurge in violence in contemporary America, random violence beyond the traditional violences, I happened to be in my bank in New York City, formerly Fun City, during the months when it is supposed to be a Summer Festival. New York offers a natural environment for thinking about random violence. I was waiting to have a check certified (speeding ticket, speedometer defective, H. Gold the Mild-Mannered Novelist feeling morose). A mousy young man came up to the desk, wrote his name and account number on a slip of paper, and said to the bank bureaucrat, "Excuse me, sir, I'd like to know how much money I have."

"How should I know?"

"I mean, in my account."

"What do you mean, don't you get a statement?"

"Yes, but there's a discrepancy—"

"Can't you add?"

"I think so, but it doesn't come out the same—"

"It'll cost you a dollar. There'll be a charge of a dollar."

Timidly the supplicant said, "Won't you tell me what I have in my account?"

It was like the tide rushing through a weak place in the wall. The put-upon, underpaid, not overbright bank clerk saw weakness and found pleasure in crushing it. "We can't just stand here all day and answer stupid questions from stupid people who can't add. I said it'll cost you a dollar. You want me to call downstairs?"

The dejected supplicant took his slip of paper with his name and number on it and walked away, gray and defeated. No matter that the bank probably wouldn't and couldn't legally charge him for the service. No matter: he believed in the authority of the Man Behind the Desk, a man exasperated and rubbed raw in the great city, a loser himself. The teller turned to me and said, "Stupid idiots, asking stupid questions, they think all I got to do here is answer them?"

I said that the supplicant walked away gray and defeated, but I'm sure there was also murder in his heart. Not against the bank or the teller, not a cop, not some authority. But against someone weaker than himself—a black man, a hippie, a kid. Isolation from power makes men look for a mob in which they can be strong.

Random violence is not really random or accidental, of course, and the man or mob, kid or gang, deciding to kill the first red-haired man in sight, is not unconnected with the rest of the fate of America and the world. There are fifty or sixty million more people in

America than there were when I was a child. The rat-sink theory holds that animals go crazy—perverse, violent, self-destructive—when the density of population increases beyond a certain needed living space. No reason to think that the anxiety of rats is sharper than that of overcrowded human beings. Every study of ambulatory psychosis and neurosis comes up with a large store of ticking time bombs walking the streets—and driving, waiting on people, directing traffic. They are damaged, we are told, by broken families and crippled families, by historical examples of cruelty, by rage and resentment, by boredom and anxiety, by jealousy and frustration. Now we also hear of chromosome damage and genetic defects leading men toward senseless attack. Prison systems all have isolation chambers for enraged men who snarl like beasts and want only to destroy, who must be kept apart, unreachable by therapy; and some of these seem to burn out and are released, and some have not yet committed acts which get them in prison. Repressed, suppressed, tormented, unconscious, the desire to kill is a part of the risk of city life, like postnasal drip. High school basketball games turn into rampages. A community in Washington protects itself from the world with fences, towers, electric eyes, dogs, guards, patrols—an armed concentration camp for suburban luxury living. The statistics about senseless crime, child beating, sniping at strangers, arson and assault, and gang sadism should make Jean Jacques Rousseau spin in his quiet Swiss grave. If man is naturally good, he is sure going against his nature more and more of the time. It sounds like a bad joke: the paranoids are after us.

Violence pours out of city men like water out of broken fire hydrants. And it's not just the city, of course. The small-town jukebox roars out Johnny Cash songs or "Happiness Is a Warm Gun," and the bouncers hit and the cops flail and the shards of plate glass decorate the pavements.

Nietzsche said: "It is only the powerful who know how to honor, it is their art, their domain for invention." In other words, power is the opposite of violence. The powerful man can respect the stranger, not fear him. The sense of being cut off makes men want to find reality through the ancient pride in bloodletting. Powerlessness corrupts; absolute powerlessness corrupts absolutely. Stabbing strange women or setting drunks on fire does not seem to be the moral equivalent of war, which William James said America needed. But if the tax man and your parents and your employer give you trouble, and you can't strike at them openly, why not declare war on their surrogates, on the weak or the strange, on humanity itself?

3

The psychiatrist Bruno Bettelheim argues that a misunderstood Freudianism has led to a hypocritical pseudo-permissiveness on the part of frightened parents, and this in turn leads to guilt and weak control in children. The kids know their parents want them to be decent human beings, but also that the parents are afraid to assert authority. The child needs authority to provide examples for learning. The childish temper tantrum is a common means of testing. It needs to be mastered, but often isn't by the time the child has an adult's body. The character-disordered or psychopathic personality may seem to be intelligent, controlled and in touch; but, in fact, all it knows is one lesson: I want, I want at once, I want only what *I* want—and I'll take it.

When a man respects no one, and not himself either, but wants wants *wants*, there is no reason to defer his hatreds and revenges; and when he doesn't really know why he hates and needs revenge, he may express his childish storm of temper with a high-powered rifle from a rooftop or a knife in a crowd. How quickly the "love generation" turns to hating yippies under pressure about Vietnam and cynicism about American virtue. The kids can throw flowers, turn on, and make lovely rock music, but if they are goal-less amid affluence, they grow impatient with a doctrinaire forever springtime designed like a record jacket. The tender communal living arrangements seem to work out fine, as they did for a sweet flower child I knew a few years ago: "We love each other, we live at peace, we share everything."

"How long has this been going on?"

"Five days," she said.

But the grooviness ended with thievery, fights, jealous rage, and a contagion of breakdowns. A Panglossian reaction might be: Okay, let's work out the violence, it's the price we pay for super-organization. The trouble with this is that violence *expresses* other feelings, but only *communicates* itself—the desire to hurt. It does no good to the victim, unlike the victim of a poem or a song, who may benefit from the composer's expressed rage. And it does no good to the perpetrator, who comes to understand nothing, but may develop a taste for blood.

A businessman in Detroit hopes that holdup men are rational and want his money; he can offer money—it's the ones who just want to kill him that are a bother. A childhood friend, a funny red-haired man from Cleveland, carries a teargas gun in his pocket. "Why?" I asked him.

"Some people don't like red hair," he said.

Mace, karate, judo, personal weapons—HELP! Stop! The police say that the worst criminals are the amateurs, out for kicks, not purses; pleasure, not gain. A presidential report on violence, released on the first anniversary of the assassination of Robert Kennedy, says that Americans are a "rather bloody-minded people." In the past, it notes, violence was generally initiated by white Anglo-Saxons against Catholics, black men, labor organizers, and pacifists. Now black violence, campus violence, antiwar violence, political assassinations, and spooky random violence are added to our turbulent past. Eric Hoffer, who hollered on television that we are not a violent people, wrote in his column in the San Francisco *Examiner* (June 9, 1969): "A day of wrath is waiting around the corner, when the saturated resentment of the long-suffering majority crystallizes in retaliation." He bemoaned an "incredible submissiveness in an age of violence," and seemed to be urging the public to rush the "foul-mouthed, bushy-faced punks." People shouldn't put limitation on the police; do-gooders are the enemy. His solution to the problem is on a similar level to the one reported in the *New York Times*, where Associate Justice Paul C. Reardon of the Massachusetts Supreme Court urged that a campaign should be mounted in the nation's schools to search "for a brief synonym for police officer and policeman to supplant that unfortunate word all Americans currently employ." The headline reads: NEW WORD FOR "COP" SOUGHT. Obviously the word "pig" won't do, but if we call the cops "angels," it won't belong until the word "angel" means what "cop" means. If there is violence and hatred in America, new words won't make them sweeter.

How can we live with random violence? Well, one way which is seldom mentioned is just to go on going on, as we do with automobiles, smog, cigarettes, airplane failures, brush-fire wars—making irritated little gestures toward improving our chances but essentially enduring what malfunction or destiny bring. In the rat-sink city we may have to think of berserk paranoids as another health hazard, like leaking stoves. Recently I visited a prisoner in California who was convicted of kidnapping and tormenting a child. He is intelligent, gentle, thoughtful, and says he doesn't mind prison so much because it gives him a chance to catch up on his reading. (It has also dried out the drugs in his blood.) But when he is caught up on his reading and ready for the world once again, and maybe ready to try speeding through his mind with the help of methedrine sulfate, are we to think of him as just another hazard, like the defective automobile or the mysterious disturbances in our lungs which come from breathing city air.

Suppose we're not content with this new hazard of sudden death by twitch and impulse?

The police, either kindly or repressive, must always be fallible solutions. Either they are not there when you need them or they are too much there. Massed police tend to riot; police power means police brutality. What about personal armament, going about with little private jets of mace, which can be bought in grocery stores and "at fine cosmetic counters everywhere." There are too many quick tempers abroad. When everyone is armed to protect himself, who will protect us from the protectors? What about that walled suburb of Washington? This sort of panic is a reversion to the life envisaged during the great fallout-shelter craze, a retreat to something fetal and subhuman in human nature. Then what?

Other styles of child rearing, deeper and truer education, meaningful work, creative interchanges among people—everyone talks about the ways that might make it possible for masses of men to live together on a limited planet. Improved medicine calms the distraught, tranquilizes the defective. The reform of cities, and a public life which is less hypocritical about suffering, war and injustice, can influence people to meet each other without rage. Drugs, cops, institutions and karate—well, these stopgap controls may be with us forever and we will use them when we must. Humankind requires deep solutions to the demand for animal and spiritual joy. Rage, violence, ulcers, twitches, crying jags, and melancholia reflect an imbalance of personal expression and opportunity in the world. A song of a few years ago claimed morosely, "I ain't got no sat-is-fac-tion," and I've heard that song danced and sung in Los Angeles, New York, Paris, and Biafra. It's a universal anthem. The dream of love and joy seems further away than ever. Doctrinaire injunctions to love one another—love! love goddammit!—clearly don't work. Nor does anarchic self-expression when *my* freedom binds *you* to pay the price. The others out there will find their pleasure in revenge.

The billions are here, and billions more coming fast, and we must learn to live with them. There will be more of everything, including red-haired men. Is the red-haired man coming toward you your brother? No, in fact, he's not. He may be your friend or your enemy. He takes up your space, he eats your food, he jostles you. He covets what you covet.

A few days ago, waiting at the post office, a sallow, irritable, self-absorbed young man tried to slip in line between a couple of women ahead of me. I reached out to put my hands on his shoulder. I smiled sweetly. I said, "Okay, fella, tell you what. You take that place in line and I'll take you, okay? agreed? fine?"

He looked at me and saw a menace to society. I wanted to kill. The ladies in line shrank away from me. I was Mother Herb from Out-of-Town. I was not rational. And worst of all, I was proud of it.

PROBING FOR
MEANING
1. What are "fascist right wing third-world meth-freak Maoist hippie deviationist paranoids"? How do they differ from "out-people wanting in"?

2. Gold puns on the title of the movie *Rebel Without a Cause* in describing the "mothers" as "rebels without a pause." How does his pun describe these violence-prone people? What examples does Gold cite of this type of rebelliousness throughout the essay?

3. How does "traditional" violence differ from random "violence"? What examples of traditional violence substantiate the author's distinction between them?

4. For what reason does Gold divide the essay into three sections?

5. Gold claims one cause of random violence stems from powerlessness. "Isolation from power makes men look for a mob in which they can be strong." Does his discussion of the "mousy young man" at the bank justify the conclusion that the young man will go out and be violent? What examples can you give to support or attack Gold's point?

6. How does the "rat-sink theory" explain random violence? What effects of overcrowding on people does Gold mention? Do you agree that "Violence pours out of city men like water out of broken fire hydrants"? Does Gold exclude small towns from his violent world?

7. A third cause Gold mentions is parental permissiveness. What argument does he give that parents have been too permissive? Why does permissiveness lead to violence? Is the hippie movement a good example of the bad aspects of permissiveness? Can you think of others?

8. "How can we live with random violence?" What answers does Gold dispense with as unworkable? What answers does he think might work?

PROBING FOR
METHOD
1. What method of introduction does Gold use? To what extent does it fulfill the requirements of a good introduction?

2. Gold employs an unusual number of examples in making his points. How effective is this abundance of anecdote?

3. Gold also uses humor at several points in the essay. What are some specific instances? What overall effect is created by his sometimes humorous approach to a very serious subject?

4. The author mentions several causes of random violence. To what extent does he also develop the effects of it?

 NORA EPHRON

Fantasies

One of the trump cards that men who are threatened by women's liberation are always dredging up is the question of whether there is sex after liberation. I have heard at least five or six experts or writers or spokesmen or some such stand up at various meetings and wonder aloud what happens to sex between men and women when the revolution comes. These men are always hooted down by the women present; in fact, I am usually one of the women present hooting them down, sniggering snide remarks to whoever is next to me like well-we-certainly-know-how-sure-of-himself-*he*-is. This fall, at the *Playboy* Writers' Convocation, an author named Morton Hunt uttered the magic words at a panel on The Future of Sex, and even in that room, full of male chauvinism and *Playboy* philosophers, the animosity against him was audible.

I spend a great deal of my energy these days trying to fit feminism into marriage, or vice versa—I'm never sure which way the priorities lie; it depends on my mood—but as truly committed as I am to the movement and as violent as I have become toward people who knock it, I think it is unfair to dismiss these men. They deserve some kind of answer. Okay. The answer is, nobody knows what happens to sex after liberation. It's a big mystery. And now that I have gotten that out of the way, I can go on to what really interests and puzzles me about sex and liberation—which is that it is difficult for me to see how sexual behavior and relations between the sexes can change at all unless our sexual fantasies change. So many of the conscious and unconscious ways men and women treat each other have to do with romantic and sexual fantasies that are deeply ingrained, not just in society but in literature. The movement may manage to clean up the mess in society, but I don't know whether it can ever clean up the mess in our minds.

I am somewhat liberated by current standards, but I have in my head this dreadful unliberated sex fantasy. One of the women in my consciousness-raising group is always referring to her "rich fantasy life," by which I suppose she means that in her fantasies she makes it in costume, or in exotic places, or with luminaries like Mao Tse-tung in a large bowl of warm Wheatena. My fantasy life is unfortunately nowhere near that interesting.

Several years ago, I went to interview photographer Philippe Halsman, whose notable achievements include a charming book containing photographs of celebrities jumping. The jumps are quite revealing in a predictable sort of way—Richard Nixon with his rigid, constricted jump, the Duke and Duchess of Windsor in a deeply dependent jump. And so forth. In the course of the interview, Halsman asked me if I wanted to jump for him; seeing it as a way to avoid possible years of psychoanalysis, I agreed. I did what I thought was my quintessential jump. "Do it again," said Halsman. I did, attempting to duplicate exactly what I had done before. "Again," he said, and I did. "Well," said Halsman, "I can see from your jump that you are a very determined, ambitious, directed person, but you will never write a novel." "Why is that?" I asked. "Because you have only one jump in you," he said.

At the time, I thought that was really unfair—I had, after all, thought he wanted to see the *same* jump, not a different one every time; but I see now that he was exactly right. I have only one jump in me. I see this more and more every day. I am no longer interested in thirty-one flavors; I stick with English toffee. More to the point, I have had the same sex fantasy, with truly minor variations, since I was about eleven years old. It is really a little weird to be stuck with something so crucially important for so long; I have managed to rid myself of all the other accoutrements of being eleven—I have pimples more or less under control, I can walk fairly capably in high heels— but I find myself with this appalling fantasy that has burrowed in and has absolutely nothing to do with my life.

I have never told anyone the exact details of my particular sex fantasy: it is my only secret and I am not going to divulge it here. I once told *almost* all of it to my former therapist; he died last year, and when I saw his obituary I felt a great sense of relief: the only person in the world who almost knew how crazy I am was gone and I was safe. Anyway, without giving away any of the juicy parts, I can tell you that in its broad outlines it has largely to do with being dominated by faceless males who rip my clothes off. That's just about all they have to do. Stare at me in this faceless way, go mad with desire, and rip my clothes off. It's terrific. In my sex fantasy, nobody ever loves me for my mind.

The fantasy of rape—of which mine is in a kind of pre-pubescent sub-category—is common enough among women and (in mirror image) among men. And what I don't understand is that with so many of us stuck with these clichéd feminine/masculine, sub-

missive/dominant, masochistic/sadistic fantasies, how are we ever
going to adjust fully to the less thrilling but more desirable reality of
equality? A few months ago, someone named B. Lyman Steward, a
urologist at Cedars of Lebanon Hospital in Los Angeles, attributed
the rising frequency of impotence among his male patients to the
women's movement, which he called an effort to dominate men. The
movement is nothing of the kind; but it and a variety of other events
in society have certainly brought about a change in the way women
behave in bed. A young man who grows up expecting to dominate
sexually is bound to be somewhat startled by a young woman who
wants sex as much as he does, and multi-orgasmic sex at that. By the
same token, I suspect that a great deal of the difficulty women report
in achieving orgasm is traceable—sadly—to the possibility that a man
who is a tender fellow with implicit capabilities for impotence hardly
fits into classic fantasies of big brutes with implicit capabilites for
violence. A close friend who has the worst marriage I know—her
husband beats her up regularly—reports that her sex life is wonderful. I am hardly suggesting that women ask their men to beat them—
nor am I advocating the course apparently preferred by one of the
most prominent members of the women's movement, who makes it
mainly with blue-collar workers and semiliterates. But I wonder how
we will ever break free from all the nonsense we grew up with; I
wonder if our fantasies can ever catch up to what we all want for our
lives.

It is possible, through sheer willpower, to stop having unhealthy sex fantasies. I have several friends who did just that. "What
do you have instead?" I asked. "Nothing," they replied. Well, I don't
know. I'm not at all sure I wouldn't rather have an unhealthy sex
fantasy than no sex fantasy at all. But my real question is whether it
is possible, having discarded the fantasy, to discard the thinking and
expectations it represents. In my case, I'm afraid it wouldn't be. I
have no desire to be dominated. Honestly I don't. And yet I find
myself becoming angry when I'm not. My husband has trouble hailing a cab or flagging a waiter, and suddenly I feel a kind of rage; ball-
breaking anger rises to my T-zone. I wish he were better at hailing
taxis than I am; on the other hand, I realize that expectation is
culturally conditioned, utterly foolish, has nothing to do with anything, is exactly the kind of thinking that ought to be got rid of in our
society; on still another hand, having that insight into my reaction
does not seem to calm my irritation.

My husband is fond of reminding me of the story of Moses,
who kept the Israelites in the desert for forty years because he knew a
slave generation could not found a new free society. The comparison
with the women's movement is extremely apt, I think; I doubt that it

will ever be possible for the women of my generation to escape from our own particular slave mentality. For the next generation, life may indeed be freer. After all, if society changes, the fantasies will change; where women are truly equal, where their status has nothing to do with whom they marry, when the issues of masculine/feminine cease to exist, some of this absurd reliance on role playing will be eliminated. But not all of it. Because even after the revolution, we will be left with all the literature. "What will happen to the literature?" Helen Dudar of the New York *Post* once asked Ti-Grace Atkinson. "What does it matter what happens?" Ms. Atkinson replied. But it does. You are what you eat. After liberation, we will still have to reckon with the Sleeping Beauty and Cinderella. Granted there will also be a new batch of fairy tales about princesses who refuse to have ladies-in-waiting because it is exploitative of the lower classes—but that sounds awfully tedious, doesn't it? Short of a mass book burning, which no one wants, things may well go on as they are now: women pulled between the intellectual attraction of liberation and the emotional, psychological, and cultural mishmash it's hard to escape growing up with; men trying to cope with these two extremes, and with their own ambivalence besides. It's not much fun this way, but at least it's not boring.

July, 1972

PROBING FOR
MEANING

1. What is the thesis of the essay? What does the author feel must change before there is a change in relations between the sexes? Why?

2. What does the author's jumping experience with Philippe Halsman tell the author about herself? In this regard, what does Ephron realize about her unliberated sexual fantasy?

3. Why does Ephron assume that equality would be less thrilling? Do you agree? Explain. What does the author feel about the continual linking of the women's movement with the increasing frequency of impotence?

4. What does the author's anger at her husband suggest? Why, although she recognizes that her anger is irrational, does she still become angry?

5. Why is the story of Moses "extremely apt" when applied to the contemporary women's movement?

6. What is the author's concluding statement on the question she has set out to investigate? What will be the influence of literature in the future? Do you believe that equality can be achieved? Explain.

PROBING FOR
METHOD   1. What function does the introduction serve? Why is the thesis
not presented until the second paragraph?

2. How would you describe Ephron's writing style? Do you feel
that she is objective? Do you feel that she is open and honest in relating
her ideas about sexual fantasies?

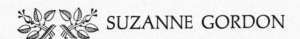 SUZANNE GORDON

The Geography of Loneliness

To be alone is to be different, to be different is to be alone,
and to be in the interior of this fatal circle is to be lonely. To be lonely
is to have failed. There is no excuse for that. It is clear to the teenager
that he or she should have a date after school, and it is clear to the
average man or woman that he or she should have a mate, family, a
circle of friends. Or a consciousness-raising group—intimacy. There
are maps to follow to get you there: grade school, high school,
perhaps college, church, company, promotion. Or the People's Yellow
Pages. We live in an era of openness and possibility. Never has there
been so much talk of sharing, so many books and courses to facilitate
smooth relating, explaining both how to begin and, in case of a mix-
up, how to end. The tight boundaries of rural, neighborhood, family-
centered America have burst, breaking the bonds of exclusiveness and
duty, freeing people for alternatives that seem to have no end, so
much do they promise. And yet—the problem of loneliness. When it
is mentioned, even the eyes of those who tend to deny its existence
flicker inward for a moment.

Life in America has exploded, and loneliness is one main
ingredient in the fallout. What was once a philosophical problem,
spoken of mainly by poets and prophets, has now become an almost
permanent condition for millions of Americans, not only for the old
or divorced but also for the men and women filling singles bars and
encounter groups, the adolescents running away from home or refusing to go to school, the corporate transients who move every two
or three years, and the people calling suicide and crisis hot-lines in
search of someone to talk to. Knowing no limits of class, race, or age,
loneliness is today a great leveler, a new American tradition.

To begin to understand the origins of the problem, one need only look at New York's high-rises, Los Angeles' pedestrianless streets, suburbia's front-porchless houses. The halls of large apartment buildings do not encourage conversation, nor do the aisles of supermarkets, the noise of factory assembly lines and factory-like offices, or the forbidding streets of the metropolitan areas that house 69 percent of the American population. Despite all the recently voiced desire for contact, there are few places where it can be made, spontaneously or otherwise. In the great rush for freedom we have lost the ability to be free together. And since personal identity seems to require the validation of another person's confirmation, many people feel faceless—empty, lonely.

In small towns or urban neighborhoods people had more than one strong relationship to affirm who they were. In their daily lives they reinforced and created networks of contacts. Doing daily chores, for instance, meant more than just purchasing the makings of the evening meal, cleaning the front stoop, or mailing a letter. These were more than just burdensome responsibilities, they were social events through which people gave each other mutual recognition. Today's American marvels at the "quaint" Europeans who still shop daily for groceries, visiting three or four small shops and taking as much time to buy food for a meal or two as an American in a supermarket might take to buy all the week's groceries. It's more than a question of pace; it's a question of people. It's pleasant to chat with your butcher or baker, to be handed a can rather than to take it off the rack in a store where efficiency has replaced humanity.

In rural settings people might, as the cliché goes, have known everybody else's business; but they were also there to help during a crisis, and one did not have to worry about calling for help in such a situation. Not so in contemporary America, as one California suburban resident vividly commented. When her husband had a stroke she hesitated before picking up the phone to call a neighbor for help. It could have been an imposition. In small towns or extended families, not to have called would have been the insult. A woman rancher living alone in Montana explained that during the winter she calls her closest neighbors, who live miles away, to tell them when she leaves to feed her cows and when she returns. "If I don't call," she said, "my neighbors are furious. They'll have to come looking for me and take care of me if I should fall from my horse or have an accident. It saves them worry. They know something is really wrong if they don't hear the phone ring." Among the most rugged of America's rugged individualists such concern is second-sense. There is an aura of community that leaves the most physically isolated people with the feeling that they *belong*.

In the past, rural areas and urban neighborhoods also provided a center where people of all ages could meet. The old could maintain contact with the young, and youth had some familiarity with aging and death. Although generational conflict has always been present, old people and young were not as radically separated, with the old set aside and doomed to loneliness in euphemistically characterized "senior citizens' communities." Today age segregation has passed all sane limits. Not only are fifteen-year-olds isolated from seventy-year-olds but social groups divide those in high school from those in junior high, and those who are twenty from those who are twenty-five. There are middle-middle-age groups, late-middle-age groups, and old-age groups—as though people with five years between them could not possibly have anything in common. Like white light going through a prism, America divides into its component parts.

Mobility has a great deal to do with this erosion of American life. People move with such astounding frequency (40 million Americans change their residence once a year, and the average person will move fourteen times in his or her lifetime) that they lose family ties, friends, and themselves. There is a myth among the most highly mobile (corporate transients, academics, and those in the armed services) that those who have met in the past will, at one point or another, meet again. They will not entirely lose touch. There are also the mails, phone lines, and air routes. Just because we live three thousand miles apart doesn't mean it's over. You can call after six o'clock, visit regularly. Technology, however, is unable to completely vanquish distance. And distance undoes the ties formed by frequent contact—the thing that makes friends friends. People do indeed lose each other, and the pain of that loss, renewed every two or three years, makes people withdraw from further contact. "I sometimes feel that I don't ever want to make friends again," the wife of a university professor said. "You find people to get close to, and then they leave or you leave. At first it seems this will happen only every once in a while. But it happens over and over again. I sometimes wish I lived in a Chinese village where nothing changes and you know everyone from birth till they die."

Mobility does more than affect close friendships; it changes the whole tone of a neighborhood. When people lived in the same place for years, residents in a community knew one another. When someone moved onto the block you brought cake or candy. Today it is not unusual for people not to know their neighbors at all. Why should one make the effort of a welcome when the new arrivals will be leaving in a year? No sense wasting the energy. I knocked on the doors of a residence hall at the New York Hospital–Cornell Medical

Center in Manhattan to ask the residents if they knew their neighbors or socialized with people living near them. All the residents in the building are doctors, nurses, or technicians; all are interested in the same things, presumably having strong interconnections. Yet very few even knew the names of the peole living directly next door, and almost none met socially. Only the women with children met—and the children made much of the effort. It seems that even where we are the closest we can neither reach nor touch.

This communal apathy is also fertile soil for crime, since people have no idea which face goes with which front door. If someone walks out of the house with a TV set, a neighbor has no idea if it is the owner taking it to the repair shop or a burglar making off with an easy haul. And crime has never been noted for its healthy effect on human relationships. You are not likely to enter into a spontaneous conversation on the street if you think the person addressing you is a potential mugger, or open your door at night to help someone in trouble if you think that person might pull a knife. In a circular swing, more distrust and more loneliness. We feel like strangers on our own streets. Where we should feel the safest, we rather feel that no one would help us if we were in trouble, that what happens to us, whether good or bad, makes no difference to the world around us— that *we* make no difference. And because we tolerate such antihuman life-styles, the encounters we have with others are more likely to be hostile than pleasant. It is not only the muggers that are frightening but the faces of shoppers waiting on lines that are too long, and the ferociousness with which commuters honk their horns and curse in heavy traffic.

Another disturbing effect of the isolation from family, friends, and community is the added difficulty it imposes on the average marriage. Besides socially inherited communication problems and increasing dissatisfaction with our work, modern marriages have to cope with the added burdens of high mobility. In the past, husband and wife were to be "the one" for each other, the perfect companion. Now a woman or man must be not only confidant and lover, but family, community, friends—all things to one other man or woman.

In the past, relationships founded on large families and close communities gave people some options if things weren't going well at home. Today, when family bonds are weaker, more and more is being asked of the nuclear unit. It is as though one loaded a table with heavier and heavier weights while shrinking the circumference of the tabletop and chopping at its legs. The table will eventually collapse— just as the nuclear family is collapsing.

Change, mobility, freedom from burdensome commitments—

all these can be exciting and enriching. Apologists for discontinuity in American life are fond of drawing upon an analogy between trees and people to support their positions. It is true, they admit, that some trees, in order to grow strong and healthy, need a great deal of time in one place so that they can send down solid, deep roots. Other varieties, however, can grow healthy despite frequent transplants and shallow roots. But the problem is that people are simply not trees. Trees, whether shallowly or deeply rooted, do not, as far as we know, need communication with other trees in order to flourish. Standing alone, they do not feel lonely.

What began as a great adventure may be turning into just another fetter. In retrospect, it is not clear from what exactly we have been running. Were small towns, for instance, suffocating or idyllic? Were ethnic, urban neighborhoods prisons or protectors? But whatever complicated reasons are behind the constant push for change and movement in urban and suburban America, people have a vision of where they are heading: toward technical and social progress—by definition a better state. What *will be* in America has generally been taken to be inherently superior to what *was*.

Our present, however, makes it abundantly clear that the price for such passionate optimism is the shattering of both personal and community life. It is a process that can only destroy much of the potential the future may hold and that is certainly demolishing any hope we may have in the present. We are paving the road forward with psychological wreckage, obstacles that make it impossible for many to make the journey and that provide a bumpy ride for those still able to travel.

Though there has been some attempt to treat the causes of the problem of "future shock," much of the emphasis has been toward disguising it—patching up the cuts, passing out the Valium,* and hoping that the patient won't cause too much trouble in the future. For the most part, however, people are left alone to deal with the traumatic loneliness in modern life. And so for many Americans life becomes a bit like playing the stock market in a time of recession: one is less concerned with maximizing one's gains than with minimizing one's losses. To borrow from Karen Horney's description of the major preoccupation of neurotics, we are forced to seek safety rather than satisfaction, despite all our claims to the contrary.

* According to a *New York Times* article of May 19, 1974, Valium is the most widely prescribed drug in the U.S., with one in ten Americans of eighteen years or over having used it at some time for various problems. Women, the article states, use the drug more frequently than men. And Valium is only one of many tranquilizers used.

It's obvious that loneliness is a human emotion common to all people in all eras. But at certain points in history, because of specific social changes, what were inevitable moments in life become, sometimes overnight, life-styles for millions of people. Mass loneliness is not just a problem that can be coped with by the particular individuals involved; it is an indication that things are drastically amiss on a societal level.

When the societal is distinguished from the psychological, as Jung has noted, an individual experience becomes a collective disturbance—a "social problem" in the sense in which Michel Philibert, the French gerontologist, uses the phrase. A social problem, says Philibert, is one that affects a category or group of people in a society, provided that the problem carries the following three qualifications:

1. It must be considered as deriving, at least in part, from the functioning of the structure of society itself.

2. It must be considered as affecting not only the category or group of people primarily involved but in some way having a pervasive influence on the rest of society, so that other people who do not face that specific difficulty are concerned about it; and it is seen as jeopardizing the whole fabric of society and endangering the development of the health of the society, so that those not directly affected are made uneasy and think something should be done about this problem.

3. It must be considered as being susceptible to some sort of treatment through the action of society itself—that is, social action, and in the long run through political action.*

People have always had to deal with hate and love, anxiety, aggression, violence, and loneliness. In certain epochs, however, these universals become the simultaneously held *preoccupation* of a major segment of the population. And the intensity of this concern is such that even those who do not feel it directly are disturbed.

To understand and begin to deal with loneliness as it exists today in America we must therefore consider more than the personal history of the particular lonely person and his or her emotional background. We cannot interpret the present problem exclusively in terms of childhood traumas: lack of affection from parents, for example, lack of openness, and thus loneliness. For present difficulties, while they encompass the problems of the past, are not simply mere reflections of it. The lonely person is not, as is commonly thought by many psychologists, lonely because he or she *needs to be lonely,* and is thus somehow enjoying it. People are lonely today because of both the psychological baggage they carry with them and the peculiar way

* From a lecture, "The Third Age," at the University of California, San Francisco, August 1973.

American society alienates the potentially closest of friends, colleagues, lovers, and workmates.*

<table>
<tr><td>

PROBING FOR
MEANING

</td><td>

1. What change has occurred in contemporary America to produce so much emphasis on intimacy and openness? Why has this change also produced loneliness?

2. In what way can loneliness be viewed as a "great leveler" and a "new American tradition"?

3. Gordon focuses attention on environment and living conditions to explain the increasing frequency of loneliness. What contrast is presented between the contemporary situation and the past? Why did past conditions promote self-affirmation and self-identity? Why did previous social conditions not lead to age segregation, while contemporary conditions do?

4. What is the effect on society of the rapidly increasing mobility of Americans? What has mobility done to friendships? Why does the author feel that distance separates people, despite modern technological advances? What effect does mobility have on crime? Finally, what added pressure has it placed on marriage?

5. The author feels that "disguising" the problem is part of the problem. How does he refute the argument of certain social observers that people can be compared to trees? With whom do you agree? Explain.

6. If, as the author readily admits, loneliness has been present in all eras, what distinguishes the contemporary situation? What, according to Philibert, are the three qualifications necessary for loneliness to be regarded as a social problem? Has Gordon sufficiently established the application of these three factors to loneliness? Is it true that contemporary loneliness is not merely a reflection of the past or previous experiences, or an expression of a need to be lonely, but an American social problem?

</td></tr>
<tr><td>

PROBING FOR
METHOD

</td><td>

1. What effect is achieved by the opening line: "To be alone is to be different, to be different is to be alone, and to be in the interior of this fatal circle is to be lonely"?

2. Give specific examples of the author's use of metaphorical language in the essay. What is the function of these comparisons?

</td></tr>
</table>

* I [am] accusing American society of various significant failings, and considering loneliness in the light of these. This is not to say that other countries do not share the same shortcomings or have the same problems. We are, however, Americans, and our major concern is with America. To excuse our problems by pointing out that things are no better elsewhere is irrelevant to any attempt at social change at home. America is, furthermore, one of the most industrially advanced countries, and the problems that result from mobility and disintegration of the family and community dominate life. Thus if we see loneliness as being inherently related to these aspects of modern life, we must admit that loneliness is more of a problem in a more advanced country such as America than in less industrially advanced societies.

3. What does the example of the Montana ranchers demonstrate about rural communities? Why does the author select this particular example?

4. Briefly, how does the author organize the essay to lead to Philibert's three qualifications? Has criteria on the second qualification been sufficiently established? What evidence for this criteria is presented by Gordon?

 TILLIE OLSEN

I Stand Here Ironing

I stand here ironing, and what you asked me moves tormented back and forth with the iron.

"I wish you would manage the time to come in and talk with me about your daughter. I'm sure you can help me understand her. She's a youngster who needs help and whom I'm deeply interested in helping."

"Who needs help." Even if I came, what good would it do? You think because I am her mother I have a key, or that in some way you could use me as a key? She has lived for nineteen years. There is all that life that has happened outside of me, beyond me.

And when is there time to remember, to sift, to weigh, to estimate, to total? I will start and there will be an interruption and I will have to gather it all together again. Or I will become engulfed with all I did or did not do, with what should have been and what cannot be helped.

She was a beautiful baby. The first and only one of our five that was beautiful at birth. You do not guess how new and uneasy her tenancy in her now-loveliness. You did not know her all those years she was thought homely, or see her poring over her baby pictures, making me tell her over and over how beautiful she had been—and would be, I would tell her—and was now, to the seeing eye. But the seeing eyes were few or nonexistent. Including mine.

I nursed her. They feel that's important nowadays. I nursed all the children, but with her, with all the fierce rigidity of first motherhood, I did like the books then said. Though her cries battered me to trembling and my breasts ached with swollenness, I waited till the clock decreed.

Why do I put that first? I do not even know if it matters, or if it explains anything.

She was a beautiful baby. She blew shining bubbles of sound. She loved motion, loved light, loved color and music and textures. She would lie on the floor in her blue overalls patting the surface so hard in ecstasy her hands and feet would blur. She was a miracle to me, but when she was eight months old I had to leave her daytimes with the woman downstairs to whom she was no miracle at all, for I worked or looked for work and for Emily's father, who "could no longer endure" (he wrote in his good-bye note) "sharing want with us."

I was nineteen. It was the pre-relief, pre-WPA world of the depression. I would start running as soon as I got off the streetcar, running up the stairs, the place smelling sour, and awake or asleep to startle awake, when she saw me she would break into a clogged weeping that could not be comforted, a weeping I can hear yet.

After a while I found a job hashing at night so I could be with her days, and it was better. But it came to where I had to bring her to his family and leave her.

It took a long time to raise the money for her fare back. Then she got chicken pox and I had to wait longer. When she finally came, I hardly knew her, walking quick and nervous like her father, looking like her father, thin, and dressed in a shoddy red that yellowed her skin and glared at the pockmarks. All the baby loveliness gone.

She was two. Old enough for nursery school they said, and I did not know then what I know now—the fatigue of the long day, and the lacerations of group life in nurseries that are only parking places for children.

Except that it would have made no difference if I had known. It was the only place there was. It was the only way we could be together, the only way I could hold a job.

And even without knowing, I knew. I knew the teacher that was evil because all these years it has curdled into my memory, the little boy hunched in the corner, her rasp, "why aren't you outside, because Alvin hits you? that's no reason, go out, scaredy." I knew Emily hated it even if she did not clutch and implore "don't go Mommy" like the other children, mornings.

She always had a reason why we should stay home. Momma, you look sick, Momma. I feel sick. Momma, the teachers aren't there today, they're sick. Momma, we can't go, there was a fire there last night. Momma, it's a holiday today, no school, they told me.

But never a direct protest, never rebellion. I think of our

others in their three-, four-year-oldness—the explosions, the tempers, the denunciations, the demands—and I feel suddenly ill. I put the iron down. What in me demanded that goodness in her? And what was the cost, the cost to her of such goodness?

The old man living in the back once said in his gentle way: "You should smile at Emily more when you look at her." What *was* in my face when I looked at her? I loved her. There were all the acts of love.

It was only with the others I remembered what he said, and it was the face of joy, and not of care or tightness or worry I turned to them—too late for Emily. She does not smile easily, let alone almost always as her brothers and sisters do. Her face is closed and sombre, but when she wants, how fluid. You must have seen it in her pantomimes, you spoke of her rare gift for comedy on the stage that rouses a laughter out of the audience so dear they applaud and applaud and do not want to let her go.

Where does it come from, that comedy? There was none of it in her when she came back to me that second time, after I had had to send her away again. She had a new daddy now to learn to love, and I think perhaps it was a better time.

Except when we left her alone nights, telling ourselves she was old enough.

"Can't you go some other time, Mommy, like tomorrow?" she would ask. "Will it be just a little while you'll be gone? Do you promise?"

The time we came back, the front door open, the clock on the floor in the hall. She rigid awake. "It wasn't just a little while. I didn't cry. Three times I called you, just three times, and then I ran downstairs to open the door so you could come faster. The clock talked loud. I threw it away, it scared me what it talked."

She said the clock talked loud again that night I went to the hospital to have Susan. She was delirious with the fever that comes before red measles, but she was fully conscious all the week I was gone and the week after we were home when she could not come near the new baby or me.

She did not get well. She stayed skeleton thin, not wanting to eat, and night after night she had nightmares. She would call for me, and I would rouse from exhaustion to sleepily call back: "You're all right, darling, go to sleep, it's just a dream," and if she still called, in a sterner voice, "now go to sleep, Emily, there's nothing to hurt you." Twice, only twice, when I had to get up for Susan anyhow, I went in to sit with her.

Now when it is too late (as if she would let me hold and comfort her like I do the others) I get up and go to her at once at her moan or restless stirring. "Are you awake, Emily? Can I get you something?" And the answer is always the same: "No, I'm all right, go back to sleep, Mother."

They persuaded me at the clinic to send her away to a convalescent home in the country where "she can have the kind of food and care you can't manage for her, and you'll be free to concentrate on the new baby." They still send children to that place. I see pictures on the society page of sleek young women planning affairs to raise money for it, or dancing at the affairs, or decorating Easter eggs or filling Christmas stockings for the children.

They never have a picture of the children so I do not know if the girls still wear those gigantic red bows and the ravaged looks on the every other Sunday when parents can come to visit "unless otherwise notified"—as we were notified the first six weeks.

Oh it is a handsome place, green lawns and tall trees and fluted flower beds. High up on the balconies of each cottage the children stand, the girls in their red bows and white dresses, the boys in white suits and giant red ties. The parents stand below shrieking up to be heard and the children shriek down to be heard, and between them the invisible wall "Not To Be Contaminated by Parental Germs or Physical Affection."

There was a tiny girl who always stood hand in hand with Emily. Her parents never came. One visit she was gone. "They moved her to Rose College," Emily shouted in explanation. "They don't like you to love anybody here."

She wrote once a week, the labored writing of a seven-year-old. "I am fine. How is the baby. If I write my leter nicly I will have a star. Love." There never was a star. We wrote every other day, letters she could never hold or keep but only hear read—once. "We simply do not have room for children to keep any personal possessions," they patiently explained when we pieced one Sunday's shrieking together to plead how much it would mean to Emily, who loved so to keep things, to be allowed to keep her letters and cards.

Each visit she looked frailer. "She isn't eating," they told us.

(They had runny eggs for breakfast or mush with lumps, Emily said later, I'd hold it in my mouth and not swallow. Nothing ever tasted good, just when they had chicken.)

It took us eight months to get her released home, and only the fact that she gained back so little of her seven lost pounds convinced the social worker.

I used to try to hold and love her after she came back, but her body would stay stiff, and after a while she'd push away. She ate little. Food sickened her, and I think much of life too. Oh she had physical lightness and brightness, twinkling by on skates, bouncing like a ball up and down up and down over the jump rope, skimming over the hill; but these were momentary.

She fretted about her appearance, thin and dark and foreign-looking at a time when every little girl was supposed to look or thought she should look a chubby blonde replica of Shirley Temple. The doorbell sometimes rang for her, but no one seemed to come and play in the house or be a best friend. Maybe because we moved so much.

There was a boy she loved painfully through two school semesters. Months later she told me how she had taken pennies from my purse to buy him candy. "Licorice was his favorite and I brought him some every day, but he still liked Jennifer better'n me. Why, Mommy?" The kind of question for which there is no answer.

School was a worry to her. She was not glib or quick in a world where glibness and quickness were easily confused with ability to learn. To her overworked and exasperated teachers she was an overconscientious "slow learner" who kept trying to catch up and was absent entirely too often.

I let her be absent, though sometimes the illness was imaginary. How different from my now-strictness about attendance with the others. I wasn't working. We had a new baby, I was home anyhow. Sometimes, after Susan grew old enough, I would keep her home from school, too, to have them all together.

Mostly Emily had asthma, and her breathing, harsh and labored, would fill the house with a curiously tranquil sound. I would bring the two old dresser mirrors and her boxes of collections to her bed. She would select beads and single earrings, bottle tops and shells, dried flowers and pebbles, old postcards and scraps, all sorts of oddments; then she and Susan would play Kingdom, setting up landscapes and furniture, peopling them with action.

Those were the only times of peaceful companionship between her and Susan. I have edged away from it, that poisonous feeling between them, that terrible balancing of hurts and needs I had to do between the two, and did so badly, those earlier years.

Oh there are conflicts between the others too, each one human, needing, demanding, hurting, taking—but only between Emily and Susan, no, Emily toward Susan that corroding resentment. It seems so obvious on the surface, yet it is not obvious. Susan, the second child, Susan, golden- and curly-haired and chubby, quick and articulate and assured, everything in appearance and manner Emily was not; Susan, not able to resist Emily's precious things, losing or sometimes clumsily breaking them; Susan telling jokes and riddles to company for applause while Emily sat silent (to say to me later: that was *my* riddle, Mother, I told it to Susan); Susan, who for all the five years' difference in age was just a year behind Emily in developing physically.

I am glad for that slow physical development that widened the difference between her and her contemporaries, though she suffered over it. She was too vulnerable for that terrible world of youthful competition, of preening and parading, of constant measuring of yourself against every other, of envy, "If I had that copper hair," "If I had that skin. . . ." She tormented herself enough about not looking like the others, there was enough of the unsureness, the having to be conscious of words before you speak, the constant caring—what are they thinking of me? without having it all magnified by the merciless physical drives.

Ronnie is calling. He is wet and I change him. It is rare there is such a cry now. That time of motherhood is almost behind me when the ear is not one's own but must always be racked and listening for the child cry, the child call. We sit for a while and I hold him, looking out over the city spread in charcoal with its soft aisles of light. *"Shoogily,"* he breathes and curls closer. I carry him back to bed, asleep. *Shoogily.* A funny word, a family word, inherited from Emily, invented by her to say: *comfort.*

In this and other ways she leaves her seal, I say aloud. And startle at my saying it. What do I mean? What did I start to gather together, to try and make coherent? I was at the terrible, growing years. War years. I do not remember them well. I was working, there were four smaller ones now, there was not time for her. She had to help be a mother, and housekeeper, and shopper. She had to set her seal. Mornings of crisis and near hysteria trying to get lunches packed, hair combed, coats and shoes found, everyone to school or Child Care on time, the baby ready for transportation. And always the paper scribbled on by a smaller one, the book looked at by Susan then mislaid, the homework not done. Running out to that huge school where she was one, she was lost, she was a drop; suffering over the unpreparedness, stammering and unsure in her classes.

There was so little time left at night after the kids were bedded down. She would struggle over books, always eating (it was in those years she developed her enormous appetite that is legendary in our family) and I would be ironing, or preparing food for the next day, or writing V-mail to Bill, or tending the baby. Sometimes, to make me laugh, or out of her despair, she would imitate happenings or types at school.

I think I said once: "Why don't you do something like this in the school amateur show?" One morning she phoned me at work, hardly understandable through the weeping: "Mother, I did it. I won,

I won; they gave me first prize; they clapped and clapped and wouldn't let me go."

Now suddenly she was Somebody, and as imprisoned in her difference as she had been in anonymity.

She began to be asked to perform at other high schools, even in colleges, then at city and statewide affairs. The first one we went to, I only recognized her that first moment when thin, shy, she almost drowned herself into the curtains. Then: Was this Emily? The control, the command, the convulsing and deadly clowning, the spell, then the roaring, stamping audience, unwilling to let this rare and precious laughter out of their lives.

Afterwards: You ought to do something about her with a gift like that—but without money or knowing how, what does one do? We have left it all to her, and the gift has as often eddied inside, clogged and clotted, as been used and growing.

She is coming. She runs up the stairs two at a time with her light graceful step, and I know she is happy tonight. Whatever it was that occasioned your call did not happen today.

"Aren't you ever going to finish the ironing, Mother? Whistler painted his mother in a rocker. I'd have to paint mine standing over an ironing board." This is one of her communicative nights and she tells me everything and nothing as she fixes herself a plate of food out of the icebox.

She is so lovely. Why did you want me to come in at all? Why were you concerned? She will find her way.

She starts up the stairs to bed. "Don't get me up with the rest in the morning." "But I thought you were having midterms." "Oh, those," she comes back in, kisses me, and says quite lightly, "in a couple of years when we'll all be atom-dead they won't matter a bit."

She has said it before. She *believes* it. But because I have been dredging the past, and all that compounds a human being is so heavy and meaningful in me, I cannot endure it tonight.

I will never total it all. I will never come in to say: She was a child seldom smiled at. Her father left me before she was a year old. I had to work her first six years when there was work, or I sent her home and to his relatives. There were years she had care she hated. She was dark and thin and foreign-looking in a world where the prestige went to blondeness and curly hair and dimples, she was slow where glibness was prized. She was a child of anxious, not proud, love. We were poor and could not afford for her the soil of easy growth. I was a young mother, I was a distracted mother. There were the other children pushing up, demanding. Her younger sister seemed all that she was not. There were years she did not want me to touch her. She kept too much in herself, her life was such she had to keep too much in herself. My wisdom came too late. She has much to her and probably nothing will come of it. She is a child of her age, of depression, of war, of fear.

Let her be. So all that is in her will not bloom—but in how many does it? There is still enough left to live by. Only help her to know—help make it so there is cause for her to know—that she is more than this dress on the ironing board, helpless before the iron.

PROBING FOR
MEANING

1. To whom is the mother attempting to "total" Emily's life? Is the person actually in the room? Explain. Do we have any clues as to why Emily's mother has been contacted? Why is this person "deeply interested" in helping Emily?

2. What difficulties and general aspects of the mother's life caused her to leave Emily with other people or not give her the attention she needed? What were Emily's reactions?

3. Both the nursery school and the convalescent home existed to help children. How did both fail Emily badly? Why does the mother say of the nursery school teacher, "even without knowing, I knew"?

4. Emily never protested her hardships, leading her mother to realize suddenly that she had demanded much more goodness from Emily than from her other children. How have the lives of her brothers and sisters been different from Emily's? Why did the mother turn a face of joy to them but not to Emily? How has being good affected Emily?

5. Why, when the mother eventually realizes that Emily needs her and attempts to be affectionate, does Emily not respond?

6. What does Emily's reaction to Susan reveal about Emily?

7. Emily invented the word "shoogily." Why is this an appropriate word for her to have invented? Why is her mother frightened when she says, "In this and other ways she leaves her seal"?

8. Can you answer the mother's question, "Where does it come from, that comedy?" What relationship often exists between suffering and comedy?

9. How can Emily, the comedienne, be "as imprisoned in her difference as she had been in anonymity"?

10. What decision does the mother make at the end of the story? Why does she choose in this way? What effect will this choice have on Emily? Do you agree with her decision?

11. How do you feel about the mother? Is she defensive? Is she to be blamed in any way? How is she in many ways as important a character in the story as Emily?

PROBING FOR
METHOD

1. Discuss the use of the iron in the story. How does ironing affect our concept of the mother? How does the iron operate on the action of the story? Does it become a symbol at any point?

2. Why does the author make Emily a "beautiful baby" and a lovely young woman, but homely in between? Does her physical appearance, in other words, mirror her experiences in any way?

3. Notice how each paragraph leads into another. Why is this an effective technique for this particular story?

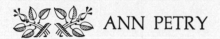 ANN PETRY

Like a Winding Sheet

He had planned to get up before Mae did and surprise her by fixing breakfast. Instead he went back to sleep and she got out of bed so quietly he didn't know she wasn't there beside him until he woke up and heard the queer soft gurgle of water running out of the sink in the bathroom.

He knew he ought to get up but instead he put his arms across his forehead to shut the afternoon sunlight out of his eyes, pulled his legs up close to his body, testing them to see if the ache was still in them.

Mae had finished in the bathroom. He could tell because she never closed the door when she was in there and now the sweet smell of talcum powder was drifting down the hall and into the bedroom. Then he heard her coming down the hall.

'Hi, babe,' she said affectionately.

'Hum,' he grunted, and moved his arms away from his head, opened one eye.

'It's a nice morning.'

'Yeah,' he rolled over and the sheet twisted around him, outlining his thighs, his chest. 'You mean afternoon, don't ya?'

Mae looked at the twisted sheet and giggled. 'Looks like a winding sheet,' she said. 'A shroud—.' Laughter tangled with her words and she had to pause for a moment before she could continue. 'You look like a huckleberry—in a winding sheet—'

'That's no way to talk. Early in the day like this,' he protested.

He looked at his arms silhouetted against the white of the sheets. They were inky black by contrast and he had to smile in spite of himself and he lay there smiling and savouring the sweet sound of Mae's giggling.

'Early?' She pointed a finger at the alarm clock on the table near the bed, and giggled again. 'It's almost four o'clock. And if you don't spring up out of there you're going to be late again.'

'What do you mean "again"?'

'Twice last week. Three times the week before. And once the week before and—'

'I can't get used to sleeping in the day time,' he said fretfully. He pushed his legs out from under the covers experimentally. Some of the ache had gone out of them but they weren't really rested yet. 'It's too light for good sleeping. And all that standing beats the hell out of my legs.'

'After two years you oughtta be used to it,' Mae said.

He watched her as she fixed her hair, powdered her face, slipping into a pair of blue denim overalls. She moved quickly and yet she didn't seem to hurry.

'You look like you'd had plenty of sleep,' he said lazily. He had to get up but he kept putting the moment off, not wanting to move, yet he didn't dare let his legs go completely limp because if he did he'd go back to sleep. It was getting later and later but the thought of putting his weight on his legs kept him lying there.

When he finally got up he had to hurry and he gulped his breakfast so fast that he wondered if his stomach could possibly use food thrown at it at such a rate of speed. He was still wondering about it as he and Mae were putting their coats on in the hall.

Mae paused to look at the calendar. 'It's the thirteenth,' she said. Then a faint excitement in her voice. 'Why it's Friday the thirteenth.' She had one arm in her coat sleeve and she held it there while she stared at the calendar. 'I oughtta stay home,' she said. 'I shouldn't go otta the house.'

'Aw don't be a fool,' he said. 'To-day's payday. And payday is a good luck day everywhere, any way you look at it.' And as she stood hesitating he said, 'Aw, come on.'

And he was late for work again because they spent fifteen minutes arguing before he could convince her she ought to go to work just the same. He had to talk persuasively, urging her gently and it took time. But he couldn't bring himself to talk to her roughly or threaten to strike her like a lot of men might have done. He wasn't made that way.

So when he reached the plant he was late and he had to wait to punch the time clock because the day shift workers were streaming out in long lines, in groups and bunches that impeded his progress.

Even now just starting his work-day his legs ached. He had to force himself to struggle past the out-going workers, punch the time clock, and get the little cart he pushed around all night because he kept toying with the idea of going home and getting back in bed.

He pushed the cart out on the concrete floor, thinking that if this was his plant he'd make a lot of changes in it. There were too many standing up jobs for one thing. He'd figure out some way most of 'em could be done sitting down and he'd put a lot more benches around. And this job he had—this job that forced him to walk ten hours a night, pushing this little cart, well, he'd turn it into a sittin'-down job. One of those little trucks they used around railroad stations would be good for a job like this. Guys sat on a seat and the thing moved easily, taking up little room and turning in hardly any space at all, like on a dime.

He pushed the cart near the foreman. He never could remember to refer to her as the forelady even in his mind. It was funny to have a woman for a boss in a plant like this one.

She was sore about something. He could tell by the way her face was red and her eyes were half shut until they were slits. Probably been out late and didn't get enough sleep. He avoided looking at her and hurried a little, head down, as he passed her though he couldn't resist stealing a glance at her out of the corner of his eyes. He saw the edge of the light colored slacks she wore and the tip end of a big tan shoe.

'Hey, Johnson!' the woman said.

The machines had started full blast. The whirr and the grinding made the building shake, made it impossible to hear conversations. The men and women at the machines talked to each other but looking at them from just a little distance away they appeared to be simply moving their lips because you couldn't hear what they were saying. Yet the woman's voice cut across the machine sounds—harsh, angry.

He turned his head slowly. 'Good Evenin', Mrs. Scott,' he said and waited.

'You're late again.'

'That's right. My legs were bothering me.'

The woman's face grew redder, angrier looking. 'Half this shift comes in late,' she said. 'And you're the worst one of all. You're always late. Whatsa matter with ya?'

'It's my legs,' he said. 'Somehow they don't ever get rested. I don't seem to get used to sleeping days. And I just can't get started.'

'Excuses. You guys always got excuses,' her anger grew and spread. 'Every guy comes in here late always has an excuse. His wife's sick or his grandmother died or somebody in the family had to go to the hospital,' she paused, drew a deep breath. 'And the niggers are the worse. I don't care what's wrong with your legs. You get in here on time. I'm sick of you niggers—'

'You got the right to get mad,' he interrupted softly. 'You got the right to cuss me four ways to Sunday but I ain't letting nobody call me a nigger.'

He stepped closer to her. His fists were doubled. His lips were drawn back in a thin narrow line. A vein in his forehead stood out swollen, thick.

And the woman backed away from him, not hurriedly but slowly—two, three steps back.

'Aw, forget it,' she said. 'I didn't mean nothing by it. It slipped out. It was a accident.' The red of her face deepened until the small blood vessels in her cheeks were purple. 'Go on and get to work,' she urged. And she took three more slow backward steps.

He stood motionless for a moment and then turned away from the red lipstick on her mouth that made him remember that the foreman was a woman. And he couldn't bring himself to hit a woman. He felt a curious tingling in his fingers and he looked down at his hands. They were clenched tight, hard, ready to smash some of those small purple veins in her face.

He pushed the cart ahead of him, walking slowly. When he turned his head, she was staring in his direction, mopping her forehead with a dark blue handkerchief. Their eyes met and then they both looked away.

He didn't glance in her direction again but moved past the long work benches, carefully collecting the finished parts, going slowly and steadily up and down, back and forth the length of the building and as he walked he forced himself to swallow his anger, get rid of it.

And he succeeded so that he was able to think about what had happened without getting upset about it. An hour went by but the tension stayed in his hands. They were clenched and knotted on the handles of the cart as though ready to aim a blow.

And he thought he should have hit her anyway, smacked her hard in the face, felt the soft flesh of her face give under the hardness of his hands. He tried to make his hands relax by offering them a description of what it would have been like to strike her because he had the queer feeling that his hands were not exactly a part of him any more—they had developed a separate life of their own over which he had no control. So he dwelt on the pleasure his hands would have felt—both of them cracking at her, first one and then the other. If he had done that his hands would have felt good now—relaxed, rested.

And he decided that even if he'd lost his job for it he should have let her have it and it would have been a long time, maybe the rest of her life before she called anybody else a nigger.

The only trouble was he couldn't hit a woman. A woman

couldn't hit back the same way a man did. But it would have been a deeply satisfying thing to have cracked her narrow lips wide open with just one blow, beautifully timed and with all his weight in back of it. That way he would have gotten rid of all the energy and tension his anger had created in him. He kept remembering how his heart had started pumping blood so fast he had felt it tingle even in the tips of his fingers.

With the approach of night fatigue nibbled at him. The corners of his mouth dropped, the frown between his eyes deepened, his shoulders sagged; but his hands stayed tight and tense. As the hours dragged by he noticed that the women workers had started to snap and snarl at each other. He couldn't hear what they said because of the sound of machines but he could see the quick lip movements that sent words tumbling from the sides of their mouths. They gestured irritably with their hands and scowled as their mouths moved.

Their violent jerky motions told him that it was getting close on to quitting time but somehow he felt that the night still stretched ahead of him, composed of endless hours of steady walking on his aching legs. When the whistle finally blew he went on pushing the cart, unable to believe that it had sounded. The whirring of the machines died away to a murmur and he knew then that he'd really heard the whistle. He stood still for a moment filled with a relief that made him sigh.

Then he moved briskly, putting the cart in the store room, hurrying to take his place in the line forming before the paymaster. That was another thing he'd change, he thought. He'd have the pay envelopes handed to the people right at their benches so there wouldn't be ten or fifteen minutes lost waiting for the pay. He always got home about fifteen minutes late on payday. They did it better in the plant where Mae worked, brought the money right to them at their benches.

He stuck his pay envelope in his pants' pocket and followed the line of workers heading for the subway in a slow moving stream. He glanced up at the sky. It was a nice night, the sky looked packed full to running over with stars. And he thought if he and Mae would go right to bed when they got home from work they'd catch a few hours of darkness for sleeping. But they never did. They fooled around—cooking and eating and listening to the radio and he always stayed in a big chair in the living room and went almost but not quite to sleep and when they finally got to bed it was five or six in the morning and daylight was already seeping around the edges of the sky.

He walked slowly, putting off the movement when he would

have to plunge into the crowd hurrying toward the subway. It was a long ride to Harlem and tonight the thought of it appalled him. He paused outside an all-night restaurant to kill time, so that some of the first rush of workers would be gone when he reached the subway.

The lights in the restaurant were brilliant, enticing. There was life and motion inside. And as he looked through the window he thought that everything within range of his eyes gleamed—the long imitation marble counter, the tall stools, the white porcelain topped tables and especially the big metal coffee urn right near the window. Steam issued from its top and a gas flame flickered under it—a lively, dancing, blue flame.

A lot of the workers from his shift—men and women—were lining up near the coffee urn. He watched them walk to the porcelain topped tables carrying steaming cups of coffee and he saw that just the smell of the coffee lessened the fatigue lines in their faces. After the first sip their faces softened, they smiled, they began to talk and laugh.

On a sudden impulse he shoved the door open and joined the line in front of the coffee urn. The line moved slowly. And as he stood there the smell of the coffee, the sound of the laughter and of the voices, helped dull the sharp ache in his legs.

He didn't pay any attention to the girl who was serving the coffee at the urn. He kept looking at the cups in the hands of the men who had been ahead of him. Each time a man stepped out of the line with one of the thick white cups the fragrant steam got in his nostrils. He saw that they walked carefully so as not to spill a single drop. There was a froth of bubbles at the top of each cup and he thought about how he would let the bubbles break against his lips before he actually took a big deep swallow.

Then it was his turn. 'A cup of coffee,' he said, just as he had heard the others say.

The girl looked past him, put her hands up to her head and gently lifted her hair away from the back of her neck, tossing her head back a little. 'No more coffee for awhile,' she said.

He wasn't certain he'd heard her correctly and he said, 'What?' blankly.

'No more coffee for awhile,' she repeated.

There was silence behind him and then uneasy movement. He thought someone would say something, ask why or protest, but there was only silence and then a faint shuffling sound as though the men standing behind him had simultaneously shifted their weight from one foot to the other.

He looked at her without saying anything. He felt his hands begin to tingle and the tingling went all the way down to his finger tips so that he glanced down at them. They were clenched tight, hard, into fists. Then he looked at the girl again. What he wanted to do was hit her so hard that the scarlet lipstick on her mouth would smear and spread over her nose, her chin, out toward her cheeks; so hard that she would never toss her head again and refuse a man a cup of coffee because he was black.

He estimated the distance across the counter and reached forward, balancing his weight on the balls of his feet, ready to let the blow go. And then his hands fell back down to his sides because he forced himself to lower them, to unclench them and make them dangle loose. The effort took his breath away because his hands fought against him. But he couldn't hit her. He couldn't even now bring himself to hit a woman, not even this one, who had refused him a cup of coffee with a toss of her head. He kept seeing the gesture with which she had lifted the length of her blonde hair from the back of her neck as expressive of her contempt for him.

When he went out the door he didn't look back. If he had he would have seen the flickering blue flame under the shiny coffee urn being extinguished. The line of men who had stood behind him lingered a moment to watch the people drinking coffee at the tables and then they left just as he had without having had the coffee they wanted so badly. The girl behind the counter poured water in the urn and swabbed it out and as she waited for the water to run out she lifted her hair gently from the back of her neck and tossed her head before she began making a fresh lot of coffee.

But he walked away without a backward look, his head down, his hands in his pockets, raging at himself and whatever it was inside of him that had forced him to stand quiet and still when he wanted to strike out.

The subway was crowded and he had to stand. He tried grasping an overhead strap and his hands were too tense to grip it. So he moved near the train door and stood there swaying back and forth with the rocking of the train. The roar of the train beat inside his head, making it ache and throb, and the pain in his legs clawed up into his groin so that he seemed to be bursting with pain and he told himself that it was due to all that anger-born energy that had piled up in him and not been used and so it had spread through him like a poison—from his feet and legs all the way up to his head.

Mae was in the house before he was. He knew she was home before he put the key in the door of the apartment. The radio was going. She had it turned up loud and she was singing along with it.

'Hello, Babe,' she called out as soon as he opened the door.

He tried to say 'hello' and it came out half a grunt and half sigh.

'You sure sound cheerful,' she said.

She was in the bedroom and he went and leaned against the door jamb. The denim overalls she wore to work were carefully draped over the back of a chair by the bed. She was standing in front of the dresser, tying the sash of a yellow housecoat around her waist and chewing gum vigorously as she admired her reflection in the mirror over the dresser.

'Whatsa matter?' she said. 'You get bawled out by the boss or somep'n?'

'Just tired,' he said slowly. 'For God's sake do you have to crack that gum like that?'

'You don't have to lissen to me,' she said complacently. She patted a curl in place near the side of her head and then lifted her hair away from the back of her neck, ducking her head forward and then back.

He winced away from the gesture. 'What you got to be always fooling with your hair for?' he protested.

'Say, what's the matter with you, anyway?' she turned away from the mirror to face him, put her hands on her hips. 'You ain't been in the house two minutes and you're picking on me.'

He didn't answer her because her eyes were angry and he didn't want to quarrel with her. They'd been married too long and got along too well and so he walked all the way into the room and sat down in the chair by the bed and stretched his legs out in front of him, putting his weight on the heels of his shoes, leaning way back in the chair, not saying anything.

'Lissen,' she said sharply. 'I've got to wear those overalls again tomorrow. You're going to get them all wrinkled up leaning against them like that.'

He didn't move. He was too tired and his legs were throbbing now that he had sat down. Besides the overalls were already wrinkled and dirty, he thought. They couldn't help but be for she'd worn them all week. He leaned further back in the chair.

'Come on, get up,' she ordered.

'Oh, what the hell,' he said wearily and got up from the chair. 'I'd just as soon live in a subway. There's be just as much place to sit down.'

He saw that her sense of humor was struggling with her anger. But her sense of humor won because she giggled.

'Aw, come on and eat,' she said. There was a coaxing note in her voice. 'You're nothing but a old hungry nigger trying to act tough and—' she paused to giggle and then continued, 'You—'

He had always found her giggling pleasant and deliberately said things that might amuse her and then waited, listening for the delicate sound to emerge from her throat. This time he didn't even hear the giggle. He didn't let her finish what she was saying. She was standing close to him and that funny tingling started in his finger tips, went fast up his arms and sent his fist shooting straight for her face.

There was the smacking sound of soft flesh being struck by a hard object and it wasn't until she screamed that he realized he had hit her in the mouth—so hard that the dark red lipstick had blurred and spread over her full lips, reaching up toward the tip of her nose, down toward her chin, out toward her cheeks.

The knowledge that he had struck her seeped through him slowly and he was appalled but he couldn't drag his hands away from her face. He kept striking her and he thought with horror that something inside him was holding him, binding him to this act, wrapping and twisting about him so that he had to continue it. He had lost all control over his hands. And he groped for a phrase, a word, something to describe what this thing was like that was happening to him and he thought it was like being enmeshed in a winding sheet—that was it—like a winding sheet. And even as the thought formed in his mind his hands reached for her face again and yet again.

PROBING FOR MEANING

1. Explain the meaning of Mae's statement in the beginning of the story, "You look like a huckleberry in a winding sheet." What further significance does the phrase acquire when Johnson uses it at the end?

2. What role does color play as a cause of the relationships between the characters in the story: Johnson and Mrs. Scott; Johnson and the girl at the coffee shop; Johnson and Mae?

3. Discuss the restrictions on men's behavior of not being able to strike a woman as it affects Johnson and as it operates in life in general. Why does he finally "hit a lady"?

4. Which is the primary cause of Johnson's behavior: that you can't hit *any* woman but you can hit your wife? Or that you can't hit a white person but you can hit another black? In either case, is man justified in releasing his frustrations on those closest to him?

PROBING FOR METHOD

1. What is the effect of beginning the story with a nebulous "He" when the reader doesn't really discover who the "he" is until much later? Is the same effect also achieved with using "he" instead of "Johnson" so often throughout the text?

2. What single effect is this story talking about? How does Petry organize the causes leading to that effect?

3. What is the author's attitude toward Mae? Toward Johnson?

How do the descriptive phrases and the thought patterns help you determine these differing attitudes?

    4. The story is organized generally according to chronological sequence, but how does Petry keep it moving forward without the time structure being obtrusive?

 GARY GILDNER

First Practice

After the doctor checked to see
we weren't ruptured,
the man with the short cigar took us
under the grade school,
where we went in case of attack
or storm, and said
he was Clifford Hill, he was
a man who believed dogs
ate dogs, he had once killed
for his country, and if   10
there were any girls present
for them to leave now.
                         No one
left. OK, he said, he said I take
that to mean you are hungry
men who hate to lose as much
as I do. OK. Then
he made two lines of us
facing each other,
and across the way, he said,   20
is the man you hate most
in the world,
and if we are to win
that title I want to see how.
But I don't want to see
any marks when you're dressed,
he said. He said, *Now*.

PROBING FOR   1. What kind of person is the coach? What words and details
MEANING   convey the man's character?

        2. What persuasive, even coercive devices does he use on the boys? Why doesn't he want to see any marks on them when they are dressed? What symbolic significance does this remark acquire?

        3. The poem does not express in so many words the effects on the boys' lives of the forces put into motion by "the man with the short cigar." These effects, however, are the real subject of the poem. What are they?

PROBING FOR   1. The poem bristles with tense drama. What are some of its
METHOD   dramatic effects? How does the poet achieve them?

        2. What attitudes does Gildner convey toward the entire incident? What was his attitude at the time? Why might it have changed?

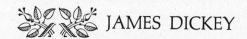 JAMES DICKEY

Adultery

We have all been in rooms
We cannot die in, and they are odd places, and sad
Often Indians are standing eagle-armed on hills

In the sunrise   open wide to the Great Spirit
Or gliding in canoes   or cattle are browsing on the walls
Far away   gazing down with the eyes of our children

Not far away   or there are men driving
The last railspike, which has turned
Gold in their hands. Gigantic forepleasure lives

Among such scenes, and we are alone with it   10
At last. There is always some weeping
Between us   and someone is always checking

A wrist watch by the bed to see how much
Longer we have left. Nothing can come
Of this   nothing can come

Of us: of me with my grim techniques
Or you who have sealed your womb
With a ring of convulsive rubber:

Although we come together,
Nothing will come of us. But we would not give   20
It up, for death is beaten

By praying Indians   by distant cows   historical
Hammers   by hazardous meetings that bridge
A continent. One could never die here

Never die   never die
While crying. My lover, my dear one
I will see you next week

When I'm in town. I will call you
If I can. Please get hold of   please don't
Oh God, Please don't any more I can't bear . . . Listen: 30

We have done it again   we are
Still living. Sit up and smile,
God bless you. Guilt is magical.

PROBING FOR
MEANING

1. How are the "rooms we cannot die in" described? Characterize the scenes that appear on the walls.

2. What is the meaning of the presence of "the eyes of our children"? Why is there weeping? Why do the two people check their wrist watches?

3. Why are the narrator's techniques "grim"? What is expressed by the fact that the woman has "sealed" her womb?

4. Although there is the recognition that "nothing can come of us," why do they continue to meet?

5. What is the meaning of the line "one could never die here"? What is being expressed about the relationship between sex and death? In this connection, why is guilt "magical"?

PROBING FOR
METHOD

1. What words and images emphasize the joyless nature of their union?

2. How does the poem's structure help emphasize the narrator's ambivalent feelings?

3. In what way does the poem build to a climax? What change in rhythm occurs in the last three lines?

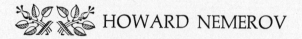

HOWARD NEMEROV

To David, About His Education

The world is full of mostly invisible things,
And there is no way but putting the mind's eye,
Or its nose, in a book, to find them out,
Things like the square root of Everest
Or how many times Byron goes into Texas,
Or whether the law of the excluded middle
Applies west of the Rockies. For these
And the like reasons, you have to go to school
And study books and listen to what you are told,
And sometimes try to remember. Though I don't know   10
What you will do with the mean annual rainfall
On Plato's Republic, or the calorie content
Of the Diet of Worms, such things are said to be
Good for you, and you will have to learn them
In order to become one of the grown-ups
Who sees invisible things neither steadily nor whole,
But keeps gravely the grand confusion of the world
Under his hat, which is where it belongs,
And teaches small children to do this in their turn.

PROBING FOR   1. What of overall significance have grown-ups received from
MEANING   their education that they pass on to their children?
        2. Does the "factual" knowledge acquired at school help children
understand the "mostly invisible things"? Explain.
        3. Do you agree with the poet's attitude? Is it possible to see
"invisible things" both "steadily" and "whole"? Or is "grand confusion"
all that is possible in the twentieth century? Explain.

PROBING FOR   1. At what point in the poem do you realize that the speaker is
METHOD   being sarcastic about David's education? What details give evidence of this
satirical tone?
        2. What justifies this as a poem?

Topics for Imitation

1. Several of the writers in this section analyze, to a greater or lesser extent, the causes of violence in the modern world. Write a cause-and-effect essay using violence as the effect and explaining its causes as presented by May, Gold, Gordon, Petry and Gildner.

2. Discuss Russell's, May's, Ephron's and Dickey's analyses of present attitudes toward sex. What are the causes of these attitudes according to the writers?

3. Poverty affects the lives of the characters in Olsen's and Petry's short stories in this chapter, in Podhoretz' essay and Ernest Gaines' story in Chapter I and in Kazin's essay in Chapter II. What are the effects of the family's poverty in each case? Are the effects similar or different from selection to selection?

4. "We have all been in rooms/We cannot die in, and they are odd places, and sad." Dickey, in his poem, and Gordon, in her essay, discuss mobility as a major cause of loneliness. Drawing on the selections as well as your own experiences, discuss the effects of mobility on human emotions.

5. The various writers in this chapter discuss the institution of marriage, primarily the causes of its disintegration. What are these causes, according to Russell, May, Ephron, Gordon and Petry? Do they include all causes? What others should be mentioned?

6. Rollo May discusses both the causes and effects of apathy. How do Gordon's essay and Nemerov's poem illuminate or supplement his discussion? Can you think of additional examples?

7. Gold and Ephron both discuss women's attitudes toward rape. To what extent are their views in agreement? In disagreement?

8. The competitive quality of American society has many effects apart from winning and losing. Discuss these side effects as Gold, Petry, Gildner and Ralbovsky (Chapter I) present them.

9. Urban life affects people in various ways. Discuss effects of city dwelling as Gold and Gordon present them. What other effects can you add?

10. Many emotional situations exist in society which have not been treated in this chapter: the crisis of belief in government, the increasing use of drugs and/or alcohol to escape from life's problems, the continual search for status and so on. Choosing any of the above, or a topic of your own, as either a cause or an effect, write an essay explaining the causes of the effect or the effect that will result from the cause(s). Limit your topic to an aspect of the broader subject that you can discuss specifically.

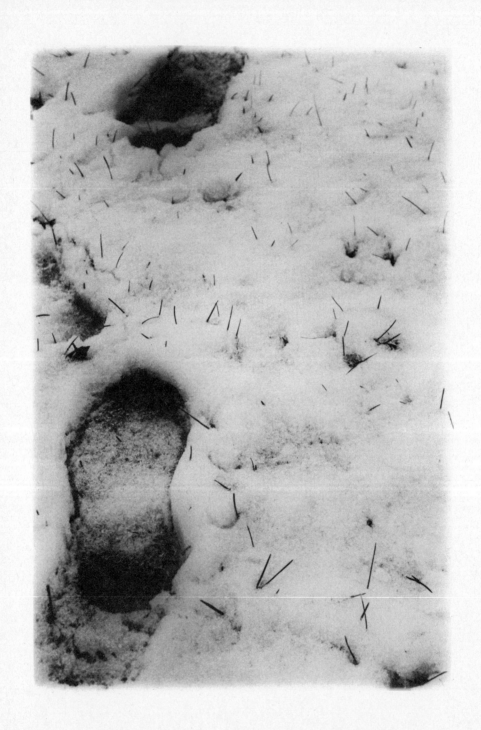

FIVE

CHOICES

"and if a man lived in obscurity . . . obscurity is not uninteresting"

"Man is the only being who refuses to be what he is," writes Albert Camus. Camus believes that we can choose to become fully human—loving and peaceful—if we wish. Other thinkers assert that our environment so shapes us that our freedom to choose to be fully human is limited. If we are violent and unloving in this latter view, we cannot always break away from environmental influences to be different. While our ability to choose to be ourselves may be restricted, the selections in this chapter present many choices open to us.

Anaïs Nin, in "Refusal to Despair," points out the fallacious choice people sometimes perceive: "there is *either* rushing virtuously to live a collective life *or else* there is this selfish introspection and concern with your own development." She believes that the creative individual can shape society more effectively than can the one blindly following it. She speaks of the "enormous radius of influence one person can have." Our choices are important, therefore, not only to ourselves, but also to the community in which we live.

Other writers also emphasize the importance of choice. Alastair Reid contrasts people who have the curiosity of cats with those as complacent as dogs. William Melvin Kelley and Doris Lessing also suggest that if we choose security as our highest value, then it is unlikely that we will discover our most interesting selves.

By comparing and contrasting alternatives, other writers suggest more specific choices. Robert Jay Lifton and William Carlos Williams compare and contrast attitudes toward death. Theodor Reik compares and contrasts love and lust; and Jack Harrison Pollack, the manner in which women teachers treat boys and girls. Santha Rama Rau points out the differences— and a few similarities—between India and Russia; and Richard Eberhart, the differences between childhood and adulthood.

Comparing and Contrasting Alternatives

All of the essays in this chapter compare and contrast the alternatives from which the writers must choose. Each essay is developed through the organizational pattern of comparison and contrast. As you read the essays, decide whether the writers have been fair in presenting the favorable or unfavorable aspects of both or all alternatives. What factors operated in the choices the writers made?

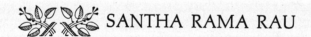 SANTHA RAMA RAU

Return to India

During the three months that my husband and I and our small son were in the Soviet Union, we lost count of the number of times Russians asked us, "Don't you think our life here is very good?"

"Yes, very good," we always replied, politely refraining from adding "for the Russians."

Inevitably the point would be pressed a little further. Life in the Soviet Union was not only good, we would be assured, but was getting better every day. Certainly on the evidence of the past few years, this was no more than the truth. Usually after this kind of opening exchange, the Russians we met proved to be intensely inquisitive about life in America, my husband's country, and the questions ranged from the price of nylons to American intentions for nuclear war. Sometimes they even showed a faintly patronizing interest in my country, India.

On one such occasion I had a brief and uninspired conversation with a chance Russian acquaintance that I was to remember much later with quite a different feeling. A young man, noticing across a restaurant dining room that I wore a sari, came over to the table where my husband and I were sitting. "Hindi-Russki bhai-bhai!" he announced proudly—a phrase Russians learned when Prime Minister Nehru visited their country, a phrase they love to use, which means in Hindi, "Indians and Russians are brothers."

"Hindi-Russki bhai-bhai," I replied dutifully, and then, after the usual opening formalities, the young man started to ask me—or rather, to tell me—about life in India.

With my husband interpreting for us, he remarked, "The Indian people are very poor."

"Yes, they are."

"I have seen photographs. They have few clothes and many have no shoes."

"That's true."

"Most of them are uneducated."

"Yes."

"Many beggars on the streets."

"Yes."

"It must be very distressing to live in such a country."

"No—" I began, suddenly feeling homesick.

But the young man was finished with the subject of India. "In Russia we have a very good life . . ."

After our stay in Russia, I returned with my son to visit my family in India. We flew from Uzbekistan in the far south of Russia, over the magnificent expanse of the Himalayas to New Delhi. The plane arrived after dark and by the time we reached my uncle's house it was quite late at night and we were too tired to do much talking or to pay much attention to our surroundings.

The next morning, with my first glimpse of the newspapers, I was sharply aware not so much that I was in India as that I was out of Russia. One paragraph was enough to convince me. It ran, as I remember, something like this: "Yesterday the Prime Minister opened the debate in parliament on the Second Five-Year Plan with a two-hour speech in his usual diffuse style." I read, and reread, and reread the words "his usual diffuse style," remembering the monotonously reverential tone of all Russian newspapers toward all Russian leaders—the ones in favor, that is.

This was trivial enough as an incident, but in the course of that first day a number of other moments—equally minor, equally transient—began to acquire a collective force. I had offered to help with the household shopping, partly because I always enjoy bazaars and partly because I wanted to show my son a little of the city. We started in the fruit market, which I'm afraid my Russian friends would have found hopelessly disorganized. No orderly queues, no rationing, no fixed prices, no stern-faced women with string shopping bags waiting in line, dutifully reading signs saying, "Drink fruit juices. They are good for you."

To me an Indian bazaar is a source of endless delight and excitement. It is usually a series of plain wooden stalls on which are piled, with unconscious artistry, brightly colored, fruits, vegetables, spices, gleaming silver jewelry, brilliant silks and cottons, or charming, grotesque painted wooden toys. The vendors who can't afford a stall sit on the sidewalk outside the market, their baskets stacked behind them, their wives in vivid cotton saris crouching in the shade, and in front of them are spread carpets of scarlet chillies drying in the sun, small hills of saffron, tumeric, coriander, ginger, cinnamon—all the magical names from the old days of the spice trade with the Indies. With a worn stone mortar and pestle the vendor or his wife will grind your spices for you, blending them according to your particular taste, and weigh them in tiny brass scales strung on twine and balanced delicately in one hand. In all transactions you receive a pleasantly individual attention—nothing standardized.

The vegetable and fruit and flower merchants are surrounded by baskets of purple eggplant, green peppers, strings of tiny silvery onions, heads of bitter Indian spinach, and a dozen Indian vegetables for which I don't even know the English names. I had forgotten about the profusion of fruit in India—it is only during the brief, intense summer that you see much variety of fruit in Moscow. In Russia as winter approaches, all vegetables except for potatoes and the pervasive cabbage in soup seem to disappear from the menus.

My son was enjoying himself, pouncing on the stacks of bananas—unobtainable in Russia—regarding with some suspicion the papayas and chikus which he had not remembered from his last stay in India. He prodded a pile of the tiny, sharp Indian limes to see if they would collapse, an action for which he would have been severely reprimanded in Russia. I was reminded of the evening when we had run into an official of the Ministry of Culture in the lobby of the Metropole, our hotel in Moscow. He had come to the hotel to buy a lemon. It seemed like an extraordinary place to come for such an item, but he explained that there were too few lemons in the winter, so that they were saved for the tourists and the foreigners and could only be obtained, if you were lucky, at an Intourist hotel.

Flowers. This was something I missed very much in Russia, where flowers are a real luxury. I can remember standing at a street corner in Russia, astonished by the sight of a flower-woman sitting in the middle of a splash of color in those gray streets. The Russians stopped to look too. Not many of them bought the flowers—too costly—but a surprising number paused in the rush to get home from offices, factories, and shops in the shadowy autumn twilight just to feast for a moment on the rare color of a few stiff bunches of chrysanthemums on a street corner.

All around us, in Delhi, there were flowers. Yes it is a tropical country, and yes, the climate makes this possible—but there was a personal pride and feminine joy in the countrywomen who tucked a marigold casually into their hair, who wove roses into small hoops to wear more formally around the knot of hair on the back of the head. I realized then that I had missed all this in Russia; the pleasure of women being women, a sense of decoration and unquestioned right of anyone to the small, cheap luxuries and gaieties.

But most impressive—to me, anyway—are the people in an Indian bazaar. First of all there is the inquisitiveness that often embarrasses foreigners. When you are engaged on an errand as prosaic as buying potatoes, in the course of the transaction your vendor may well ask you any variety of what my American friends would call personal questions. How old are you? How many children do you have? Only one? (A commiserating shake of the head.) Better hurry and have another before you are too old. Where do you live? Is your mother-in-law alive? Inevitably I made the comparison with Russia, where this kind of passing, interested exchange (between Russians) is so suspect. The right to express ordinary human curiosity about a fellow countryman came to seem like an unusual privilege.

Meanwhile, the brisk, canny routine of bargaining would be going on, and the whole performance would be interspersed with jokes and cracks and comments. Next to me a man, bargaining for a basket of tangerines, remarked to the old woman standing behind the stall, "Clearly you believe in the soak-the-rich program." This was the popular description of India's new taxation policy. The woman looked amused and replied dryly, "Give me your income and I will gladly pay your taxes." And the bargaining went on without rancor—it was all very Indian, or rather, un-Russian.

We finished our shopping and summoned a boy to carry our purchases out of the bazaar—another small, cheap luxury.

On our way out of the market, we had to pass the familiar barrage of beggars on the sidewalk and, as usual, gave them the small change left over from shopping. Even my son was struck with the contrast to Moscow. "Why are they asking for money, Mummy?"

"Because they are poor, darling."

"Why are they poor, Mummy?"

"India is a poor country, darling. Too many people and not enough food."

"We could give them some of our fruit."

"Well, that's what we've done in another way. We've given them some money to buy whatever they choose."

Then I was left wondering, as so often in the past, about the ethics of begging and giving. It is easy to win approval from foreigners by deploring two elements of Indian life—the caste structure and begging for a livelihood. The best that can be said about either of them is that it is gradually disappearing. However, it would be less than honest to pretend that social malaise is all that is involved in either system. The goals in the Hindu view of life are not the same as those of Russia or the western world. Indeed, India's highest caste, the Brahmans, are traditionally sworn to poverty. Ambition, getting ahead, comfort, success are obstacles, not aims, in the Hindu concept of a good life. Enlightenment is reached, if it is reached, when you have detached yourself from worldly considerations and emotional drives of any sort, so it is not surprising that many of India's most respected "holy men" are, in fact, beggars, or perhaps live on unsolicited contributions from strangers, disciples, casual visitors.

What in the West is almost always a degrading occupation can, in India, be a high achievement. Not, of course, that all beggars are religious mendicants. Many are simply poor, or sick, or unemployed, or seeking a little extra income. If, to a westerner, they are an embarrassment or raise guilts about his own privileged life, to an Asian they are more likely to engender a down-to-earth recognition of conditions as they are and an urge to contribute in a small way to a social responsibility. This is combined with the knowledge that there is no society, including the Russian, in which privilege is unknown. Money, birth, education, accomplishment, something makes a class (or caste) structure. The Hindu view is not to rise to a higher level of privilege but to rise beyond the concern with privilege and levels altogether. It is hard enough to explain this attitude to a sympathetic, philosophic westerner; it is impossible to describe to the average Russian, to whom spiritual values seem to be mysterious, unacceptable, or discredited.

Could the Indian government, like the Russian or the Chinese, abolish beggars with a sweeping compulsory measure? I suppose it could. Would the cost in undemocratic forcefulness be too high? I think it might. We are committed to raising the standard of living in India, but by different methods, at a different pace—a pace designed to preserve other important aspects of our life. Although a number of these thoughts occurred to me that day at the bazaar, luckily I hadn't the time to try and explain many of them to my son because he was thirsty and was more concerned with demanding a limonad of the sort he had liked in Russia. We stopped at a nearby coffee shop.

An Indian coffeehouse, like an Indian bazaar, has its own peculiar atmosphere. It is a cheerful, unpretentious place in which to dawdle, encounter friends, talk, discuss, gossip. Students make fiery speeches to each other; women meet for a break in a morning's shopping; idlers stop by for a rest, to watch the world go by, to pick up a chance colleague. The actual drinking of coffee is the least important part of the whole affair. Looking around at the animated groups of uninhibited talkers at the tables, I couldn't help thinking that this particular sort of place doesn't exist in Moscow. There, one can find restaurants (mostly rather expensive by any standard), or "Parks of Culture and Rest," or hotel dining rooms, and several varieties of bar ranging from the pivnaya, where as a rule you can't even sit down, where women are seldom seen, and where the customers walk to the bar, order a drink, down it and leave, all within the space of five minutes, to the stolovoye, which is considered more refined, more suitable for women, and where ordinary vodka is not served, though wines and brandy are brought to your table. But India is not a drinking country—even in the states where there is no prohibition. The sight of drunks being thrown out of restaurants with the offhand ruthlessness that the Russians employ for such occasions is extremely rare in India.

Indians meet in public places for sociability, and though poor housing contributes, as it does in Russia, to the life of cafés and restaurants and street corners, still Indians do not meet for the dedicated purpose of getting drunk. They are incurable talkers. At the coffeehouse I found myself once again cozy and amused in the endless stream of comments, criticism, scandal, anecdote, and analysis that accompanies one's days in any Indian society. I like the idea that one can be interested, amused, or disapproving of the activities or remarks of one's neighbors, friends, and acquaintances, or of political figures, college professors, taxi drivers, and artists. I like the idea that one's concern, malicious or pleasant, in one's fellow countrymen cannot lead to their political harassment.

Listening that morning in the coffeehouse to the flurry of debate that rose from the students' tables about the latest political controversy, interspersed with the social chit-chat of the ladies or the shop talk of secretaries, office workers, and clerks, I thought of the sad, sly exchanges we had shared with our Russian acquaintances. I remembered the way conversation with a Russian in a restaurant would stop cold whenever a waiter came to the table or strangers walked by. At first I was astonished to find that Russians are much more willing to talk than I had expected, that people will come up to you in parks, restaurants, on the street, drawn by curiosity to a foreigner, eager to ask and answer questions. But we soon learned, after hearing some deeply intimate confidences from Russians we scarcely knew, that our relations with them were very much in the nature of a shipboard romance. It can be intimate because it is so brief. "I can talk to you frankly," one of our friends said, not wistfully, merely as a statement of fact, "because you are in Moscow only a short time. Soon you will go and we will never meet again."

I remembered a waiter at the Metropole Hotel who had seen us so often in the dining room that one day he drifted unobtrusively over to our table to ask us in muttered conversation and scribbled notes about foreign writers. In return for whatever fragments of information we could give him, he told us about his favorite poet, Valery Bryusov. We had never heard of him, and then learned that he was banned in the Soviet Union. "You see," the waiter whispered, "he is a symbolist." In the rowdy air of the coffeehouse, it seemed incredible that there were places where poetry, even symbolist poetry, was considered too dangerous for the fragile human intellect.

After those early days in India, both the novelty of being home and the continual contrasts with Russia began to wear thin. Soon I slipped back in the slow pace and familiar daily life of India. My son no longer noticed beggars. I no longer thought of a trip to the bazaar or the coffeehouse as an occasion. I even remembered the cold blue evenings of Moscow with some nostalgia as the Indian climate warmed up to its early spring. But once during that time I had reason to think of my trip to Moscow and of India as a nation with a shock of rediscovery. It was during the Independence Day parade that takes place in New Delhi every January 26.

It is an immense celebration and villagers from all the surrounding areas of the city had been walking into the town or arriving in their bullock carts for days before. As the day grew closer all the open spaces of New Delhi were gradually filled with impromptu camps. Carts were unhitched, oxen grazed in the parks, the evening air was filled with the haze of open-air cooking fires for the scanty dinners of the travelers. On the streets you saw everywhere the brilliantly colored full ankle-length skirts and tight bodices of the village women. Each footstep (yes, barefoot, I would have had to admit to my Russian acquaintance) was emphasized by the metallic clink of silver anklets or toe rings. Every time a small child was hitched into a more comfortable position on his mother's hip, the sound of silver bracelets would accompany the movement. The fathers, proudly carrying sons on a tour of the city's sights or carefully washing their oxen at a public fountain, were less decorative but good-humored and ready for a festival. The streets were full of color and excitement and nobody checked the wanderings of the villagers as they looked around their capital.

In Russia you need a permit to travel even within the country, an identity card and an official permit before you may stay at a hotel. For most non-Muscovites, the only way to get to Moscow is to come, as a reward for outstanding service, on a brief "workers' tour" or as a member of some delegation. Chekhov's yearning phrase "To Moscow, to Moscow . . ." has just as intense a meaning now.

The day of the parade brought thousands of villagers and citizens of Delhi to the parade route, lining the roads in a dense, active crowd of mothers, fathers, children, babies, donkeys, oxen. Many families had their lunches tied up in pieces of cloth. Children clutched balloons or candy sticks. Little stalls selling nuts, tea, sweets, and fruit sprang up everywhere. I was lucky enough to have a seat on one of the bleachers outside the president's house where the procession started, and next to me was an old man in a worn khaki sweater and army trousers. A faded patch on his arm said "Engineers." He was obviously a veteran, obviously now retired, and obviously he had never been higher in rank than the equivalent of a sergeant.

When the procession began with the arrival of the Indian president, the old man stood up to get a better view. All the pomp and ceremony of viceregal days surrounded the appearance of the president—the outriders, the cavalry escort, the great coach drawn by matched horses, guarded by lancers. Out of the coach stepped a small thin man in a brown achkan (the Indian jacket), narrow trousers wrinkled at the ankles, a Gandhi cap on his head. He looked embarrassed by the flashy display that surrounded him. Smiling shyly, he brought his hands together in a namaskar, the Indian greeting, and hurried to his place on the reviewing platform. This in no way discouraged the old man next to me. He raised his hands in a namaskar above the heads of the people around him. With tears streaming down his face, he yelled (apparently convinced that the president could hear him), "Namaste ji! Jai Hind!" and continued with such fervor that the rest of us near him suddenly found ourselves joining in a tribute from an Indian who had spent all his life in the British Army to an Indian who represented, at last, the fact that all this and India itself belonged to all of us.

The parade was splendid as such things go—a vast cavalcade of camels, elephants, ski troops, horsemen, the tough Gurkhas, the bearded colorful Sikhs—all the diversity and pageantry of India. But I am not really very keen on parades. They worry and depress me, and while this fantastic procession was going on, in my mind I had slipped back to the day of the fortieth anniversary of the Russian Revolution in Moscow. Another parade. Of a very different sort. There were no crowds lining the sidewalks—the streets had been cleared for security reasons. There was none of the good-humored pushing and shoving and wriggling of small children to get to the front where they could see best. Color? Pageantry? No, a few people in the factory workers' groups in the procession carried paper flowers, and one realized in a moment how seldom one saw color on the streets in Moscow, how rarely the drab grays and browns of the city were ever lightened by even so much as a pretty shop window. Mostly the Russian parade was grimly military, tanks and guns and huge rockets, and ranks and ranks of marching soldiers.

At the end of our parade the tribesmen from the Naga hills came by to do a dance in the street in front of the president. Predictably (it couldn't happen in Russia), they were late in getting started. Consequently they clashed with the flypast of the new Indian jets. Watching the two performances simultaneously, I could only think I would never have been able to explain to that anonymous Russian acquaintance of mine the appeal of Indian casualness, of the need for color, ease, humor—the joy of an Indian festival.

Poor and undernourished and undereducated, yes. But in India, people turn out every election day in a larger percentage than anywhere else in the world to choose a government. They make a real holiday of it, decorating their oxcarts and dressing in their best clothes to go to the polls. Certainly one cannot pretend that there is nothing in India that needs to be changed, but somewhere in all this is a confidence and pleasure in being Indian, and in the country's ways. And, yes, those ways are very different from Russian ways.

Well, it never fails: one always sounds sentimental in trying to say things like this. Perhaps it is just as well that I never got a chance to explain to that remote young man in Moscow how I feel about India.

PROBING FOR   1. Santha Rama Rau has limited her discussion of Indian life to
MEANING   three aspects: the bazaar, the coffeehouse and the parade. Why does her
limiting her topic to these particular featues of life in her native land fulfill
her purpose of proving that for her India is preferable to Russia?

2. At what points does she contrast India with Russia? Does she indicate any similarities? If so, what are they?

3. How does she answer foreigners' charges that Indian society creates beggars and maintains a caste system? Do you think her answer would silence India's accusers? Why or why not?

4. Which of her points of comparison and contrast are political? Economic? Aesthetic? Social? Intellectual? Does she indicate which are more important to her? Which do you feel carry more weight?

5. To what extent do her criticisms of Russia apply to America? Which of India's good points do we share? Which do we lack? What advantages and disadvantages do we have which neither India nor Russia share? Which of the three countries would an objective observer prefer? Why?

PROBING FOR
METHOD

1. Since she is describing three places in India and her experiences at these places, what other methods of development besides contrast and comparison does Rau use in writing her essay?

2. What effect is achieved by developing this essay in the first person pronoun?

3. In one sentence the author writes, "At the coffeehouses I found myself once again cozy and amused in the endless stream of comment, criticism, scandal, anecdote and analysis that accompanies one's days in any Indian society." Find other sentences in the essay where she has also used alliteration this effectively.

4. In what way does Rau end her essay with a framing technique? How does she pick up an idea in the final paragraph that goes back to her introduction, in other words?

Comparing and Contrasting Alternatives

ILLUS-
TRATION

How does Santha Rama Rau develop her comparison and contrast essay? Travelers set the wheels of comparison and contrast spinning as soon as they arrive in a foreign country. How is the new country similar to and different from their own? Santha Rama Rau, in visiting Russia, noticed the points of contrast (not many similarities evidently) between Russia and India, and, wearing a sari, she also evoked comparison and contrast questions about her country in the Russians.

In writing her essay, she chooses three areas of Indian life through which she most clearly distinguishes India from Russia: the bazaar, the coffeehouse and the parade. Her basic discussion of comparisons and contrasts is as follows:

I. The Bazaar
   A. Russia lacks fruit; India has plenty.
   B. In Russia, service is standardized; in India one receives individual attention.

C. Flowers are seldom seen in Russia but grow in profusion in India.

D. Women do not wear ornaments in Russia, but Indian women are gaily decorated.

E. Russia has no beggars, but they are a way of life in India.

II. The Coffeehouse

A. There are few public meeting places in Russia, but in India coffeehouses abound.

B. Russia has numerous drunks; India has none.

C. Talk is inhibited in Russia, but is constant and free in India.

III. The Parade

A. Russians need permits to travel, but there is much freedom of movement in India.

B. Russian parades lack color, but Indian parades are joyful pageants.

C. Precision is the keyword of Russian parades, casualness, even tardiness, that of Indian.

INDUCTION   *Principles of the comparison and contrast essay.* Comparison and contrast is used by the writer who wishes to compare and/or contrast two or more ideas, objects, methods or people, usually for the purpose of advancing one over the other(s) by demonstrating ways in which it is better than its counterpart(s). This method may also be used in defining one idea by distinguishing it from another.

In organizing a comparison and contrast essay, the writer may take one of three approaches: the whole-by-whole method, the part-by-part method, or a combination of the two. In the first method, the writer looks at all aspects of one subject first and then examines all aspects of the other subject(s) with which he is making the comparison. In this method, no direct comparing and contrasting is done; similarities and differences are only implied.

In adopting a part-by-part structure, the writer looks at one phase of the first subject and then compares it to a corresponding phase of the other subject(s); next, he examines a second phase of both; then, a third phase, and so on. In this method, direct relationships are clearly indicated. The combination method divides the subject into three but also either directly compares and contrasts the parts within each whole or discusses one subject as a whole but the second subject part by part, i.e., directly comparing and contrasting.

How does a writer choose which method will be most effective in presenting his topic? The whole-by-whole method is useful when simply presenting two subjects and not endorsing one or the other. This method can often work better for shorter papers. The part-by-part method is valuable when the writer is advocating one subject over another. By directly comparing and contrasting various aspects of his subjects, he can demonstrate the superiority of one over the other(s). This method requires greater detail and is most appropriate for longer papers.

The combination method also is appropriate when the subject matter demands it. If a writer, for example, were advocating a new idea over an old one, he might introduce the former before comparing and contrasting the two specifically to demonstrate how one is superior to the other.

To illustrate the differences among the methods of organization, consider the following sample outlines:

A sample outline using the whole-by-whole method might be:
    I. Choice of Vice President by Presidential Candidate
       A. Plus factors
       B. Minus factors
   II. Choice of Vice President by Convention Delegates
       A. Plus factors
       B. Minus factors

A part-by-part outline on this subject might be:
    I. Reliability of Candidate as Potential President
       A. If chosen by presidential candidate
       B. If chosen by convention delegates
   II. Usefulness of Candidate on Ticket
       A. If chosen by presidential candidate
       B. If chosen by convention delegates
  III. Redefined and Enlarged Role of Vice President

An outline combining these two methods might be:
    I. Choice of Vice President by Presidential Candidate (whole-by-whole)
       A. Plus factors
       B. Minus factors
   II. Choice of Vice President by Convention Delegates (part-by-part)
       A. Reliability; as compared and contrasted with reliability of selection by presidential candidate
       B. Usefulness on ticket; as compared and contrasted with usefulness of selection by presidential candidate
       C. Redefined and Enlarged Role of Vice Presidential Candidate; as compared and contrasted with role chosen by presidential candidate

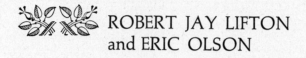 ROBERT JAY LIFTON
and ERIC OLSON

Death—The Lost Season

The sun she dies so quietly
So sure of resurrection
And I am dying in the street
Crying for connection.
               —Tom Rush*

And some cease feeling
Even themselves or for themselves.
           —Wilfred Owen†

Historical struggles strongly influence the subjects psychologists choose for study. In our time, massive violence and absurd death have made this century one of horror for millions of people. Death has become unmanageable for our culture, and for us as individuals.

While death has never been fully "manageable" for anyone, death and life are painfully out of joint in our time. In choosing to write a book about death and the continuity of life, we realize we are deeply affected by the present historical situation. What is needed now, we believe, is an approach to death that is both sensitive to personal experience and responsible to broader currents of thought. . . .

Seventy years ago, around the turn of the century, sex was more problematic than death as a cultural and psychological dilemma. In 1900 Freud published a book that many people consider the most important of the twentieth century. In that book, *The Interpretation of Dreams*, Freud examined his own dreams and found in their sexual symbolism what he regarded as the deepest sources of human motivation—and the roots of mental disorder.

* From "Starlight" by Tom Rush; used with permission.
† From "Insensibility," in Wilfred Owen, *Collected Poems.* © Chatto & Windus, Ltd., 1946, © 1963. Reprinted by permission of New Directions Publishing Corp.

294

Freud developed most of his ideas during the late Victorian era. At that time there had as yet been no world wars. The atomic bomb did not yet exist. Science and industry were growing rapidly; people had reason to hope that the fruits of research and economic expansion would solve the world's problems. What people seemed unable to deal with was their own sexuality.

In the Victorian age sexuality was something that polite middle-class people never mentioned. Babies, however, continued to be born, and so we can assume that men and women did have sexual relations. Moreover, the era gave rise to a notably rich pornographic literature. But for much of Victorian society, the less said about such things the better; if one did not think about sex at all, that was better still. The Victorian custom of covering the legs of tables with skirts because of their "similarity" to the human body (no part of which was to be left uncovered) reflects the anxiety, indeed the terror, surrounding sex in many segments of European society at that time.

The patients Freud treated were victims of this social situation. They suffered from anxiety and guilt about their inability to express their sexuality. Sexual impulses repressed by day emerged in dreams at night and in such symptoms as headaches or paralyzed arms. Freud believed that such repression frequently led to disabling psychological conflicts. In working to cure his patients, he emphasized how important it was for them to recognize and accept these sexual feelings.

Much that Freud wrote seventy years ago remains true today. Certainly, people continue to have difficulties with sexual expression. But it is also clear that the times have changed. Rather than ignore sex, we are more likely to flaunt it, experiment with it, or seek new kinds of experience through it. Whatever our relationship to sex, it is no longer taboo.

There is much else that differentiates our time from the era when Freud was writing. We live with the legacy of the atomic bomb and the violent deaths of one hundred million people in this century's wars and death camps. The same high technology employed for this massive killing tends to distance us from virtually all human problems. We are most distanced from the reality of human death. We don't talk about it; we try to conceal, deny, and "bury" it. But—like repressed sexuality in Freud's day—death does not go away. And we too have our symptoms, though they are not the same ones that Freud described.

Death was not always so distant. When people died at home rather than in hospitals, the sight of death was not uncommon. The deaths of grandparents, infants, and mothers giving birth were more frequent. There were no "old people's homes"; old and young people lived together in the same house. Children saw family members and friends die of one ailment or another. The full cycle of life was more visible, and growth, sickness, aging, and death were understood to be part of that cycle. In refusing to face death—as individuals and as a culture—we living today close off a part of life.

Many things have come together now to make death the most central and troubling fact of modern existence. Throughout history, man has feared premature death. The death of a child, a youth, a man or woman in the midst of family rearing and creative work: These images of incomplete, unfulfilled life have always aroused terror. What is new is the awareness that premature death is possible now, not only for an individual man or woman, but for the entire human race. In the past, such apocalyptic visions have been the stuff of nightmares and the prophecy of madmen or religious zealots. That is no longer exclusively the case.

Man is now capable of annihilating himself as a species with his technology. This capacity means that no firm boundary can be drawn anymore between wild fantasy and a sober assessment of real danger. Joyce Maynard, when she was eighteen, wrote about her discovery of the contemporary meaning of death. In her book *Looking Back: A Chronicle of Growing Up Old in the Sixties*, this is what she says:

> People talked about fallout shelters in their basements and one family on our street packed their car to go to the mountains. I couldn't understand that. If everybody was going to die, I certainly didn't want to stick around, with my hair falling out and—later— a plague of thalidomide-type babies. I wanted to go quickly, with my family. Dying didn't bother me so much—I'd never known anyone who died, and death was unreal, fascinating. (I wanted Dr. Kildare to have more terminal cancer patients and fewer love affairs.)
>
> What bothered me was the business of immortality. Sometimes growing-up concepts germinate slowly, but the full impact of death hit me like a bomb in the night. Not only would my body be gone—that I could take—but I would cease to think. That I would no longer be a participant I had realized before; now I saw that I wouldn't even be an observer. What especially alarmed me about the Bomb (always singular like, later, the Pill) was the possibility of total obliteration. All traces of me would be destroyed. There would be no grave and, if there were, no one left to visit it.

The atomic bomb does not merely destroy; it destroys the boundaries of destruction. With older weapons—an arrow shot from a bow, a bullet from a gun, a bomb dropped from a plane—people are killed or injured, family and community life are upset, but there remains a sense of limits. Some people suffer and die, others recover, and history continues.

The atomic bomb is different. The first atomic bomb used on a human population fell on Hiroshima, Japan, on August 6, 1945. The destruction inflicted by that blast was so nearly total and so longlasting that the survivors of the bomb have experienced a *permanent encounter with death*. No one knows how many people were killed. Estimates vary from 63,000 to 240,000. But even those who survived were left with a devastated city and with fears that their bodies were permanently contaminated from exposure to atomic radiation.

That first atomic bomb was a very small one by today's standards. The world's nuclear arsenal now holds bombs thousands of times more powerful than that one. Such destructive power is not imaginable, not comprehensible. We can contemplate the death of an individual man or woman but not the death of everyone, because we have no images adequate to the possibility of total extinction.

The Vietnam war, like nuclear holocaust, has had a quality of incomprehensibility. Statistics of "kill ratios" and fatalities and even pictures of maimed people have constantly appeared in newspapers and on television. But Americans have not been convinced that all the killing and destruction are necessary. Returning Vietnam veterans have been looked upon, not as heroic warriors, but rather as the unfortunate agents of a policy of death which no one has understood.

Both Hiroshima and the air war in Vietnam are examples of highly technologized violence. In both cases, the use of massive air power has revealed the destructive capacity of technology and the absurdity of the experience of death in modern warfare: unseen victims suffering and dying without ever having met their opponents.

No American military effort prior to Vietnam has been so strongly condemned as immoral. Without the notion that they were fighting for a noble cause or suffering for a higher good, American soldiers have had great difficulty accepting the risks of fighting in Vietnam. The "I-Feel-Like-I'm-Fixin'-to-Die Rag" of Country Joe MacDonald became *the* song of the war. Its wildly mocking refrain expresses the sense of absurdity of dying in Vietnam:

> And it's 1, 2, 3, what are we fighting for?
> Don't ask me I don't give a damn
> Next stop is Vietnam
> And it's 5, 6, 7, open up the Pearly Gates
> Well there ain't no time to wonder why
> Whoopee we're all gonna die.*

* From "I-Feel-Like-I'm-Fixin'-to-Die Rag" by Country Joe MacDonald; © by Tradition Music Co. (BMI).

When killing is absurd—because of either the nature of the weapons or the illegitimacy of the enterprise—death becomes unacceptable. To a degree, any form of dying is perceived as absurd, but to live in the face of inevitable death, man requires a sense that his life has continuity and significance.

While the holocausts of twentieth-century warfare have rendered death absurd, the dislocations of the modern world had already rendered life's meaning problematic. People in advanced industrial culture have become so mobile, so rootless, so cut off from traditional sources of meaning that life appears to hold no certainties or reliable values. All of the institutions which throughout history have organized and given meaning to life—family, religion, government, work—are now in crisis.

We live in a time when people find increasing difficulty in giving significant form to their ideas, aspirations, and lives. The subjective experience of psychological and historical (or "psychohistorical") dislocation is precisely a sense of not having a place. The Beatles express this in the line "Once there was a way to get back home"*; Tom Rush, in the phrase "crying for connection."†

When a society's values and institutions are seriously questioned, life transitions become anxious and traumatic. What does it mean to face the time of marriage when divorce is so common and alternative living arrangements, such as communes and cohabitation, are so widely explored? What does it mean to choose a vocation when all forms of work, and the idea of work itself, are so severely criticized? What does it mean to grow up when adulthood implies being locked into support of a violent, directionless culture? What does it mean to grow old when old people are isolated, put off by themselves in "homes" or institutions, apart from family and ongoing community? What does it mean to die when science has challenged sacred religious beliefs and in the place of spiritual comfort has left only the "scientific method"?

There was a time when Americans could face the transitions of life, if not with ease, at least with some poise and grace. The confidence and candor of these lines composed by Benjamin Franklin for his gravestone reveal no hesitancy to look squarely at death—and beyond it:

The Body of
B. Franklin Printer,
(Like the cover of an Old Book
Its contents torn out
And stript of its Lettering and Gilding)
Lies here, Food for Worms.
But the work shall not be lost;
For it will, (as he believ'd) appear
once more
In a new and more elegant Edition
Revised and Corrected
By the Author.

Such a relaxed wit, made possible by the prevailing belief in resurrection, is rare now. Our lack of meaningful rituals and beliefs makes dying the more desperate and fearsome, and impoverishes life as well.

The tumultuous history of America in the last ten years has intensified the crisis in cultural symbols and values that has been visible since the Industrial Revolution, but whose origins date back to Europe's emergence from the Middle Ages. The assassinations of John Kennedy, Malcolm X, Robert Kennedy, and Martin Luther King gave rise to a feeling that America was without leadership, without direction. The black uprisings and ghetto burnings in cities across the country expressed angry disillusionment as increasing numbers of people came to doubt whether America was capable of extending humane treatment to all citizens. Vietnam and Watergate have brought a sense of bitter mockery to the American dream.

These years have been particularly difficult for young people. Asked to fight in a war they did not believe in but could not stop, struggling to define for themselves and the country a new form of political consciousness, the young have agonized over how to grow up in America. For a brief moment in 1969 it appeared that the music and good vibes of the Woodstock rock festival would give birth to a new "Woodstock Nation." But over the course of less than a year the collapse of that hope was symbolized by a violent death at the next large festival at Altamont, the drug-related deaths of Jimi Hendrix, Janis Joplin, and Jim Morrison, and the students killed at Jackson State and Kent State universities after the U.S. invasion of Cambodia. Euphoric visions quickly gave way to despair and, above all, confusion.

John Lennon expressed all this when he wrote, "The dream is

over, what can I say?"* Without a cultural context in which life has continuity and boundaries, death seems premature whenever it comes. Whatever the age and circumstances, it is always "untimely." But when individual life appears to lack significance beyond itself, death becomes profoundly threatening, unacceptable.

Death is simply a fact—the inevitable end of biological life. The *acceptability* of death depends upon the psychological context in which it occurs. Death has now become unacceptable because it is associated with images of absurd holocaust and annihilation and because our lives have become rootless and disconnected. A well-known study (done, in part, by Sigmund Freud's daughter Anna) explored the responses of children to the bombing and destruction of London during World War II. The children's encounter with death was mediated and profoundly influenced by the responses of the adults around them. Mothers and children huddled together for shelter in dark cellars as bombs fell. During this time of crisis, some children became extremely terrified and anxious, while others were not greatly alarmed. The children seemed to respond more to the emotional attitudes of their mothers than to the bombing itself. Those children who were fortunate enough to have comforting mothers were themselves likely to remain calm. Children whose mothers were not calm became overwhelmed with fear.

The times in which we now live provide no ready emotional context or system of meaning to render death acceptable. We might compare our situation with that of the children in the World War II study whose mothers were terrified by the bombing and conveyed that anxiety to their children. We, too, lack a meaningful and reassuring emotional context.

How might death and life relate to each other in less troubled times? Ideally, death might be seen as life's final season—as autumn is to the summer green of a forest. In late September and October, when the days become cooler and shorter and the angle of sunlight changes slightly, the leaves rapidly begin to change color. They fall quickly, and few are left on the trees by November. Leaves do not cling to the trees when autumn signals a time of change—"The sun she dies so quietly."

It has long been an aspiration of men to experience the ebb and flow of human existence as rhythmically as the passages and changes in the rest of nature. This comparison of the changes in the life of a human being with the seasons of nature is compellingly expressed in the words of Ecclesiastes. In the early 1960's when these verses were put to music in the song "Turn, Turn, Turn," first recorded by Pete Seeger and later in a rock version by the Byrds, many people were surprised to discover that the lyrics are from the Bible:

> For everything there is a season, and a time to every purpose under heaven:
>   a time to be born and a time to die;
>   a time to plant, and a time to pluck up what is planted;
>   a time to kill, and a time to heal;
>   a time to break down, and a time to build up;
>   a time to weep, and a time to laugh;
>   a time to mourn, and a time to dance;
>   a time to cast away stones, and a time to gather stones together;
>   a time to embrace, and a time to refrain from embracing;
>   a time to seek, and a time to lose;
>   a time to keep, and a time to cast away;
>   a time to rend, and a time to sew;
>   a time to keep silence, and a time to speak;
>   a time to love, and a time to hate;
>   a time for war, and a time for peace.
>
> Ecclesiastes 3:1-8

At the time Pete Seeger put a modified version of these lines to music he had been carrying the Biblical passage around for months on a folded piece of paper in his wallet. They are strong words, and they move us because they suggest something we know to be true but generally avoid confronting.

For most people the process of change—accepting the disappearance of the old and welcoming the arrival of the new—is not as graceful and rhythmical as the change of seasons in nature. In India, the passage of life is perceived in "stages": from student to householder to the wisdom of age. Each time of life has a specified activity that is sanctified by religious tradition. For us in the West, and for many contemporary Indians, the rituals and rites of passage which facilitated these changes in earlier times have been lost along with religious faith. Movement from one stage to another, therefore, becomes accompanied by confusion and anxiety—an occasion for trauma rather than celebration.

. . . [Here] we approach these questions through a focus on the formative (or psychoformative) process—by which we mean the continuous creation and re-creation of images and symbols. We view this process as essential to human mental life. A sense of vitality can proceed only so long as the symbolizing process provides forms and images adequate to guide behavior and render it meaningful.

Twentieth-century holocaust and dislocation have combined to create for modern man a kind of "symbolic gap": Our capacity to interpret experience symbolically has not kept pace with the rapidity of historical change. The systems of symbols through which man has traditionally comprehended the world, and the institutions through which he has been active in it no longer provide comfortable images or channels for life. The family, work, religion, government, military service, educational institutions—all these, and even the sequence of the human life cycle itself, are widely criticized and doubted now. The Vietnam war and the Watergate crisis are representative in this sense of a much wider crisis of all of our cultural forms.

When the psychoformative function is disturbed, man becomes desensitized, numb. This happens when historical events are too large or absurd or terrifying to be given meaningful expression through the culture's available symbols. People feel distant from their own lives: "Some cease feeling/Even themselves or for themselves."

Numbing is the characteristic psychological problem of our age. Jet pilots who coolly drop bombs on people they never see tend not to feel what goes on at the receiving end. Those of us who watch such bombing on TV undergo a different though not unrelated desensitization. To the extent that numbing entails a blockage of feeling, it resembles death. Life itself (or part of it) becomes deadened. Under extreme conditions numbing takes an extreme form, such as in the death camps of World War II, where men and women were turned into what have been described as walking corpses.

The mind cannot take in or absorb those experiences that cannot be meaningfully symbolized and inwardly re-created. In this way, a certain degree of numbing can operate to protect one from great psychological suffering. When numbing is slowly replaced by full awareness, a traumatic experience may be confronted gradually, rather than all at once. But numbing which goes too far and does not cease implies a permanent incapacity to feel.

The process of accepting the death of a loved person usually involves an initial numbness ("I can't believe it") which gradually gives way to awareness. Survivors are confronted with the psychological task of accepting their loss and continuing to live.

In Western culture, when someone dies there is usually a funeral to which family and friends come to mourn for the deceased. Traditionally, the bereaved family was expected to mourn for a full year, to wear black, and to maintain a somber attitude. Many psychological investigators have emphasized how vital the mourning period is for survivors, how necessary it is for their own psychological health. People rarely mourn for a year any more, but there was considerable psychological wisdom in the tradition prescribing that length of time.

During the course of a year, through the full change of seasons and holidays, a family could gradually come to accept the absence of the dead person. Our memories of people are so closely bound up with memories of the times and places they have shared with us that the process of "remembering that someone has died" takes time. For a child gradually coming to believe that the death of a father is real, the largely unspoken psychological process of mourning would be something like this: "It's summer and Daddy is not here when I go swimming; it's fall and Daddy is not here when we eat Thanksgiving dinner; it's Christmas and Daddy is not here when we open the presents." Slowly a child accepts the repeated evidence of his senses and concludes to himself, "Daddy will not be here with me any more." A similar process takes place for mourners of any age.

The ease with which a child, or anyone else, accepts the death of someone close depends upon many things. Generally, if a child feels part of a loving family and is given emotional support and the chance to express in his own way his sorrows and fears, he will begin again to play and study and carry on his own young life with a minimum of self-pity and self-blame.

For survivors' mourning process, the "grief work" requires an initial loss of feeling which persists until new images and feelings take shape that allow the loss to be accepted. If the mourning process is not carried through, a person may remain inwardly numb indefinitely. In historical times when religion played a larger role, the comfort of a church and belief in God were of great help to people in mourning. For us now, such support is less available; this loss is part of contemporary psychohistorical dislocation.

We attempt to conceal what we can neither face nor escape. The Forest Lawn Memorial Park cemetery in southern California epitomizes our attempt to "bury death." There, at the world's largest cemetery, death itself is a dirty word. The "loved ones" (never referred to as "the dead") are elaborately embalmed, decorated with cosmetics and smiles to appear alive and happy, and then "laid to rest" (not "buried").

Even in hospitals, death is embarrassing and has no place. The doctors and technicians are committed to using their science and equipment to keep people alive—at least to keep them breathing. Death becomes a defeat for medical science, an unwanted intrusion, and is not accepted as a human event that has its place in the seasons of life. As one prominent engineer said, "We will lick the problem of aging completely so that accidents will be the only cause of death."

The most absolute effort to stave off final extinction is the freezing of bodies immediately after death. The dubious rationale behind this "cryonics" movement is the assumption that these bodies can be cured and brought back to life when cures are discovered for the diseases responsible for these deaths. The more common techniques of organ transplantation are now extending the lives of people whose hearts or kidneys no longer function.

Though new medical techniques have brought much relief from suffering, their more extreme manifestations reflect our difficulty in accepting death as part of the life cycle. They then lead us further to deny that there is "a time to be born and a time to die." Dylan Thomas urged his father:

> Do not go gentle into that good night,
> Old age should burn and rave at close of day;
> Rage, rage against the dying of the light.

But rather than raging against the dying light of life, we find ourselves refusing to believe that the light ever dies. We hide from ourselves the very fact of death.

The historian Arnold Toynbee once said that death is un-American. He meant that in a culture that places so much emphasis on progress, strength, and the vitality and beauty of youth, and so little on the wisdom and dignity of age, death has no place. In such a society, dying can be a terribly lonely and desperate experience—as indeed it often is.

The repression of sexuality led to an underground and often perverse fascination with sex known as pornography. Our denial of death has resulted now in movies, books, and magazines which exhibit what the English anthropologist Geoffrey Gorer has called "the pornography of death." Though this kind of pornography includes much exploitation, it also reflects the attempt to create meaningful psychological ideas around death and expose false ones. This development reveals both the persistence of the human tendency to formulate experience and our overwhelming need to confront death honestly.

In agrarian communities of the past, death could not be concealed. Man's earliest villages and cities were in fact built around burial sites for dead ancestors. Hunting and gathering peoples made pilgrimages to the burial places to honor the dead who could no longer travel. Such fixed places eventually became cities. What began as cities for the dead became cities for the living as well.

Modern cities are for the living only. Those who are old or weak or dead have, like obsolete cars, no place in them. But there is a growing sense that the fact of human death can no longer be denied. Psychiatrists are becoming increasingly concerned about patients left amid the tubes and machines of the modern hospital to face death alone. People everywhere are coming to an awareness that man's new capacity to destroy himself requires new thinking about death if we are to comprehend our current historical crisis.

The extremity and danger of the present historical moment suggest that we need the theme of death to reconstitute our lives. In the words of Ecclesiastes, there is "a time to every purpose under heaven." Now is the time to ponder the words of the novelist E. M. Forster: "Death destroys a man; the idea of Death saves him."

PROBING FOR MEANING

1. What differentiates the contemporary attitude toward death from the attitude of previous eras?

2. What are the similarities between the Victorian attitude toward sex and the contemporary attitude toward death? In what way have we "repressed" our feelings about death according to Lifton? Do you agree? Explain.

3. How has the development of the atomic bomb contributed to our repression of death? What is the difference between the atomic bomb and previous means of destruction in their effect on the cultural attitude toward death? How have Hiroshima and Vietnam revealed the "absurdity of the experience of death in modern warfare"?

4. What other factors in the modern world have contributed to our repression of death? What is the effect of alienation and the lack of "a cultural context in which life has continuity and boundaries"?

5. What conditions need to be present for death to be acceptable? Why were the reactions of their mothers so important for children during the bombings of London in World War II?

6. What attitude does Lifton suggest is appropriate for accepting death? Why are images and symbols so important? What is the "symbolic gap" of the contemporary era?

7. Why does Lifton consider "numbing" to be the characteristic psychological problem of our age? How are certain cemeteries and hospitals attempting to conceal death? What is the effect of the freezing of bodies and other medical advances? What did Toynbee mean when he said "death is un-American"?

8. Why are funerals and rituals necessary to soften the impact of death? What does Lifton suggest is the benefit of mourning for a full year?

9. Why does Lifton feel that we need "the theme of death to reconstitute our lives"? Do you agree? Explain.

10. Having read Suzanne Gordon's essay on loneliness, do you feel that our repression of death merits consideration as a social problem, given the three qualifications she presents?

1. Why does Lifton draw such an elaborate parallel between the Victorian view of sex and our view of death? Does he ever return to this idea? Where? For what purpose?

2. Why does Lifton offer quotations from contemporary artists and songwriters?

3. In paragraph 21, Lifton begins a series of questions with "What does it mean to . . ." What is the purpose of this parallel structure?

4. What is shown by the words on Benjamin Franklin's gravestone? Similarly, what is the effect of the quotation from Ecclesiastes?

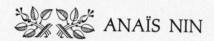 ANAÏS NIN

Refusal to Despair

I think we are living now in a period which in some ways resembles the time of the plague. It sounds like a very exaggerated image, but we are confronted every day with despair and horror. There is the nightmare of the war and the fear of the bomb, but you know as well as I all the events that cause our universal anxiety. So the feeling I wanted to give you tonight is that during these events, during these happenings, it is as important for us to step out of history as it is for us to live within it. We have to step out of it in order to find the strength with which to participate in it, with which to live in it, and with which to achieve what I was finally able to achieve in the later diaries, which is a *refusal to despair*. This has meant creativity on the one hand and relationship on the other—the obsession with establishing intimate contact, with friendship, with every form of relationship to man, woman, child, to people close to us and to people in other countries.

It's not only the artist who talks about creativity. We can begin to create in a desert of life, we can begin to create with those that we live with, we can begin to create as children do—immediately writing poems or painting when they can hardly hold a brush or a pen. This creativity is a constant interaction between our life and the struggle with larger issues such as history, whose victim we can become. And in order not to be victimized by it we also have to learn to live apart from it. It's not escape, it's having a place that we return to in order to regain our strength, in order to regain our values, in order not to be shattered by events.

It's almost like the man who goes to the bottom of the ocean and takes with him some oxygen to equalize the pressure. I'm talking about equalizing the pressure between outer actions and events which are shattering and devastating to us and then the place where we recompose and reconstruct ourselves, where we finally achieve what Jung called the second birth. The second birth we are entirely responsible for; it's a self-creation. This second birth is the one that *you* can make, and the discovery of that to me was always a great relief. As long as we expect the changes to come only from the outside or from action outside or from political systems, then we are bound to feel helpless, to feel sometimes that reality is bigger and stronger than we are. But if suddenly we begin to feel that there is one person *we* can change, simultaneously we change many people around us. And as a writer I suddenly discovered the enormous radius of influence that one person can have.

So when we make this interior change we do affect the external world. Now everybody separated that and said: there is *either* rushing virtuously to live a collective life *or else* there is this selfish introspection and concern with your own development. But the two are completely interdependent, they are completely interactive; and the more you have this response to life, the more you have a source to respond with, then of course the more enrichment you pass around you. Why we made a dichotomy between those two—saying that the two wouldn't enrich each other—I don't know. Because whatever the individual does for himself and by himself is something that ultimately flows back again like a river into the collective unconscious. So if we are disappointed today in the external changes it's because not enough of us have worked at raising a better quality of human being: one who is more aware, more able to evaluate, judge others, judge the characters of our leaders.

That is the kind of responsibility I think we have to take. For example, when I got hysterical over the assassination of Dr. King, what I felt was guilt, a kind of total guilt. Though I am incapable of such an act of hostility, still I felt it came from all our hostilities. I wrote at the end of one diary about war. When war came in '39, I said: "I have never been responsible for an act of war and yet I am now involved in this thing that has happened to the whole world." And even then I felt that this was an aggregate of all our hostilities, and that's why I fight hostility.

We have to work upon ourselves because, as Loren Eisley said, every time we come to terms with hostility within ourselves we are creating the possibility of someday not having war. In other words, I'm putting back into the self the responsibility for the collective life. If each one of us took very seriously the fact that every little act, every little word we utter, every injury we do to another human being is really what is projected into larger issues; if we could once begin to think of it that way, then each one of us, like a small cell, would do the work of creating a human self, a kind of self who wouldn't have ghettos, a kind of self that wouldn't go to war. Then we could begin to have the cell which would influence an enormous amount of cells around you. I don't think we can measure the radius of the personal influence of one person, within the home, outside of the home, in the neighborhood, and finally in national affairs.

We never connected those two; we always thought we had to approach the larger issues directly; we never thought we could transform the larger issues by transforming ourselves. If first of all every individual had taught himself lucidity about character, the knowledge of psychological disturbances in depth, and had learned to go inside of himself, he could learn to perceive the workings of others, he would be able to choose better leaders. He would be able to do whatever it is that he does in his profession far better if he had this added lucidity, this clairvoyance that the recognition of other people's subtlety and complexity gives.

As recently as a few weeks ago, I was reading a book called *Future Shock*—which gave *me* a shock! Because it implied that because of technology and our world's accelerated rhythm, we were doomed not to relate to each other. Because things were happening so fast and we were moving from town to town and we were uprooted and we were transients, we didn't have time really for relation. What shocked me was the concept that technology should dictate to us what our human relations should be and decide that because our life has been accelerated we have no time for relationship. This is the unfortunate consequence of the false concept we had about *contact*. And what helped us to distort the sense of contact was the media, which gave us the illusion that we were in touch with all the world and everything that was happening in the world. The media fabricate personalities and offer as false a vision of the world as we can possibly have. Although sometimes it serves us, most of the time it deceives us. So, ultimately it comes back to the way we conceive of human beings or events or history or wars or other nations or other races; only from some kind of evaluation from within, not from the media, do we really come to an understanding of others. The media give us a false sense of communication and of contact.

We talk about media and we talk about new sensitive tapes and we think about all kinds of ways of recording, but we never think of our bodies and our mind and our hearts as receptors. And that can only happen when we develop a sensitivity, when we get rid of the defenses which I call the calluses of the soul. R. D. Laing has a beautiful long paragraph explaining that while we all have a hope of authentic encounters and relationships taking place, they will not take place until we unmask ourselves, until we get rid of the persona, until we get rid of the defenses, the projections and introjections. He mentions all the interferences; and the diary revealed to me, when I finally opened it up to you, what those interferences were. They were mostly fear, fear of other human beings—which I suddenly lost the moment that I published the diaries. So the gamble proved to me that if we gamble in depth, if we offer the deep and the genuine part of ourselves, then it's not destructible. We cannot be destroyed.

Alvin Toffler also says in *Future Shock* that the students who are turning toward astrology, toward mysticism, toward the East, toward anything of the spirit, are *dropping out* of technology. I say: "No, they are trying to find a source of strength and a center so that technology doesn't enslave us, so that we are the captains of our own lives." So I don't agree with him at all. The turning toward other things is really an attempt to create a self which can then survive in the air in which we live. He lays great stress on what he calls the acceleration of our lives, and he argues that this is ruining the possibility of contact, of friendships. But I was able to disprove that this year because I took an unusually heavy load of lectures. I couldn't say no; I said yes, yes, yes and I went all over the country. Finally it became very accelerated. I saw so many people, and they passed by so quickly. Yet in spite of that, seeing thousands of people, I was able to select friends and make friendships in those few minutes of passing. So it isn't necessary for us to be victims of accelerated living or of transience or of moving away. It is a question of how deep the contact is when the contact is made.

I always had the wish to commune with others, despite the fact that during childhood, what I call my bridge to the world was broken by the desertion of the father, a situation which usually instills a great deal of mistrust. Traumas create this mistrust of human beings, because a human being can hurt you, can desert you, can betray you. Yet I still say that it's a million times better to risk being deserted or betrayed than to withdraw into a fortress of aliena-tion, shut the door and break the contact with others. Because then we really die. That is death. That is emotional death. It is mistrust that makes us do that, mistrust and fear of pain, which I expressed in the diary very often. As a child of eleven, I said I never wanted to love again because whatever you love you lose—I was thinking of my Spanish grandmother whom I would never see again. So I learned that mistrust was the root of the separation between human beings.

I struggled all my life—now with the women's studies, with

the women's movement, with men—to involve everyone in this connection, this contact which comes out of feeling for others. For though I experienced mistrust, I did not let that make me insensitive. Yet what *Future Shock* says, specifically almost, is that we are bound to become insensitive; that since we receive too much information, are battered by too many events, and are confronted with the whole universe, the best thing to do and the thing we will ultimately do is to shut off the source of feeling. That's why it's a dangerous book, I think. It's a shocking book because it is accepting what technology might do to us instead of saying we have to struggle against this tendency, against the dehumanization and loss of contact occasioned by the acceleration of life or the fact that we move about so much.

I read a remarkable statement the other day about Aldous Huxley who, toward the end of his life when he was invited to speak at Berkeley, said, "I expect that you think I will talk about very scholarly things and give you the sum of all my life's knowledge." And he went on and on about what he knew people expected of him. But then he said: "Tonight I only feel like coming to ask you to be a little kinder to each other."

This warmth is something we all need, we need nourishment, we need encouragement. Our culture, however, made us ashamed of paying compliments, of saying beautiful things to other people. We were not supposed to. A compliment was a falsity in itself to the Puritan. You never said anything complimentary. Now the Latin races encourage compliments. They believe that if someone looks beautiful today one should say it. Why do we eliminate that? Why should we consider it false to give each other the nourishing encouragement which sustains us, which is the obverse of destructive criticism, of hostility?

Messages are conveyed by the eyes, sometimes by no words at all. It is no excuse to say that technology has accelerated our life to the point where we pass others without noticing them, without contacting, or without a real meeting. A real meeting can take place in one instant. But how does that come about? How do we reach a moment when in one instant we can communicate with another human being?

The most beautiful metaphor I know for this connecting with others I discovered when I was invited to Stanford by the electrical engineers to talk about the integrated circuits. I couldn't understand first of all why I was invited. I didn't know anything about integrated circuits. I tried to read the book by the professor who invited me and finally had to ask my friends for explanations. When I got there I was shown through the laboratory and finally talked with the fifteen electrical engineers who do electronic circuits. They showed me the drawings on the walls, the large drawings that they start with and which become smaller and smaller. And then I understood that as a metaphor this was really a wonderful thing. Of course when the artist is ignorant of science then he turns science into a metaphor. And I always said that the artist today will use the images of science, that he will use all the marvelous metaphors of science when he really begins to understand them. So I began to understand the integrated circuit, and I began to think of it as an image of our psychic problem, which was really to find all these fine, terribly delicate connections with other human beings.

Now these circuits are damaged very often in childhood and we don't receive anything. These circuits very often are damaged by the culture or they become insensitive to stimuli. There is also in *Future Shock* the theory that, as a result of technology, we are receiving too many messages, too much information which we cannot cope with, too much devastating news of everything that is happening in the world, and that the way human beings protect themselves from too much emotional receptivity is by trying not to feel at all. And Toffler points out the dangers, just as the psychologists have, of what corresponds to the physical shock in the face of an accident or a sudden death or a sudden tragedy: the body ceases in a sense to be really alive or conscious, and this condition, known as psychic shock, is the way we protect ourselves when we see, for instance, the war in Vietnam on television. The way we have learned to protect ourselves is *not to feel*, which is a terrible danger because then we really become sub-human or non-human and are as far away from our real connection with other human beings as we possibly can be. So we have to fight these dangerous elements in technology which come with an expanded universe and the illusion the media give us of being in touch with everything simply because we are given so much to *see*. You can only be in touch by feeling.

So the integrated circuit is really for the human being quite different from the scientific integrated circuit. It is really the channel of feeling that has to be kept open. Now how do we do that when we want to protect ourselves from feeling too much or from being devastated or being disintegrated by experience? Well, my suggestion was that you build up a sufficient inner spiritual resistance—what I call "the spirit house." We must not close off the circuits, the emotional circuits. That's not the way. Because then we become arid and we really die, psychically. So all those words we used so carelessly before, such as alienation, dropping out, all those words really had a very fatal meaning. Because it is really a kind of death to separate from others, to separate from what is happening in the world, to separate from feeling.

I think if we came back to the concept of a small and intimate universe and then realized that what we call the communal life or mass movements are really aggregates of individuals and that the more marvelous, the more developed, the more expanded, the deeper, the more poetic, the more free the individual is, then the mass, the larger movements, would take on a different character. We would not be subjected then to the will or to the distorted power-thoughts of other people. Somehow we felt that the best thing for the community was to abdicate our individuality, not to think for ourselves or to examine ourselves, never realizing that what we could bring to the group and what we brought to the communal life was really the summary of our own self-development, our own growth, and that the more we bring something that *we* have already worked out to the collective life, the more we bring to this mass movement. If we brought something besides our problems or our difficulties or the unsolved parts of our lives, then these tremendously large movements would have another character. They would not serve for war and they wouldn't serve for separations between races and they wouldn't divide us. We wouldn't have so much hostility as we have in our society, a frightening amount of hostility. It's almost a blind hostility that doesn't even know where it comes from, blind anger which strikes out at others and blames others always for whatever trouble we find ourselves in.

To me war is a multiplication of our own hostilities, and possibly we are beginning to realize that. For example, when I went to Germany, invited to the Book Fair, I went with a tight heart because so many of my friends are Jews, and I felt very full of hatred of Germany. But on the radio they had a philosopher, who is now the head of the government of the new Germany, saying that we had to combat hostility, individually, every one of us, if we didn't want a war again. *He was saying that, over the radio.* That was my first inkling that possibly there was a new Germany—this consciousness of what hostility or of what passivity toward the leader could lead to.

So we can't go on just marching and expecting the change to come always from outside. We tried and we saw that some external changes could be made: the abortion laws, women's rights. There are some changes that can be effected from the outside. But the greatest and most important change must be inner; we must change ourselves as human beings. Because we have really caused minor wars and minor types of violence right amongst ourselves, within our immediate and personal situations: in the family, in relationships, in school, and through our hostility towards the stranger. I experienced that very strongly when I first came to America. The foreigner was an outsider. This feeling belongs to the American culture, and until recently (now I've been adopted) they always used to say "Paris-born

Anaïs Nin"—as they say "Russian-born Nabokov" or "Polish-born Kozinski." That is a way of saying that you are an outsider.

Then the anger about blaming society for the situation in which we find ourselves—blaming, say, man for the situation in which woman finds herself. I don't believe in that because I believe very much our double responsibility, that we engage ourselves in destructive relationships, that we have a part of the responsibility, unconsciously. When I engaged in a destructive relationship with Gonzalo, there was a part of me that was living through him—the rebel—which I refused to live out myself. I wasn't a victim of anything. There was something going on there which happened to be a destructive alliance. But there was also a positive thing; he was showing me how destructive explosions were, how destructive that kind of rebellion was, the kind of rebellion he manifested. So that I was learning, I was experiencing, I was testing that through another person.

I'll tell you one thing I do feel. I feel we do have a surplus of hostility, of undirected hostility, because we refuse to take part of the responsibility for the things we find ourselves caught in, and that we despair because we only live on the external part of history. If we are going to live in history then we are going to have despair; if we find absolutely no nourishing, no revitalizing, no recharging power in ourselves, then we're going to be bitter and we are always going to be shifting the blame either to society or to the other—or on man, as some women are doing at the moment. You see this makes us feel helpless. If we are helpless, we are angry and if we are angry, we're violent.

I came to realize that our need and hunger for closeness, after the terrible period of alienation, occurred because we always blamed alienation on every possible cause except the right one. We were alienated from *ourselves*. How could we love, how could we give, how could we trust, how could we share what we didn't have to give? If we did not spend some time in creating ourselves in depth and power, with what were we going to relate to others?

And of course when you're interested in growth, you're interested in the growth of those around you. They are absolutely interdependent. You grow only insofar as people around you are also growing and expanding and becoming freer. It is something that is interactive, something that you give to each other.

It isn't something that you accomplish alone. What you accomplish alone and what you have to do first of all is to *exist*, to *be*, so that you can be then a friend or a lover or a mother or a child. In other words, what our culture was saying was something so illogical, so impossible. It was saying: "Don't concern yourself with yourself. Be generous, be active in the world, give yourself to causes and all that *without a self!"* What can you give when there is no self, when you have no sensitivity, no receptivity, no warmth, nothing to contact others *with?* And this error grew and grew.

In our twenties we have conflicts. We think everything is either-or, black or white; we are caught between them and we lose all our energy in the conflicts. My answer, later on in maturity, was to do them all. Not to exclude any, not to make a choice. I wanted to be a woman, I wanted to be an artist, I wanted to be everything. And I took everything in, and the more you take in the more strength you find waiting to accomplish things and to expand your life, instead of the other (which is what we have been taught to do) which is to look for structure and to fear change, *above all to fear change.* Now I didn't fear change, and that is another thing I learned from psychology, that we evolve. We don't need revolutions provided we evolve, provided we are constantly open to new experience, provided we are open to other human beings and what they have to give us.

There is a beautiful book, entitled *Out of Africa*, by Isak Dinesen, who had a coffee farm and lived a long time with the Africans. Natural disasters played a central role in the court of justice of the Africans and were used as evidence, whether in the case of an accident or a deliberate act like murder. This is a totally different idea of justice, absolutely different from ours, and she had a very difficult time trying to see things as the Africans saw them. But she conceded that it was part of their culture and it was sincere. It was their concept of justice, and it had to be carried out. She didn't try to impose white justice on the African village. The recognition of other cultures and other forms of thought, knowing when to yield, I think is part of our gift for relationship. There is a time when yielding is not conceding but acceptance of the other's existence and also of the motivation for what he does.

This is a good night to talk about the source of strength which we need when the outer changes fail us. Before, when I talked about that, people said I was referring to the Ivory Tower, to a great concern and obsession with art and a turning away from action. But I never meant that. I meant that they were interrelated and that when we can't act in the outside or the outside doesn't change and we want to break our heads against the things that we can't change, then it is time just simply to move back to the center of ourselves. I discovered this source of strength in the way all of us discover a source of strength, which is during the first traumatic experiences, the first handicaps, the first difficulties. Coming from what the social welfare calls the broken home, being uprooted, knowing what poverty is, coming to a country whose language I didn't know—all these things taught me simply to put my roots in the self. As I said, I became "a lady with transportable roots." This is very important to all of us because our culture gave us a false impression of the value of living completely in history, completely objectively, completely outside in what was happening—that there was something almost evil about subjectivity. . . . So I like to have this image of a place where you construct some source of strength, some way of resisting outer pressures. And I didn't mean the Ivory Tower. I often say if you write me a letter to the Ivory Tower, I won't answer.

I started with a conviction which I've never had to retract: that all of us can be hurt or in trouble. I had another conviction, which came from Baudelaire, that in all of us there is a man, a woman, and child—which solves all the question of militancy! In all of us there is a man, a woman, and a child, and the child is usually an orphan. So we have a tremendous task to do: we have to take care of this orphan in ourselves and in others; we have to act out our creativity in every moment of our life. And I remember doing something which was considered very silly at the time. When war was imminent in '39, I was living on a houseboat. I hadn't finished painting and fixing it and so I was still working on it while my friends were collapsing and saying: "The war is coming. Why are you painting and fixing the boat?" I said: "Well, I'm only doing it to sustain my own defiance of catastrophe." It was really a spiritual thing. I had to do that to maintain myself from collapsing—as they were collapsing *in my boat!* It was just a challenge. You see, I knew the war was coming. It wasn't lack of a sense of reality, it wasn't schizophrenia. I knew perfectly well what was coming. But I wanted to make a gesture which strengthened *me*, which strengthened this capacity to endure catastrophe.

This is why I have been able to speak, for instance at City College in Los Angeles, which is almost entirely Black. They are the most underprivileged students that you could possibly imagine, their backgrounds are so very difficult. But they understood when I spoke. They had a student paper, and all the paper said was: the world is falling apart. That was their image of the world—that it was hopeless. They had lost faith in any social change, and the only thing they did understand was that I asked them to put their stability in themselves. They understood that, the search, in an unstable world, for a place of stability and clarity and faith. Some place to recover their faith. Because they feel that the external is immovable.

Walter Lippmann said that "the discontent that is shocking the world cannot be dealt with by politics only, or on the periphery of life, but must touch the central and intimate places of personal life. What has been wrecked cannot be restored by some new political gadget." This has been the substance of all my talks this year.

1. What does Nin mean by a "refusal to despair"? Why does she object to viewing personal development as an escape? Why does she also object to the dichotomy of the collective life and personal development?

2. How can one effect external changes by developing one's own personal life? What can be accomplished by individual growth to reduce the amount of hostility in the world?

3. What does Nin suggest is the reason for an individual's inability to establish authentic relationships? What was the result of the publication of her diaries? How does she describe her childhood? What did she learn from her experiences?

4. What are Nin's objections to Alvin Toffler's *Future Shock*? Why does she object to Toffler's thesis? What does she think about the influence of technology and the media?

5. What are the effects of technology? What measures does Nin suggest to combat these effects? What does she feel is the result of anger toward society? Why does she object to the term "dropping out"?

6. What external changes have been accomplished through collective action, according to the author? Why aren't revolutions necessary to effect changes?

7. What is implied by the term "Ivory Tower"? Why does Nin object to being identified with the Ivory Tower? Why did her message receive a favorable response from the black City College students? What is your reaction to her message? Explain.

1. What aspects of this article distinguish it as a speech? What factors make a speech different from an essay? Do you believe that this selection would be more effective if spoken by Anaïs Nin?

2. Why does the author feel that the metaphor of integrated circuits appropriately expresses her thesis?

3. Why is she so impressed by the speech made by the head of the German government? Why is this example a reason for optimism?

4. What symbolism is involved in Nin's rebuilding her houseboat just before World War II? How does this exemplify her message?

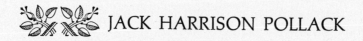 JACK HARRISON POLLACK

Are Teachers Fair to Boys?

Boys generally aren't treated as fairly as girls in the crucial elementary grades, according to a series of studies recently reported in the *National Elementary School Principal*, published by the National Education Association. Countless teachers, the overwhelming majority of whom are women, expect boy pupils to behave, react, and learn like girls. Even though frequently unaware of it, many of these women teachers value neatness and cleanliness above individual initiative. They prefer conformity, mental passivity, and gentle obedience—at which girls excel—to the aggressive drive and originality of many boys.

In discipline especially, girls get the breaks. Sixth-grade boys receive infinitely more disapproval or blame than girls, getting into eight times more trouble in the classroom's "control" or "managerial" aspects, reveals psychologist Philip W. Jackson of the University of Chicago.

No less shocking, men as well as women teachers generally use a harsher or angrier tone of voice when scolding boys. Girls are criticized in a more normal tone, Dr. Robert L. Spaulding found in a 2-year study for the U.S. Office of Education.

Typical of this discrimination in discipline, a 12-year-old Pennsylvania boy recalls, "One day when all of us were joking in class, the teacher told two of the girls just to keep quiet but sent three of us boys to the principal."

Twice as many boys as girls are reported to principals for behavior and learning problems. Three times as many develop stuttering difficulties. Nearly two-thirds of all grade-repeaters are boys.

Women principals sometimes share this unconscious bias against boys. In a Southern state recently, a class of second-grade boys and girls were marching in separate lines to the playground, led by their young woman teacher. All of the children were happily sauntering, laughing, jogging, dancing, or gaily fingering the walls and railings. Suddenly, the fiftyish woman principal appeared and sternly rebuked one sex: "Why aren't you boys in a straight line? Don't you have any respect for your teacher?"

Paradoxically, such female teacher and principal hostility usually leads to counter-aggression in boys. Pauline S. Sears, Stanford University education professor who has intensively probed the problem, concludes: "Quite possibly, the harsh tones intended to cause boys to conform actually foster a defiant, independent attitude which reinforces the very behavior the teacher wishes to subdue."

The "trouble" caused by many independent, questioning boys results from their not being able to adjust to a classroom's institutional aspects. Elementary school too often is based on being able to sit at a desk and listen—which many restless boys find difficult. Teachers feel kindlier toward pupils whose behavior and talents facilitate their own pedagogic satisfactions. This teacher approval is more important to parrot-like girls than to boys. Bright boys are generally liked by a teacher if they are friendly, self-sufficient, *and* obedient.

But for the average woman teacher, most grammar school boys are harder to teach than girls. "Boys have greater manipulative curiosity than girls," explains a third-grade New York female teacher. "When controls are released, boys take advantage of them more. They go hog wild faster than girls, who have greater listening and looking skills."

Boys are also harder to handle. Not long ago a tall, 13-year-old, picked-on California boy finally said to his young eighth-grade substitute teacher in front of the class: "You're not as good as the last teacher we had." Tears rolled down the hurt teacher's cheeks. "If nobody appreciates me," she sobbed, "I'll leave. I don't have to teach here." She left the room and it was several minutes before she returned, composed.

"If there's a ruckus in my classroom," admits a fifth-grade Massachusetts woman teacher, "my eyes automatically turn to the boys I *expect* to be troublesome. But if it's a girl who happens to be making the noise, I tend to condone her behavior by saying to myself: 'Well, it's good for her to come out of her shell.' "

In grades, girls are likewise favored. Even when boys score as well on standardized achievement tests, they tend to receive lower report-card marks. "Though the evidence isn't conclusive," points out Professor Sears, "it seems that girls are given higher grades than boys, despite the fact that boys achieve at least as well as girls, and in some cases better."

University of Minnesota educational psychologist E. P. Torrance suggests that girls receive their higher academic rewards because of their conforming behavior. It isn't that girls *really* achieve better than boys in school—their teachers just *think* they do. "One wonders if girls receive the implicit message that creative thinking is for boys and conformity for girls," asks Professor Sears.

An 18-year-old, now a college freshman, reflects, "My boyfriend Ben used to crack jokes all through grammar and high school and got his women teachers mad—so they gave him poor marks. But he was brilliant. He took an exam and won a scholarship and also became a chess champion. Unlike grammar school teachers, most high school women teachers like boys. But Ben bothered them with his nagging questions. Frankly, I'm not half as smart as Ben even though I got better grades all through high school."

University of Maryland vice president Walter B. Waetjen contends, "Doing well in school doesn't make a girl more intellectual or interested in intellectual pursuits."

As early as the first grade, boys and girls are aware of this sex discrimination in areas other than discipline and marks. First-grade boys and girls studied in reading groups by University of California (UCLA) psychologist John D. McNeil agreed that boys had fewer chances to respond. And when they did, they received more negative comments from the teachers on their answers and reading performances.

Is it any wonder that, by the second grade, small boys often consider school a female institution—and therefore hostile to them!

Much of this sex stereotyping stems from the popular belief that there are certain things boys "should" do and other things girls "should" do. Parents unwittingly begin this sex differentiation—and most teachers perpetuate it. Artistic achievement, for example, isn't *expected* of boys; problem-solving isn't *expected* of girls. American boys aren't *expected* to be interested in the ballet, even though teenage Russian boys are because of their heritage. But America would be richer if boys and girls developed *all* of these skills to the fullest.

In many other ways, we stereotype the behavior of males and females. Boys aren't *expected* to cry because it is considered unmasculine. Only sissies—and females—cry, it is commonly believed. "The little boy is deprived of the pleasure of tears—he is reminded that boys are brave," observes Dr. Irene M. Josselyn, Phoenix psychoanalyst.

Typical of this sex stereotyping is the case of the five-year-old Eastern kindergarten boy whose woman teacher asked him what kind of a toy he wanted to play with.

"The doll's house," he said.

"Oh, no," she retorted. "Boys aren't *supposed* to do that. That's for girls. Go play with the fire engine."

The young boy—whose father happened to be a doll manufacturer—felt there was something wrong and abnormal about his interest.

Similarly, a studious eight-year-old Ohio boy was taunted by his woman teacher for remaining in the classroom and reading during his recess period instead of playing with the other children in the schoolyard. Anxious to prove his "masculinity" to his teacher, he started a fight with another boy one day in the hallway and later became a serious delinquency problem.

Boys and girls don't learn how to be different—they just naturally are—physically, intellectually, and emotionally. Yet we stereotype boys and girls almost from birth. Hospital delivery rooms usually wrap a newborn infant in either blue or pink blanket. From that moment on a child's maleness or femaleness is reinforced.

Scientists agree that these differences—which some teachers fail to recognize while they insist upon conformity and obedience—appear shortly after birth and in the weeks that follow.

The lesser maturity of infant boys was demonstrated by Dr.

Howard Moss, a National Institute of Mental Health researcher. He observed three-week- and three-month-old infants for seven and eight hours at a time. His findings: Boy babies slept less, cried more, demanded more attention. And many of the male infants seemed to be much more inconsolable than the girls—also a sign of lesser maturity.

These differences result in considerable unwitting discrimination against boys by women teachers.

Boys mature more slowly than girls. At age six, physically they are at least a year behind. Yet women teachers often *expect* boy first-graders to write as well as girls, even though their hand muscles are less developed.

Edward Feeney, elementary school supervisor in Prince Georges County, Maryland, reminds us: "We expect boys in the first grade to use the pencil and shape letters just as well as girls. But right in the first grade we begin to frustrate some of these boys by making them do something which isn't natural. Why is it so important that their writing be neat, perfectly shaped, and lovely to display in the classroom?"

A summary of 900 studies edited by Stanford educational psychology professor Eleanor E. Maccoby in her *The Development of Sex Differences* reveals:

Little boys start more fights, make more noise, take more risks, think more independently, are harder to educate than girls, and are more fragile. They are more likely to stutter, to have reading problems, and to suffer emotional quirks of every kind. They lag behind girls in physical development, and even at the start of school, their hand control is less mature.

Little girls, on the other hand, are more robust and mature, yet more dependent, submissive, conforming, and unadventurous. They are more interested in people than in things, show more concern for others, are more sensitive to others' reactions, and are far more likely to remember names and places.

While there is no difference in IQ levels in early childhood, girls excel in verbal abilities. They talk earlier, spell better, and write more. Boys outclass them in mathematics, science, and creative thinking.

A teacher's inability or unwillingness to recognize these differences in styles of thinking and learning—and to act accordingly—can be responsible, in part at least, for the seeds of hate and rebellion that sprout into delinquency.

In school, women teachers tend to ask questions and demand answers which favor female patterns of thinking. For example, a girl is more likely to remember the details of a presidential campaign. By contrast, a boy is more likely to question its purposes.

This questioning quality of boys often disturbs many women teachers.

Studies by Harvard psychologist Jerome Bruner and others reveal that the nurturing warmth of a woman in a boy's early years can aid him immeasurably in later life. Thousands of dedicated women teachers, especially those trained in modern child development, are fulfilling this vital role magnificently.

But what can be done to give boys a better break in women-oriented schools where the teachers are frustrated, hostile, and male-resenting? "Too many woman elementary teachers and principals have an unconscious 'getting-even' attitude toward boys," claim University of Maryland professors Jean D. Grambs and Walter B. Waetjen. "Their overinsistence on boy conformity may in effect be reflected in the feeling: 'My father, brother, and male superintendent all think I'm less than they are. Well, I'll show them. Johnny, behave yourself! You are bad and, besides, that was a stupid question!' "

A hopeful trend is that the traditional old-maid school marm is fast being replaced by a married woman in kindergarten and first grade—25 per cent of whom have their own children under age 10, according to a recent survey by *Grade Teacher* magazine.

Everyone agrees that more male teachers are needed in elementary schools. "But we drive them away because we try to make them fit into a female mold," observes supervisor Edward Feeney. "We want them to have nice potted plants in their classrooms and murals on the wall. Why is it so important to get men to behave like women?"

But since male teachers for the lower grades are so hard to get, authorities now suggest that males could be added to elementary school staffs as co-principals, psychologists, counselors, and teacher-researchers. This would not hurt a man's self-esteem—any more than it does a doctor's working with young children. Their presence would not only give reassurance to boy pupils, but could often comfort a fretting Miss Jones who could come to them with her teacher problems.

Another suggestion is hiring young male teacher aides, possibly youths needing jobs through the Neighborhood Youth Corps, who could be assigned playground and lunch-room duty and ride the school buses.

Still another proposal is getting older boy pupils—sixth-graders perhaps—to volunteer as tutors and companions in kindergartens and first and second grades. "They might be better able to think *with* the very young boys than women teachers can," suggests Dr. Waetjen. "The use of older tutors has been successfully demonstrated in some poverty programs as a way of getting low achieving children to achieve better. Certainly the average and able boy in the upper grades can find satisfaction in being helpful to younger children."

This male restructuring of elementary schools can also benefit girls. Girls need an environment which permits them to view men and boys as colleagues, not as competitors—which allows them access to the lure of science and the puzzles of mathematics. Boys, of course, need freedom and encouragement to enjoy the esthetics of creativity, and the opportunity and guidance to develop sensitivity to human motivations and feelings.

Aware that boys mature slower than girls, Maryland curriculum director Elizabeth Wilson says, "Our schools are factory oriented. We put all the boys and girls together in square boxes and try to make them come out the same shapes at the other end of the educational process. We try to produce assembly-line children—all children in fifth grade should be like so; all six-year-olds should do such and such. Why shouldn't boys take longer to go through elementary school? Why should it be a disgrace?"

Aware that boys mature more slowly than girls, researchers at the Gesell Institute of Child Development recommend that most boys should be fully five and a half years old before starting kindergarten and fully six and a half before entering first grade. Says Dr. Louise Bates Ames, director of research: "Of course, many teachers favor girls because the girls are sitting there and learning while the boys aren't. But give boys an extra six months or a year and you'll see our first and second grades revolutionized, with fewer dropouts and less delinquency later."

A unique experiment in separate classes for boys and girls, as in most European and U.S. private schools, has enjoyed satisfactory results at the Wakefield Forest Elementary School in Fairfax County, Virginia. Ever since the program was started seven years ago, these sex-separated classes have been continued and expanded, but the boys and girls are not isolated from one another. They come together for assemblies, lunch periods, recesses, and some physical-education activities.

"There are now fewer serious discipline problems," explains principal Thomas B. Lyles. "The behavior of the boys in separate classes seems more normal and more acceptable to teachers. Children who have been withdrawn become more outgoing, more confident. This is true of both boys and girls. Students are more willing to ask questions if they do not understand something and feel freer to discuss ideas which otherwise might be embarrassing. In health classes, for example, both boys and girls are more at ease in studying the body. Boys are more thoughtful and considerate of each other, wanting to help each other. The lack of distractions from the opposite sex results in better work habits. Boys take part more freely in art and music and do better work in foreign languages when in separate classes. Both boys and girls overcome their fear of standing in front of a class to give reports and oral readings.

"In all-boy and all-girl classes, we have used different songs and rhythms. For girls, we use quieter games, fairy stories, and games and songs which emphasize feminine activities such as sewing and housekeeping. For boys, we use more active physical games which involve noise and muscle movement and are based on a transportation theme.

"Different reading series are also used. Girls enjoy all stories in readers, even those about boys, but boys do not like stories about girls. Boys prefer adventure tales and stories about industry and vocations. We plan many discussions and round-table talks for the girls because they need this practice in independent thinking."

But since it isn't practical today to separate boys and girls in most school systems, all-boy or all-girl debates, contests, dramatic and musical clubs might give pupils the confidence and enthusiasm of separate classes. Limited separation, for special ages and subjects, also has been recommended.

Mixed or sex-separated classes, there still is no basic solution to the cramping and frustrating of millions of little Johnnies who get the short end of the stick in so many woman-oriented American schools.

What can be done about teacher? Is there any way to resolve her irritation, impatience, and often nervous crises because boys are loud, noisy, slow learners, and full of animal spirits that bring on her migraines? How deep is the antagonism which makes her snap harshly at boys even when no offense has been meant? Is the pain initially in her own nature? Are boy pupils her unconscious victims because she may hate men?

Shortsighted parents don't help matters. Studies at Stanford and elsewhere reveal that many parents actually encourage greater aggression in their sons than daughters by reinforcing the "sex roles" stereotype. This aggression, in turn, becomes part of a boy's character—which often contributes to his classroom cacophony.

For parents of boys, a psychiatrist has a helpful suggestion. "If you don't expect your son's reading or handwriting to be the best, it may take some unnecessary pressure off him," advises Dr. Stanley F. Yolles, director of the National Institute of Mental Health.

Children do best in school, Stanford's Eleanor Maccoby found, when boys are less bold and impulsive than the "real" boy— and when girls are less timid and conforming than the "real" girl. Sure, little boys and girls are made of different things and not just sugar and spice and puppy tails. But the brightest girls are those with the *widest* interests, including such "masculine" subjects as mathematics, motors, and abstract problems. Similarly, the smartest boys respond to such "feminine" traits as child-rearing and homemaking.

A wise father reveals, "I always try to answer my daughter's naïve questions about business and science, though frankly it isn't always easy." An equally intelligent mother admits, "Whenever my son shows an interest in cooking, I encourage him to experiment himself. I'm sure this won't make him a sissy, but just a better and more understanding husband and father."

In life as well as in school, possessing so-called attributes and interests of the opposite sex is an advantage. "Children should be helped to accept their own sex with a sense of fulfillment and value the complementary role of the opposite sex," suggests psychoanalyst Dr. Irene M. Josselyn. As shrewd old Ben Franklin pointed out, "It is the man and woman united that makes the complete human being."

The America of tomorrow needs men who are not limited to aggressive "masculine" characteristics but capable of showing the more "feminine" traits of warmth and sensitivity to others' feelings. And we need women who are less conforming, more original and daring in their thinking.

Unhappily, in too many of the nation's female-oriented schools we are still planting the seeds which may be making millions of Johnnies low-achievers, dropouts, truants, delinquents, and maladjusted members of society.

PROBING FOR MEANING

1. On what differences in treatment between boys and girls in the lower grades does Pollack concentrate? Why are boys disciplined more harshly than girls? Why is neatness a central aspect of the problem?

2. What does Pollack suggest are the reasons for the differences in treatment? In what way do sex-role stereotypes contribute to the problem?

3. What are the differences between boys and girls in adolescence? What are the specific differences in general learning abilities?

4. What solutions to the problem of female teachers who are biased against males does Pollack suggest? What is his solution to the problem? What reasons does he give to support sex-separated classes?

5. What suggestions does Pollack present for parents?

6. Judging from your school experiences, do you concur with Pollack's view of the problem? Do you also feel it is necessary for boys and girls to be encouraged to possess the attributes and interests of the opposite sex? For example, do you feel boys should be taught child rearing and homemaking?

1. Why does the author include so many quotations? In general terms, what is the reason for the exact quotation of a source? In your opinion, does the emphasis on sources detract from the originality of an essay?

2. Why does Pollack present so many short paragraphs? Briefly, how does he develop transitions between paragraphs?

3. What is the tone of the essay? What kind of audience is Pollack attempting to reach?

 THEODOR REIK

From *Of Love and Lust*

[Sigmund Freud assumed] that sex includes love, tenderness, charity and sympathy. What superficially appears to be of the same kind shows profound differences upon finer analysis. The situation can be compared with that of chemists who for a long time thought a certain substance to be homogeneous until a new examination showed this not to be so. The substance turned out to be a mixture of two different substances, a fusion of very dissimilar components.

I choose a very simple instance: our common table salt. The example is not at all inappropriate.

Was not salt considered a precious and sacred substance through the ages? It was the symbol of friendship, loyalty and affection. The Arabs say, "There is salt between us," when they mean an affectionate and loyal friendship. The "covenant of salt" which you find in the Bible was recognized as full of sacredness and deep meaning. For almost two thousand years salt was considered a coherent and homogeneous substance. We know now that is chemically a compound of sodium and chlorine. Any high-school pupil today knows that these two elements are different, and he would be able to demonstrate to you that salt is a fusion of both. He also knows that these two substances can be isolated and can be used for various purposes separately.

What are the facts? We first want to get hold of them. We can put them together later on. We want to discriminate between sex and love as the chemist would isolate the sodium element from chlorine in the combination, salt. To make the differences clear and clean-cut it is best to contrast love and sex in their extreme manifestations, where they do not yet appear fused.

Sex is an instinct, a biological need, originating in the organism, bound to the body. It is one of the great drives, like hunger and thirst, conditioned by chemical changes within the organism. The time is not far distant when we shall think of libido in chemical terms, and in chemical terms only. The sex urge is dependent on inner secretions. It can be localized in the genitals and in other erogenic zones. Its aim is the disappearance of a physical tension. It is originally objectless. Later on the sexual object is simply the means by which the tension is eased.

None of these characteristics can be found in love. If we do not accept the opinion of the ordinary man and woman that love lives in the heart we are unable to place it. It certainly is not a biological need, because there are millions of people who do not feel it and many centuries and cultural patterns in which it is unknown. We cannot name any inner secretions or specific glands which are responsible for it. Sex is originally objectless. Love certainly is not. It is a very definite, emotional relationship between a Me and a You.

What is the aim of sex? We have already stated it: the disappearance of a *physical* tension, a discharge and a *release*. What is the aim of the desire we call love? Disappearance of a *psychical* tension, *relief*. In this contrast between release and relief lies one of the most decisive differences. Sex wants satisfaction; love wants happiness.

Sex appears as a phenomenon of nature, common to men and beasts. Love is the result of a cultural development and is not even found among all men. We know that the sex urge is subject to periodic fluctuations of increase and decrease. This is of course quite obvious among the beasts, but survivals of its original nature are easily recognized in men. Nothing of this kind is known about love. Sex can be casual about its object. Love cannot. Love is always a personal relationship. This is not necessarily so with sex.

The object of sex may become of no account, boring or even hateful immediately after satisfaction is reached and the tension reduced. Not so the love-object. Referring to the extreme and crudest cases, the sexual partner can appear as a kind of appendage to the other's sexual parts, as a sexual object only. The object of love is always seen as a person and a personality. The sexual object has to have certain physical qualities which excite or arouse one. If they are lacking one remains indifferent. Not so the love object. It has to have certain psychical qualities which are highly valued, the existence of which is not demanded from a mere sexual object. Even when your object is both loved and sexually desired you can often discriminate between the sex appeal and the appeal of personality, and you know that they are different things. The sex urge hunts for lustful pleasure; love is in search of joy and happiness.

Again considering only extreme types, sex is utterly selfish, using the object only in order to get satisfaction. Love is not unselfish, but it is very difficult to name its selfish aims, other than that of being happy in the happiness of the beloved person. In no case can love be only selfish, or as selfish as sex. Then it would not be love. It is always concerned with the welfare or happiness of the other person, regrets the other's absence, wants to be together with the object, feels lonely without it, fears calamity or danger for it. There is nothing of this kind in crude sex. If the individual is not aroused by sexual wishes the presence of the sex object is not desired and its absence not regretted. The same is true after sexual satisfaction is reached. I have heard men say that the only wish they felt after a satisfactory intercourse was to be left alone—alone meaning that the sexual object should leave them. One man said, "Women should be like stars—rise late in the evening and disappear early in the morning." No such wish is imaginable toward a loved object.

Sex (always considering the crudest types) is undiscriminating. It wants "a woman." It is modest in its demands. But love always makes a choice. It is highly discriminating. It insists on "this woman" and no other. There is no such thing as an impersonal love. The sensually desired person and the adored one, the sex object and the love object, can be two different persons. The sex object can become the center of all one's wishes under the pressure of sexual needs. It can, for moments, be idolized. It cannot be idealized. Only love can work that. The other day an American girl, disgusted with the rumor that Australian girls exercised a strong fascination upon the American soldiers stationed overseas, wrote to her boy friend, "What have they got that we haven't?" He answered, "Nothing, except one thing. They are here." This answer you certainly would not expect from love, but you would very readily expect it from sex. Absence makes the heart grow fonder. There is—in normal cases, at least—no similar effect of absence on the sexual partner. Sex gives satisfaction. Love gives comfort.

The sex aim is not identical with the love aim. Recently a patient said of her partner, "He is not the person I love, but the person who gives me sexual gratification." Sex is a passionate interest in another body; love a passionate interest in another personality, or in his life. Sex does not feel pain if its object is injured, nor joy when it is happy. It is possible to possess another person in sex, but not in love. In love you cannot possess another person, you can only belong to another person. You can force another person to sexual activity, but not to love.

Could you speak of sex partners as "two hearts that beat as one"? Would you not rather be concerned with other parts of the body? Could you, without being ridiculous, say that aim-inhibited sex never ends? Could you swear eternal sex attraction? Jupiter laughs at the oaths of lovers, but at such sex-inspired oaths all gods and mortals would laugh. Would it not sound funny for the young Cherubino in Mozart's opera to ask us, "Say, is it sex now which in me burns?" You might think there would be certain signs that would help a young man to decide the question very easily so that there could be no doubt about it in his mind. The only doubt there could be—and which there is—is whether it is merely sex desire that he feels or love.

Sex is bound up with the time element, with the rhythm of the ebb and flow of the urge. After the orgasm sexual desire sharply or slowly vanishes. There is nothing comparable to that in love. There is need of variety in sex, but not in love. The sex object can be easily replaced, but not the love-object. There are many possible sexual objects, but only one who is loved. "The world is full of folks, it's true, but there was only one of you."

Its relation to time reveals the nature of sex as a drive, because in it we realize the cyclical character of the tissue needs as for hunger and thirst. We here see the results of the activity of internal stimuli which are activated by chemical changes within the body. Hunger is connected with contraction of the muscles of the walls of the stomach. Thirst springs from the dryness of the mucous membrane of the mouth; sex from organic pressures. Where are the organic stimuli for love, where the needs within the organism, the physical tension that drives the organism to remove the painful and unpleasant stimuli? Where is the analogy with hunger? When you are hungry the sight and smell of food rouses strong desire. After satiation your appetite disappears for the time being. The sight and smell of the dish you enjoyed a few minutes ago now leaves you cold. In this respect sex is distinctly comparable to hunger. The urge disappears after being satisfied. There is a tension, a spasm, a discharge and an anticlimax, sharply defined in time. Time does not play the same role in love. Lovers become aware of it only in the hour of parting. "It is the nightingale and not the lark."

Sex and love are so different that they belong to distinct realms of research fields; sex to the domain of biochemistry and physiology, love to the domain of the psychology of emotions. Sex is an urge, love is a desire.

But is not love a passion? Yes, of course it is, but do passions originate only in sex? Are there not other passions in us mortals as ardent and powerful as the sex urge? Is it not possible that they can blend with the sexual desires? The fact that all philosophers from Plato to Schopenhauer, all psychologists from Spencer to Havelock Ellis and Freud, have asserted that love is sexual in its origin and nature does not make the statement true. All their views have to face a set of facts and undergo the test for truth or falsity.

That love is aim-inhibited sex is more an escape from than an insight into the problem. Love is not a blurred carbon of sex, unconsciously sexual in its essence, derived from the same organic drive. Love can exist before sexual desire is felt for a person. It can outwear and outlive sex. There are old couples in whom the sex desire has vanished and who still love each other dearly. There are other cases in which sexual satisfaction with a particular partner is no longer desired, but where love continues. There are instances in which the sexual desire remains very vivid, while love has long since died. If love were only aim-inhibited sex its existence would not be imaginable with men and women who have no such inhibitions, who gratify their sexual wishes to the point of orgies. Nor would it be possible if all sex urge had vanished. And why should there be an intense desire for love in addition to the desire for a full and satisfactory sex life? If love is just a kind of arrested development of sex, how could the wish to love co-exist beside sexual exhaustion or the fulfillment of every normal and perverted impulse? The peak of sex gratification is ecstasy; the peak of love is beatitude.

Let us not be deceived by the logical fallacy that love and sex are so often united. Even where they overlap and are fused, even where sensual urge and tenderness melt into each other, a finer observation will recognize their qualities as discernible and differentiable. Are we not capable of thinking of love without sex and of sex without love? Even if it were true that there is an element of sex in every affection, it might be so infinitesimal as to be of no importance.

There are basic differences between a person who is sex-starved and one who is love-starved. Love is not a washed-out version of sex, not an anemic remnant, but something entirely different.

I know that sex meant something other to Freud than it means to most of his students, to whom it signifies sex and nothing more; but the word has proved stronger than his will to change its meaning. The result of the confusion has been disastrous.

What is hidden behind the emotions of love is not the sublimated or arrested sexual drive. When the cat is out of the bag it will be recognized as a different animal altogether.

PROBING FOR
MEANING

1. What are the major differences between sex and love, particularly in terms of their origins, their aims, their causes and effects, and their periods of occurrence? How is the object of love different from the sexual object?

2. Why does Reik believe that love is a cultural phenomenon?

3. Why does Reik feel it is important to differentiate between love and sex? What did Freud assume to be the relationship between love and sex? What influence has Freud's view had on following generations?

4. What does Reik mean when he says, "The peak of sex gratification is ecstasy; the peak of love is beatitude"? What is the difference between the two states?

PROBING FOR
METHOD

1. What is the basis for the analogy between common table salt and sex and love? Why does Reik establish the analogy at the beginning of the essay?

2. Give some examples of Reik's use of parallel structure to emphasize the contrast between love and sex.

3. Why does Reik repeatedly emphasize that he is considering sex and love "in their extreme manifestations"?

4. What is the analogy between sex and hunger? Why is this an important aspect of Reik's argument?

 DORIS LESSING

Notes for a Case History

Maureen Watson was born at 93 Nelson's Way, N.1., in 1942. She did not remember the war, or rather, when people said "The War," she thought of Austerity: couponed curtains, traded clothes, the half pound of butter swapped for the quarter of tea. (Maureen's parents preferred tea to butter.) Further back, at the roots of her life, she *felt* a movement of fire and shadow, a leaping and a subsidence of light. She did not know whether this was a memory or a picture she had formed, perhaps from what her parents had told her of the night the bomb fell two streets from Nelson's Way and they had all stood among piles of smoking rubble for a day and night, watching firemen hose the flames. This feeling was not only of danger, but of fatality, of being helpless before great impersonal forces; and was how she most deeply felt, saw, or thought an early childhood which the social viewer would describe perhaps like this: "Maureen Watson, conceived by chance on an unexpected granted-at-the-last-minute leave, at the height of the worst war in history, infant support of a mother only occasionally upheld (the chances of war deciding) by a husband she had met in a bomb shelter during an air raid: poor baby, born into a historical upheaval which destroyed forty million and might very well have destroyed her."

As for Maureen, her memories and the reminiscences of her parents made her dismiss the whole business as boring, and nothing to do with her.

It was at her seventh birthday party she first made this clear. She wore a mauve organdy frock with a pink sash, and her golden hair was in ringlets. One of the mothers said: "This is the first unrationed party dress my Shirley has had. It's a shame, isn't it?" And her own mother said: "Well of course these war children don't know what they've missed." At which Maureen said: "*I* am not a war child." "What are you then, love?" said her mother, fondly exchanging glances.

"I'm Maureen," said Maureen.

"And I'm Shirley," said Shirley, joining cause.

Shirley Banner was Maureen's best friend. The Watsons and the Banners were better than the rest of the street. The Watsons lived in an end house, at higher weekly payments. The Banners had a sweets-paper-and-tobacco shop.

Maureen and Shirley remembered (or had they been told?) that once Nelson's Way was a curved terrace of houses. Then the ground-floor level had broken into shops: a grocer's, a laundry, a hardware, a baker, a dairy. It seemed as if every second family in the street ran a shop to supply certain defined needs of the other families. What other needs were there? Apparently none; for Maureen's parents applied for permission to the Council, and the ground floor of their house became a second grocery shop, by way of broken-down walls, new shelves, a deepfreeze. Maureen remembered two small rooms, each with flowered curtains where deep shadows moved and flickered from the two small fires that burned back to back in the centre wall that divided them. These two rooms disappeared in clouds of dust from which sweet-smelling planks of wood stuck out. Strange but friendly men paid her compliments on her golden corkscrews and asked her for kisses, which they did not get. They gave her sips of sweet tea from their canteens (filled twice a day by her mother) and made her bracelets of the spiralling fringes of yellow wood. Then they disappeared. There was the new shop. Maureen's Shop. Maureen went with her mother to the sign shop to arrange for these two words to be written in yellow paint on a blue ground.

Even without the name, Maureen would have known that the shop was connected with hopes for her future; and that her future was what her mother lived for.

She was pretty. She had always known it. Even where the shadows of fire and dark were, they had played over a pretty baby. "You were such a pretty baby, Maureen." And at the birthday parties: "Maureen's growing really pretty, Mrs. Watson." But all babies and little girls are pretty, she knew that well enough . . . no, it was something more. For Shirley was plump, dark—pretty. Yet their parents'—or rather, their mothers'—talk had made it clear from the start that Shirley was not in the same class as Maureen.

When Maureen was ten there was an episode of importance. The two mothers were in the room above Maureen's Shop and they were brushing their little girls' hair out. Shirley's mother said: "Maureen could do really well for herself, Mrs. Watson." And Mrs. Watson nodded, but sighed deeply. The sigh annoyed Maureen, because it contradicted the absolute certainty that she felt (it had been bred into her) about her future. Also because it had to do with the *boring* era which she remembered, or thought she did, as a tiger-striped movement of fire. *Chance:* Mrs. Watson's sigh was like a prayer to the gods of Luck: it was the sigh of a small helpless thing being tossed about by big seas and gales. Maureen made a decision, there and then, that she had nothing in common with the little people who were prepared to be helpless and tossed about. For she was going to be quite different. She was already different. Not only The War but the shadows of war had long gone, except for talk in the newspapers which had nothing to do with her. The shops were full of everything. The Banners' sweets-tobacco-paper shop had just been done up; and Maureen's was short of nothing. Maureen and Shirley, two pretty little girls in smart mother-made dresses, were children of plenty, and knew it, because their parents kept saying (apparently they did not care how tedious they were): "These kids don't lack for anything, do they? They don't know what it can be like, do they?" This, with the suggestion that they ought to be grateful for not lacking anything, always made the children sulky, and they went off to flirt their full many-petticoated skirts where the neighbours could see them and pay them compliments.

Eleven years. Twelve years. Already Shirley had subsided into her role of pretty girl's plainer girl friend, although of course she was not plain at all. Fair girl, dark girl, and Maureen by mysterious birthright was the "pretty one," and there was no doubt in either of their minds which girl the boys would try first for a date. Yet this balance was by no means as unfair as it seemed. Maureen, parrying and jesting on street corners, at bus stops, knew she was doing battle for two, because the boys she discarded Shirley got: Shirley got far more boys than she would have done without Maureen who, for her part, needed—more, *had* to have—a foil. Her role demanded one.

They both left school at fifteen, Maureen to work in the shop. She was keeping her eyes open: her mother's phrase. She wore a slim white overall, pinned her fair curls up, was neat and pretty in her movements. She smiled calmly when customers said: "My word, Mrs. Watson, your Maureen's turned out, hasn't she?"

About that time there was a second moment of consciousness. Mrs. Watson was finishing a new dress for Maureen, and the fitting was taking rather long. Maureen fidgeted and her mother said: "Well, it's your capital, isn't it? You've got to see that, love." And she added the deep unconscious sigh. Maureen said: "Well don't go on about it, it's not very nice, is it?" And what she meant was, not that the idea was not very nice, but that she had gone beyond needing to be reminded about it; she was feeling the irritated embarrassment of a child when it is reminded to clean its teeth after this habit has become second nature. Mrs. Watson saw and understood this, and sighed again; and this time it was the maternal sigh which means: Oh dear, you are growing up fast! "Oh *Mum*," said Maureen, "sometimes you just make me tired, you do really."

Sixteen. She was managing her capital perfectly. Her assets were a slight delicate prettiness, and a dress sense that must have been a gift from God, or more probably because she had been reading the fashion magazines since practically before consciousness. Shirley had put in six months of beehive hair, pouting scarlet lips, and an air of sullen disdain; but Maureen's sense of herself was much finer. She modelled herself on film stars, but with an understanding of how far she could go—of what was allowable to Maureen. So the experience of being Bardot, Monroe, or whoever it was, refined her: she took from it an essence, which was learning to be a vehicle for other people's fantasies. So while Shirley had been a dozen stars, but really *been* them, in violent temporary transmogrifications, from which she emerged (often enough with a laugh) Shirley—plump, good-natured, and herself—Maureen remained herself through every role, but creating her appearance, like an alter ego, to meet the expression in people's eyes.

Round about sixteen, another incident: prophetic. Mrs. Watson had a cousin who worked in the dress trade, and this man, unthought-of for many years, was met at a wedding. He commented on Maureen, a vision in white gauze. Mrs. Watson worked secretly on this slender material for some weeks; then wrote to him: Could

Maureen be a model? He had only remote connections with the world of expensive clothes and girls, but he dropped into the shop with frankly personal aims. Maureen in a white wrapper was still pretty, very; but her remote air told this shrewd man that she would certainly not go out with him. She was saving herself; he knew that air of self-esteem very well from other exemplars. Such girls do not go out with middle-age cousins, except as a favour or to get something. However, he told Mrs. Watson that Maureen was definitely model material, but that she would have to do something about her voice. (He meant her accent of course; and so Mrs. Watson understood him.) He left addresses and advice, and Mrs. Watson was in a state of quivering ambition. She said so to Maureen: "This is your chance, girl. Take it." What Maureen heard was: "This is *my* chance."

Maureen, nothing if not alert for her Big Chance, for which her whole life had prepared her, accepted her mothers gift of a hundred pounds (she did not thank her, no thanks were due) and actually wrote to the school where she would be taught voice training.

Then she fell into sullen withdrawal, which she understood so little that a week had gone by before she said she must be sick—or something. She was rude to her mother: very rare, this. Her father chided her for it: even rarer. But he spoke in such a way that Maureen understood for the first time that this drive, this push, this family effort to gain her a glamorous future, came from her mother, her father was not implicated. For him, she was a pretty-enough girl, spoiled by a silly woman.

Maureen slowly understood she was not sick, she was growing up. For one thing: if she changed her "voice" so as to be good enough to mix with new people, she would no longer be part of this street, she would no longer be *Our Maureen*. What would she be then? Her mother knew: she would marry a duke and be whisked off to Hollywood. Maureen examined her mother's ideas for her and shrank with humiliation. She was above all no fool, but she had been very foolish. For one thing: when she used her eyes, with the scales of illusion off them, she saw that the million streets of London blossomed with girls as pretty as she. What, then, had fed the illusion in herself and in other people? What accounted for the special tone, the special looks that always greeted her? Why, nothing more than that she, Maureen, because of her mother's will behind her, had carried herself from childhood as something special, apart, destined for a great future.

Meanwhile (as she clearly saw) she was in 93 Nelson's Way, serving behind the counter of Maureen's Shop. (She now wondered what the neighbours had thought—before they got used to it—about her mother's fondness so terribly displayed.) She was dependent on nothing less than that a duke or a film producer would walk in to buy a quarter of tea and some sliced bread.

Maureen sulked. So her father said. So her mother complained. Maureen was—thinking? Yes. But more, a wrong had been done her, she knew it, and the sulking was more of a protective silence while she grew a scab over a wound.

She emerged demanding that the hundred pounds should be spent on sending her to secretarial school. Her parents complained that she could have learned how to be a secretary for nothing if she had stayed on at school another year. She said: "Yes, but you didn't have the sense to make me, did you? What did you think—I was going to sell butter like you all my life?" Unfair, on the face of it; but deeply fair, in view of what they had done to her. In their different ways they knew it. (Mr. Watson knew in his heart, for instance, that he should never have allowed his wife to call the shop "Maureen's.") Maureen went, then, to secretarial school for a year. Shirley went with her: she had been selling cosmetics in the local branch of a big chain store. To raise the hundred pounds was difficult for Shirley's parents: the shop had done badly, had been bought by a big firm; her father was an assistant in it. For that matter, it wasn't all that easy for the Watsons: the hundred pounds was the result of small savings and pinchings over years.

This was the first time Maureen had thought of the word capital in connection with money, rather than her own natural assets: it was comparatively easy for the Watsons to raise money, because they had capital: the Banners had no capital. (Mrs. Watson said the Banners had had *bad luck*.) Maureen strengthened her will; and as a result the two families behaved even more as if the girls would have different futures—or, to put it another way, that while the two sums of a hundred pounds were the same, the Watsons could be expected to earn more on theirs than the Banners.

This was reflected directly in the two girls' discussions about boys. Shirley would say: "I'm more easygoing than you."

Maureen would reply: "I only let them go so far."

Their first decisions on this almighty subject had taken place years before, when they were thirteen. Even then Shirley went further ("let them go further") than Maureen. It was put down, between them, to Shirley's warmer temperament—charitably; for both knew it was because of Maureen's higher value in the market.

At the secretarial school they met boys they had not met before. Previously boys had been from the street or the neighbourhood, known from birth, and for this reason not often gone out with—that would have been boring (serious, with possibilities of marriage). Or boys picked up after dances or at the pictures. But now there were new boys met day after day in the school. Shirley went out with one for weeks, thought of getting engaged, changed her mind, went out with another. Maureen went out with a dozen, chosen carefully. She knew what she was doing—and scolded Shirley for being so *soft*. "You're just stupid, Shirl—I mean, you've got to get on. Why don't you do like me?"

What Maureen did was to allow herself to be courted, until she agreed at last, as a favour, to be taken out. First, lunch—a word she began to use now. She would agree to go out to lunch two or three times with one boy, while she was taken out to supper (dinner) by another. The dinner partner, having been rewarded by a closed-mouth kiss for eight, ten, twelve nights, got angry or sulky or reproachful, according to his nature. He dropped her, and the lunch partner was promoted to dinner partner.

Maureen ate free for the year of her training. It wasn't that she planned it like this: but when she heard other girls say they paid their way or liked to be independent, it seemed to Maureen wrong-headed. To pay for herself would be to let herself be undervalued: even the idea of it made her nervous and sulky.

At the end of the training Maureen got a job in a big archi-tect's office. She was a junior typist. She stuck out for a professional office because the whole point of the training was to enable her to meet a better class of people. Of course she had already learned not to use the phrase, and when her mother did snubbed her with: "I don't know what you mean, better *class*, but it's not much point my going into that hardware stuck upstairs in an office by myself if I can get a job where there's some life about."

Shirley went into a draper's shop where there was one other typist (female) and five male assistants.

In Maureen's place there were six architects, out most of the time, or invisible in large offices visited only by the real secretaries; a lower stratum of young men in training, designers, draftsmen, man-agers, etc., and a pool of typists.

The young men were mostly of her own class. For some months she ate and was entertained at their expense; and at each week's end there was a solemn ceremony, the high point of the week, certainly the most exciting moment in it, when she divided her wage. It was seven pounds (rising to ten in three years) and she allocated two pounds for clothes, four for the post office, and one pound for the week's odd expenses.

At the end of a year she understood two things. That she had saved something like two hundred pounds. That there was not a young man in the office who would take her out again. They regarded her, according to their natures, with resentment or with admiration for her cool management of them. But there was nothing doing *there*—so they all knew.

Maureen thought this over. If she were not taken out to meals and entertainment, she must pay for herself and save no money, or she must never go out at all. If she was going to be taken out, then she must give something in return. What she gave was an open mouth, and freedom to the waist. She calculated that because of her prettiness she could give much less than other girls.

She was using her *capital* with even more intelligence than before. A good part of her time—all not spent in the office or being taken out—went in front of her looking glass, or with the better-class fashion magazines. She studied them with formidable concentration. By now she knew she could have gone anywhere in these islands, except for her voice. Whereas, months before, she had sulked in a sort of fright at the idea of cutting herself off from her street and the neighbours, now she softened and shaped her voice, listening to the clients and the senior architects in the office. She knew her voice had changed when Shirley said: "You're talking nice, Maureen, much nicer than me."

There was a boy in the office who teased her about it. His name was Tony Head. He was in training to be an accountant for the firm, and was very much from her own background. After having taken her out twice to lunch, he had never asked her again. She knew why: he had told her. "Can't afford you, Maureen," he said. He earned not much more than she did. He was nineteen, ambitious, serious, and she liked him.

Then she was nineteen. Shirley was engaged to one of the assistants in her shop, and would be married next Christmas.

Maureen took forty pounds out of her savings and went on a tour to Italy. It was her first time out of England. She hated it: not Italy, but the fact that half the sixty people on the tour were girls, like herself, looking for a good time, and the other half elderly couples. In Rome, Pisa, Florence, Venice, the Italians mooned over Maureen, courted her with melting eyes, while she walked past them, distant as a starlet. They probably thought she was one. The courier, a sharp young man, took Maureen out to supper one night after he had finished his duties, and made it clear that her mouth, even if opened, and her breasts, were not enough. Maureen smiled at him sweetly through the rest of the trip. No one paid for her odd coffees, ices and drinks. On the last night of the trip, in a panic because the forty-pound investment had yielded so little, she went out with an Italian boy who spoke seven words of English. She thought him crude, and left him after an hour.

But she had learned a good deal for her forty pounds.

Quietly, in her lunch hour, she went off to the National Gallery and to the Tate. There she looked, critical and respectful, at pictures, memorising their subjects, or main colours, learning names. When invited out, she asked to be taken to "foreign" films, and when she got back home wrote down the names of the director and the stars. She looked at the book page of the *Express* (she made her parents buy it instead of the *Mirror*) and sometimes bought a recommended book, if it was a best seller.

Twenty. Shirley was married and had a baby. Maureen saw little of her—both girls felt they had a new world of knowledge the other couldn't appreciate.

Maureen was earning ten pounds a week, and saved six.

There came to the office, as an apprentice architect, Stanley Hunt, from grammar school and technical college. Tallish, well-dressed, fair, with a small moustache. They took each other's measure, knowing they were the same kind. It was some weeks before he asked her out. She knew, by putting herself in his place, that he was looking for a wife with a little money or a house of her own, if he couldn't get a lady. (She smiled when she heard him using this word about one of the clients.) He tried to know clients socially, to be accepted by them as they accepted the senior architects. All this Maureen watched, her cool little face saying nothing.

One day, after he had invited a Miss Plast (Chelsea, well-off, investing money in houses) to coffee, and been turned down, he asked Maureen to join him in a sandwich lunch. Maureen thanked him delightfully, but said she already had an engagement. She went off to the National Gallery, sat on the steps, froze off wolves and pickups, and ate a sandwich by herself.

A week later, invited to lunch by Stanley, she suggested the Trattoria Siciliana which was more expensive, as she knew quite well, than he had expected. But this meal was a success. He was impressed with her, though he knew (how could he not, when his was similar?) her background.

She was careful to be engaged for two weeks. Then she agreed to go to the pictures—"a foreign film, if you don't mind, I think the American films are just boring." She did not offer to pay, but remarked casually that she had nearly six hundred pounds in the post office. "I'm thinking of buying a little business, sometime. A dress shop. I've got a cousin in the trade."

Stanley agreed that "with your taste" it would be a sure thing.

Maureen no longer went to the Palais, or similar places (though she certainly did not conceal from Stanley that she had "once"), but she loved to dance. Twice they went to the West End together and danced at a Club which was "a nice place." They danced well together. On the second occasion she offered to pay her share, for the first time in her life. He refused, as she had known he would, but she could see he liked her for offering: more, was relieved; in the office they said she was mean, and he must have heard them. On that night, taken home lingeringly, she opened her mouth for him and let his hands go down to her thighs. She felt a sharp sexuality which made her congratulate herself that she had never, like Shirley, gone "halfway" before. Well of course, girls were going to get married to just anybody if they let themselves be all worked up every time they were taken out!

But Stanley was not at all caught. He was too cool a customer, as she was. He was still looking for something better.

He would be an architect in a couple of years; he would be in a profession; he was putting down money for a house; he was good-looking, attractive to women, and with these assets he ought to do better than marry Maureen. Maureen agreed with him.

But meanwhile he took her out. She was careful often to be engaged elsewhere. She was careful always to be worth taking somewhere expensive. When he took her home, while she did not go so far as "nearly the whole way," she went "everything but"; and she was glad she did not like him better, because otherwise she would have been lost. She knew quite well she did not really like him, although her mind was clouded by her response to his hands, his moustache, his clothes and his new car.

She knew, because meanwhile a relationship she understood very well, and regretted, had grown up with Tony. He, watching this duel between the well-matched pair, would grin and drop remarks at which Maureen coloured and turned coldly away. He often asked her out—but only for a "Dutch treat"—expecting her to refuse. "How's your savings account, Maureen? I can't save, you girls get it all spent on you." Tony took out a good many girls: Maureen kept a count of them. She hated him; yet she liked him, and knew she did. She relied on him above all for this grinning, honest understanding of her: he did not approve of her, but perhaps (she felt in her heart) he was right? During this period she several times burst into tears when alone, without apparent reason; afterwards she felt that life had no flavour. Her future was narrowing down to Stanley; and at these times she viewed it through Tony Head's eyes.

One night the firm had a party for the senor members of the staff. Stanley was senior, Maureen and Tony were not. Maureen knew that Stanley had previously asked another girl to go, and when he asked herself, was uncertain whether she could make it until the very last moment: particularly as his inviting her, a junior, meant that he was trying out on the senior members the idea of Maureen as a wife. But she acquitted herself very well. First, she was the best-looking woman in the room by far, and the best-dressed. Everyone looked at her and commented: they were used to her as a pretty typist; but tonight she was using all her will to make them look at her, to make her face and body reflect what they admired. She made no mistakes. When the party was over Stanley and two of the younger architects suggested they drive out to London airport for breakfast, and they did. The two other girls were middle-class. Maureen kept silent for the most part, smiling serenely. She had been to Italy, she remarked, when a plane rose to go to Italy. Yes, she had liked it, though she thought the Italians were too noisy; what she had enjoyed best was the Sistine Chapel and a boat trip on the Adriatic. She hadn't cared for Venice much, it was beautiful, but the canals smelled, and there were far too many people; perhaps it would be better to go in winter? She said all this, having a right to it, and it came off. As she spoke she remembered Tony, who had once met her on her way to the National Gallery. "Getting yourself an education, Maureen? That's right, it'll pay off well, that will."

She knew, thinking it all over afterwards, that the evening had been important for her with Stanley. Because of this, she did not go out with him for a week, she said she was busy talking to her cousin about the possibilities of a dress shop. She sat in her room thinking about Stanley, and when thoughts of Tony came into her mind, irritatedly pushed them away. If she could succeed with Stanley, why not with someone better? The two architects from that evening had eyed her all the following week: they did not, however, ask her out. She then found that both were engaged to marry the girls they had been with. It was bad luck: she was sure that otherwise they would have asked her out. How to meet more like them? Well, that was the trouble—the drive to the airport was a bit of a fluke; it was the first time she had actually met the seniors socially.

Meanwhile Stanley showed an impatience in his courtship— and for the first time. As for her, she was getting on for twenty-one, and all the girls she had grown up with were married and had their first or even their second babies.

She went out with Stanley to a dinner in the West End at an Italian restaurant. Afterwards they were both very passionate. Maureen, afterwards, was furious with herself: some borderline had been crossed (she supposed she still could be called a virgin?) and now decisions would have to be made.

Stanley was in love with her. She was in love with Stanley. A week later he proposed to her. It was done with a violent moaning intensity that she knew was due to his conflicts over marrying her.

She was not good enough. He was not good enough. They were second-best for each other. They writhed and moaned and bit in the car, and agreed to marry. Her eight hundred pounds would make it easier to buy the house in a good suburb. He would formally meet her parents next Sunday.

"So you're engaged to Stanley Hunt?" said Tony.

"Looks like it, doesn't it?"

"Caught him—good for you!"

"He's caught me, more like it!"

"Have it your way."

She was red and angry. He was serious.

"Come and have a bite?" he said. She went.

It was a small restaurant, full of office workers eating on luncheon vouchers. She ate fried plaice ("No chips, please") and he ate steak-and-kidney pudding. He joked, watched her, watched her intently, said finally: "Can't you do better than that?" He meant, and she knew it, better in the sense she would use herself, in her heart: he meant *nice*. Like himself. But did that mean that Tony thought *she* was nice? Unlike Stanley? She did not think she was, she was moved to tears (concealed) that he did. "What's wrong with him then?" she demanded, casual. "What's wrong with *you*? You need your head examined." He said it seriously, and they exchanged a long look. The two of them sat looking goodbye at each other: the extremely pretty girl at whom everyone in the room kept glancing and remarking on, and the good-looking, dark, rather fat young accountant who was brusque and solemn with disappointment in her. With love for her? Very likely.

She went home silent, thinking of Tony. When she thought of him she needed to cry. She also needed to hurt him.

But she told her parents she was engaged to Stanley, who would be an architect. They would have their own house, in (they thought) Hemel Hampstead. He owned a car. He was coming to tea on Sunday. Her mother forgot the dukes and the film producers before the announcement ended: her father listened judiciously, then congratulated her. He had been going to a football match on Sunday, but agreed, after persuasion, that this was a good-enough reason to stay home.

Her mother then began discussing, with deference to Maureen's superior knowledge, how to manage next Sunday to best advantage. For four days she went on about it. But she was talking to herself. Her husband listened, said nothing. And Maureen listened, critically, like her father. Mrs. Watson began clamouring for a definite opinion on what sort of cake to serve on Sunday. But Maureen had no opinion. She sat, quiet, looking at her mother, a largish ageing woman, her ex-fair hair dyed yellow, her flesh guttering. She was like an excited child, and it was not attractive. *Stupid, stupid, stupid—* that's all you are, thought Maureen.

As for Maureen, if anyone had made the comparison, she was "sulking" as she had before over being a model and having to be drilled out of her "voice." She said nothing but: "It'll be all right, Mum, don't get so worked up." Which was true, because Stanley knew what to expect: he knew why he had not been invited to meet her parents until properly hooked. He would have done the same in her place. He *was* doing the same: she was going to meet his parents the week after. What Mrs. Watson, Mr. Watson, wore on Sunday; whether sandwiches or cake were served; whether there were fresh or artificial flowers—none of it mattered. The Watsons were part of the bargain: what he was paying in return for publicly owning the most covetable woman anywhere they were likely to be; and for the right to sleep with her after the public display.

Meanwhile Maureen said not a word. She sat on her bed looking at nothing in particular. Once or twice she examined her face in the mirror, and even put cream on it. And she cut out a dress, but put it aside.

On Sunday Mrs. Watson laid tea for four, using her own judgement since Maureen was too deeply in love (so she told every- one) to notice such trifles. At four Stanley was expected, and at 3:55 Maureen descended to the living room. She wore: a faded pink dress from three summers before; her mother's cretonne overall used for housework; and a piece of cloth tied round her hair that might very well have been a duster. At any rate, it was a faded grey. She had put on a pair of her mother's old shoes. She could not be called plain; but she looked like her own faded elder sister, dressed for a hard day's spring cleaning.

Her father, knowledgeable, said nothing: he lowered the paper, examined her, let out a short laugh, and lifted it again. Mrs. Watson, understanding at last that this was a real crisis, burst into tears. Stanley arrived before Mrs. Watson could stop herself crying. He nearly said to Mrs. Watson: "I didn't know Maureen had an older sister." Maureen sat listless at one end of the table; Mr. Watson sat grinning at the other, and Mrs. Watson sniffed and wiped her eyes between the two.

Maureen said: "Hello, Stanley, meet my father and mother." He shook their hands and stared at her. She did not meet his eyes: rather, the surface of her blue gaze met the furious, incredulous, hurt pounce of his glares at her. Maureen poured tea, offered him sand- wiches and cake, and made conversation about the weather, and the prices of food, and the dangers of giving even good customers credit in the shop. He sat there, a well-set-up young man, with his brushed hair, his brushed moustache, his checked brown cloth jacket, and a face flaming with anger and affront. He said nothing, but Maureen talked on, her voice trailing and cool. At five o'clock, Mrs. Watson again burst into tears, her whole body shaking, and Stanley brusquely left.

Mr. Watson said: "Well, why did you lead him on, then?" and turned on the television. Mrs. Watson went to lie down. Maureen, in her own room, took off the various items of her disguise, and returned them to her mother's room. "Don't cry, Mum. What are you carrying on like that for? What's the matter?" Then she dressed extremely carefully in a new white linen suit, brown shoes, beige blouse. She did her hair and her face, and sat looking at herself. The last two hours (or week) hit her, and her stomach hurt so that she doubled up. She cried; but the tears smeared her makeup, and she stopped herself with the side of a fist against her mouth.

It now seemed to her that for the last week she had simply not been Maureen; she had been someone else. What had she done it for? Why? Then she knew it was for Tony: during all that ridiculous scene at the tea table, she had imagined Tony looking on, grinning, but understanding her.

She now wiped her face quite clear of tears, and went quietly out of the house so as not to disturb her father and mother. There was a telephone booth at the corner. She stepped calm and aloof along the street, her mouth held (as it always was) in an almost smile. Bert from the grocer's shop said: "Hey, Maureen, that's a smasher. Who's it for?" And she gave him the smile and the toss of the head that went with the street and said: "You, Bert, it's all for you." She went to the telephone booth thinking of Tony. She felt as if he already knew what had happened. She would say: "Let's go and dance, Tony." He would say: "Where shall I meet you?" She dialled his number, and it rang and it rang and it rang. She stood holding the receiver, waiting. About ten minutes—more. Slowly she replaced it. *He had let her down.* He had been telling her, in words and without, to be something, to stay something, and now he did not care, he had let her down.

Maureen quietened herself and telephoned Stanley.

All right then, if that's how you want it, she said to Tony.

Stanley answered, and she said amiably: "Hello."

Silence. She could hear him breathing, fast. She could see his affronted face.

"Well, aren't you going to say anything?" She tried to make this casual, but she could hear the fear in her voice. Oh yes, she could lose him and probably had. To hide the fear she said: "Can't you take a joke, Stanley?" and laughed

"A joke!"

She laughed. Not bad, it sounded all right.

"I thought you'd gone off your nut, clean off your rocker. . . ." He was breathing in and out, a rasping noise. She was reminded of his hot breathing down her neck and her arms. Her own breath quickened, even while she thought: I don't like him, I really don't like him at all . . . and she said softly: "Oh Stan, I was having a bit of a giggle, that's all."

Silence. Now, this was the crucial moment.

"Oh Stan, can't you see—I thought it was all just boring, that's all it was." She laughed again.

He said: "Nice for your parents, I don't think."

"Oh they don't mind—they laughed after you'd left, though first they were cross." She added hastily, afraid he might think they were laughing at him: "They're used to me, that's all it is."

Another long silence. With all her willpower she insisted that he should soften. But he said nothing, merely breathed in and out, into the receiver.

"Stanley, it was only a joke, you aren't really angry, are you, Stanley?" The tears sounded in her voice now, and she judged it better that they should.

He said, after hesitation: "Well, Maureen, I just didn't like it, I don't like that kind of thing, that's all." She allowed herself to go on crying, and after a while he said, forgiving her in a voice that was condescending and irritated: "Well, all right, all right, there's no point in crying, is there?"

He was annoyed with himself for giving in, she knew that, because she would have been. He had given her up, thrown her over, during the last couple of hours: he was pleased, really, that something from outside had forced him to give her up. Now he could be free for the something better that would turn up—someone who would not strike terror into him by an extraordinary performance like this afternoon's.

"Let's go off to the pictures, Stan. . . ."

Even now, he hesitated. Then he said, quick and reluctant: "I'll meet you at Leicester Square, outside the Odeon, at seven o'clock." He put down the receiver.

Usually he came to pick her up in the car from the corner of the street.

She stood smiling, the tears running down her face. She knew she was crying because of the loss of Tony, who had let her down. She walked back to her house to make up again, thinking that she was in Stanley's power now: there was no balance between them, the advantage was all his.

PROBING FOR
MEANING

1. Characterize Maureen. What is she like as a child? As a teen-ager? As a young adult? What is her goal in life? When does she first begin to formulate this goal?

2. Describe Maureen's relationship with her parents. How do Maureen's mother and father view her differently?

3. The story takes place in London, just after World War II. What role does "The War" play in the story? Why does Maureen insist that she is not a "war child"?

4. What significance do Maureen's moods of "sullen withdrawal" have? What is their cause and effect?

5. Why would Maureen consider spending 100£ (about $200) to improve her "voice"? What attempts at self-education does Maureen make? With what success? In general, what role does social class play in the story?

6. Compare and contrast Stanley and Tony. How do Maureen's relationships with these males differ?

7. Why does Maureen behave as she does when Stanley visits her parents' house?

8. What is the significance of the last line of the story?

PROBING FOR
METHOD

1. What is the symbolism of "Maureen's Shop"? In this connec-tion, what is Maureen's "capital" throughout the story? Why is this a particularly appropriate description of her "assets"?

2. At one point, the author comments, "Maureen . . . needed—more, *had* to have—a foil. Her role demanded one." In what ways is Shirley a "foil" for Maureen? In other words, how does the author use Shirley as a contrast to the heroine to tell us something about Maureen? Why does Maureen herself feel she needs a foil?

3. What is a "case history"? Who might write a case history? In what way does the style of the story reflect a case history? In this con-nection, how are the transitions between the parts of Maureen's life presented?

4. Why does the story end as it does? In other words, what is implied by ending the case history at this point in Maureen's life?

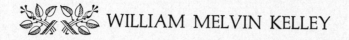 WILLIAM MELVIN KELLEY

Saint Paul and The Monkeys

Standing just inside the metal door of her hospital room, Chig Dunford tried to decide if she was too sick to be kissed. "How are you, Avis?"

She opened her arms to him. "Come and kiss me."

He did, then inspected her again. She had the smooth face of a Polynesian. Her complexion, the rich brown of tarnished copper, seemed the slightest bit gray. Her large brown eyes looked tired. Her mouth was soft, a baby's. In her rust-colored hair were two small blue ribbons. Under her light blue pajamas, she wore no bra, and her small breasts were flat. "How are you?" He held her hand.

"I'm supposed to be pretty sick. The doctor at school said my blood was going crazy. He thought it was Mono, but he wanted me in the hospital to make sure." She had phoned him the night before to tell him she was in town and had been in the hospital since that morning.

He started to sit down, but instead kissed her again, lightly. She grabbed him around the neck and kissed him hard. He sat down, holding her hand. "Why didn't your parents want me to come last night?"

She turned away and did not answer. He thought he saw her shake with fighting tears, and reached to pat her back.

"Come on, now. You can tell me."

Suddenly she was staring at him. "They don't want me to see you any more, Chig." As soon as she spoke, the threat of tears disappeared.

"They can't *do* that." He realized they could, felt desperate; and echoed himself softly. "They *can't* do that." Sensing what the answer would be, he asked: "What did you say?"

She turned away again. "I tried to, Chig. Honestly, I really wanted to—"

"But you didn't say anything." He sighed.

"I couldn't, Chig."

"But you could let them make us stop seeing each other?"

Her answer was flat and definite. "Yes." He knew what was

coming next and hardened himself against it. "I'd do it just not to hurt them. You know how much I owe them. They've done an awful lot for me, put me through school and all."

"But they're your parents. They're supposed to do that kind of stuff."

"You always say that, Chig."

"Okay, if they're not supposed to, then they *wanted* to. They were happy doing it. Avis, you can only owe them so much."

"I owe them for everything." She was very calm now.

He did not want to argue about her parents, and changed the subject. "What's so bad about me anyway? Why don't they want me around any more?"

"They like you very much, Chig. It isn't that. But they don't think you're serious about me."

"Is going steady with you for three years not serious?"

"But you haven't spoken to them yet." It seemed almost as if she too doubted him. "You haven't asked my father for my hand or even mentioned it."

"What did you say to that?"

"I told them we were planning to get married some day. But . . ."

"Well?"

"But they said speaking to *me* wasn't enough. They said boys were apt to say anything to be intimate with a girl." When she spoke of her parents, she used their expressions. "Then they asked me if we had been intimate."

"What did you tell them?"

"You don't actually think I told them the truth, *do* you?"

"No, I guess not. But God, they should have enough sense to take it for granted. You're not a little girl any more, Avis."

She said nothing and he searched her face for a long moment. She had become timid and insecure. "Chig, will you . . . will you talk to Daddy about us getting married?"

He stared off into a dustless corner. "Avis, you know I want to marry you, but after I graduate in June, I still have three years of law school. I can't possibly support you. And you have to finish college too."

"But they don't even want us to set a date. They just want you to say something to them. You can do that."

"Sure I can. But I don't see why I should have to. I know they'll say Okay. Even if they didn't, wouldn't you marry me?"

"Of course I would." She believed it, but, for an instant, he did not. She leaned toward him. "But since they'll say Yes, it doesn't matter if you ask them or not. Aren't you sure of us?" Her face was troubled.

"Of course I am!" He decided quickly. "Okay, I'll ask him." It sounded right, but still he felt uncomfortable. He gripped her hand. "You know I want to marry you, don't you?"

Her eyes were a trifle pink. "I know that, Chig." She smiled.

"I'm only thinking of you. I want you to have everything."

"I will. I'll be marrying you."

He felt like sighing, but held it back. "When does he want me to speak to him?"

"Any time you feel like it. They really like you very much." She was trying to encourage him.

He had always hoped that their engagement would come about in a more romantic way. But her parents had robbed him of the perfect night and setting. He tried now to salvage a particle of his romantic dream. "You got an extra hairpin? The wire kind."

"Sure." She leaned over to the other side of the bed, opened a drawer, and handed it to him.

"Let me have your . . . right hand." She extended it to him, and he bent the hair pin around the knuckle of her ring finger.

"What are you doing?"

He searched her soft face to see if she was pretending ignorance, but could not tell. He put the hairpin into his pocket. "It's a surprise."

Before knocking, he inspected himself. This was a special day and he wanted his clothes in perfect order. He was not surprised to find his efforts had come to nothing. He still looked as if he had dressed in the panic of fleeing a burning house. As usual, his shirt was creeping out of his pants, his knees were bagging, his socks were sliding into his shoes. He sighed and knocked at her door.

Avis, propped on two pillows, was reading. In her hair, yellow ribbons had replaced yesterday's blue bows. She gave him her nicest smile. He asked her how she felt.

"Better. But I want to get out of here." She spoke as if he could do something about it.

He removed his overcoat, sneaking the ring box to his jacket pocket, and pulled up a chair.

"What kind of day did you have?"

"All right." He belittled the thrill of what he had done, and was about to do, trying to detect if she had any idea why he had wanted the hair pin. "Avis," he started, but bogged down in muddy nervousness.

She studied him. "Yes."

He tried again. "Avis, I always had a dream of how . . . I always thought I'd do this after something good happened to me that would sort of guarantee our security . . . and that it would be a surprise to you." He searched her face again. She knew now. "But none of that happened. So, anyway, it doesn't matter. Will you marry me?"

"Yes, Chig. I love you, Chig."

He reached into his pocket, produced the ring box, and handed it to her. She opened it, leaned toward him, and kissed him sweetly. Her tears were oily on his cheek. "It's beautiful, Chig. It didn't cost too much, did it?" She looked at it once more, then handed back the box.

A feeling like eating lemons spread through him. "What's wrong, Avis?" His voice cracked.

She did not notice. "*You* have to put it on me."

He did it; it was small and cold, and fit perfectly.

"*I'll never* take it off. Only you can take it off."

"Then you're stuck with it." Smiling, he sat back in his chair, tired. It was finished, settled; he was engaged. He began to think of the wonderful life that one day they would have with each other.

She interrupted his dreams. "I spoke to my parents, last night, Chig." The happiness in her eyes had fled while he was dreaming.

He leaned forward, "What did they say?"

She hesitated. "They want us to set a definite date. They want us to get married in August. They—"

"In August! What do they think I am?" He was standing, glaring down at her. "Didn't you tell them what I said?"

"Chig, don't shout."

He fell into his chair, and attempted to rein his feelings by whispering. "Avis, how can I marry you in August? What'll we live on?"

She brightened. "That's no problem. Your parents are going to see you through law school, aren't they? And mine'll see me through college. I'll transfer to wherever you are."

He could not arrange all his different emotions, but one picture kept exploding in his mind—of a baby monkey he had seen once on television that shivered and whimpered in the corner of a wire cage, as lights flashed and the arms of a weird contrivance clawed and battered the air. The monkey had been part of a psychological experiment. Stress had destroyed its mind.

Avis was quite calm.

"Don't you see why it would be bad for us to get married so soon, Avis?"

"I know, Chig. But we don't have to worry about money. And I didn't think you minded *that* much." She looked down at the ring sparkling on her finger, and sighed. "Three years is a long time to wait, Chig."

"I know." He stared at the springs of the high bed. "But . . . I'm . . . You really want to get married in August, don't you."

She answered with thoughts they had often expressed. "You always have to go home, go away from me, go back some place. It'd be nice to lock our door and say good-night to the world together."

He nodded. "Have you got enough time to transfer? How do you know you'll get into a school near me?"

"I'll just apply to all the places you do. I'll get in." Her face was beaming. "It can be so *nice*, Chig."

"Yes it can." He had forgotten about his cornered, frightened monkey, and begun to think now of a small attic apartment in a university town. He slapped the heel of his hand against his forehead. "God, how can I be so stupid! I worry about all the bad things when everything'll be so good."

"You just want it to be perfect, Chig. That's not bad." She smiled at him. "You're just a worrier."

"I'm stupid too." He shook his head and began to laugh, sensing, for an instant, that his laughter was not completely free or happy.

Avis did not laugh. "When are you going to ask my father?" Her voice was completely emotionless.

He was confused. "You just told me *he* wants us to get married."

"But he still expects you to ask him." She was annoyed with him. "He said he won't know you're sincere until you look him in the eye and ask him."

"Would I go out and buy a God-damned engagement ring if I wasn't sincere?" Again, he saw his monkey, shivering.

"It's the custom to ask him."

"Custom? Oh boy!" He rolled his eyes at the ceiling.

"Don't be disrespectful of my father!" She was too serious, and beginning to get red.

He did not want her angry at him. "I'll go see him right now. Is he in his office?"

She glared at him. "Yes, he is and you don't have to be sarcastic."

"I'm not being sarcastic," he whined.

"Look, do you really want to marry me?"

"Come on, don't be silly. I only want to get this junk out of the way."

"It is not junk. Why do you always have to be so disagreeable!"

"All right, Avis. I'm sorry." He sighed. "It's not junk. I'll go see him tonight—now."

"Don't go if you don't want to." She picked up the book she had been reading when first he came.

"I want to go." Suddenly he was so tired he could not hold up his head. The bones and muscles in his neck no longer existed.

"I'm sorry, Chig. I guess it's been a hard day for you." The tone of her voice made him feel better.

"It's just me. Look, I *will* go see him. Okay?"

She smiled. "Yes."

He put on his coat and came back to the edge of the bed. "I hope I didn't upset you. For a minute I forgot you were sick. I mean, that's taking advantage of you."

"Oh, Chig, I feel fine." She looked at her left hand, holding it before her proudly. "I'm engaged! It's a beautiful ring!"

He kissed her good-by. Closing the door, he turned back and found her gazing at the ring so intently she did not hear him whisper that he loved her.

The memory of the enchanted look on her face helped him survive his thirty-minute interview with her father, who finally consented to their August marriage.

At dinner, he told his parents and his sister he was engaged, and would be married in August if his parents would help financially as Avis's parents were planning to do. His father shook his hand. His mother kissed him. They said that of course they would help.

His sister, Connie, who was sixteen, sat across from him, silent, for a while. "Are you really marrying Avis, Chig?"

At times, Connie asked ridiculous questions. "Sure." He nodded, puzzled.

Connie stared at him, unblinking. "Oh." She was disappointed.

Avis was dismissed from the hospital a week later. The doctors wanted her to stay at home and rest, rather than return to school. She and Chig planned an engagement party for the Friday before Christmas. He wanted to keep the party small and quiet, and to invite only their closest friends. Avis wanted it large and noisy. They compromised. He invited his two best friends; Avis invited sixty people and told them to bring their friends. This upset him. But finally he decided the act of getting married was, after all, by and for women. It would not hurt to let her have a gathering she would always remember.

The party, held at her house in Westchester, was to begin at eight, but Chig arrived in the early afternoon to help decorate. He began to drink immediately, but did not feel anything until well past nine. He discovered he was drunk when he mixed himself, instead of bourbon and soda, bourbon and scotch. He drank it anyway. He knew most of the people by sight, if not by name, but still felt lost, out of place, and began to lurk in the least crowded corners of the house.

Connie, feeling overmatched because of her age, found him on the enclosed porch, where, at the end of the day, there was a fine view of the sun being devoured by the rock cliffs on the western side of the Hudson. She sat beside him.

Chig squinted at her. "Having a good time?" He could not quite make out her face.

"All right." She smiled. "You look like you are. What gallon you drinking now?" She did not let him answer. "You shouldn't drink so much, Chig. You have to drive us home."

He raised his hand, pledging. "Promise to stop after this one. I know my limit." He took a swallow, and inspected his glass. "Good-by, last drink. You have served me well."

"What's wrong, Chig?" She had not yet dropped all her baby fat and her chubby face was more comic than earnest.

"What do you mean? God, was I like this when I was sixteen?" He was talking to his glass.

"Well, if you're so fine, what are you doing sitting out here when everybody else is having such a good time?"

"I'm having a good time."

"About as good a time as a rat in a cage."

He thought about that. Several times, sitting alone on the porch, he had thought about his monkey, wondering too why the stupid little creature clung to his thoughts. "Not a rat, sister dear, a monkey."

"What?"

"A baby monkey. Were you around that Sunday they had the monkey show?"

"What?"

"The Wisconsin monkey show." Her face was blank. He went on. "In Wisconsin . . . the University . . . they got these monkeys . . . in cages . . . away from their mothers. There was this one baby monkey in particular, sleeping on a blanket. Every day they took the blanket out to clean it and when they did the baby monkey would crawl into a corner and whimper and cry and shake." Connie did not understand. "Don't you see? The blanket was his mother!" The porch was lighted only by yellow party lamps from inside the house. Chig stared at his drink. "If that monkey has anything to do with people, they really showed what loneliness can do to you. People'll do anything not to be lonely, you know? I almost cried when they showed that monkey without his blanket." He shook his head.

Connie was staring at him. "Chig, you really love Avis?"

He shot her a glance. "Of course, I love her. Why do you ask such stupid questions?"

"You sure you love her?" She shifted toward him. Her voice seemed closer now. "No fooling?"

"What's wrong with you anyway?"

"How can you love her?"

"What do you mean?"

"She's all the things you don't like in anybody else. I've heard you make speeches about it." She stopped. "She's a phony, Chig."

He could not take her seriously. She was probably jealous of Avis. He and Connie had been very close up until three years before, when he started to go steady with Avis. "Why do you say that?" He heard himself being indulgent.

"It's clear as anything." She did not sound at all jealous. "Aren't you supposed to have a good time at your own engagement party?"

"I guess so."

She had a puzzled expression on her face. "You don't seem happy."

"I don't feel so hot."

She was silent for a while. "Chig, you better watch out. She'll eat you alive."

He was angry now and snapped at her. "What do you know about it?"

"I know you've changed a lot. You can't even blow your nose without wondering if you're doing it the right way. And you're getting to be a liar."

"What are you talking about?"

"You know you feel fine, but all this is making you feel bad. You can't even be honest with me any more."

Chig got up. "I want to see Avis." He left Connie sitting on the porch.

He went downstairs into the cellar playroom, carrying his glass and sloshing liquor on his shoes. He laughed to himself about it, then out loud, and several people turned around to greet him. "Where's Avis?"

Someone pointed to where people danced under soft lights to loud music.

Avis, in a billowing orange dress with long sleeves, spun

around the floor. Chig could not identify her partner. An undirected jealously hummed through him. Chig did not dance very well. At most parties they attended, he watched her stepping with someone else. Avis loved to dance and did so expertly.

He did not want to see her now, and returned to the porch. Connie had disappeared. He thought how nice it would be if Avis broke away from the people downstairs and came to sit quietly with him.

He did not know how long he brooded on the porch, but all at once people were thundering up from downstairs and filing into the dining room, talking and laughing.

Then Avis was standing by him, her hand on his shoulder. "Where have you been?"

"Right here." With her hair up, she was beautiful in the faint light. "You been looking for me?" He desperately hoped she had.

"Not until now. Come on." She grabbed his hand, attempting to pull him to his feet.

"Where?" He did not feel like moving.

"Daddy's going to announce our engagement." She tried again to rouse him. "You'll have to make a speech."

"Okay." He sighed and struggled to his feet. "Okay."

She led him into the dining room. The guests stood around a huge table upon which was a large square cake, small forks, pink napkins, and a stack of shining plates. Her father waited at the far end, his hands knit in front of him like a minister's. He was tall and lean, wore perfectly round spectacles, and a black suit. His hair was long, and brushed straight back in the style of a British diplomat.

Avis led Chig around the table, several people propelling him along with heavy smacks on the back. Her father took a step forward, as the murmuring guests quieted. He said he was proud to announce his daughter's engagement to Charles Dunford (only her father called him Charles), who he knew as a fine young man with a great future. Everyone applauded and the man shook Chig's hand for the first time since they had been introduced three years before.

Someone hollered for Chig to make a speech; the motion received a round of applause.

Chig lumbered forward. "Well, you know, I've been hanging around here for a long time. And I got to like Avis a lot." He looked at her and smiled. "But I have to say I was surprised when she asked me to marry her." Everyone laughed as Chig scanned faces.

"I didn't really know about that. But she put up a good fight . . ." There was more laughter. Connie stood far back on his right, her face grave. Chig went on. "So finally I told her Yes, and . . ." He became very serious now. "And I think it's the best decision I ever made in my life. Thanks very much for coming." He put his arm around Avis and kissed her high on the forehead. There was more applause. At that instant, he remembered that Connie had called him a liar. If he had not known before what she meant, he did now, and it frightened him.

At her house, slouching on a sofa, Chig watched Avis, who stood across the room, her back to him, looking at the river. "Avis, what would you say if I decided I didn't want to be a lawyer?" He tried to sound relaxed.

She did not turn around. "Okay. What do you want to be?"

He was delighted, wondering why he had expected opposition. "That's just it. I don't know. I'm not even sure I don't want to be a lawyer. But I'm . . ." He stopped.

She had turned to him, her lips parted. "You're actually serious?" She advanced on him.

Panic heated his body. "Well, I'm sort of serious."

She was standing in front of him, over him. He could not look her in the eye. The engagement ring winked on her finger. "How could you be serious?" Her voice was soft and baffled.

"Wouldn't it be wrong for me to do something I didn't really want to do? I mean, wouldn't it?" He tilted his head back, willed himself to look at her face, but quickly returned to the ring. "I mean, wrong for me?"

Her hands were knit in front of her. "Sure, it would. But you've always wanted to be a lawyer so much, ever since I've known you."

For an instant, he could not remember if he actually had stepped into her house wanting to be a lawyer. "I know that. But lately I've been having doubts. I don't even know why." He wished she would sit down beside him. He would feel less uncomfortable, more as if they were solving his problem together.

She smiled. He did not want her to smile just then. "Well, why all of sudden, do you—?"

"Hell, I don't know." Her right hand hid her left and he could no longer see the ring. "Well, yes, I do. I was talking to my father a few nights ago and he told me how he felt about medicine—"

"What does medicine have to do with law?"

"Let me finish, will you?" His voice was whiny and high; his tone surprised him.

Her eyes became just the slightest bit cloudy. "All right, Chig."

"I'm sorry." He sighed. "I just realized how much a profession *can* mean to a person and that I don't look forward to being a lawyer nearly as much as he did to being a doctor. He said he doesn't even need people. He enjoys medicine as a . . . a body of knowledge. You know what I mean? Kind of abstract."

"He doesn't want to make people well?"

"Not exactly. I mean, that isn't his only consideration . . ." He wanted to say something more, but did not know what.

"I don't think that's right." She scowled. "He should care about them."

"He cares about them, Avis." He was impatient with her lack of understanding. He wanted her very much to understand. "It's like when you do something well, it gives you a good feeling whether anybody else benefits or not."

"That's a terrible attitude!" She was being huffy. "You can't just walk all over people."

He raised his voice. "He doesn't walk all over people, for God's sake. He just doesn't live or die on everything people say and think! He has private reasons for being a doctor."

"He can have them!" She was angry now. Chig was startled to discover he did not care, did not feel the urge to calm her.

"Look, does it make him any less a doctor? His patients still like and respect him. He still helps them."

"I can't see how—with his attitude."

"Avis, don't be so f---ing stupid!"

She was stunned; when she spoke her voice was wet. "My being stupid doesn't give you the right to curse at me."

"You're not stupid. I am. I can't make you understand." He was not trying to soothe her; he believed it. But realizing that if he did not stop it soon, it would go too far, he lost all taste for the discussion, and sighed. "Look, let's forget it now." He reached for her waist.

She stepped away, her back curled. "We can't forget it. If you're having doubts about . . . *things*, then we ought to find out . . . before it's too late."

He knew exactly what she meant, and thought it childish. "Avis, a minor difference between us doesn't all of a sudden mean I don't want to marry you. I asked a simple question: How would you feel if I decided not to be a lawyer? I wanted to know what you thought. Now you're making a big thing out of it."

"It *is* a big thing. It's important." She was standing too far from him. He could feel cold distance between them. "If you need time to think things over, I shouldn't push you into marrying me. Marriage is a big responsibility, Chig. I should give you time. There are things you have to decide a-*lone*."

This was crazy. He had never once said to her or even to himself that he definitely did not want to be a lawyer. It was simply that since the night of the party, when he realized he had lied, thanking the guests for coming, he had thought a great deal about himself, and had questioned many of his long-cherished goals. But now, it was getting out of hand.

He found himself staring at Avis. "How can I be so God-damned dense!" He started to laugh.

She was puzzled. She took a step toward him, but said nothing.

"I was getting set to botch up my whole life." He was still laughing. "God!"

"What happened?" She came a bit closer.

"Nothing. Not a God-damned thing!" He was serious now. "I read too many books. I just realized I want everything in my life to be like Saint Paul's Conversion." He started to giggle.

"What?" She smiled quizzically.

"Saint Paul's Conversion, Avis. Saint Paul was on his way to Damascus to suppress the Christians and God knocked him off his horse and made him see the light." Giggling overwhelmed him now.

Avis began to laugh too and collapsed beside him on the sofa. "Chig, you're so silly sometimes."

"I know. But most of the time I'm not even here." He hit his head to straighten out his brains. "Most of the time I'm not in real life. I'm living in a dream world of Saint Pauls and baby monkeys."

"What?"

"Forget it." He waved it all away. "Just remember I love you more than anything in the world." He put his arm around her shoulder. She turned to him and let him kiss her.

In January, Chig began to wonder again whether he actually wanted to be a lawyer, but he convinced himself that he was only doubting because he missed Avis so much. If he could see her, everything would be all right. He had not seen her since she returned to school after the holidays, a week or so after their discussion, which he had not been able to forget.

Early in March, Chig went up the Hudson River to visit Avis at school. On the train, he passed Sing Sing Prison. He wondered about prison life.

Avis had a single room and a key to her door. Chig was allowed in her room from twelve-thirty until seven in the evening. Behind the locked door, they made love.

She lived on the top floor of the tallest building on campus; they did not have to draw the blinds for privacy. The early afternoon sun warmed their bare feet and legs. She lay beside him, perfume mingling with sweat. They talked aimlessly about their marriage. Both were tired and happy.

"I found the nicest silverware." Avis babbled, whispering. "It's so simple and light and beautiful." She kissed him.

"Pull up the sheet. You'll catch cold." He reached down, untangled the bedclothes, and covered both of them. He smoothed her hair, which sweat had made kinky. "You'll have to do something about that."

"Does it look horrible?" She sounded worried.

"It looks beautiful. Don't get upset." He kissed the short baby hair that fringed her forehead.

"Are you sure?"

"Yes." He rolled onto his stomach.

On a bookcase beside the bed, was a secondhand copy of *Huckleberry Finn*. Just to see it there made him feel good. He had read it five times since first discovering it. Reaching out, he took it in his hand and smiled to himself.

She felt him move. "What are you doing?" She rolled over and put her arm around his waist.

"I didn't know you had this." There was admiration for her in his voice.

"I had to read it for school." Her eyes closed lazily. "I wrote a paper on it."

"This is the greatest book ever—American anyway." He leafed through it, turning to his favorite chapter, and started to read aloud:

> . . . So I got a piece of paper and a pencil, all glad and excited, and set down and wrote:
>
> Miss Watson, your runaway nigger Jim is down here two mile below Pikesville, and Mr. Phelps has got him and he will give him up for the reward if you send.
>
> Huck Finn.
>
> I felt good and all washed clean of sin for the first time I had ever felt so in my life, and I knowed I could pray now. But I didn't do it straight off, but laid the paper down and set there thinking—thinking how good it was all this happened so, and how near I come to being lost and going to hell. And went on thinking. And got to thinking over our trip down the river; and I see Jim before me all the time: in the day and in the night time, sometimes moonlight, sometimes storms, and we a-floating along, talking and singing and laughing. But somehow I couldn't seem to strike no places to harden me against him, but only the other kind.

Beside him, Avis yawned and stretched. He tried to ignore, forgive what she had done, and continued reading:

. . . and then I happened to look around and see that paper.

It was a close place. I took it up, and held it in my hand. I was a-trembling, because I'd got to decide, forever, betwixt two things, and I knowed it. I studied a minute, sort of holding my breath, and then says to myself:

"All right, then, I'll go to hell"—and tore it up.

Chig closed his eyes. It had always made him feel slightly melancholy, and warm. "That's great!" he sighed.

Avis was silent for a second. "It's nice how Twain spells out his own moral dilemma. Did you know he ran away to the West so as not to decide which side to fight on in the Civil War?"

"I don't mean it that way, Avis. I . . ." He did not know how to go on. He closed the book.

"Oh, you mean the way he sets up the conflict by having Huck do something he's been taught is wrong—the irony of it." She had propped herself on her elbows and her small breasts hung down between her arms.

He let his head fall on the pillow, turning away. "I mean, how does it make you feel?" He tried not to sound earnest.

"Okay, I guess. Chig, let's not talk about school any more. Not now."

He turned suddenly toward her and kissed her desperately, trying to chase away his own evil thoughts.

Later, they came out into the sun, onto mud-spongy ground. In shadowed corners, there was still snow crusted in dirty mounds. Other couples, holding mittened hands, ambled across the campus.

Avis was skipping. "Come on. I want to show you the lake."

There was still thin ice floating in the black water. Near the edges, dead leaves were frozen into the ice.

"Avis, I'm not going to law school."

"Oh, Chig, not again. I thought we had that settled."

"Does it really matter so much?"

"Of course it does." She stared at him. "You should want to be *something*. God, why do you have to be so melodramatic all the time?"

"I'm not being melodramatic, Avis. I just want to—"

"What's wrong with you anyway?" Tears popped into her eyes. She clenched her fists; her voice, louder now, bounced across the lake and back. There was no one else in sight. "What do you expect me to do?"

"I don't expect you to do anything but have some faith in me." He was pleading with her and did not mind.

"Chig, I'll have faith in you. You tell me you don't want to be a lawyer. All right! But what *do* you want to be?"

He felt foolish, put his hands in his pockets, and stared at the muddy toes of his shoes. "I don't know."

She pounced on that. "You don't know! And you're giving up . . . ? Chig, you're acting crazy. This isn't a movie. You have to know where you're going. You have to have some ambition and direction. Nobody gets anywhere without a goal, and ambition. Not my father . . . or even yours."

"But they love what they're doing. I wouldn't like being a lawyer."

"Suppose you wait and nothing hits you like your precious saint?" She had stopped crying now.

"I . . . I don't know." He realized he was defending an impossible position. He would defend it anyway.

"That's what I'm talking about. You don't know anything. You're like a girl who can't decide what dress to wear to a party and so she goes naked!"

Perhaps what she said was true. He hated the thought of it being true. "But, Avis, I have a right to want something to hit me like that. I'm asking you to have some faith in me. That's all."

"It's too much to ask." Her right hand covered her left. The fingers on her left hand were very straight as she slid off the engagement ring and held it in her right palm.

"Please, Avis, don't take it off." He stared at the ring. "Give me some space to breathe in."

"You mean, some space to be a *bum* in." She held out the ring.

He heard his voice crying. "I don't want to be a bum. I just want to be something I love being."

"Be a lawyer." Her arm, her hand holding the ring looked stiff and grotesque.

"I can't, Avis." He plucked up the ring. It was warm.

He had never actually seen a person faint before. His first impulse, not a cruel one, was to laugh—at the fluttering eyelids, at the sudden blue paleness that rushed into her baby's lips, at the buckling knees, at the comic, floating way she crumpled at his feet. She lay on her back, her arms spread wide, her feet twisted under her awkwardly.

Then he was angry. She was faking. People did not faint. She had threatened him, and now she was trying to keep him in line, using his own pity as a weapon.

"Come on, Avis, get up." He looked down, furious at her. "Get up." If she was awake and listening, she would know he was not being moved by her performance.

Still she remained, sprawled, mud in her hair. Avis would never have allowed mud to get in her hair.

He knelt beside her, frightened, not knowing what to do. He wanted now to gather her, like a dead child, into his arms. But if he touched her, he would kiss her. He knew that. And if he kissed her, he would slide the ring on her finger, and would go to law school.

He sat a short distance away from her, mud seeping through his wool pants, waiting patiently for her large brown eyes to open, hoping that when they did, he would have enough strength not to touch her when he walked her back to the dormitory.

PROBING FOR
MEANING

1. The story involves several conflicts between Avis and Chig. How does each arise and how is each resolved?

2. Chig's sister calls Avis a "phony" and Chig a "liar." What role do these remarks play in the story?

3. What significance do the stories of the baby monkey and of the conversion of St. Paul have for Chig?

4. Explain the meaning of the scene from "Huck Finn" in relation to Chig's growing awareness of a need to make a choice.

5. Will Chig be strong enough to sever his relationship with Avis? Compare and contrast the two kinds of life which Chig must choose between.

PROBING FOR
METHOD

1. Does the dialogue between Avis and Chig seem realistic to you? Why or why not?

2. Several sections of the story are physically identified by spacing within the story. What is the narrative function of these story sections? What cohesive devices bind them all together?

3. How does Kelley use chronology in this story? Are the chronological markers effective? Do they ever intrude too much into the story?

 WILLIAM CARLOS WILLIAMS

Tract

I will teach you my townspeople
how to perform a funeral
for you have it over a troop
of artists—

unless one should scour the world—
you have the ground sense necessary.

See! the hearse leads.
I begin with a design for a hearse.
For Christ's sake not black—
nor white either—and not polished!   10
Let it be weathered—like a farm wagon—
with gilt wheels (this could
be applied fresh at small expense)
or no wheels at all:
a rough dray to drag over the ground.

Knock the glass out!
My God—glass, my townspeople!
For what purpose? Is it for the dead
to look out or for us to see
how well he is housed or to see   20
the flowers or the lack of them—
or what?
To keep the rain and snow from him?
He will have a heavier rain soon:
pebbles and dirt and what not.
Let there be no glass—
and no upholstery, phew!
and no little brass rollers
and small easy wheels on the bottom—
my townspeople what are you thinking of?   30
A rough plain hearse then
with gilt wheels and no top at all.
On this the coffin lies
by its own weight.

                        No wreaths please—
especially no hot-house flowers.
Some common memento is better,
something he prized and is known by:
his old clothes—a few books perhaps—
God knows what! You realize   40
how we are about these things
my townspeople—
something will be found—anything
even flowers if he had come to that.
So much for the hearse.

For heaven's sake though see to the driver!
Take off the silk hat! In fact
that's no place at all for him—
up there unceremoniously
dragging our friend out to his own dignity!   50
Bring him down—bring him down!
Low and inconspicuous! I'd not have him ride
on the wagon at all—damn him—
the undertaker's understrapper!
Let him hold the reins
and walk at the side
and inconspicuously too!

Then briefly as to yourselves:
Walk behind—as they do in France,
seventh class, or if you ride   60
Hell take curtains! Go with some show
of inconvenience; sit openly—
to the weather as to grief.
Or do you think you can shut grief in?
What—from us? We who have perhaps
nothing to lose? Share with us
share with us—it will be money
in your pockets.

Go now
I think you are ready.   70

PROBING FOR
MEANING

1. Why do the townspeople "have it over a troop/of artists"? What does the poet mean by "ground sense"?

2. To what funeral customs does Williams object? What are the reasons for his objections?

3. What does the poet feel about grief in relation to death? What does he mean by "share with us—it will be money/in your pockets"?

4. Do you agree with Williams' criticisms? Explain. Do you feel that awareness of death is important? Why?

PROBING FOR
METHOD

1. What is a tract? How does the title apply to what follows?

2. What is the tone of the poem? How would you describe the attitude of the "I" of the poem toward the townspeople? Why are so many exclamation marks used in the poem?

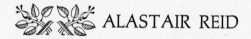 ALASTAIR REID

Curiosity

may have killed the cat; more likely
the cat was just unlucky, or else curious
to see what death was like, having no cause
to go on licking paws, or fathering
litter on litter of kittens, predictably.

Nevertheless, to be curious
is dangerous enough. To distrust
what is always said, what seems,
to ask odd questions, interfere in dreams,
leave home, smell rats, have hunches   10
do not endear cats to those doggy circles
where well-smelt baskets, suitable wives, good lunches
are the order of things, and where prevails
much wagging of incurious heads and tails.

Face it. Curiosity
will not cause us to die—
only lack of it will.
Never to want to see
the other side of the hill
or that improbable country   20
where living is an idyll
(although a probable hell)
would kill us all.
Only the curious
have, if they live, a tale
worth telling at all.

Dogs say cats love too much, are irresponsible,
are changeable, marry too many wives,
desert their children, chill all dinner tables
with tales of their nine lives.   30
Well, they are lucky. Let them be
nine-lived and contradictory,

curious enough to change, prepared to pay
the cat price, which is to die
and die again and again,
each time with no less pain.
A cat minority of one
is all that can be counted on
to tell the truth. And what cats have to tell
on each return from hell
is this: that dying is what the living do,
that dying is what the loving do,
and that dead dogs are those who do not know
that dying is what, to live, each has to do.

40

PROBING FOR
MEANING

1. The poet finds many instances in which to apply the old saying "curiosity killed the cat" to human life. What kind of people are cats? Why is curiosity dangerous for people?

2. Why does the poet state, "Only the curious/have, if they live, a tale/worth telling at all"?

3. What kind of people are dogs? What criticism do they have of cats? Why does the poet say dogs are dead? What does living entail?

4. The poet uses paradox when he says, "dying is what the living do." What does this paradox mean?

PROBING FOR
METHOD

1. What is the tone of the poem? How does the tone contribute to the meaning?

2. The title of the poem also serves as the first line. Why might the poet choose to structure the poem in this way?

3. How does the line structure contribute to the poem's statement?

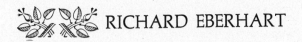 RICHARD EBERHART

If I could only live at the pitch
that is near madness

If I could only live at the pitch that is near madness
When everything is as it was in my childhood
Violent, vivid, and of infinite possibility:
That the sun and the moon broke over my head.

Then I cast time out of the trees and fields,
Then I stood immaculate in the Ego;
Then I eyed the world with all delight,
Reality was the perfection of my sight.

And time has big handles on the hands,
Fields and trees a way of being themselves.   10
I saw battalions of the race of mankind
Standing stolid, demanding a moral answer.

I gave the moral answer and I died
And into a realm of complexity came
Where nothing is possible but necessity
And the truth wailing there like a red babe.

PROBING FOR   1. Do you agree with the description of childhood in the first
MEANING   stanza as "violent, vivid, and of infinite possibility"?
       2. What further descriptions of childhood are added by each of
the four lines in the second stanza?
       3. In what sense did the poet "die" in stanza 4? Why is his
"death" the result of giving the "moral answer"? What role does "truth"
have in the "realm of complexity"?
       4. What is this "realm of complexity"? How does this realm com-
pare with living "at the pitch that is near madness"? What does "necessity" mean to the poet?

PROBING FOR   How does the third stanza contrast with the first two? What has
METHOD   happened to time in line 9? To the fields and trees in line 10?

Topics for Imitation

       1. Compare and contrast the viewpoints of Reik (this chapter)
and May (Chapter IV) on the differences between love and lust. Do
you agree with their points? Disagree?
       2. Compare and contrast Nin's concept of the individual in
society with that of Lifton, Lessing, Gold (Chapter IV) and Gordon
(Chapter IV). Do you agree with Nin's optimism or the pessimism of
the others?
       3. To what extent does the "madness" of childhood in Eber-
hart's poem correspond to the curiosity of the cats in Reid's? Compare and contrast Eberhart's adulthood with Reid's dog-like existence.

4. How similar are Maureen's and Chig's choices about mates in the Lessing and Kelley short stories? How different?

5. Compare the ideas expressed in Reid's poem and Nin's essay on the role of imagination in the individual personality.

6. Compare the viewpoints of Williams and Lifton on society's attitudes toward death. How similar are the writers' attitudes? Different? Do you agree with either? Both?

7. Compare and contrast Burgess's idea (Chapter III) that in America the individual is separate from the community with Nin's idea that the individual must assume responsibility for the collective life. With which writer do you agree?

8. In Chapter III, Burgess contrasts Italian and American cultures. To what extent do the contrasts Rau points out between Russia and India correspond to those between Italy and America?

9. Both Maynard (Chapter III) and Pollack discuss the tendency of teachers to stereotype and thereby control students. Compare and contrast their discussions, drawing on your own educational experiences as well.

10. To what extent do the characters in the Lessing and Kelley short stories dramatize Reik's thesis about love and lust?

11. Many choices present themselves to us daily. Choose any one of the following pairs of alternatives and compare and contrast the choices. Be sure to devote equal space to each alternative; if you have a preference for one of the alternatives, indicate your choice only in your conclusion. In other words, use comparison and contrast rather than argumentation as your structure.

    a. Marriage or living together

    b. Paternal or maternal custody of children in divorce cases

    c. Women working or attending college before marriage and a family or doing so after marriage and a family

    d. Obtaining a college education or on-the-job training

    e. Choosing a major based on the job market or a major based on your own interests and abilities

    f. Going away to school or commuting to school from home

    g. Specializing in college or taking a varied course of study

SIX

 # PHILOSOPHIES

"not people die but worlds die in them"

Plato, in his "Allegory of the Cave," compares man's search for sense and significance in life to his leaving the safe, dark but warm cave of illusions for the blinding light of the sun of truth. Most people prefer to remain in the cave and lead a life patterned for them by others, but some need the greater fulfillment resulting from the search for a personal philosophy of life.

"Techniques of living" is how Anne Morrow Lindbergh describes what she is looking for. Henry David Thoreau is in search of himself. Other writers use other phrases—"enlightened nature," "values of life" and "self-development"—but all are searching for a philosophy of existence.

Several writers, while searching, turn to nature: Walt Whitman contemplates the grass; Thoreau moves to Walden Pond; the son in Pär Lagerkvist's story spends an afternoon in the woods, as does E. M. Forster; Anne Morrow Lindbergh visits the seashore; Daru, in Albert Camus' story, inhabits a barren Algerian plateau. Conversely, Helen Keller searches for meaning in New York City.

Each writer's truth is different. Keller finds significance in friendship; Thoreau, in solitude; Whitman, in nature itself; Lindbergh, in simplicity; Lagerkvist's boy, in courage before the unknown; Camus, in brotherhood; Forster, in compromise; Sexton, in God. Edna St. Vincent Millay finds no answer at all: "Life in itself/Is nothing."

369

While we may remain behind in Plato's cave or Thoreau's village, in order to enrich our lives we must search for the sunlight or leave the village for the solitude of the woods. As Thoreau says, "Not till we are lost, in other words not till we have lost the world, do we begin to find ourselves. . . ."

Illustrating Ideas

Each writer in this chapter is presenting an idea or a series of ideas that form his or her philosophy of life. As you read, notice the concrete comparisons and examples the writers use to make the abstract ideas more concrete and vivid.

 ANNE MORROW LINDBERGH

Channelled Whelk

The shell in my hand is deserted. It once housed a whelk, a snail-like creature, and then temporarily, after the death of the first occupant, a little hermit crab, who has run away, leaving his tracks behind him like a delicate vine on the sand. He ran away, and left me his shell. It was once a protection to him. I turn the shell in my hand, gazing into the wide open door from which he made his exit. Had it become an encumbrance? Why did he run away? Did he hope to find a better home, a better mode of living? I too have run away, I realize, I have shed the shell of my life, for these few weeks of vacation.

But his shell—it is simple; it is bare, it is beautiful. Small, only the size of my thumb, its architecture is perfect, down to the finest detail. Its shape, swelling like a pear in the center, winds in a gentle spiral to the pointed apex. Its color, dull gold, is whitened by a wash of salt from the sea. Each whorl, each faint knob, each criss-cross vein in its egg-shell texture, is as clearly defined as on the day of creation. My eye follows with delight the outer circumference of that diminutive winding staircase up which this tenant used to travel.

My shell is not like this, I think. How untidy it has become!

Blurred with moss, knobby with barnacles, its shape is hardly recognizable any more. Surely, it had a shape once. It has a shape still in
my mind. What is the shape of my life?

The shape of my life today starts with a family. I have a
husband, five children and a home just beyond the suburbs of New
York. I have also a craft, writing, and therefore work I want to
pursue. The shape of my life is, of course, determined by many other
things; my background and childhood, my mind and its education,
my conscience and its pressures, my heart and its desires. I want to
give and take from my children and husband, to share with friends
and community, to carry out my obligations to man and to the world
as a woman, as an artist, as a citizen.

But I want first of all—in fact, as an end to these other
desires—to be at peace with myself. I want a singleness of eye, a
purity of intention, a central core to my life that will enable me to
carry out these obligations and activities as well as I can. I want, in
fact—to borrow from the language of the saints—to live "in grace"
as much of the time as possible. I am not using this term in a strictly
theological sense. By grace I mean an inner harmony, essentially
spiritual, which can be translated into outward harmony. I am seeking
perhaps what Socrates asked for in the prayer from the *Phaedrus*
when he said, "May the outward and inward man be at one." I would
like to achieve a state of inner spiritual grace from which I could
function and give as I was meant to in the eye of God.

Vague as this definition may be, I believe most people are
aware of periods in their lives when they seem to be "in grace" and
other periods when they feel "out of grace," even though they may
use different words to describe these states. In the first happy condition, one seems to carry all one's tasks before one lightly, as if borne
along on a great tide; and in the opposite state one can hardly tie a
shoe-string. It is true that a large part of life consists in learning a
technique of tying the shoe-string, whether one is in grace or not. But
there are techniques of living too; there are even techniques in the
search for grace. And techniques can be cultivated. I have learned by
some experience, by many examples, and by the writings of countless
others before me, also occupied in the search, that certain environ-
ments, certain modes of life, certain rules of conduct are more conducive to inner and outer harmony than others. There are, in fact,
certain roads that one may follow. Simplification of life is one of
them.

I mean to lead a simple life, to choose a simple shell I can
carry easily—like a hermit crab. But I do not. I find that my frame of
life does not foster simplicity. My husband and five children must
make their way in the world. The life I have chosen as wife and

mother entrains a whole caravan of complications. It involves a house in the suburbs and either household drudgery or household help which wavers between scarcity and non-existence for most of us. It involves food and shelter; meals, planning, marketing, bills, and making the ends meet in a thousand ways. It involves not only the butcher, the baker, the candlestickmaker but countless other experts to keep my modern house with its modern "simplifications" (electricity, plumbing, refrigerator, gas-stove, oil-burner, dish-washer, radios, car, and numerous other labor-saving devices) functioning properly. It involves health; doctors, dentists, appointments, medicine, cod-liver oil, vitamins, trips to the drugstore. It involves education, spiritual, intellectual, physical; schools, school conferences, carpools, extra trips for basket-ball or orchestra practice; tutoring; camps, camp equipment and transportation. It involves clothes, shopping, laundry, cleaning, mending, letting skirts down and sewing buttons on, or finding someone else to do it. It involves friends, my husband's, my children's, my own, and endless arrangements to get together; letters, invitations, telephone calls and transportation hither and yon.

For life today in America is based on the premise of ever-widening circles of contact and communication. It involves not only family demands, but community demands, national demands, international demands on the good citizen, through social and cultural pressures, through newspapers, magazines, radio programs, political drives, charitable appeals, and so on. My mind reels with it. What a circus act we women perform every day of our lives. It puts the trapeze artist to shame. Look at us. We run a tight rope daily, balancing a pile of books on the head. Baby-carriage, parasol, kitchen chair, still under control. Steady now!

This is not the life of simplicity but the life of multiplicity that the wise men warn us of. It leads not to unification but to fragmentation. It does not bring grace; it destroys the soul. And this is not only true of my life, I am forced to conclude; it is the life of millions of women in America. I stress America, because today, the American woman more than any other has the privilege of choosing such a life. Woman in large parts of the civilized world has been forced back by war, by poverty, by collapse, by the sheer struggle to survive, into a smaller circle of immediate time and space, immediate family life, immediate problems of existence. The American woman is still relatively free to choose the wider life. How long she will hold this enviable and precarious position no one knows. But her particular situation has a significance far above its apparent economic, national or even sex limitations.

For the problem of the multiplicity of life not only confronts the American woman, but also the American man. And it is not merely the concern of the American as such, but of our whole modern civilization, since life in America today is held up as the ideal of a large part of the rest of the world. And finally, it is not limited to our present civilization, though we are faced with it now in an exaggerated form. It has always been one of the pitfalls of mankind. Plotinus was preaching the dangers of multiplicity of the world back in the third century. Yet, the problem is particularly and essentially woman's. Distraction is, always has been, and probably always will be, inherent in woman's life.

For to be a woman is to have interests and duties, raying out in all directions from the central mother-core, like spokes from the hub of a wheel. The pattern of our lives is essentially circular. We must be open to all points of the compass; husband, children, friends, home, community; stretched out, exposed, sensitive like a spider's web to each breeze that blows, to each call that comes. How difficult for us, then, to achieve a balance in the midst of these contradictory tensions, and yet how necessary for the proper functioning of our lives. How much we need, and how arduous of attainment is that steadiness preached in all rules for holy living. How desirable and how distant is the ideal of the contemplative, artist, or saint—the inner inviolable core, the single eye.

With a new awareness, both painful and humorous, I begin to understand why the saints were rarely married women. I am convinced it has nothing inherently to do, as I once supposed, with chastity or children. It has to do primarily with distractions. The bearing, rearing, feeding and educating of children; the running of a house with its thousand details; human relationships with their myriad pulls—woman's normal occupations in general run counter to creative life, or contemplative life, or saintly life. The problem is not merely one of *Woman and Career, Woman and the Home, Woman and Independence.* It is more basically: how to remain whole in the midst of the distractions of life; how to remain balanced, no matter what centrifugal forces tend to pull one off center; how to remain strong, no matter what shocks come in at the periphery and tend to crack the hub of the wheel.

What is the answer? There is no easy answer, no complete answer. I have only clues, shells from the sea. The bare beauty of the channelled whelk tells me that one answer, and perhaps a first step, is in simplification of life, in cutting out some of the distractions. But how? Total retirement is not possible. I cannot shed my responsibilities. I cannot permanently inhabit a desert island. I cannot be a nun in the midst of family life. I would not want to be. The solution for me, surely, is neither in total renunciation of the world, nor in total acceptance of it. I must find a balance somewhere, or an alternating rhythm between these two extremes; a swinging of the pendulum between solitude and communion, between retreat and return. In my periods of retreat, perhaps I can learn something to carry back into my worldly life. I can at least practice for these two weeks the simplification of outward life, as a beginning. I can follow this superficial clue, and see where it leads. Here, in beach living, I can try.

One learns first of all in beach living the art of shedding; how little one can get along with, not how much. Physical shedding to begin with, which then mysteriously spreads into other fields. Clothes, first. Of course, one needs less in the sun. But one needs less anyway, one finds suddenly. One does not need a closet-full, only a small suitcase-full. And what a relief it is! Less taking up and down of hems, less mending, and—best of all—less worry about what to wear. One finds one is shedding not only clothes—but vanity.

Next, shelter. One does not need the airtight shelter one has in winter in the North. Here I live in a bare sea-shell of a cottage. No heat, no telephone, no plumbing to speak of, no hot water, a two-burner oil stove, no gadgets to go wrong. No rugs. There were some, but I rolled them up the first day; it is easier to sweep the sand off a bare floor. But I find I don't bustle about with unnecessary sweeping and cleaning here. I am no longer aware of the dust. I have shed my Puritan conscience about absolute tidiness and cleanliness. Is it possible that, too, is a material burden? No curtains. I do not need them for privacy; the pines around my house are enough protection. I want the windows open all the time, and I don't want to worry about rain. I begin to shed my Martha-like anxiety about many things. Washable slipcovers, faded and old—I hardly see them; I don't worry about the impression they make on other people. I am shedding pride. As little furniture as possible; I shall not need much. I shall ask into my shell only those friends with whom I can be completely honest. I find I am shedding hypocrisy in human relationships. What a rest that will be! The most exhausting thing in life, I have discovered, is being insincere. That is why so much of social life is exhausting; one is wearing a mask. I have shed my mask.

I find I live quite happily without those things I think necessary in winter in the North. And as I write these words, I remember, with some shock at the disparity in our lives, a similar statement made by a friend of mine in France who spent three years in a German prison camp. Of course, he said, qualifying his remark, they did not get enough to eat, they were sometimes atrociously treated, they had little physical freedom. And yet, prison life taught him how little one can get along with, and what extraordinary spiritual freedom and peace such simplification can bring. I remember again, ironically, that today more of us in America than anywhere else in the world have the luxury of choice between simplicity and complication of life. And for the most part, we, who could choose simplicity, choose complication. War, prison, survival periods, enforce a form of simplicity on man. The monk and the nun choose it of their own free will. But if one accidentally finds it, as I have for a few days, one finds also the serenity it brings.

Is it not rather ugly, one may ask? One collects material possessions not only for security, comfort or vanity, but for beauty as well. Is your sea-shell house not ugly and bare? No, it is beautiful, my house. It is bare, of course, but the wind, the sun, the smell of the pines blow through its bareness. The unfinished beams in the roof are veiled by cobwebs. They are lovely, I think, gazing up at them with new eyes; they soften the hard lines of the rafters as grey hairs soften the lines on a middle-aged face. I no longer pull out grey hairs or sweep down cobwebs. As for the walls, it is true they looked forbidding at first. I felt cramped and enclosed by their blank faces. I wanted to knock holes in them, to give them another dimension with pictures or windows. So I dragged home from the beach grey arms of driftwood, worn satin-smooth by wind and sand. I gathered trailing green vines with floppy red-tipped leaves. I picked up the whitened skeletons of conchshells, their curious hollowed-out shapes faintly reminiscent of abstract sculpture. With these tacked to walls and propped up in corners, I am satisfied. I have a periscope out to the world. I have a window, a view, a point of flight from my sedentary base.

I am content. I sit down at my desk, a bare kitchen table with a blotter, a bottle of ink, a sand dollar to weight down one corner, a clam shell for a pen tray, the broken tip of a conch, pink-tinged, to finger, and a row of shells to set my thoughts spinning.

I love my sea-shell of a house. I wish I could live in it always. I wish I could transport it home. But I cannot. It will not hold a husband, five children and the necessities and trappings of daily life. I can only carry back my little channelled whelk. It will sit on my desk in Connecticut, to remind me of the ideal of a simplified life, to encourage me in the game I played on the beach. To ask how little, not how much, can I get along with. To say—is it necessary?—when I am tempted to add one more accumulation to my life, when I am pulled toward one more centrifugal activity.

Simplification of outward life is not enough. It is merely the outside. But I am starting with the outside. I am looking at the outside of a shell, the outside of my life—the shell. The complete answer is not to be found on the outside, in an outward mode of living. This is only a technique, a road to grace. The final answer, I know, is always inside. But the outside can give a clue, can help one to find the inside answer. One is free, like the hermit crab, to change one's shell.

Channelled whelk, I put you down again, but you have set my mind on a journey, up an inwardly winding spiral staircase of thought.

1. Why does Lindbergh compare the shell just deserted by a hermit crab to her life and the hermit crab to herself? How is the shell different from the life she is living?

2. What does she mean by "being at peace with" herself? What does it mean to be "out of grace"? How serious a state is the latter?

3. What is the technique for living that she talks about? Do you agree with her that it is a very difficult technique to learn? What has contributed to this difficulty?

4. Do you agree with her that multiplicity leads to fragmentation? What evidence does she cite for this statement?

5. "Distraction is, always has been, and probably always will be, inherent in woman's life." Why is a woman's life more fragmented than a man's? Why is this particularly true in America? Why is it enviable, as Lindbergh claims it is, to be fragmented if fragmentation destroys the soul?

6. She discusses what she calls "the art of shedding." To what is this analogous? Which people have perfected this art? How possible is it for most people to "shed"?

7. What stages in "shedding" does Lindbergh delineate? How did she avoid making shedding ugly?

8. What does she hope to accomplish in her cottage at the seashore? Why does she think her concentration on physical shedding will affect her spiritually or emotionally (in other words, that the "outside" will affect the "inside")?

1. What method does Lindbergh use in introducing her essay? Does her first paragraph include a thesis statement? If so, what is it?

2. What parallel exists between the whelk shell and her life? On how many levels does this parallel work? How does using the shell to refer to her life help convey her point? What other comparisons might she have used?

3. What techniques are employed in the conclusion? How effective is the conclusion?

4. What writing techniques does Lindbergh employ to achieve a simplicity of style which underscores her theme of the simplicity of life?

Illustrating Ideas

How does Lindbergh use illustration in her essay? Lindbergh uses many techniques of illustration, several of which are evident on the first page. *Simile,* in which one subject is illustrated through a direct comparison with another using "like" or "as," can be seen in the hermit crab's running away, "leaving his *tracks* behind him like a delicate *vine* on the sand." While we may not have seen the tracks of a hermit crab, we have seen a trailing vine, and therefore the picture is made much more vivid by the comparison.

Metaphor, a less direct form of comparison, forms the basis of another illustration: "I have shed the shell of my life." The complexities of Lindbergh's life are indirectly compared to the shell of the whelk, providing again a vivid illustration of her meaning.

She uses many other similes and metaphors in her essay. Can you find them?

Lindbergh also uses *example,* another illustrative device, in paragraph 7 when she lists all her involvements as a wife and mother: providing food and shelter, health care and education, maintaining household appliances, socializing, and so on. For each involvement, she lists several examples, thus making very specific her statement that her life is complex.

She also uses illustration, which is an extended example. Seeking simplicity in a world of complexity, she uses her vacation at the seashore as an illustration of how one could live a simple life.

Her entire essay is organized around another illustrative device: *analogy* or extended metaphor. As we have seen, her essay begins with a comparison of her life with that of the shell in a simple metaphor: "I have shed the shell of my life." This metaphor is extended throughout the essay at various points: she compares their shapes, their simplicity, the shelter of shell and seaside cottage, the change both experience. What begins as a simple metaphor extends throughout the essay to become an analogy.

Lindbergh is discussing an idea—that of the need for simplicity of life—by using many concrete examples and comparisons to make her idea vivid.

INDUCTION
Principles of illustration. As we saw in Chapter I, specific topics and vivid language help forge the best writing. Another sharp tool at the writer's disposal is illustration. Illustration further hones the abstract and general into the concrete and particular shape of good writing.

A. The writer may use example—a logical illustration of his point in which the part represents the whole: "A luscious orange is an example of fruit."

B. Another logical method of illustrating an abstract principle is to tell a story or create a hypothetical situation which through its narrative qualities makes the abstract concrete. This method can be called, simply, illustration: "The cycle of fruit from seed to ripening can be illustrated through the story of the orange."

C. Or the writer may, as in metaphor or simile, use a totally unrelated illustration which still offers some information about the subject: "A *poem* is palpable and mute as globed *fruit.*"

D. Analogy and allegory, which also form unrelated comparisons, extend throughout a paragraph or an essay. An analogy is an extended metaphor. Analogy is used to describe a poem throughout an essay as having many properties of fruit: beauty, nourishment, sweetness, and so on.

In allegory, the two points of comparison are not directly mentioned. Allegory is used to describe fruit in such a way as to suggest that the writer is talking, not about nature, but about art, specifically poetry. Two levels of meaning exist simultaneously: the literal level (a description of fruit) and the abstract level (a description of poetry). Again, an abstraction is made concrete. See Plato's "Allegory of the Cave" in this chapter as an example of allegory. Compare and contrast the Plato and Lindbergh selections to distinguish between allegory and analogy.

IMITATION   *Procedures to follow in using illustration.*

A. Any topic can be most successfully developed through the use of one or more illustrative devices. Alfred Kazin uses metaphor and analogy to describe his mother's kitchen in Chapter II. Also in Chapter II, Eldridge Cleaver describes the jailer's keys as sounding like Christmas bells when the jailer brings him mail. In Chapter IV, Rollo May uses many examples from newspaper files to support his thesis that we are an apathetic society. Santha Rama Rau's essay on India in Chapter V is based on illustrations from Indian life. In this chapter, a very important use of the methods of illustration has been elucidated: as a way of making the abstract idea concrete.

B. A major method of paragraph development (see Chapter III) is the use of examples. Almost any paragraph topic can be developed through the use of examples. As you write each paragraph of your essay, ask yourself what example can be cited to support and concretize more fully that paragraph topic. An extended example or illustration may form the foundation of your entire essay (see Helen Keller's essay in this chapter).

C. Metaphors and similes also can and should be included in any writing. Whenever making a point, ask yourself what comparisons might make your point more vivid. Be sure to avoid clichés, however. Comparisons too often used lose their effectiveness.

D. Analogy and allegory refer to the entire structure of an essay and require careful planning. A writer's creativity can be developed through use of these techniques. While most writing today tends to be factual and does not therefore lend itself to allegory, analogy can be utilized to illustrate any type of writing. An aerospace engineer, for example, might compare a new spacecraft to an insect in order to familiarize readers with its appearance.

Writers often look to the insect or animal world for illustrative material. A fable, for example, is a form of allegory which depicts animals as having human qualities. Thoreau, in *Walden*, uses analogy to compare ants to men.

If your topic is abstract, not requiring factual documentation, you should consider the possibility of using allegory or analogy.

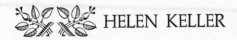 HELEN KELLER

Three Days to See

All of us have read thrilling stories in which the hero had only a limited and specified time to live. Sometimes it was as long as a year; sometimes as short as twenty-four hours. But always we were interested in discovering just how the doomed man chose to spend his last days or his last hours. I speak, of course, of free men who have a choice, not condemned criminals whose sphere of activities is strictly delimited.

Such stories set us thinking, wondering what we should do under similar circumstances. What events, what experiences, what associations should we crowd into those last hours as mortal beings? What happiness should we find in reviewing the past, what regrets?

Sometimes I have thought it would be an excellent rule to live each day as if we should die tomorrow. Such an attitude would emphasize sharply the values of life. We should live each day with a gentleness, a vigor, and a keenness of appreciation which are often lost when time stretches before us in the constant panorama of more days and months and years to come. There are those, of course, who would adopt the epicurean motto of "Eat, drink, and be merry," but most people would be chastened by the certainty of impending death.

In stories, the doomed hero is usually saved at the last minute by some stroke of fortune, but almost always his sense of values is changed. He becomes more appreciative of the meaning of life and its permanent spiritual values. It has often been noted that those who live, or have lived, in the shadow of death bring a mellow sweetness to everything they do.

Most of us, however, take life for granted. We know that one day we must die, but usually we picture that day as far in the future. When we are in buoyant health, death is all but unimaginable. We seldom think of it. The days stretch out in an endless vista. So we go about our petty tasks, hardly aware of our listless attitude toward life.

The same lethargy, I am afraid, characterizes the use of all our faculties and senses. Only the deaf appreciate hearing, only the blind realize the manifold blessings that lie in sight. Particularly does this observation apply to those who have lost sight and hearing in adult life. But those who have never suffered impairment of sight or hearing seldom make the fullest use of these blessed faculties. Their eyes and ears take in all sights and sounds hazily, without concentration and with little appreciation. It is the same old story of not being grateful for what we have until we lose it, of not being conscious of health until we are ill.

I have often thought it would be a blessing if each human being were stricken blind and deaf for a few days at some time during his early adult life. Darkness would make him more appreciative of sight; silence would teach him the joys of sound.

Now and then I have tested my seeing friends to discover what they see. Recently I was visited by a very good friend who had just returned from a long walk in the woods, and I asked her what she had observed. "Nothing in particular," she replied. I might have been incredulous had I not been accustomed to such reponses, for long ago I became convinced that the seeing see little.

How was it possible, I asked myself, to walk for an hour through the woods and see nothing worthy of note? I who cannot see find hundreds of things to interest me through mere touch. I feel the delicate symmetry of a leaf. I pass my hands lovingly about the smooth skin of a silver birch, or the rough shaggy bark of a pine. In spring I touch the branches of trees hopefully in search of a bud, the first sign of awakening Nature after her winter's sleep. I feel the delightful, velvety texture of a flower, and discover its remarkable convolutions; and something of the miracle of Nature is revealed to me. Occasionally, if I am fortunate, I place my hand gently on a small tree and feel the happy quiver of a bird in full song. I am delighted to have the cool waters of a brook rush through my open fingers. To me a lush carpet of pine needles or spongy grass is more welcome than the most luxurious Persian rug. To me the pageant of seasons is a thrilling and unending drama, the action of which streams through my finger tips.

At times my heart cries out with longing to see all these things. If I can get so much pleasure from mere touch, how much more beauty must be revealed by sight. Yet, those who have eyes apparently see little. The panorama of color and action which fills the world is taken for granted. It is human, perhaps, to appreciate little that which we have and to long for that which we have not, but it is a great pity that in the world of light the gift of sight is used only as a mere convenience rather than as a means of adding fullness to life.

If I were the president of a university I should establish a compulsory course in "How to Use Your Eyes." The professor would try to show his pupils how they could add joy to their lives by really seeing what passes unnoticed before them. He would try to awake their dormant and sluggish faculties.

Perhaps I can best illustrate by imagining what I should most like to see if I were given the use of my eyes, say, for just three days. And while I am imagining, suppose you, too, set your mind to work on the problem of how you would use your own eyes if you had only three more days to see. If with the oncoming darkness of the third night you knew that the sun would never rise for you again, how would you spend those three precious intervening days? What would you most want to let your gaze rest upon?

I, naturally, should want most to see the things which have become dear to me through my years of darkness. You, too, would want to let your eyes rest long on the things that have become dear to you so that you could take the memory of them with you into the night that loomed before you.

If, by some miracle I were granted three seeing days, to be followed by a relapse into darkness, I should divide the period into three parts.

On the first day, I should want to see the people whose kindness and gentleness and companionship have made my life worth living. First I should like to gaze long upon the face of my dear teacher, Mrs. Anne Sullivan Macy, who came to me when I was a child and opened the outer world to me. I should want not merely to see the outline of her face, so that I could cherish it in my memory, but to study that face and find in it the living evidence of the sympathetic tenderness and patience with which she accomplished the difficult task of my education. I should like to see in her eyes that strength of character which has enabled her to stand firm in the face of difficulties, and that compassion for all humanity which she has revealed to me so often.

I do not know what it is to see into the heart of a friend through that "window of the soul," the eye. I can only "see" through my finger tips the outline of a face. I can detect laughter, sorrow, and many other obvious emotions. I know my friends from the feel of their faces. But I cannot really picture their personalities by touch. I know their personalities, of course, through other means, through the thoughts they express to me, through whatever of their actions are revealed to me. But I am denied that deeper understanding of them which I am sure would come through sight of them, through watching their reactions to various expressed thoughts and circumstances, through noting the immediate and fleeting reactions of their eyes and countenance.

Friends who are near to me I know well, because through the

months and years they reveal themselves to me in all their phases; but of casual friends I have only an incomplete impression, an impression gained from a handclasp, from spoken words which I take from their lips with my finger tips, or which they tap into the palm of my hand.

How much easier, how much more satisfying it is for you who can see to grasp quickly the essential qualities of another person by watching the subtleties of expression, the quiver of a muscle, the flutter of a hand. But does it ever occur to you to use your sight to see into the inner nature of a friend or acquaintance? Do not most of you seeing people grasp casually the outward features of a face and let it go at that?

For instance, can you describe accurately the faces of five good friends? Some of you can, but many cannot. As an experiment, I have questioned husbands of long standing about the color of their wives' eyes, and often they express embarrassed confusion and admit that they do not know. And, incidentally, it is a chronic complaint of wives that their husbands do not notice new dresses, new hats, and changes in household arrangements.

The eyes of seeing persons soon become accustomed to the routine of their surroundings, and they actually see only the startling and spectacular. But even in viewing the most spectacular sights the eyes are lazy. Court records reveal every day how inaccurately "eyewitnesses" see. A given event will be "seen" in several different ways by as many witnesses. Some see more than others, but few see everything that is within the range of their vision.

Oh, the things that I should see if I had the power of sight for just three days!

The first day would be a busy one. I should call to me all my dear friends and look long into their faces, imprinting upon my mind the outward evidences of the beauty that is within them. I should let my eyes rest, too, on the face of a baby, so that I could catch a vision of the eager, innocent beauty which precedes the individual's consciousness of the conflicts which life develops.

And I should like to look into the loyal, trusting eyes of my dogs—the grave, canny little Scottie, Darkie, and the stalwart, understanding Great Dane, Helga, whose warm, tender, and playful friendships are so comforting to me.

On that busy first day I should also view the small simple things of my home. I want to see the warm colors in the rugs under my feet, the pictures on the walls, the intimate trifles that transform a house into home. My eyes would rest respectfully on the books in raised type which I have read, but they would be more eagerly interested in the printed books which seeing people can read, for during the long night of my life the books I have read and those which have been read to me have built themselves into a great shining lighthouse, revealing to me the deepest channels of human life and the human spirit.

In the afternoon of that first seeing day, I should take a long walk in the woods and intoxicate my eyes on the beauties of the world of Nature, trying desperately to absorb in a few hours the vast splendor which is constantly unfolding itself to those who can see. On the way home from my woodland jaunt my path would lie near a farm so that I might see the patient horses plowing in the field (perhaps I should see only a tractor!) and the serene content of men living close to the soil. And I should pray for the glory of a colorful sunset.

When dusk had fallen, I should experience the double delight of being able to see by artificial light, which the genius of man has created to extend the power of his sight when Nature decrees darkness.

In the night of that first day of sight, I should not be able to sleep, so full would be my mind of the memories of the day.

The next day—the second day of sight—I should arise with the dawn and see the thrilling miracle by which night is transformed into day. I should behold with awe the magnificent panorama of light with which the sun awakens the sleeping earth.

This day I should devote to a hasty glimpse of the world, past and present. I should want to see the pageant of man's progress, the kaleidoscope of the ages. How can so much be compressed into one day? Through the museums, of course. Often I have visited the New York Museum of Natural History to touch with my hands many of the objects there exhibited, but I have longed to see with my eyes the condensed history of the earth and its inhabitants displayed there— animals and the races of men pictured in their native environment; gigantic carcasses of dinosaurs and mastodons which roamed the earth long before man appeared, with his tiny stature and powerful brain, to conquer the animal kingdom; realistic presentations of the processes of evolution in animals, in man, and in the implements which man has used to fashion for himself a secure home on this planet; and a thousand and one other aspects of natural history.

I wonder how many readers of this article have viewed this panorama of the face of living things as pictured in that inspiring museum. Many, of course, have not had the opportunity, but I am sure that many who *have* had the opportunity have not made use of it. There, indeed, is a place to use your eyes. You who see can spend many fruitful days there, but I, with my imaginary three days of sight, could only take a hasty glimpse, and pass on.

My next stop would be the Metropolitan Museum of Art, for

just as the Museum of Natural History reveals the material aspects of the world, so does the Metropolitan show the myriad facets of the human spirit. Throughout the history of humanity the urge to artistic expression has been almost as powerful as the urge for food, shelter, and procreation. And here, in the vast chambers of the Metropolitan Museum, is unfolded before me the spirit of Egypt, Greece, and Rome, as expressed in their art. I know well through my hands the sculptured gods and goddesses of the ancient Nile-land. I have felt copies of Parthenon friezes, and I have sensed the rhythmic beauty of charging Athenian warriors. Apollos and Venuses and the Winged Victory of Samothrace are friends of my finger tips. The gnarled, bearded features of Homer are dear to me, for he, too, knew blindness.

My hands have lingered upon the living marble of Roman sculpture as well as that of later generations. I have passed my hands over a plaster cast of Michelangelo's inspiring and heroic Moses; I have sensed the power of Rodin; I have been awed by the devoted spirit of Gothic wood carving. These arts which can be touched have meaning for me, but even they were meant to be seen rather than felt, and I can only guess at the beauty which remains hidden from me. I can admire the simple lines of a Greek vase, but its figured decorations are lost to me.

So on this, my second day of sight, I should try to probe into the soul of man through his art. The things I knew through touch I should now see. More splendid still, the whole magnificent world of painting would be opened to me, from the Italian Primitives, with their serene religious devotion, to the Moderns, with their feverish visions. I should look deep into the canvases of Raphael, Leonardo da Vinci, Titian, Rembrandt. I should want to feast my eyes upon the warm colors of Veronese, study the mysteries of El Greco, catch a new vision of Nature from Corot. Oh, there is so much rich meaning and beauty in the art of the ages for you who have eyes to see!

Upon my short visit to this temple of art I should not be able to review a fraction of that great world of art which is open to you. I should be able to get only a superficial impression. Artists tell me that for a deep and true appreciation of art one must educate the eye. One must learn through experience to weigh the merits of line, of composition, of form and color. If I had eyes, how happily would I embark upon so fascinating a study! Yet I am told that, to many of you who have eyes to see, the world of art is a dark night, unexplored and unilluminated.

It would be with extreme reluctance that I should leave the Metropolitan Museum, which contains the key to beauty—a beauty so neglected. Seeing persons, however, do not need a Metropolitan to find this key to beauty. The same key lies waiting in smaller museums, and in books on the shelves of even small libraries. But naturally, in my limited time of imaginary sight, I should choose the place where the key unlocks the greatest treasures in the shortest time.

The evening of my second day of sight I should spend at a theater or at the movies. Even now I often attend theatrical performances of all sorts, but the action of the play must be spelled into my hand by a companion. But how I should like to see with my own eyes the fascinating figure of Hamlet, or the gusty Falstaff amid colorful Elizabethan trappings! How I should like to follow each movement of the graceful Hamlet, each strut of the hearty Falstaff! And since I could see only one play, I should be confronted by a many-horned dilemma, for there are scores of plays I should want to see. You who have eyes can see any you like. How many of you, I wonder, when you gaze at a play, a movie, or any spectacle, realize and give thanks for the miracle of sight which enables you to enjoy its color, grace, and movement?

I cannot enjoy the beauty of rhythmic movement except in a sphere restricted to the touch of my hands. I can vision only dimly the grace of a Pavlova, although I know something of the delight of rhythm, for often I can sense the beat of music as it vibrates through the floor. I can well imagine that cadenced motion must be one of the most pleasing sights in the world. I have been able to gather something of this by tracing with my fingers the lines in sculptured marble; if this static grace can be so lovely, how much more acute must be the thrill of seeing grace in motion.

One of my dearest memories is of the time when Joseph Jefferson allowed me to touch his face and hands as he went through some of the gestures and speeches of his beloved Rip Van Winkle. I was able to catch thus a meager glimpse of the world of drama, and I shall never forget the delight of that moment. But, oh, how much I must miss, and how much pleasure you seeing ones can derive from watching and hearing the interplay of speech and movement in the unfolding of a dramatic performance! If I could see only one play, I should know how to picture in my mind the action of a hundred plays which I have read or had transferred to me through the medium of the manual alphabet.

So, through the evening of my second imaginary day of sight, the great figures of dramatic literature would crowd sleep from my eyes.

The following morning, I should again greet the dawn, anxious to discover new delights, for I am sure that, for those who

have eyes which really see, the dawn of each day must be a perpetually new revelation of beauty.

This, according to the terms of my imagined miracle, is to be
my third and last day of sight. I shall have no time to waste in regrets
or longings; there is too much to see. The first day I devoted to my
friends, animate and inanimate. The second revealed to me the history
of man and Nature. Today I shall spend in the workaday world of the
present, amid the haunts of men going about the business of life. And
where can one find so many activities and conditions of men as in
New York? So the city becomes my destination.

I start from my home in the quiet little suburb of Forest Hills,
Long Island. Here, surrounded by green lawns, trees, and flowers, are
neat little houses, happy with the voices and movements of wives and
children, havens of peaceful rest for men who toil in the city. I drive
across the lacy structure of steel which spans the East River, and I get
a new and startling vision of the power and ingenuity of the mind of
man. Busy boats chug and scurry about the river—racy speed boats,
stolid, snorting tugs. If I had long days of sight ahead, I should spend
many of them watching the delightful activity upon the river.

I look ahead, and before me rise the fantastic towers of New
York, a city that seems to have stepped from the pages of a fairy
story. What an awe-inspiring sight, these glittering spires, these vast
banks of stone and steel—structures such as the gods might build for
themselves! This animated picture is a part of the lives of millions of
people every day. How many, I wonder, give it so much as a second
glance? Very few, I fear. Their eyes are blind to this magnificent sight
because it is so familiar to them.

I hurry to the top of one of those gigantic structures, the
Empire State Building, for there, a short time ago, I "saw" the city
below through the eyes of my secretary. I am anxious to compare my
fancy with reality. I am sure I should not be disappointed in the
panorama spread out before me, for to me it would be a vision of
another world.

Now I begin my rounds of the city. First, I stand at a busy
corner, merely looking at people, trying by sight of them to understand something of their lives. I see smiles, and I am happy. I see
serious determination, and I am proud. I see suffering, and I am
compassionate.

I stroll down Fifth Avenue. I throw my eyes out of focus so
that I see no particular object but only a seething kaleidoscope of
color. I am certain that the colors of women's dresses moving in a
throng must be a gorgeous spectacle of which I should never tire. But
perhaps if I had sight I should be like most other women—too
interested in styles and the cut of individual dresses to give much

attention to the splendor of color in the mass. And I am convinced, too, that I should become an inveterate window shopper, for it must be a delight to the eye to view the myriad articles of beauty on display.

From Fifth Avenue I make a tour of the city—to Park Avenue, to the slums, to factories, to parks where children play. I take a stay-at-home trip abroad by visiting the foreign quarters. Always my eyes are open wide to all the sights of both happiness and misery so that I may probe deep and add to my understanding of how people work and live. My heart is full of the images of people and things. My eye passes lightly over no single trifle; it strives to touch and hold closely each thing its gaze rests upon. Some sights are pleasant, filling the heart with happiness; but some are miserably pathetic. To these latter I do not shut my eyes, for they, too, are part of life. To close the eye on them is to close the heart and mind.

My third day of sight is drawing to an end. Perhaps there are many serious pursuits to which I should devote the few remaining hours, but I am afraid that on the evening of that last day I should again run away to the theater, to a hilariously funny play, so that I might appreciate the overtones of comedy in the human spirit.

At midnight my temporary respite from blindness would cease, and permanent night would close in on me again. Naturally in those three short days I should not have seen all I wanted to see. Only when darkness had again descended upon me should I realize how much I had left unseen. But my mind would be so crowded with glorious memories that I should have little time for regrets. Thereafter the touch of every object would bring a glowing memory of how that object looked.

Perhaps this short outline of how I should spend three days of sight does not agree with the program you would set for yourself if you knew that you were about to be stricken blind. I am, however, sure that if you actually faced that fate your eyes would open to things you had never seen before, storing up memories for the long night ahead. You would use your eyes as never before. Everything you saw would become dear to you. Your eyes would touch and embrace very object that came within your range of vision. Then, at last, you would really see, and a new world of beauty would open itself before you.

I who am blind can give one hint to those who see—one admonition to those who would make full use of the gift of sight: Use your eyes as if tomorrow you would be stricken blind. And the same method can be applied to the other senses. Hear the music of voices, the song of a bird, the mighty strains of an orchestra, as if you would be stricken deaf tomorrow. Touch each object you want to touch as if tomorrow your tactile sense would fail. Smell the perfume of flowers, taste with relish each morsel, as if tomorrow you could never smell and taste again. Make the most of every sense; glory in all the facets of pleasure and beauty which the world reveals to you through the several means of contact which Nature provides. But of all the senses, I am sure that sight must be the most delightful.

PROBING FOR
MEANING

1. Do you agree with Keller's statement that "most people would be chastened by the certainty of impending death" rather than adopting the motto of "Eat, drink, and be merry"? Is it true that the only people who appreciate life are those who live or have lived near death, either their own or someone else's?

2. Do we take our senses for granted as well as our life? Do only the deaf and blind appreciate hearing and seeing? What would be the curriculum of a college course in "How to Use Your Eyes"?

3. What priorities does Keller establish for what she would like to see in her three allotted days of sight? She says others would not agree with her program. How would your priorities compare with hers?

4. Do you agree that you have to see people to really know them? Why does she think so? Do you agree that we are as unobservant about even our close friends as she claims?

5. Why would she visit museums on her second day of sight? Why does she say that man's "urge to artistic expression has been almost as powerful as the urge for food, shelter, and procreation"? How does her desire to visit the theater relate to her visit to the museums?

6. How would your tour of New York or any other large city differ from hers? Why does she choose a city?

7. Helen Keller was both deaf and blind, yet she chose sight as "the most delightful" of all the senses. Do you agree with her choice?

PROBING FOR
METHOD

1. Where does Keller's introduction end? Where does her thesis statement occur? What technique does she employ in this rather lengthy introduction?

2. Why does she choose three days rather than two, four or any other number?

3. What is her purpose in constantly referring to and asking questions of the reader?

4. Her illustration of how to appreciate life grows very naturally out of her own experience as a person blind from birth. What other illustrations of her theme does she mention? Can you think of illustrations other than those she mentioned of having only three days to live or see?

5. To what extent does her conclusion build a frame around her essay? Does it refer to the introduction in any way?

 PLATO

The Allegory of the Cave

Next, said I, here is a parable to illustrate the degrees in which our nature may be enlightened or unenlightened. Imagine the condition of men living in a sort of cavernous chamber underground, with an entrance open to the light and a long passage all down the cave. Here they have been from childhood, chained by the leg and also by the neck, so that they cannot move and can see only what is in front of them, because the chains will not let them turn their heads. At some distance higher up is the light of a fire burning behind them; and between the prisoners and the fire is a track with a parapet built along it, like the screen at a puppet-show, which hides the performers while they show their puppets over the top.

I see, said he.

Now behind this parapet imagine persons carrying along various artificial objects, including figures of men and animals in wood or stone or other materials, which project above the parapet. Naturally, some of these person will be talking, others silent.

It is a strange picture, he said, and a strange sort of prisoners.

Like ourselves, I replied; for in the first place prisoners so confined would have seen nothing of themselves or of one another, except the shadows thrown by the fire-light on the wall of the Cave facing them, would they?

Not if all their lives they had been prevented from moving their heads.

And they would have seen as little of the objects carried past.

Of course.

Now, if they could talk to one another, would they not suppose that their words referred only to those passing shadows which they saw?

Necessarily.

And suppose their prisoner had an echo from the wall facing them? When one of the people crossing behind them spoke, they could only suppose that the sound came from the shadow passing before their eyes.

No doubt.

In every way, then, such prisoners would recognize as reality nothing but the shadows of those artificial objects.

Inevitably.

Now consider what would happen if their release from the chains and the healing of their unwisdom should come about in this way. Suppose one of them set free and forced suddenly to stand up, turn his head, and walk with eyes lifted to the light; all these movements would be painful, and he would be too dazzled to make out the objects whose shadows he had been used to see. What do you think he would say, if someone told him that what he had formerly seen was meaningless illusion, but now, being somewhat nearer to reality and turned towards more real objects, he was getting a truer view? Suppose further that he were shown the various objects being carried by and were made to say, in reply to questions, what each of them was. Would he not be perplexed and believe the objects now shown him to be not so real as what he formerly saw?

Yes, not nearly so real.

And if he were forced to look at the fire-light itself, would not his eyes ache, so that he would try to escape and turn back to the things which he could see distinctly, convinced that they really were clearer than these other objects now being shown to him?

Yes.

And suppose someone were to drag him away forcibly up the steep and rugged ascent and not let him go until he had hauled him out into the sunlight, would he not suffer pain and vexation at such treatment, and, when he had come out into the light, find his eyes so full of its radiance that he could not see a single one of the things that he was now told were real?

Certainly he would not see them all at once.

He would need, then, to grow accustomed before he could see things in that upper world. At first it would be easiest to make out shadows, and then the images of men and things reflected in water, and later on the things themselves. After that, it would be easier to watch the heavenly bodies and the sky itself by night, looking at the light of the moon and stars rather than the Sun and the Sun's light in the daytime.

Yes, surely.

Last of all, he would be able to look at the Sun and contemplate its nature, not as it appears when reflected in water or any alien medium, but as it is in itself in its own domain.

No doubt.

And now he would begin to draw the conclusion that it is the Sun that produces the seasons and the course of the year and controls everything in the visible world, and moreover is in a way the cause of all that he and his companions used to see.

Clearly he would come at last to that conclusion.

Then if he called to mind his fellow prisoners and what passed for wisdom in his former dwelling-place, he would surely think himself happy in the change and be sorry for them. They may have had a practice of honouring and commending one another, with prizes for the man who had the keenest eye for the passing shadows and the best memory for the order in which they followed or accompanied one another, so that he could make a good guess as to which was going to come next. Would our released prisoner be likely to covet those prizes or to envy the men exalted to honour and power in the Cave? Would he not feel like Homer's Achilles, that he would far sooner be on earth as a hired servant in the house of a landless man or endure anything rather than go back to his old beliefs and live in the old way?

Yes, he would prefer any fate to such a life.

Now imagine what would happen if he went down again to take his former seat in the Cave. Coming suddenly out of the sunlight, his eyes would be filled with darkness. He might be required once more to deliver his opinion on those shadows, in competition with the prisoners who had never been released, while his eyesight was still dim and unsteady; and it might take some time to become used to the darkness. They would laugh at him and say that he had gone up only to come back with his sight ruined; it was worth no one's while even to attempt the ascent. If they could lay hands on the man who was trying to set them free and lead them up, they would kill him.

Yes, they would.

Every feature in this parable, my dear Glaucon, is meant to fit our earlier analysis. The prison dwelling corresponds to the region revealed to us through the sense of sight, and the fire-light within it to the power of the Sun. The ascent to see the things in the upper world you may take as standing for the upward journey of the soul into the region of the intelligible; then you will be in possession of what I surmise, since that is what you wish to be told. Heaven knows whether it is true; but this, at any rate, is how it appears to me. In the world of knowledge, the last thing to be perceived and only with great difficulty is the essential Form of Goodness. Once it is perceived, the conclusion must follow that, for all things, this is the cause of whatever is right and good; in the visible world it gives birth to light and to the lord of light, while it is itself sovereign in the intelligible world and the parent of intelligence and truth. Without having had a vision of this Form no one can act with wisdom, either in his own life or in matters of state.

PROBING FOR
MEANING

    1. An allegory or parable is a concrete story on one level and an explication of abstract, moral truths on another. Plato explains at the end what each part of his story symbolizes on the moral level. What correspondences does he establish?

    2. If we assume the people in the cave represent mankind, why does Plato call them "prisoners"? Plato is not specific as to who placed the people in chains, but who seems to be the jailer when the freed prisoner returns to free the others?

    3. Plato equates making the "ascent to see things in the upper world" on the story level with gaining knowledge on the abstract level. Why, instead of making the ascent, would people prefer to remain in the cave with illusions of what is real? Do you agree with Plato's analysis of human nature here? Explain.

    4. Plato says of the man who returns to the cave after seeing the sun, "If they could lay hands on him they would kill him." Are there historical or contemporary situations which fulfill this prediction?

PROBING FOR
METHOD

    1. Plato's essay is presented as a dialogue between teacher and student. What contribution to structure and theme is made by the brief comments of the student?

    2. What logical plan of organization can be seen at work within this essay?

    3. Why is Plato's language so simple? How does it compare with Lindbergh's in "Channelled Whelk"? What purpose does his language serve?

    4. Is Plato's final comment upon the allegory necessary, or would you be able to fit together its features without this ending?

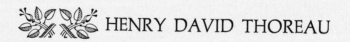 HENRY DAVID THOREAU

The Village

After hoeing, or perhaps reading and writing, in the forenoon, I usually bathed again in the pond, swimming across one of its coves for a stint, and washed the dust of labor from my person, or smoothed out the last wrinkle which study had made, and for the afternoon was absolutely free. Every day or two I strolled to the village to hear some of the gossip which is incessantly going on there, circulating either from mouth to mouth, or from newspaper to newspaper, and which, taken in homœopathic doses, was really as refreshing in its way as the rustle of leaves and the peeping of frogs. As I walked in the woods to see the birds and squirrels, so I walked in the village to see the men and boys; instead of the wind among the pines I heard the carts rattle. In one direction from my house there was a colony of muskrats in the river meadows; under the grove of elms and buttonwoods in the other horizon was a village of busy men, as curious to me as if they had been prairie-dogs, each sitting at the mouth of its burrow, or running over to a neighbor's to gossip. I went there frequently to observe their habits.

The village appeared to me a great news room; and on one side, to support it, as once at Redding & Company's on State Street, they kept nuts and raisins, or salt and meal and other groceries. Some have such a vast appetite for the former commodity, that is, the news, and such sound digestive organs, that they can sit forever in public avenues without stirring, and let it simmer and whisper through them like the Etesian winds, or as if inhaling ether, it only producing numbness and insensibility to pain,—otherwise it would often be painful to hear,—without affecting the consciousness. I hardly ever failed, when I rambled through the village, to see a row of such worthies, either sitting on a ladder sunning themselves, with their bodies inclined forward and their eyes glancing along the line this way and that, from time to time, with a voluptuous expression, or else leaning against a barn with their hands in their pockets, like caryatides, as if to prop it up. They, being commonly out of doors, heard whatever was in the wind. These are the coarsest mills, in which all gossip is first rudely digested or cracked up before it is emptied into finer and more delicate hoppers within doors.

I observed that the vitals of the village were the grocery, the bar-room, the post-office, and the bank; and, as a necessary part of the machinery, they kept a bell, a big gun, and a fire-engine, at convenient places; and the houses were so arranged as to make the most of mankind, in lanes and fronting one another, so that every traveller had to run the gauntlet, and every man, woman, and child might get a lick at him. Of course, those who were stationed nearest to the head of the line, where they could most see and be seen, and have the first blow at him, paid the highest prices for their places; and the few straggling inhabitants in the outskirts, where long gaps in the line began to occur, and the traveller could get over walls or turn aside into cow-paths, and so escape, paid a very slight ground or window tax. Signs were hung out on all sides to allure him; some to catch him by the appetite, as the tavern and victualling cellar; some by the fancy, as the dry goods store and the jeweller's; and others by the hair or the feet or the skirts, as the barber, the shoemaker, or the tailor. Besides, there was a still more terrible standing invitation to call at every one of these houses, and company expected about these times.

For the most part I escaped wonderfully from these dangers, either by proceeding at once boldly and without deliberation to the goal, as is recommended to those who run the gauntlet, or by keeping my thoughts on high things, like Orpheus, who, "loudly singing the praises of the gods to his lyre, drowned the voices of the Sirens, and kept out of danger." Sometimes I bolted suddenly, and nobody could tell my whereabouts, for I did not stand much about gracefulness, and never hesitated at a gap in a fence. I was even accustomed to make an irruption into some houses, where I was well entertained, and after learning the kernels and very last sieveful of views,—what had subsided, the prospects of war and peace, and whether the world was likely to hold together much longer,—I was let out through the rear avenues, and so escaped to the woods again.

It was very pleasant, when I stayed late in town, to launch myself into the night, especially if it was dark and tempestuous, and set sail from some bright village parlor or lecture room, with a bag of rye or Indian meal upon my shoulder, for my snug harbor in the woods, having made all tight without and withdrawn under hatches with a merry crew of thoughts, leaving only my outer man at the helm, or even tying up the helm when it was plain sailing. I had many a genial thought by the cabin fire "as I sailed." I was never cast away nor distressed in any weather, though I encountered some severe storms. It is darker in the woods, even in common nights, than most suppose. I frequently had to look up at the opening between the trees above the path in order to learn my route, and, where there was no cartpath, to feel with my feet the faint track which I had worn, or steer by the known relation of particular trees which I felt with my hands, passing between two pines for instance, not more than eighteen inches apart, in the midst of the woods, invariably, in the darkest night. Sometimes, after coming home thus late in a dark and muggy night, when my feet felt the path which my eyes could not see, dreaming and absent-minded all the way, until I was aroused by having to raise my hand to lift the latch, I have not been able to recall a single step of my walk, and I have thought that perhaps my body would find its way home if its master should forsake it, as the hand finds its way to the mouth without assistance.

Several times, when a visitor chanced to stay into evening, and it proved a dark night, I was obliged to conduct him to the cartpath in the rear of the house, and then point out to him the direction he was to pursue, and in keeping which he was to be guided rather by his feet than his eyes. One very dark night I directed thus on their way two young men who had been fishing in the pond. They lived about a mile off through the woods, and were quite used to the route. A day or two after one of them told me that they wandered about the greater part of the night, close by their own premises, and did not get home till toward morning, by which time, as there had been several heavy showers in the meanwhile, and the leaves were very wet, they were drenched to their skins. I have heard of many going astray even in the village streets, when the darkness was so thick that you could cut it with a knife, as the saying is. Some who live in the outskirts, having come to town a-shopping in their wagons, have been obliged to put up for the night; and gentlemen and ladies making a call have gone half a mile out of their way, feeling the sidewalk only with their feet, and not knowing when they turned.

It is a surprising and memorable, as well as valuable experience, to be lost in the woods any time. Often in a snow-storm, even by day, one will come out upon a well-known road and yet find it impossible to tell which way leads to the village. Though he knows that he has travelled it a thousand times, he cannot recognize a feature in it, but it is as strange to him as if it were a road in Siberia. By night, of course, the perplexity is infinitely greater. In our most trivial walks, we are constantly, though unconsciously, steering like pilots by certain well-known beacons and headlands, and if we go beyond our usual course we still carry in our minds the bearing of some neighboring cape; and not till we are completely lost, or turned round,—for a man needs only to be turned round once with his eyes shut in this world to be lost,—do we appreciate the vastness and strangeness of nature. Every man has to learn the points of compass again as often as he awakes, whether from sleep or any abstraction. Not till we are lost, in other words not till we have lost the world, do we begin to find ourselves, and realize where we are and the infinite extent of our relations.

One afternoon, near the end of the first summer, when I went to the village to get a shoe from the cobbler's, I was seized and put into jail, because, as I have elsewhere related, I did not pay a tax to, or recognize the authority of, the State which buys and sells men, women, and children, like cattle, at the door of its senate-house. I had gone down to the woods for other purposes. But, wherever a man goes, men will pursue and paw him with their dirty institutions, and, if they can, constrain him to belong to their desperate odd-fellow society. It is true, I might have resisted forcibly with more or less effect, might have run "amok" against society; but I preferred that society should run "amok" against me, it being the desperate party. However, I was released the next day, obtained my mended shoe, and returned to the woods in season to get my dinner of huckleberries on Fair Haven Hill. I was never molested by any person but those who represented the State. I had no lock nor bolt but for the desk which held my papers, not even a nail to put over my latch or windows. I never fastened my door night or day, though I was to be absent several days; not even when the next fall I spent a fortnight in the woods of Maine. And yet my house was more respected than if it had been surrounded by a file of soldiers. The tired rambler could rest and warm himself by my fire, the literary amuse himself with the few books on my table, or the curious, by opening my closet door, see what was left of my dinner, and what prospect I had of a supper. Yet, though many people of every class came this way to the pond, I suffered no serious inconvenience from these sources, and I never missed anything but one small book, a volume of Homer, which perhaps was improperly gilded, and this I trust a soldier of our camp has found by this time.

I am convinced, that if all men were to live as simply as I then did, thieving and robbery would be unknown. These take place only in communities where some have got more than is sufficient while others have not enough. The Pope's Homers would soon get properly distributed.

"Nec bella fuerunt,
Faginus astabat dum scyphus ante dapes."

"Nor wars did men molest,
When only beechen bowls were in request."

"You who govern public affairs, what need have you to employ punishments? Love virtue, and the people will be virtuous. The virtues of a superior man are like the wind; the virtues of a common man are like the grass; the grass, when the wind passes over it, bends."

PROBING FOR
MEANING

1. What impression of life in his cabin in the woods around Walden Pond does Thoreau give in the first sentence of the essay?

2. What comparisons and contrasts does he make between the pond and the village? What does "homœopathic" mean? How does its meaning further convey his attitudes toward woods and village?

3. What characteristics of the village does he mention? Why does he say he "escaped" to the woods again?

4. How is he able to find his way through the woods in the dark?

Many travellers, he says, lose their way at night. How does this relate to Helen Keller's theory about our not using all our senses?

5. "Not till we are lost, in other words not till we have lost the world, do we begin to find ourselves, and realize where we are and the infinite extent of our relations." To what extent is this the thesis statement of Thoreau's essay? How does it relate to the thesis statement of Helen Keller's essay?

6. Notice that near the end of the essay when Thoreau recounts his imprisonment for not paying his taxes, he equates the village with "the State." To what extent is the essay an allegory of civilization versus nature, with the village representing civilization and the woods near Walden Pond symbolizing nature? What is Thoreau saying about civilization? About living apart from it?

7. What major complaint does Thoreau have against the village? Why did the village become "the desperate party" in its dealings with him? How and why is the pond (or woods) existence preferable?

8. How similar are Thoreau's and Anne Morrow Lindbergh's notions of simplicity?

PROBING FOR METHOD

1. Thoreau uses many comparisons—metaphors and similes—to convey more vividly his various points. What comparisons, for example, does he make in describing the similarities between village and pond?

2. Locate the story of Orpheus and the Sirens from Greek mythology. How does this myth help to convey Thoreau's attitude toward the village?

3. Thoreau uses two metaphors in describing his jaunt through the village and later his journey home through the woods. What are these metaphors? How successful are they?

4. Compare his introduction with his conclusion. Are they similar in theme? What accounts for their dissimilarity in tone?

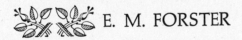 E. M. FORSTER

My Wood

A few years ago I wrote a book which dealt in part with the difficulties of the English in India. Feeling that they would have no difficulties in India themselves, the Americans read the book freely. The more they read it the better it made them feel, and a cheque to the author was the result. I bought a wood with the cheque. It is not a large wood—it contains scarcely any trees, and it is intersected, blast it, by a public footpath. Still, it is the first property that I have owned, so it is right that other people should participate in my shame, and should ask themselves, in accents that will vary in horror, this very important question: What is the effect of property upon the character? Don't let's touch economics; the effect of private ownership upon the community as a whole is another question—a more important question, perhaps, but another one. Let's keep to psychology. If you own things, what's their effect on you? What's the effect on me of my wood?

In the first place, it makes me feel heavy. Property does have this effect. Property produces men of weight, and it was a man of weight who failed to get into the Kingdom of Heaven. He was not wicked, that unfortunate millionaire in the parable, he was only stout; he stuck out in front, not to mention behind, and as he wedged himself this way and that in the crystalline entrance and bruised his well-fed flanks, he saw beneath him a comparatively slim camel passing through the eye of a needle and being woven into the robe of God. The Gospels all through couple stoutness and slowness. They point out what is perfectly obvious, yet seldom realized: that if you have a lot of things you cannot move about a lot, that furniture requires dusting, dusters require servants, servants require insurance stamps, and the whole tangle of them makes you think twice before you accept an invitation to dinner or go for a bathe in the Jordan. Sometimes the Gospels proceed further and say with Tolstoy that property is sinful; they approach the difficult ground of asceticism here, where I cannot follow them. But as to the immediate effects of property on people, they just show straightforward logic. It produces men of weight. Men of weight cannot, by definition, move like the lightning from the East unto the West, and the ascent of a fourteen-stone bishop into a pulpit is thus the exact antithesis of the coming of the Son of Man. My wood makes me feel heavy.

In the second place, it makes me feel it ought to be larger.

The other day I heard a twig snap in it. I was annoyed at first, for I thought that someone was blackberrying, and depreciating the value of the undergrowth. On coming nearer, I saw it was not a man who had trodden on the twig and snapped it, but a bird, and I felt pleased. My bird. The bird was not equally pleased. Ignoring the relation between us, it took fright as soon as it saw the shape of my face, and flew straight over the boundary hedge into a field, the property of Mrs. Henessy, where it sat down with a loud squawk. It had become Mrs. Henessy's bird. Something seemed grossly amiss here, something that would not have occurred had the wood been larger. I could not afford to buy Mrs. Henessy out, I dared not murder her, and limitations of this sort beset me on every side. Ahab did not want that vineyard—he only needed it to round off his property, preparatory to plotting a new curve—and all the land around my wood has become necessary to me in order to round off the wood. A boundary protects. But—poor little thing—the boundary ought in its turn to be protected. Noises on the edge of it. Children throw stones. A little more, and then a little more, until we reach the sea. Happy Canute! Happier Alexander! And after all, why should even the world be the limit of possession? A rocket containing a Union Jack, will, it is hoped, be shortly fired at the moon. Mars. Sirius. Beyond which . . . But these immensities ended by saddening me. I could not suppose that my wood was the destined nucleus of universal dominion—it is so very small and contains no mineral wealth beyond the blackberries. Nor was I comforted when Mrs. Henessy's bird took alarm for the second time and flew clean away from us all, under the belief that it belonged to itself.

In the third place, property makes its owner feel that he ought to do something to it. Yet he isn't sure what. A restlessness comes over him, a vague sense that he has a personality to express— the same sense which, without any vagueness, leads the artist to an act of creation. Sometimes I think I will cut down such trees as remain in the wood, at other times I want to fill up the gaps between them with new trees. Both impulses are pretentious and empty. They are not honest movements towards money-making or beauty. They spring from a foolish desire to express myself and from an inability to enjoy what I have got. Creation, property, enjoyment form a sinister trinity in the human mind. Creation and enjoyment are both very, very good, yet they are often unattainable without a material basis, and at such moments property pushes itself in as a substitute, saying, "Accept me instead—I'm good enough for all three." It is not enough. It is, as Shakespeare said of lust, "The expense of spirit in a waste of shame"; it is "Before, a joy proposed; behind, a dream." Yet we don't know how to shun it. It is forced on us by our economic system as the alternative to starvation. It is also forced on us by an internal defect in the soul, by the feeling that in property may lie the germs of self-development and of exquisite or heroic deeds. Our life on earth is, and ought to be, material and carnal. But we have not yet learned to manage our materialism and carnality properly; they are still en- tangled with the desire for ownership, where (in the words of Dante) "Possession is one with loss."

And this brings us to our fourth and final point: the black- berries.

Blackberries are not plentiful in this meagre grove, but they are easily seen from the public footpath which traverses it, and all too easily gathered. Foxgloves, too—people will pull up the foxgloves, and ladies of an educational tendency even grub for toadstools to show them on the Monday in class. Other ladies, less educated, roll down the bracken in the arms of their gentlemen friends. There is paper, there are tins. Pray, does my wood belong to me or doesn't it? And, if it does, should I not own it best my allowing no one else to walk there? There is a wood near Lyme Regis, also cursed by a public footpath, where the owner has not hesitated on this point. He has built high stone walls each side of the path, and has spanned it by bridges, so that the public circulate like termites while he gorges on the blackberries unseen. He really does own his wood, this able chap. Dives in Hell did pretty well, but the gulf dividing him from Lazarus could be traversed by vision, and nothing traverses it here. And perhaps I shall come to this in time. I shall wall in and fence out until I really taste the sweets of property. Enormously stout, endlessly avaricious, pseudo-creative, intensely selfish, I shall weave upon my forehead the quadruple crown of possession until those nasty Bolshies come and take it off again and thrust me aside into the outer darkness.

PROBING FOR MEANING

1. Why does Forster say that the effect of private ownership upon the community is another, perhaps more important, question than its effect on character?

2. How do the examples Forster uses in his second paragraph illustrate the first effect of property on character? Do you agree that property produces men of weight? Are people more virtuous if they have fewer possessions?

3. Who are Ahab, Canute and Alexander? From what you know or can learn about their lives, why are they good examples of Forster's second effect? Does ownership always make one more greedy?

4. What effect does the last sentence in the fourth paragraph have on the meaning of the paragraph? Compare this sentence with William Stafford's poem in Chapter II, "The Star in the Hills." What are both writers saying about the material world and man's attempts to possess it?

5. "Creation, property, enjoyment form a sinister trinity in the human mind." What does Forster mean by this statement? What examples does he give to explain it? What examples can you add of your own? Is property in your opinion a substitute for creativity?

6. How can "possession" be "one with loss"?

7. What point does Forster make with the example of the blackberries? Do you agree that property generally has this effect?

8. Who are the "nasty Bolshies" mentioned in the last paragraph? What does this sentence contribute to the essay?

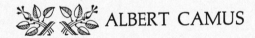

1. Forster leads into his introduction by commenting that Americans provided him with the money to purchase his wood. For what reason does Forster mention Americans in an introduction to an essay on materialism? What attitude does he have toward them?

2. What attitude toward his wood does Forster have? Do the words "shame" and "horror" used in paragraph 1 describe his tone in any way? How does the last sentence of the essay contribute to tone?

3. Forster's organization is perfectly clear. What device does he use to convey the movement of the essay? Is this device effective? Why don't all writers mark each section of their essays as clearly?

4. What would the essay have been like without all the examples Forster uses? Would it have been as effective?

5. While Forster's essay uses concrete example throughout, his thesis is the abstract one that property affects us adversely. Much of his language is also abstract; what, for example, do words like "crystalline," "antithesis," "trinity," "carnality," "traversed," "avaricious" and "pseudo-creative" mean? How, in each case, do they relate either to his thesis or to his example?

ALBERT CAMUS

The Guest

The schoolmaster was watching the two men climb toward him. One was on horseback, the other on foot. They had not yet tackled the abrupt rise leading to the schoolhouse built on the hillside. They were toiling onward, making slow progress in the snow, among the stones, on the vast expanse of the high, deserted plateau. From time to time the horse stumbled. Without hearing anything yet, he could see the breath issuing from the horse's nostrils. One of the men, at least, knew the region. They were following the trail although it had disappeared days ago under a layer of dirty white snow. The schoolmaster calculated that it would take them half an hour to get onto the hill. It was cold; he went back into the school to get a sweater.

He crossed the empty, frigid classroom. On the blackboard the four rivers of France, drawn with four different colored chalks,

had been flowing toward their estuaries for the past three days. Snow
had suddenly fallen in mid-October after eight months of drought
without the transition of rain, and the twenty pupils, more or less,
who lived in the villages scattered over the plateau had stopped
coming. With fair weather they would return. Daru now heated only
the single room that was his lodging, adjoining the classroom and
giving also onto the plateau to the east. Like the class windows, his
window looked to the south too. On that side the school was a few
kilometers from the point where the plateau began to slope toward
the south. In clear weather could be seen the purple mass of the
mountain range where the gap opened onto the desert.

Somewhat warmed, Daru returned to the window from which
he had first seen the two men. They were no longer visible. Hence
they must have tackled the rise. The sky was not so dark, for the snow
had stopped falling during the night. The morning had opened with a
dirty light which had scarcely become brighter as the ceiling of clouds
lifted. At two in the afternoon it seemed as if the day were merely
beginning. But still this was better than those three days when the
thick snow was falling amidst unbroken darkness with little gusts of
wind that rattled the double door of the classroom. Then Daru had
spent long hours in his room, leaving it only to go to the shed and
feed the chickens or get some coal. Fortunately the delivery truck
from Tadjid, the nearest village to the north, had brought his supplies
two days before the blizzard. It would return in forty-eight hours.

Besides, he had enough to resist a siege, for the little room
was cluttered with bags of wheat that the administration left as a
stock to distribute to those of his pupils whose families had suffered
from the drought. Actually they had all been victims because they
were all poor. Every day Daru would distribute a ration to the
children. They had missed it, he knew, during these bad days. Possibly one of the fathers or big brothers would come this afternoon
and he could supply them with grain. It was just a matter of carrying
them over to the next harvest. Now shiploads of wheat were arriving
from France and the worst was over. But it would be hard to forget
that poverty, that army of ragged ghosts wandering in the sunlight,
the plateaus burned to a cinder month after month, the earth
shriveled up little by little, literally scorched, every stone bursting
into dust under one's foot. The sheep had died then by thousands and
even a few men, here and there, sometimes without anyone's
knowing.

In contrast with such poverty, he who lived almost like a
monk in his remote schoolhouse, nonetheless satisfied with the little
he had and with the rough life, had felt like a lord with his white-
washed walls, his narrow couch, his unpainted shelves, his well, and
his provision of water and food. And suddenly this snow, without

warning, without the foretaste of rain. This is the way the region was, cruel to live in, even without men—who didn't help matters either. But Daru had been born here. Everywhere else, he felt exiled.

He stepped out onto the terrace in front of the schoolhouse. The two men were now halfway up the slope. He recognized the horseman as Balducci, the old gendarme he had known for a long time. Balducci was holding on the end of a rope an Arab who was walking behind him with hands bound and head lowered. The gendarme waved a greeting to which Daru did not reply, lost as he was in contemplation of the Arab dressed in a faded blue jellaba, his feet in sandals but covered with socks of heavy raw wool, his head surmounted by a narrow, short *chèche*. They were approaching. Balducci was holding back his horse in order not to hurt the Arab and the group was advancing slowly.

Within earshot, Balducci shouted: "One hour to do the three kilometers from El Ameur!" Daru did not answer. Short and square in his thick sweater, he watched them climb. Not once had the Arab raised his head. "Hello," said Daru when they got up onto the terrace. "Come in and warm up." Balducci painfully got down from his horse without letting go the rope. From under his bristling mustache he smiled at the schoolmaster. His little dark eyes, deep-set under a tanned forehead, and his mouth surrounded with wrinkles made him look attentive and studious. Daru took the bridle, led the horse to the shed, and came back to the two men, who were now waiting for him in the school. He led them into his room. "I am going to heat up the classroom," he said. "We'll be more comfortable there." When he entered the room again, Balducci was on the couch. He had undone the rope tying him to the Arab, who had squatted near the stove. His hands still bound, the *chèche* pushed back on his head, he was looking toward the window. At first Daru noticed only his huge lips, fat, smooth, almost Negroid; yet his nose was straight, his eyes were dark and full of fever. The *chèche* revealed an obstinate forehead and, under the weathered skin now rather discolored by the cold, the whole face had a restless and rebellious look that struck Daru when the Arab, turning his face toward him, looked him straight in the eyes. "Go into the other room," said the schoolmaster, "and I'll make you some mint tea." "Thanks," Balducci said. "What a chore! How I long for retirement." And addressing his prisoner in Arabic: "Come on, you." The Arab got up and, slowly, holding his bound wrists in front of him, went into the classroom.

With the tea, Daru brought a chair. But Balducci was already enthroned on the nearest pupil's desk and the Arab had squatted against the teacher's platform facing the stove, which stood between the desk and the window. When he held out the glass of tea to the prisoner, Daru hesitated at the sight of his bound hands. "He might

perhaps be untied." "Sure," said Balducci. "That was for the trip." He
started to get to his feet. But Daru, setting the glass on the floor, had
knelt beside the Arab. Without saying anything, the Arab watched
him with his feverish eyes. Once his hands were free, he rubbed his
swollen wrists against each other, took the glass of tea, and sucked
up the burning liquid in swift little sips.

"Good," said Daru. "And where are you headed?"

Balducci withdrew his mustache from the tea. "Here, son."

"Odd pupils! And you're spending the night?"

"No. I'm going back to El Ameur. And you will deliver this
fellow to Tinguit. He is expected at police headquarters."

Balducci was looking at Daru with a friendly little smile.

"What's this story?" asked the schoolmaster. "Are you pulling my leg?"

"No, son. Those are the orders."

"The orders? I'm not . . ." Daru hesitated, not wanting to
hurt the old Corsican. "I mean, that's not my job."

"What! What's the meaning of that? In wartime people do all
kinds of jobs."

"Then I'll wait for the declaration of war!"

Balducci nodded.

"O.K. But the orders exist and they concern you too. Things
are brewing, it appears. There is talk of a forthcoming revolt. We are
mobilized, in a way."

Daru still had his obstinate look.

"Listen, son," Balducci said. "I like you and you must understand. There's only a dozen of us at El Ameur to patrol throughout
the whole territory of a small department and I must get back in a
hurry. I was told to hand this guy over to you and return without
delay. He couldn't be kept there. His village was beginning to stir;
they wanted to take him back. You must take him to Tanguit tomorrow before the day is over. Twenty kilometers shouldn't faze a husky
fellow like you. After that, all will be over. You'll come back to your
pupils and your comfortable life."

Behind the wall the horse could be heard snorting and pawing
the earth. Daru was looking out the window. Decidedly, the weather
was clearing and the light was increasing over the snowy plateau.
When all the snow was melted, the sun would take over again and
once more would burn the fields of stone. For days, still, the un-
changing sky would shed its dry light on the solitary expanse where
nothing had any connection with man.

"After all," he said, turning around toward Balducci, "what
did he do?" And, before the gendarme had opened his mouth, he
asked: "Does he speak French?"

"No, not a word. We had been looking for him for a month, but they were hiding him. He killed his cousin."

"Is he against us?"

"I don't think so. But you can never be sure."

"Why did he kill?"

"A family squabble, I think. One owed the other grain, it seems. It's not at all clear. In short, he killed his cousin with a billhook. You know, like a sheep, *kreezk!*"

Balducci made the gesture of drawing a blade across his throat and the Arab, his attention attracted, watched him with a sort of anxiety. Daru felt a sudden wrath against the man, against all men with their rotten spite, their tireless hates, their blood lust.

But the kettle was singing on the stove. He served Balducci more tea, hesitated, then served the Arab again, who, a second time, drank avidly. His raised arms made the jellaba fall open and the schoolmaster saw his thin, muscular chest.

"Thanks, kid," Balducci said. "And now, I'm off."

He got up and went toward the Arab, taking a small rope from his pocket.

"What are you doing?" Daru asked dryly.

Balducci, disconcerted, showed him the rope.

"Don't bother."

The old gendarme hesitated. "It's up to you. Of course, you are armed?"

"I have my shotgun."

"Where?"

"In the trunk."

"You ought to have it near your bed."

"Why? I have nothing to fear."

"You're crazy, son. If there's an uprising, no one is safe, we're all in the same boat."

"I'll defend myself. I'll have time to see them coming."

Balducci began to laugh, then suddenly the mustache covered the white teeth.

"You'll have time? O.K. That's just what I was saying. You have always been a little cracked. That's why I like you, my son was like that."

At the same time he took out his revolver and put it on the desk.

"Keep it; I don't need two weapons from here to El Ameur."

The revolver shone against the black paint of the table. When the gendarme turned toward him, the schoolmaster caught the smell of leather and horseflesh.

"Listen, Balducci," Daru said suddenly, "every bit of this

disgusts me, and first of all your fellow here. But I won't hand him over. Fight, yes, if I have to. But not that."

The old gendarme stood in front of him and looked at him severely.

"You're being a fool," he said slowly. "I don't like it either. You don't get used to putting a rope on a man even after years of it, and you're even ashamed—yes, ashamed. But you can't let them have their way."

"I won't hand him over," Daru said again.

"It's an order, son, and I repeat it."

"That's right. Repeat to them what I've said to you: I won't hand him over."

Balducci made a visible effort to reflect. He looked at the Arab and at Daru. At last he decided.

"No, I won't tell them anything. If you want to drop us, go ahead; I'll not denounce you. I have an order to deliver the prisoner and I'm doing so. And now you'll just sign this paper for me."

"There's no need. I'll not deny that you left him with me."

"Don't be mean with me. I know you'll tell the truth. You're from hereabouts and you are a man. But you must sign, that's the rule."

Daru opened his drawer, took out a little square bottle of purple ink, the red wooden penholder with the "sergeant-major" pen he used for making models of penmanship, and signed. The gendarme carefully folded the paper and put it into his wallet. Then he moved toward the door.

"I'll see you off," Daru said.

"No," said Balducci. "There's no use being polite. You insulted me."

He looked at the Arab, motionless in the same spot, sniffed peevishly, and turned away toward the door. "Good-by, son," he said. The door shut behind him. Balducci appeared suddenly outside the window and then disappeared. His footsteps were muffled by the snow. The horse stirred on the other side of the wall and several chickens fluttered in fright. A moment later Balducci reappeared outside the window leading the horse by the bridle. He walked toward the little rise without turning around and disappeared from sight with the horse following him. A big stone could be heard bouncing down. Daru walked back toward the prisoner, who, without stirring, never took his eyes off him. "Wait," the schoolmaster said in Arabic and went toward the bedroom. As he was going through the door, he had a second thought, went to the desk, took the revolver, and stuck it in his pocket. Then, without looking back, he went into his room.

For some time he lay on his couch watching the sky gradually close over, listening to the silence. It was this silence that had seemed painful to him during the first days here, after the war. He had requested a post in the little town at the base of the foothills separating the upper plateaus from the desert. There, rocky walls, green and black to the north, pink and lavender to the south, marked the frontier of eternal summer. He had been named to a post farther north, on the plateau itself. In the beginning, the solitude and the silence had been hard for him on these wastelands peopled only by stones. Occasionally, furrows suggested cultivation, but they had been dug to uncover a certain kind of stone good for building. The only plowing here was to harvest rocks. Elsewhere a thin layer of soil accumulated in the hollows would be scraped out to enrich paltry village gardens. This is the way it was: bare rock covered three quarters of the region. Towns sprang up, flourished, then disappeared; men came by, loved one another or fought bitterly, then died. No one in this desert, neither he nor his guest, mattered. And yet, outside this desert neither of them, Daru knew, could have really lived.

When he got up, no noise came from the classroom. He was amazed at the unmixed joy he derived from the mere thought that the Arab might have fled and that he would be alone with no decision to make. But the prisoner was there. He had merely stretched out between the stove and the desk. With eyes open, he was staring at the ceiling. In that position, his thick lips were particularly noticeable, giving him a pouting look. "Come," said Daru. The Arab got up and followed him. In the bedroom, the schoolmaster pointed to a chair near the table under the window. The Arab sat down without taking his eyes off Daru.

"Are you hungry?"

"Yes," the prisoner said.

Daru set the table for two. He took flour and oil, shaped a cake in a frying-pan, and lighted the little stove that functioned on bottled gas. While the cake was cooking, he went out to the shed to get cheese, eggs, dates, and condensed milk. When the cake was done he set it on the window sill to cool, heated some condensed milk diluted with water, and beat up the eggs into an omelette. In one of his motions he knocked against the revolver stuck in his right pocket. He set the bowl down, went into the classroom, and put the revolver in his desk drawer. When he came back to the room, night was falling. He put on the light and served the Arab. "Eat," he said. The Arab took a piece of the cake, lifted it eagerly to his mouth, and stopped short.

"And you?" he asked.

"After you. I'll eat too."

The thick lips opened slightly. The Arab hesitated, then bit into the cake determinedly.

The meal over, the Arab looked at the schoolmaster. "Are you the judge?"

"No, I'm simply keeping you until tomorrow."

"Why do you eat with me?"

"I'm hungry."

The Arab fell silent. Daru got up and went out. He brought back a folding bed from the shed, set it up between the table and the stove, perpendicular to his own bed. From a large suitcase which, upright in a corner, served as a shelf for papers, he took two blankets and arranged them on the camp bed. Then he stopped, felt useless, and sat down on his bed. There was nothing more to do or to get ready. He had to look at this man. He looked at him, therefore, trying to imagine his face bursting with rage. He couldn't do so. He could see nothing but the dark yet shining eyes and the animal mouth.

"Why did you kill him?" he asked in a voice whose hostile tone surprised him.

The Arab looked away.

"He ran away. I ran after him."

He raised his eyes to Daru again and they were full of a sort of woeful interrogation. "Now what will they do to me?"

"Are you afraid?"

He stiffened, turning his eyes away.

"Are you sorry?"

The Arab stared at him openmouthed. Obviously he did not understand. Daru's annoyance was growing. At the same time he felt awkward and self-conscious with his big body wedged between the two beds.

"Lie down there," he said impatiently. "That's your bed."

The Arab didn't move. He called to Daru:

"Tell me!"

The schoolmaster looked at him.

"Is the gendarme coming back tomorrow?"

"I don't know."

"Are you coming with us?"

"I don't know. Why?"

The prisoner got up and stretched out on top of the blankets, his feet toward the window. The light from the electric bulb shone straight into his eyes and he closed them at once.

"Why?" Daru repeated, standing beside the bed.

The Arab opened his eyes under the blinding light and looked at him, trying not to blink.

"Come with us," he said.

In the middle of the night, Daru was still not asleep. He had gone to bed after undressing completely; he generally slept naked. But when he suddenly realized that he had nothing on, he hesitated. He felt vulnerable and the temptation came to him to put his clothes back on. Then he shrugged his shoulders; after all, he wasn't a child and, if need be, he could break his adversary in two. From his bed he could observe him, lying on his back, still motionless with his eyes closed under the harsh light. When Daru turned out the light, the darkness seemed to coagulate all of a sudden. Little by little, the night came back to life in the window where the starless sky was stirring gently. The schoolmaster soon made out the body lying at his feet. The Arab still did not move, but his eyes seemed open. A faint wind was prowling around the schoolhouse. Perhaps it would drive away the clouds and the sun would reappear.

During the night the wind increased. The hens fluttered a little and then were silent. The Arab turned over on his side with his back to Daru, who thought he heard him moan. Then he listened for his guest's breathing, become heavier and more regular. He listened to that breath so close to him and mused without being able to go to sleep. In this room where he had been sleeping alone for a year, this presence bothered him. But it bothered him also by imposing on him a sort of brotherhood he knew well but refused to accept in the present circumstances. Men who share the same rooms, soldiers or prisoners, develop a strange alliance as if, having cast off their armor with their clothing, they fraternized every evening, over and above their differences, in the ancient community of dream and fatigue. But Daru shook himself; he didn't like such musings, and it was essential to sleep.

A little later, however, when the Arab stirred slightly, the schoolmaster was still not alseep. When the prisoner made a second move, he stiffened, on the alert. The Arab was lifting himself slowly on his arms with almost the motion of a sleepwalker. Seated upright in bed, he waited motionless without turning his head toward Daru, as if he were listening attentively. Daru did not stir; it had just occurred to him that the revolver was still in the drawer of his desk. It was better to act at once. Yet he continued to observe the prisoner, who, with the same slithery motion, put his feet on the ground, waited again, then began to stand up slowly. Daru was about to call out to him when the Arab began to walk, in a quite natural but extraordinarily silent way. He was heading toward the door at the end of the room that opened into the shed. He lifted the latch with precaution and went out, pushing the door behind him but without shutting it. Daru had not stirred. "He is running away," he merely thought. "Good riddance!" Yet he listened attentively. The hens were not fluttering; the guest must be on the plateau. A faint sound of water reached him, and he didn't know what it was until the Arab again stood framed in the doorway, closed the door carefully, and came back to bed without a sound. Then Daru turned his back on him and fell asleep. Still later he seemed, from the depths of his sleep, to hear furtive steps around the schoolhouse. "I'm dreaming! I'm dreaming!" he repeated to himself. And he went on sleeping.

When he awoke, the sky was clear; the loose window let in a cold, pure air. The Arab was asleep, hunched up under the blankets now, his mouth open, utterly relaxed. But when Daru shook him, he started dreadfully, staring at Daru with wild eyes as if he had never seen him and such a frightened expression that the schoolmaster stepped back. "Don't be afraid. It's me. You must eat." The Arab nodded his head and said yes. Calm had returned to his face, but his expression was vacant and listless.

The coffee was ready. They drank it seated together on the folding bed as they munched their pieces of the cake. Then Daru led the Arab under the shed and showed him the faucet where he washed. He went back into the room, folded the blankets and the bed, made his own bed and put the room in order. Then he went through the classroom and out onto the terrace. The sun was already rising in the blue sky; a soft, bright light was bathing the deserted plateau. On the ridge the snow was melting in spots. The stones were about to reappear. Crouched on the edge of the plateau, the schoolmaster looked at the deserted expanse. He thought of Balducci. He had hurt him, for he had sent him off in a way as if he didn't want to be associated with him. He could still hear the gendarme's farewell and, without knowing why, he felt strangely empty and vulnerable. At that moment, from the other side of the schoolhouse, the prisoner coughed. Daru listened to him almost despite himself and then, furious, threw a pebble that whistled through the air before sinking into the snow. That man's stupid crime revolted him, but to hand him over was contrary to honor. Merely thinking of it made him smart with humiliation. And he cursed at one and the same time his own people who had sent him this Arab and the Arab too who had dared to kill and not managed to get away. Daru got up, walked in a circle on the terrace, waited motionless, and then went back into the schoolhouse.

The Arab, leaning over the cement floor of the shed, was washing his teeth with two fingers. Daru looked at him and said: "Come." He went back into the room ahead of the prisoner. He slipped a hunting-jacket on over his sweater and put on walking-shoes. Standing, he waited until the Arab had put on his *chèche* and sandals. They went into the classroom and the schoolmaster pointed to the exit, saying: "Go ahead." The fellow didn't budge. "I'm coming," said Daru. The Arab went out. Daru went back into the room and made a package of pieces of rusk, dates, and sugar. In the classroom, before going out, he hesitated a second in front of his desk, then crossed the threshold and locked the door. "That's the way," he said. He started toward the east, followed by the prisoner. But, a short distance from the schoolhouse, he thought he heard a slight sound behind them. He retraced his steps and examined the surroundings of the house; there was no one there. The Arab watched him without seeming to understand. "Come on," said Daru.

They walked for an hour and rested beside a sharp peak of limestone. The snow was melting faster and faster and the sun was drinking up the puddles at once, rapidly cleaning the plateau, which gradually dried and vibrated like the air itself. When they resumed walking, the ground rang under their feet. From time to time a bird rent the space in front of them with a joyful cry. Daru breathed in deeply the fresh morning light. He felt a sort of rapture before the vast familiar expanse, now almost entirely yellow under its dome of blue sky. They walked an hour more, descending toward the south. They reached a level height made up of crumbly rocks. From there on, the plateau sloped down, eastward, toward a low plain where there were a few spindly trees and, to the south, toward outcroppings of rock that gave the landscape a chaotic look.

Daru surveyed the two directions. There was nothing but the sky on the horizon. Not a man could be seen. He turned toward the Arab, who was looking at him blankly. Daru held out the package to him. "Take it," he said. "There are dates, bread, and sugar. You can hold out for two days. Here are a thousand francs too." The Arab took the package and the money but kept his full hands at chest level as if he didn't know what to do with what was being given him. "Now look," the schoolmaster said as he pointed in the direction of the east, "there's the way to Tinguit. You have a two-hour walk. At Tinguit you'll find the administration and the police. They are expecting you." The Arab looked toward the east, still holding the package and the money against his chest. Daru took his elbow and turned him rather roughly toward the south. At the foot of the height on which they stood could be seen a faint path. "That's the trail across the plateau. In a day's walk from here you'll find pasturelands and the first nomads. They'll take you in and shelter you according to their law." The Arab had now turned toward Daru and a sort of panic was visible in his expression. "Listen," he said. Daru shook his head: "No, be quiet. Now I'm leaving you." He turned his back on him, took two long steps in the direction of the school, looked hesitantly at the motionless Arab, and started off again. For a few minutes he heard nothing but his own step resounding on the cold ground and did not turn his head. A moment later, however, he turned around. The Arab was still there on the edge of the hill, his arms hanging now, and he was looking at the schoolmaster. Daru felt something rise in his throat. But he swore with impatience, waved vaguely, and started off again. He had already gone some distance when he again stopped and looked. There was no longer anyone on the hill.

Daru hesitated. The sun was now rather high in the sky and was beginning to beat down on his head. The schoolmaster retraced his steps, at first somewhat uncertainly, then with decision. When he reached the little hill, he was bathed in sweat. He climbed it as fast as he could and stopped, out of breath, at the top. The rock-fields to the south stood out sharply against the blue sky, but on the plain to the east a steamy heat was already rising. And in that slight haze, Daru, with heavy heart, made out the Arab walking slowly on the road to prison.

A little later, standing before the window of the classroom, the schoolmaster was watching the clear light bathing the whole surface of the plateau, but he hardly saw it. Behind him on the blackboard, among the winding French rivers, sprawled the clumsily chalked-up words he had just read: "You handed over our brother. You will pay for this." Daru looked at the sky, the plateau, and, beyond, the invisible lands stretching all the way to the sea. In this vast landscape he had loved so much, he was alone.

PROBING FOR
MEANING   1. "Cruel to live in" is the way Daru describes his part of Algeria. What details indicate the truth of his description? Why doesn't he leave? Where in the story does he indicate his attitude toward the land?

2. What does Daru think of mankind? What connection exists between his attitude toward people and his profession?

3. Describe the relationship between Balducci and Daru. What does this relationship further reveal about Daru's attitude toward others?

4. Daru, the French Algerian, must play host to an Arab. What kind of host is he? How would you describe his behavior toward, and thoughts about, the Arab?

5. How does the guest respond to the host? What details of conversation and action indicate this response?

6. "That man's stupid crime revolted him, but to hand him over was contrary to honor." Why does Daru's philosophy make it dishonorable to turn in a murderer?

7. Why does Daru give the Arab a choice, rather than setting him on the path to freedom? Why does the Arab choose to walk to prison? Daru observes the Arab's choice "with heavy heart." Why?

8. "In this vast landscape he had loved so much, he was alone."

For what reason does Camus add the ironic touch of the Arab threat scrawled on the blackboard? Was Daru ever not alone? Does he want to be alone?

PROBING FOR
METHOD

1. To what extent do we see the action through Daru's eyes? Do we enter the mind of any characters other than Daru? Could the story have been written in the first person? What different effect would a first person narration create?

2. Why is the natural setting so appropriate for a story dramatizing the author's philosophy that life is meaningless except as people choose to make it meaningful?

3. How do the snowstorm and sunlight—dark and light—serve as an ironic symbolic background to the actions of Daru and the Arab?

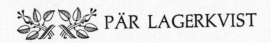 PÄR LAGERKVIST

Father and I

When I was getting on toward ten, I remember, Father took me by the hand one Sunday afternoon, as we were to go out into the woods and listen to the birds singing. Waving good-bye to Mother, who had to stay at home and get the evening meal, we set off briskly in the warm sunshine. We didn't make any great to-do about this going to listen to the birds, as though it were something extra special or wonderful; we were sound, sensible people, Father and I, brought up with nature and used to it. There was nothing to make a fuss about. It was just that it was Sunday afternoon and Father was free. We walked along the railway line, where people were not allowed to go as a rule, but Father worked on the railway and so he had a right to. By doing this we could get straight into the woods, too, without going a round-about way.

Soon the bird song began and all the rest. There was a twittering of finches and willow warblers, thrushes and sparrows in the bushes, the hum that goes on all around you as soon as you enter a wood. The ground was white with wood anemones, the birches had just come out into leaf, and the spruces had fresh shoots; there were scents on all sides, and underfoot the mossy earth lay steaming in the sun. There was noise and movement everywhere; bumblebees came out of their holes, midges swarmed wherever it was marshy, and birds darted out of the bushes to catch them and back again as quickly.

All at once a train came rushing along and we had to go down on to the embankment. Father hailed the engine driver with two fingers to his Sunday hat and the driver saluted and extended his hand. It all happened quickly; then on we went, taking big strides so as to tread on the sleepers and not in the gravel, which was heavy going and rough on the shoes. The sleepers sweated tar in the heat, everything smelled, grease and meadowsweet, tar and heather by turns. The rails glinted in the sun. On either side of the line were telegraph poles, which sang as you passed them. Yes, it was a lovely day. The sky was quite clear, not a cloud to be seen, and there couldn't be any, either, on a day like this, from what Father said.

After a while we came to a field of oats to the right of the line, where a crofter we knew had a clearing. The oats had come up close and even. Father scanned them with an expert eye and I could see he was satisfied. I knew very little about such things, having been born in a town. Then we came to the bridge over a stream, which most of the time had no water to speak of but which now was in full spate. We held hands so as not to fall down between the sleepers. After that it is not long before you come to the platelayer's cottage lying embedded in greenery, apple trees and gooseberry bushes. We called in to see them and were offered milk, and saw their pig and hens and fruit trees in blossom; then we went on. We wanted to get to the river, for it was more beautiful there than anywhere else; there was something special about it, as farther upstream it flowed past where Father had lived as a child. We usually liked to come as far as this before we turned back, and today, too, we got there after a good walk. It was near the next station, but we didn't go so far. Father just looked to see that the semaphore was right—he thought of every-thing.

We stopped by the river, which murmured in the hot sun, broad and friendly. The shady trees hung along the banks and were reflected in the backwater. It was all fresh and light here; a soft breeze was blowing off the small lakes higher up. We climbed down the slope and walked a little way along the bank, Father pointing out the spots for fishing. He had sat here on the stones as a boy, waiting for perch all day long; often there wasn't even a bite, but it was a blissful life. Now he didn't have time. We hung about on the bank for a good while, making a noise, pushing out bits of bark for the current to take, throwing pebbles out into the water to see who could throw farthest; we were both gay and cheerful by nature, Father and I. At last we felt tired and that we had had enough, and we set off for home.

It was beginning to get dark. The woods were changed—it wasn't dark there yet, but almost. We quickened our steps. Mother would be getting anxious and waiting with supper. She was always afraid something was going to happen. But it hadn't; it had been a lovely day, nothing had happened that shouldn't. We were content with everything.

The twilight deepened. The trees were so funny. They stood listening to every step we took, as if they didn't know who we were. Under one of them was a glow-worm. It lay down there in the dark staring at us. I squeezed Father's hand, but he didn't see the strange glow, just walked on. Now it was quite dark. We came to the bridge over the stream. It roared down there in the depths, horribly, as though it wanted to swallow us up; the abyss yawned below us. We trod carefully on the sleepers, holding each other tightly by the hand so as not to fall in. I thought Father would carry me across, but he didn't say anything; he probably wanted me to be like him and think nothing of it.

We went on. Father was so calm as he walked there in the darkness, with even strides, not speaking, thinking to himself. I couldn't understand how he could be so calm when it was so murky. I looked all around me in fear. Nothing but darkness everywhere. I hardly dared take a deep breath, for then you got so much darkness inside you, and that was dangerous. I thought it meant you would soon die. I remember quite well that's what I thought then. The embankment sloped steeply down, as though into chasms black as night. The telegraph poles rose, ghostly, to the sky. Inside them was a hollow rumble, as though someone were talking deep down in the earth and the white porcelain caps sat huddled fearfully together listening to it. It was all horrible. Nothing was right, nothing real; it was all so weird.

Hugging close to Father, I whispered, "Father, why is it so horrible when it's dark?"

"No, my boy, it's not horrible," he said, taking me by the hand.

"Yes, Father, it is."

"No, my child, you mustn't think that. Not when we know there is a God."

I felt so lonely, forsaken. It was so strange that only I was afraid, not Father, that we didn't think the same. And strange that what he said didn't help me and stop me from being afraid. Not even what he said about God helped me. I thought he too was horrible. It was horrible that he was everywhere here in the darkness, down under the trees, in the telegraph poles which rumbled—that must be he—everywhere. And yet you could never see him.

We walked in silence, each with his own thoughts. My heart

contracted, as though the darkness had got in and was beginning to squeeze it.

Then, as we were rounding a bend, we suddenly heard a mighty roar behind us! We were awakened out of our thoughts in alarm. Father pulled me down on to the embankment, down into the abyss, held me there. Then the train tore past, a black train. All the lights in the carriages were out, and it was going at frantic speed. What sort of train was it? There wasn't one due now! We gazed at it in terror. The fire blazed in the huge engine as they shovelled in coal; sparks whirled out into the night. It was terrible. The driver stood there in the light of the fire, pale, motionless, his features as though turned to stone. Father didn't recognize him, didn't know who he was. The man just stared straight ahead, as though intent on rushing into the darkness, far into the darkness that had no end.

Beside myself with dread, I stood there panting, gazing after the furious vision. It was swallowed up by the night. Father took me up on to the line; we hurried home. He said, "Strange, what train was that? And I didn't recognize the driver." Then we walked on in silence.

But my whole body was shaking. It was for me, for my sake. I sensed what it meant: it was the anguish that was to come, the unknown, all that Father knew nothing about, that he wouldn't be able to protect me against. That was how this world, this life, would be for me; not like Father's, where everything was secure and certain. It wasn't a real world, a real life. It just hurtled, blazing, into the darkness that had no end.

PROBING FOR MEANING

1. What quality of the males in the family does the narrator stress in the first paragraph? What additional quality of his father does he emphasize in paragraphs 3 and 4?

2. At what point does the son begin to feel that his father cannot protect him from the unknown? What foreshadows his fear?

3. What objects and experiences which formed part of their daytime walk are repeated at night? How do they differ?

4. Why does the father not react to the dark in the same way as the son? What is his reaction to the black train?

5. What does the black train symbolize for the son? Is his reaction justified? Is it temporary? Will he one day be as "secure and certain" as his father? In other words, do you think the father was as afraid when he was a child? Why or why not?

PROBING FOR METHOD

1. How does the narrator's personal use of pronouns differ in the day and night sections of the story? How does this difference underline the content of the story?

2. Are the two trains effective metaphors for what the narrator wants to convey? What other metaphors might he have used?

3. The more difficult words in Lagerkvist's essay, like "sleeper," "semaphore," "anemones" and "crofter" are very closely related to his themes. What do the words mean? Why did he need to use them?

 WALT WHITMAN

What Is the Grass?

A child said *What is the grass?* fetching it to me with full
    hands,
How could I answer the child? I do not know what it is any
    more than he.

I guess it must be the flag of my disposition, out of hopeful
    green stuff woven.

Or I guess it is the handkerchief of the Lord,
A scented gift and remembrancer designedly dropt,

Bearing the owner's name someway in the corners, that we
    may see and remark, and say *Whose?*

Or I guess the grass is itself a child, the produced babe of the
    vegetation.

Or I guess it is a uniform hieroglyphic,
And it means, Sprouting alike in broad zones and narrow
    zones,
Growing among black folks as among white,   10
Kanuck, Tuckahoe, Congressman, Cuff, I give them the same,
    I receive them the same.

And now it seems to me the beautiful uncut hair of graves.

Tenderly will I use you curling grass,
It may be you transpire from the breasts of young men,
It may be if I had known them I would have loved them,
It may be you are from old people, or from offspring taken
     soon out of their mothers' laps,
And here you are the mothers' laps.
This grass is very dark to be from the white heads of old
     mothers,
Darker than the colorless beards of old men,
Dark to come from under the faint red roofs of mouths.   20
O I perceive after all so many uttering tongues,
And I perceive they do not come from the roofs of mouths
     for nothing.

I wish I could translate the hints about the dead young men
     and women,
And the hints about old men and mothers, and the offspring
     taken soon out of their laps.

What do you think has become of the young and old men?
And what do you think has become of the women and chil-
     dren?

They are alive and well somewhere,
The smallest sprout shows there is really no death,
And if ever there was it led forward life, and does not wait at
     the end to arrest it,
And ceas'd the moment life appear'd.   30
All goes onward and outward, nothing collapses,
And to die is different from what any one supposed, and
     luckier.

PROBING FOR   1. In this poem, Walt Whitman strikes the pose of an old man
MEANING   pondering the questions of youth. Wise but not omniscient, age fumbles for
          adequate answers. What evidence in the poem indicates the poet is groping
          for answers, rather than having them "on the tip of his tongue"?
                2. In responding to the child's question, Whitman postulates sev-
          eral answers. What are they?
                3. One answer seems more satisfactory to the poet than the others
          because he emphasizes it in an obvious way. Which answer is this and how
          does the poet emphasize it?
                4. Analyze Whitman's philosophy of death as he presents it in this
          poem.

1. How does the structure of this poem enhance its meaning? What is the significance of those lines printed completely separated from the others: lines 3 and 6, for example?

2. Does anything about this poem remind you of the technique used by Plato in his allegory? Explain.

3. Parts of the poem depend upon contrasts for meaning. What are some of these parts? How does the study in contrasts give additional impact to the poet's ideas?

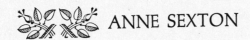 ANNE SEXTON

The Rowing Endeth

I'm mooring my rowboat
at the dock of the island called God.
This dock is made in the shape of a fish
and there are many boats moored
at many different docks.
"It's okay," I say to myself,
with blisters that broke and healed
and broke and healed—
saving themselves over and over.
And salt sticking to my face and arms like   10
a glue-skin pocked with grains of tapioca.
I empty myself from my wooden boat
and onto the flesh of The Island.

"On with it!" He says and thus
we squat on the rocks by the sea
and play——— can it be true———
a game of poker.
He calls me.
I win because I hold a royal straight flush.
He wins because He holds five aces.   20
A wild card had been announced
but I had not heard it
being in such a state of awe

when He took out the cards and dealt.
As He plunks down His five aces
and I sit grinning at my royal flush,
He starts to laugh,
the laughter rolling like a hoop out of His mouth
and into mine,
and such laughter that He doubles right over me   30
laughing a Rejoice-Chorus at our two triumphs.
Then I laugh, the fishy dock laughs
the sea laughs. The Island laughs.
The Absurd laughs.

Dearest dealer,
I with my royal straight flush,
love you so for your wild card,
that untamable, eternal, gut-driven *ha-ha*
and lucky love.

PROBING FOR   1. What has the poet evidently gone through to moor "at the dock
MEANING   of the island called God"? What does her rowing to God symbolize?
                    2. What effect is created by her representation of God as a gambler
whose announcement of a wild card is not heard by his opponent? What
is her image of God? What does God's attitude toward her seem to be?
                    3. Despite her loss in the poker game, the poet seems quite happy
with her royal straight flush and shares in God's laughter at their "two
triumphs." In what sense has the poet won? Why is she not resentful
about God's wild card? How do the last two lines contribute to the reader's
understanding of her attitude?
                    4. Can you paraphrase the poem? What is its religious meaning?
What is the "Absurd"?

PROBING FOR   1. How effective is the poet's comparison of God with an island
METHOD   to which we must row? Why is the dock shaped like a fish?
                    2. The poet uses unusual combinations of words. What do the
expressions "glue-skin" and "gut-driven" mean? Can you find any other
unusual uses of words?
                    3. How would you categorize the poet's vocabulary? Is it formal?
Informal? Colloquial? Slang? Select words from the poem to defend your
answer. What effect does her vocabulary have on the meaning of the
poem?

EDNA ST. VINCENT MILLAY

Spring

To what purpose, April, do you return again?
Beauty is not enough.
You can no longer quiet me with the redness
Of little leaves opening stickily.
I know what I know.
The sun is hot on my neck as I observe
The spikes of the crocus.
The smell of the earth is good.
It is apparent that there is no death.
But what does that signify?   10
Not only under ground are the brains of men
Eaten by maggots.
Life in itself
Is nothing,
An empty cup, a flight of uncarpeted stairs.
It is not enough that yearly, down this hill,
April
Comes like an idiot, babbling and strewing flowers.

PROBING FOR
MEANING
1. What characteristics usually associated with April does the poet mention?
2. What does the line "It is apparent that there is no death" mean?
3. Why, despite the beauty of April, is the poet angry? Why does she say, "Beauty is not enough"?
4. Why is the poet deliberately reversing the usual attitude toward Spring?

PROBING FOR
METHOD
1. Observe the comparisons in the poem. What do they contribute to your understanding of the meaning?
2. Why has the poet formed line length as she has? What is the effect, for example, of the shorter lines? Why, near the end of the poem,

does the poet make the word "April" a separate line? What relationship exists between content and line length?

Topics for Imitation

1. Property "makes me feel heavy," says Forster in "My Wood." Lindbergh and Thoreau also discuss materialism in this chapter. Discuss their attitudes toward possessions or, in Thoreau's case, commercialism.

2. Many writers discuss man's reluctance to confront reality. What do Keller, Plato, Lagerkvist and Millay contribute to this discussion?

3. The difficulties women who are artists encounter in their pursuit of creativity are discussed by Lindbergh, Rich (Chapter III) and Nin (Chapter V). What obstacles have these women encountered? To what extent have they resolved the problems?

4. Compare and contrast the views of religion of Lagerkvist, Whitman and Sexton.

5. Compare and contrast the attitudes toward nature of Lindbergh, Whitman and Millay.

6. "Sometimes I have thought it would be an excellent rule to live each day as if we should die tomorrow. Such an attitude would emphasize sharply the values of life." Thoreau in "The Village" and Daru in "The Guest" share Helen Keller's keen awareness that people should utilize their freedom to appreciate life. Discuss what each writer values in life.

7. Plato, Thoreau and Daru in "The Guest" chose to live apart from society. What are the effects on them of their philosophies of individualism?

8. Write an essay of your own using one of the methods of illustration to make an abstract idea concrete. The following are some possible approaches:

a. Choose an object of nature, as Lindbergh did the channelled whelk, and use it to illustrate an idea of your own.

b. Find an illustration other than Plato's cave to represent truth versus illusion and develop it either as an analogy or as an allegory.

c. Find your own way of illustrating Helen Keller's idea of the necessity of living life in the present moment.

d. Write about an idea of yours, including, as Thoreau does, many metaphors and similes. Be sure not to use clichés but to create fresh comparisons.

e. Use a possession of yours to illustrate your attitude toward possessions. Use Forster's essay as a model.

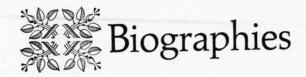# Biographies

SHERWOOD ANDERSON (1876–1941) American novelist and short story writer whose collection of short stories *Winesburg, Ohio* (1919) reflecting life in a small Midwestern town brought him instant recognition. Anderson was convinced that the growth of urban centers would result in the disintegration of the personal life. His interest in the latter subject is reflected in his autobiographical essay "Discovery of a Father."

W. H. AUDEN (1907–1974) British poet whose work in the 1930's expressed his hope that social injustices could be corrected by the "right" political system. "The Unknown Citizen" reflects his critique of capitalism. He gradually abandoned his belief in Marxism, and his later poems are essentially humanistic reflections on the importance of all aspects of human love.

DEE BROWN (b. 1908) American journalist and novelist whose works reflect his interest in the American frontier. This enthusiasm was fostered by his grandmother, who told him tales of the California gold rush and the Civil War. His works include *The Settler's West* (1955), *The Galvanized Yankees* (1963) and *Bury My Heart at Wounded Knee* (1971), from which the selection in this anthology is taken.

ANTHONY BURGESS (b. 1917) English novelist and essayist. His most famous novel, *A Clockwork Orange* (1962), was later made into a film. In recent years Burgess has been a visiting professor at City University of New York and has written several essays about his impressions of American life.

JACK ANDREW CADY (b. 1932) American author and educator. From 1961 to the present he has been a writer-in-residence at Knox College. In 1965 he received an award from the *Atlantic Monthly*. Several of his short stories have been anthologized, and a collection entitled *The Burning and Other Stories* was published in 1972.

ALBERT CAMUS (1913–1960)   French novelist, dramatist, essayist and journalist whose work had a significant impact on his contemporaries. He was a member of the French Resistance movement during World War II and the editor of *Combat*, an underground publication. Although he has been identified with existentialism, Camus' profound humanism distinguishes him from many purely existentialist writers. Convinced of the absurdity of life, Camus, nevertheless, in his art and in his life, struggled with the paradoxical aspirations of personal freedom and social justice, solitude and solidarity and reason and passion. He was awarded the Nobel Prize in 1957 for his philosophical essays, which include "The Myth of Sisyphus" (1942) and "The Rebel" (1953), and for his fiction, which includes *The Stranger* (1942), *The Plague* (1948) and *The Fall* (1957). He was killed in an automobile accident at the height of his literary career.

ELDRIDGE CLEAVER (b. 1935)   Born in the American South, Cleaver spent most of the years from 1947 to 1966 in reformatories and prisons. During his time in San Quentin he educated himself, became an editor of *Ramparts* and in 1968 published *Soul on Ice*, a collection of essays and letters, including "A Day in Folsom Prison," many of which were written while he was in prison. In the mid-1960's he became a leader of the Black Panther party, and in 1968 ran for president as the candidate of the Peace and Freedom party. In November, 1968 he left America, settling first in Havana and then in Algeria. In 1976 Cleaver returned to America disillusioned with his former philosophical beliefs. He faces a prison sentence for his former activities with the Black Panthers. He is currently very interested in religion and claims to have undergone a "conversion" experience.

JAMES DICKEY (b. 1923)   Southern American poet and author of best-selling novel, *Deliverance* (1970), which was later made into a film. He attempts to make his poetry, which deals with events in everyday life, "the kind of thing that means something to people in their life situations" rather than a purely literary exercise.

EMILY DICKINSON (1830–1886)   American poet whose reclusive life contrasted sharply with her radical thoughts. Although few of her 1,000 poems were published in her lifetime, Dickinson is now regarded as an important influence in modern poetry

because of her unorthodox poetic techniques and her preoccupation with the irrational in the human psyche.

RICHARD EBERHART (b. 1904)   American poet and teacher whose collected work was published in 1960. His poetry is characterized by short lines, few rhymes and the use of objects from
everyday life to suggest metaphysical truths.

NORA EPHRON (b. 1941)   She began her writing career as a reporter
for the *New York Post* and in 1968 became a free-lance writer
for numerous magazines. From 1972 to 1973 she was a columnist for *Esquire* where a year later she became a senior
editor. Her publications include *Wallflower at the Orgy*
(1970) and *Crazy Salad* (1975), from which "Fantasies" was
taken.

KENNETH FEARING (1902–1961)   American poet who published much
of his work during the Depression. His many volumes of
poetry may be primarily classified as social satire.

E. M. FORSTER (1879–1970)   English novelist and essayist known for
his humanistic philosophy expressed in the novel *A Passage
to India* (1924), which exposes the prejudices and injustices
that existed under British domination of colonial India. With
his subtle irony he reveals the moral and emotional emptiness
of British middle class life. He believes that the bourgeoisie
bury their capacity for passion and intuition and have to re-
capture those qualities in order to make life vital. He has also
written seven books of literary criticism and in 1951 published a collection of sociological essays entitled *Two Cheers
for Democracy.*

ERNEST GAINES (b. 1933)   A black American writer who was born
in the Deep South and spent most of his formative years
working in the fields. Gaines draws from his own life experiences and depicts in a most realistic style the conditions under
which his people have lived. His works include *Catherine
Carmier* (1964), his first novel; *Of Love and Dust* (1967) and
Bloodline (1968), a volume of short stories. His novel *The
Autobiography of Miss Jane Pittman* (1971) won him national acclaim. The television adaptation of it provided him
with the recognition that was long overdue.

GARY GILDNER (b. 1938)   His collected works include *First Practice*
(1970) and *Digging for Indians* (1972). He currently teaches

creative writing at the University of Iowa and is working on a collection of short stories.

HERBERT GOLD (b. 1924)   An American novelist who sometimes aspires to the existentialist school of thought but only insofar as he is concerned with man's capacity for creating values. He is essentially an optimist, which comes out most clearly in his novels *Birth of a Hero* (1951) and *The Prospect Before Us* (1954). His essays reflect his interest in contemporary American culture.

SUZANNE GORDON (b. 1945)   New Yorker who started her career teaching in Baltimore. In 1970 she became a reporter and photographer for United Press International. She has also contributed essays and short stories to *Ms., Ramparts* and *Newsweek*. For her book *Loneliness in America* (1976), she has received critical acclaim as a perceptive sociological writer.

ALEX HALEY (b. 1921)   Haley's literary career was launched with his collaboration on the *Autobiography of Malcolm X*, published in 1956. Extensive research and writing over a number of years culminated in the 1976 publication of *Roots*, which was later televised and very well received. The selection in this anthology is an account of the events which led to the writing of *Roots*.

ERNEST HEMINGWAY (1898–1961)   American novelist who was part of the Lost Generation of post–World War I writers who settled in Paris. Under the tutelage of Gertrude Stein and F. Scott Fitzgerald, Hemingway emerged as a major novelist and influence on twentieth-century fiction. His novels include *The Sun Also Rises* (1926), *A Farewell to Arms* (1929), *For Whom the Bell Tolls* (1940) and *The Old Man and the Sea* (1952), for which he was awarded the Nobel Prize. In his life and works Hemingway portrayed his vacillation between faith and despair. He committed suicide in 1961.

TED HUGHES (b. 1930)   British poet whose first volume, *The Hawk in the Rain* (1957), was published in America. His later work contains violent animal symbolism suggestive of a vision of man in a savage world confronting a hostile God.

KAZIN, ALFRED (b. 1915)   American literary critic and teacher. In 1951 Kazin published *A Walker in the City*, a series of recollections of his childhood in Brooklyn from which "The Kitchen" is taken. His critical writings include *On Native Grounds* (1942) and *Contemporaries* (1962). Most recently he has been involved in a study of the literature and films of the holocaust.

HELEN KELLER (1880–1968)   American essayist and advisor on international relations for the blind. Although deprived of her sight and hearing from the age of nineteen months, she learned to communicate first by using sign language and later through voice lessons. Despite her physical handicaps, Keller had a keen awareness and insight into human nature and the world around her. She graduated with honors from Radcliffe and received critical acclaim for her autobiography, *Story of My Life* (1902). Among her other written achievements are *Optimism* (1903), *The World I Live In* (1908) and *Out of the Dark* (1913).

WILLIAM MELVIN KELLEY (b. 1937)   A black American writer educated at Harvard who is best noted for his novel *A Different Drummer* (1962). Kelley has also published a collection of short stories entitled *Dancers on the Shore* (1964), from which "Saint Paul and The Monkeys" is taken. He currently lives in Jamaica, West Indies.

PÄR LAGERKVIST (b. 1891)   A Swedish poet, novelist and playwright whose humanism and agonized honesty led him to actively oppose the Nazi regime of the 1930's and all forms of tyranny and totalitarianism. His determination to probe deeply and honestly into the human heart and mind brought him acclaim for his novel *The Hangman* (1935), a poignant and revealing portrait of the destructive nature of violence. As a testament to his genius, he won the Nobel Prize for Literature in 1951. His best known works internationally are *The Dwarf* (1945), *Barabbas* (1950) and *The Sibyl* (1956).

DORIS LESSING (b. 1919)   English novelist and short story writer born in Rhodesia. Her intense commitment to socialism and other social causes, including the women's movement, is expressed in many of her works. Her most experimental novel, *The Golden Notebook* (1962), reflects the anguish of a "liberated" woman in finding herself.

ROBERT JAY LIFTON (b. 1926)   American psychiatrist who teaches at
   Yale Medical School and is a frequent contributor to psychological journals, writing about such subjects as the psychological effects of brainwashing. He has also written several
   books about death, including a study of the survivors of Hiroshima. The essay in this anthology is from his book *Living
   and Dying* (1974), which was coauthored by Eric Olson, Lifton's research assistant.

ANNE MORROW LINDBERGH (b. 1906)   American writer who is best
   known for her controversial essay "The Wave of the Future"
   (1940), which was regarded as a defense of Fascism. In 1955
   she wrote *Gift from the Sea* which was especially addressed
   to women. Her novel *Dearly Beloved* (1962) comments on
   marriage and in *Earth Shine* (1969) she writes of the launch-
   ing of the Apollo moon mission. She has also published several volumes of her diaries and letters.

CARSON McCULLERS (1917–1967)   American southern writer whose
   first novel, *The Heart Is a Lonely Hunter* (1940), won her
   immediate critical acclaim. Her fiction, focusing on the alienated, has been praised for its sensitive characterization and
   effective communication of sense impressions. "The Sojourner" is from a collection entitled *The Ballad of the Sad
   Café* (1951).

BERNARD MALAMUD (b. 1914)   American fiction writer who was born
   in Brooklyn, New York, the setting for many of his works. In
   The Assistant (1957) he presents the struggle of a good man,
   Morris Bober, who fails in society's terms to attain success.
   For his collection of short stories *The Magic Barrel* (1958) he
   received the National Book Award. His other novels include
   A New Life (1961) and *The Fixer* (1966). He currently teaches
   at Bennington College.

ROLLO MAY (b. 1909)   An American psychotherapist who began his
   studies in Vienna and completed his education and psychoanalytic training in New York. He has published several
   books on his psychoanalytic theories including *Man's Search
   for Himself* (1953), *Love and Will* (1969), to which "Our
   Schizoid World" is an introduction, and *Power and Innocence* (1972). His latest publication, *The Courage to Create*
   (1975), explores the role of creativity.

JOYCE MAYNARD (b. 1954)   One of the youngest writers to be published in the *New York Times* where she is currently on the editorial staff. In her freshman year at Yale she wrote an autobiography, *Looking Back: A Chronicle of Growing Up Old in the Sixties* (1973), from which "The Lion Tamers" is taken.

EDNA ST. VINCENT MILLAY (1892–1950)   American poet whose volume *The Harp Weaver and Other Poems* was awarded the Pulitzer Prize in 1923. Famous for her use of the sonnet form, Millay's early poems celebrated love and life, while her later work was more concerned with social issues. Her use of traditional poetic forms creates an interesting juxtaposition with her radical ideas such as those expressed in the poem "Spring."

HOWARD NEMEROV (b. 1920)   American poet and fiction writer whose poems often discuss American society and its various institutions. His collected poems include *The Image and The Law* (1947), *Guide to the Ruins* (1950), *The Salt Garden* (1955), *Mirrors and Windows* (1958) and *New and Selected Poems* (1960).

ANAÏS NIN (1903–1977)   American writer born in Paris. Her father was the Spanish composer Joaquin Nin. Her vast published works include several volumes of a diary as well as numerous novels and short stories reflecting her sensitive and psychologically perceptive analyses of human relationships.

TILLIE OLSEN (b. 1913)   Born in Nebraska, Olsen has spent most of her life in San Francisco. She has been a writer-in-residence at Amherst College and Stanford University. Her collection of short stories *Tell Me a Riddle* received much critical acclaim. Her novel *Yonnondio* reflects life in Wyoming during the Depression.

GEORGE ORWELL (1903–1950)   British novelist born in India who served for several years with the Indian Imperial Police in Burma. He then moved to Europe, working first as a dishwasher in Paris, then living like a tramp in England. His first autobiographical publication, *Down and Out in Paris and London*, records his experiences. A Socialist, Orwell criticized middle class exponents of the philosophy who, while living comfortably, pretended to identify with the working class.

His best known novels, *Animal Farm* (1945) and *1984* (1949), are satirical depictions of the evils of totalitarianism.

ANN PETRY (b. 1911)   A black novelist, journalist and short story writer who spent most of her life in Harlem. Her fiction reflects the naturalist school. In keeping with this tradition, many of her works are drawn from her experience in an urban setting. She received critical acclaim for her novel, *The Street* (1946), from which "Like a Winding Sheet" is taken.

PLATO (427–348 B.C.)   Greek philosopher and writer who became actively involved in the politics of the Athenian state. He rebelled against the tyranny which had permeated Athenian democracy. His reaction to the death of his teacher and friend Socrates led him to search for an alternative life style. He is best known for his philosophic dialogues. His philosophic and political ideas have had a significant and lasting impact on Western thought.

NORMAN PODHORETZ (b. 1930)   A native of Brooklyn, New York, Podhoretz became associate editor of *Commentary* in 1958 and editor-in-chief in 1960. "The Brutal Bargain" is taken from his autobiography, *Making It* (1968).

JACK HARRISON POLLACK   An expert in ESP and former professor of journalism at New York University, Pollack is also founder of the Society of Magazine Writers and has published more than 500 articles on such varied topics as Daniel Ellsberg, Angela Davis, education, divorce and medicine. His most recent book, published in 1977, is a biography of former Chief Justice Earl Warren.

MARTIN PAUL RALBOVSKY (b. 1942)   A native of New York who describes himself as an atheist and as a "Marxist-Leninist with no place to go." He has been a sportswriter for numerous periodicals and newspapers including the *New York Times*. He has also written several books on the role of sports in American society.

SANTHA RAMA RAU (b. 1923)   Indian writer educated in England and America. She has traveled widely in Europe and Asia. Her works include a dramatization of E. M. Forster's *Passage to India* (1956). She has also written several collections of essays including *My Russian Journey* (1959) and *Gifts of Passage* (1961).

ALASTAIR REID (b. 1926)   Born in Scotland and currently living in Spain, Reid has taught at Sarah Lawrence College in New York. He has published several volumes of poetry and is a frequent contributor to various periodicals including the *Atlantic, Encounter*, and the *New Yorker*.

THEODOR REIK (1888–1969)   Austrian psychoanalyst who was influenced by Freud but also differed from him. He was forced to leave Europe during the Nazi regime and settled in New York. He published many books on his psychoanalytic theories, particularly on his ideas about the role of the unconscious, including *The Search Within* (1956), *Of Love and Lust* (1957) and *The Need to Be Loved* (1963).

ADRIENNE RICH (b. 1928)   American poet who received the National Book Award in 1974 for her volume *Diving into the Wreck*. Her poetry expresses the conflicts that she confronted as she sought to express herself artistically while struggling with her roles as wife and mother. In the early seventies she taught at City College of New York. Her most recent book, *Of Woman Born*, is an analysis of motherhood.

THEODORE ROETHKE (1908–1963)   American poet whose collected works were awarded the Pulitzer Prize in 1954. Experimenting with traditional and free poetic forms, sometimes tending toward the surrealistic, Roethke's poems frequently reflect his preoccupation with childhood and old age.

BERTRAND RUSSELL (1872–1970)   British mathematician and philosopher who was also a social reformer interested in education and pacifism. A voluminous writer, he was awarded the Nobel Prize in 1950. His works include *Marriage and Morals* (1929), *History of Western Philosophy* (1945) and *Human Society in Ethics and Politics* (1954).

ANNE SEXTON (1928–1974)   American poet who published several volumes, receiving the Pulitzer Prize in 1966 for *Live or Die*. Sexton is a confessional poet; her work is a poignant expression of her personal struggle. Her poetry, full of concrete and vivid images, reflects the relationship between the personal and the metaphysical, including the elusiveness of God. She committed suicide on October 4, 1974.

WILLIAM STAFFORD (b. 1914)   American poet and teacher who was a conscientious objector during World War II and has been active since in pacifist movements. He received the National Book Award in 1963. He defines the role of the poet as "finding out what the world is trying to be."

HENRY DAVID THOREAU (1817–1862)   American essayist and poet who was part of the American romantic literary movement. In 1845 he built a cabin at Walden Pond in Massachusetts where he lived for the next two years. In *Walden* (1854), from which "The Village" is taken, he describes his daily experiences. A nonconformist, Thoreau was imprisoned for failing to pay his taxes and recorded the episode in his essay on civil disobedience. He is recognized today not only for his prose style but for his individualism, which not only challenged the social status quo of his contemporaries but challenges ours today as well. He was a major influence on Gandhi.

JAMES THURBER (1894–1961)   American essayist, humorist and short story writer who began his career as a journalist and worked with E. B. White on the *New Yorker*. His many essays and short stories satirize the follies of men and women. "The Secret Life of Walter Mitty," the most well known of his writings, has been made into a film.

CHAD WALSH (b. 1914)   American poet, teacher and critic who is concerned with religious and social issues. He is currently teaching at Beloit College and writing drama for television.

HANA WEHLE (b. 1917)   A native of Czechoslovakia, Wehle spent several years in Terezin/Theresienstadt, Birkenau-Auschwitz, and Stutthof. Her first husband was killed by the SS in Terezin. When she returned to Prague after the defeat of the Nazis, she met and married Kurt Wehle, who survived Terezin/Theresienstadt, Birkenau-Auschwitz and Schwarzheide concentration camps. His first wife died in Stutthof. They now live in New York and have four children. Wehle will graduate in January, 1978 from City University of New York with a degree in art therapy.

E. B. WHITE (b. 1899)   American humorist and essayist who began his career as a journalist. He was for many years on the editorial staff of the *New Yorker*. His essays are primarily social commentaries on contemporary life written in witty and succinct prose.

WALT WHITMAN (1819–1892)   American poet and journalist famous for the original poetic techniques in his volume *Leaves of Grass* (1855), which was considered an "immoral" book because of its frank treatment of sexuality. Whitman is now regarded as the poet of democracy whose verse reflects his love of man, beauty and nature.

TOM WICKER (b. 1926)   American southern journalist who edited several newspapers including the *Nashville Tennessean*. In 1960 he joined the staff of the *New York Times* where since 1968 he has been an associate editor. The excerpt in this anthology is from his book *Kennedy Without Tears* (1964). He has also written an analysis of the Attica prison rebellion entitled *A Time to Die* (1975) and has recently published a novel.

WILLIAM CARLOS WILLIAMS (1883–1963)   American poet who was a physician by profession. His poetry deals with everyday events in urban life which are expressed in vivid and concrete imagery. He was awarded the Pulitzer Prize posthumously in 1963.

TOM WOLFE (b. 1931)   American journalist and novelist who has worked on the staff of the *Washington Post* and the *New York Herald Tribune*. He is also a frequent contributor to *Esquire* and *Harper's*. In 1968 he published *The Electric Kool-Aid Acid Test*. His writing has often been criticized for its "supercontemporary" attitudes and styles.

YEVGENY YEVTUSHENKO (b. 1933)   Russian poet who became prominent in the Soviet Union in the 1960's. With the publication of his poem "Babi Yar" (1962) he was criticized by the Soviet regime for his censure of its anti-Semitic actions. He has subsequently toured the United States and Europe, drawing record audiences to his poetry readings.

AL YOUNG (b. 1939)   Free-lance musician who later became interested in poetry and dance. He is currently on the staff of Stanford University's Creative Writing Center. He has published several volumes of poetry and his work is anthologized in several books including *The New Black Poetry*.